But First, These Messages . . . The Selling of Broadcast Advertising

Barton C. White
Western Kentucky University

N. Doyle Satterthwaite
Western Kentucky University

Allyn and Bacon
Boston   London   Sydney   Toronto

Copyright © 1989 by Allyn and Bacon
A Division of Simon & Schuster
160 Gould Street
Needham Heights, Massachusetts 02194-2310

Series Editor: Mylan Jaixen
Series Editorial Assistant: Susan S. Brody
Production Administrator: Annette Joseph
Production Coordinator: Susan Freese
Editorial-Production Service: Editing, Design & Production, Inc.
Cover Administrator: Linda K. Dickinson
Cover Designer: Suzi Wojdyslawski

Library of Congress Cataloging-in-Publication Data

White, Barton.
  But first, these messages . . . : the selling of broadcast
advertising / Barton C. White, N. Doyle Satterthwaite.
  p.   cm.
  Bibliography: p.
  Includes index.
  ISBN 0-205-11687-6
  1. Selling—Broadcast advertising.   I. Satterthwaite, N. Doyle.
II. Title.
HF5439.B67W45 1989
659.14′068′8—dc19   88-19354
                                           CIP

Printed in the United States of America

10 9 8 7 6 5 4 3 2 1   93 92 91 90 89 88

Contents

Preface

This book came into being as a result of continuing conversations between the authors beginning in 1983 concerning the need for a more comprehensive book on the overall field of sales for the electronic media—radio, television, and cable. The conversations evolved into a resolution to produce a book that would be useful for two principal audiences: the student in higher education studying the practice of broadcasting and the professional salesperson of limited experience in radio, television, or cable television sales.

This beginning evolved into a step-by-step approach that aims at pointing out the similarities of selling different kinds of electronic media as well as adaptations to accommodate the differences among these media. It is based on our more than 30 years of broadcast media experience and honed by use in the broadcast sales course at Western Kentucky University.

Radio, television, and cable television are, first of all, businesses that produce a product (service) that must be sold for the media outlet to stay in business and succeed. Competent, professional salespeople are needed, and will continue to be needed, to accomplish this task. In this book we aim to foster competence and professionalism among broadcast media sales practitioners in markets of all sizes.

Students and practicing professionals should find the MEDIA system useful in planning and presenting their direct sales proposals to prospective clients. The chapters preceding and following the presentation of this system provide important planning techniques, a needed understanding of ratings and rates, and material on promotion and contest selling. The student or beginning salesperson should find the material on selling against or with other media very helpful in recognizing the competition and deciding how to deal with it. The interviews with media sales managers bring the beginner additional insight into the field of broadcast sales as a career. The appendices include the Radio Advertising Bureau sales consultant approach and a conversation with a cable television sales pioneer. We emphasize the markets where most openings for beginning salespeople occur, but the book includes material to enhance the professionalism of salespeople in markets of any size.

In short, our desire is that this book will continue to improve the capability and professionalism of those working in and those entering the broadcast sales field. As representatives of the industry's product, better salespeople enhance the stature and profitability of the industry in which they work.

Acknowledgments

The material within this book is dedicated to the personal success and professionalism of the coming generation of salespeople in radio, television, and cable television.

So many people have helped our development in our broadcast media careers that individual thanks would not be possible. Similarly, we cannot individually thank the students in Broadcast Communication 385—Broadcast Sales who were the testing ground for content and arrangement as the idea of this book moved to reality.

However, we must single out for our thanks Carl Kell, Professor of Speech Communication at Western Kentucky University, for his help in bringing our manuscript to the attention of Allyn and Bacon and for his suggestions, including the title of the book, during the manuscript preparation; Robert Leffingwell of Slippery Rock State University for his review and comments, which made the final manuscript better; and Jack Hogan, General Manager, WVEZ AM & FM, Louisville, Kentucky, who also provided invaluable comments that improved manuscript content.

We also thank the professional sales managers who agreed to share their thoughts and insights with readers: Tom Bornhauser, WHAS-TV, Louisville; Sandra Kennedy, WSM-AM and FM, Nashville; Vicki Knight, KLIF and KPLX-FM, Dallas–Fort Worth; Jeff Kuether, WTMJ, Milwaukee; John F. Lee, WBBM-TV, Chicago; Carl McNeil, WRVA, Richmond; Carol Quereau Netter, WCAU-TV, Philadelphia; Al Rothstein, WTVJ (TV), Miami; Kelly Seaton, WGN, Chicago; Larry Shrum, KPRC-TV, Houston; and cable sales pioneer Bill Ryan, Palmer Communications, Inc., Des Moines.

The Radio Advertising Bureau, Television Advertising Bureau, Arbitron Ratings Company, A. C. Nielsen Company, and AGB Research, Inc., provided invaluable aid.

To Project Editor Lilliane Chouinard of Editing, Design & Production, Inc. whose capable and careful editing always found the right words to delete as well as to add.

Much appreciation is also extended to artist Kendall Hart, whose characterizations of co-author Bart White during classroom lectures led to a contract to provide the drawings for this text.

Finally, our thanks to our wives, Dot Satterthwaite and Carol White, for their patience, tolerance, and encouragement during the planning and completion of this project.

Bart White
N. Doyle Satterthwaite

During the final editing of this project, my friend, colleague, and co-author Doyle Satterthwaite died following a year-long battle with cancer. Doyle was a veteran radio and television journalist who also possessed a strong sales background. His knack for research and organization enabled him to produce the detailed Ratings and Rates material and the brilliant chapter on "Selling against (and with) Other Media." His remaining contributions to the writing of this project—especially the organization of several interviews we conducted into one cohesive chapter—were invaluable. Doyle served as the editor of our first draft written two years ago and kept the challenge of preparing a book-length manuscript in perspective for both of us during many months of writing.

Thanks, Doyle. This book is dedicated to your memory. We'll all miss you.

Bart White
May 1988

Chapter 1

INTRODUCTION TO THE SELLING PROCESS

IN THE BEGINNING

The old saying promises that if you build a better mousetrap, the world will beat a path to your door. Don't believe it! First, the world has to be told of your invention. Second, it must be convinced that your mousetrap really is better at solving the mouse problem. Third, the world has to believe that your invention is a real value in terms of how much you expect to be paid for it and what benefits the world will derive from this payment.

The elements between the invention of the better mousetrap and the purchase of it in huge quantities make up the field of salesmanship. Failure to utilize salesmanship in convincing the world that the invention is a real value—a product that works well in accomplishing its aims at a price that makes it a value—can mean failure in the marketplace for the invention.

Salesmanship began in *barter*, the process of one person trading surplus goods for another person's surplus goods. One distant ancestor, after returning from a successful hunt with lots of meat, most likely persuaded another ancestor with no meat and lots of fur skins to trade some of those extra pelts for dinner.

Barter became more difficult as society grew more complex. More people had more types of surplus goods, and finding mutually beneficial matches became problematic. Some intermediate medium of exchange was necessary, something a person could accept for surplus goods and then trade to a third person for desirable goods at a later time. Salt served this purpose in some societies, as did gold in others; some North American Indians used shell beads called *wampum*.

Optimum Level Production

The economic system in the United States (and in the rest of the free world) is founded on producing at the optimum level, which means that markets must be established for the products to enable production to continue at that optimum level. A brief explanation of the process will help.

A company beginning business has a fixed overhead—the cost of plant, management, machinery, and the like—the cost of which must be met no matter how many products are produced or sold. Add to the fixed costs a variable factor that includes the wages of the workers and the operating costs of the machinery. The company must strive at first to meet the *breakeven point*, that point at which the price for which the product can be sold exactly matches the cost of its production. Sales of enough units to match this breakeven point is the first milestone the beginning company must reach. The company no longer is losing money on each product unit at this point, but neither is it making a profit on each product unit sold. Thus, the company is not making money for its investors.

After reaching the breakeven point, the next aim of the company is to reach the *optimum level production point*, that point at which the cost of producing the product, including the fixed and variable costs of overhead and production, is lowest in relation to the selling price for the product. Beyond this optimum point, the cost of adding additional workers or shifts of workers, additional machinery, and/or expanded plant facilities causes the unit price of production to rise. This increase lowers the amount and percentage of profit for each product unit or, if the profit is to remain the same, causes a rise in price.

The company wants to produce at the optimum level. To do this, it must sell the number of units of product necessary to maintain production at this optimum level. Creation of markets and salesmanship to supply those markets with the company's product become necessary.

The Early Settlers

In *Salesmanship: Modern Principles and Practices*, U. Grant Marsh says the first settlers on the North American continent found the native forest hostile, and nature not always hospitable. Each family had to be self-sufficient. Marsh says,

> It is conceivable that little Martha said to her father one day in the spring after the snow had melted, "You know, Papa, my shoes are worn out. When you make me some new ones, will you make them like Charity Abbott's? Her shoes are still pretty."
>
> Stirred by her persuasive approach, Martha's father visited his neighbor, Henry Abbott.
>
> "Tell me, Henry, how long did it take to make Charity's shoes?"

Henry's traveling shoestore

"Maybe half a day."

"Hm. Tell you what. You make boots for Martha, Henry, and I'll hoe your corn for two days."

It was a deal. Before long, Henry Abbott was a part-time farmer and a part-time shoemaker.[1]

Taking Marsh's story further, suppose other farmers approached Henry in the same manner as Martha's father. Soon, Henry was getting his potatoes planted and hoed, as well as the corn, and Henry was spending more time making boots and shoes. As time went on, Henry discovered ways to shorten the time spent on each boot and trained a helper.

Need for Expansion

Now Henry could produce more boots than his immediate neighbors needed and yet he would need to produce even more if he were going to spend all his work time producing boots and shoes and keep his trained helper. After all, he had a good product that was in demand by those who knew of it. Would it not also be in demand by others, if only they knew of its benefits for them?

So, Henry took to the road in his wagon one or two days a week to show his boots to people farther from his homestead. At this point, Henry was letting the "world" know about his "better mousetrap." He visited people to tell them about the benefits of his boots and shoes and to explain how

Henry's shoe factory

those benefits would fill these people's needs, which they may not have perceived until Henry pointed out the inadequacies of their homemade boots.

Assume that Henry brought back enough orders through these trips that he had to train a second helper. With further expansion, buying materials, seeing that orders were filled and delivered promptly, and supervising his helpers in the bootmaking operation took too much of Henry's time to allow him to continue making his rounds in the wagon. Having the vision that an entrepreneur must have, Henry hired his first salesperson and laid the foundation for what would become one of the first shoe factories in the United States.

Fiction? Dreaming? Situations similar to the mythical one described were the starting points of many of what are the largest businesses in this country today.

Salesmanship

Note how quickly the success of the company becomes dependent on the elements of salesmanship. As soon as Henry had decided that his future lay in bootmaking and not in farming, he had to expand sales beyond those people who asked for his boots by seeking to build additional markets

Mass production made goods faster and cheaper

among people who were not familiar with his product. After seeing the boots, these people had to be shown why this was the "better mousetrap," or the product for them, and why they should pay the price asked.

Producing a good product and offering it for sale are not enough. The mere offering of the product is a rudimentary form of salesmanship, but more than this is required to move the products from the producer to the user in sufficient volume for the business to prosper. This moving of the product from producer to user is the field of the salesperson—*salesmanship*.

Henry Ford's Automobile

Automobiles were expensive and few in number when Henry Ford decided he could make more of them faster and at a cheaper unit price through mass production. The market for automobiles at that time was severely limited. However, Ford saw potential markets that would justify mass production. The problem was the cultivation of these additional markets. The product was produced, salesmanship moved the products into the hands of dealers, after which salesmanship moved the same products from dealer to customer-user, and the rest is history—the history of the American automobile industry.

When Henry the bootmaker wanted to go beyond producing boots just for his neighors and when Henry Ford wanted to go beyond producing automobiles as playthings for the rich, both faced the two prime problems ad-

The drummer created a bad reputation for salespeople

dressed by salesmanship: (1) the expansion of the existing market to absorb more of the products to be produced and (2) the identification (or creation) of new markets to push beyond the volume that could be absorbed by the existing markets.

Expansion of the existing market does not mean hiring salespersons to sell things that people do not need or cannot use or that should not be sold. This has too often been the perception of the salesperson by much of society: someone who comes into an area and sells lots of gadgets to people who had no need for them and will not find them useful. This "salesperson" then moves on to more fertile areas to repeat the process. For a long time many people put salespeople in the same category they would a carnival pitchman: not believable and not dependable.

The Drummer

The Music Man capitalized on such a negative impression of the salesperson of the turn of the century. This individual was sometimes called the *drummer* because his job was to drum up business. Some of these early traveling salespeople actually did use drums and other noisemakers to attract a crowd to hear the pitch for their products. In the movie cited, the traveling salesperson set out to sell band instruments and uniforms without a care as to whether the town's youth could utilize the items being sold. The idea was "load 'em up with the merchandise and get out of town quickly" before the townspeople found out they had been taken. Some so-called salespeople pursue the same course today, and some of this breed are likely to remain as long as there are people who are gullible enough to be easily separated from their money.

In these earlier days, the salesperson generally did not project a professional image, and by and large salesmanship was not a respected profession or craft. However, even then some prided themselves on being the forerunners of progress and the introducers of new products to people or businesses who had a real need for the new product, whether they knew it or not.

Imagine what society might have been like without these "pioneers of progress" to sell automobiles, sewing machines, farm plows, and the myriad other products that salesmanship has moved from the production line to the consumer.

THE SALES PROCESS

The sales process model below defines the theory of selling.

$$\text{Definition of Product Potential} + \frac{\text{Definition of Potential Customers} + \text{Potential Customer Needs}}{\text{Price Related to Benefits}} = \text{Sales Success}$$

The model shown is not intended to be a precise mathematical formula that quantifies each potential sale and precisely predicts in advance the odds of success for the sales attempt. Because two of the variables (the salesperson and the potential customer) are human factors, a precise formula for the sales effort outcome is impossible.

The prospective salesperson should look closely at the four major elements shown in the model as parts of the sales process. Although none of the four elements aims directly at the salesperson's revenue or profit, the combination of the four directly affects the success, and thus the income, of the salesperson.

Product Potential

The first element in the model is the *definition of product potential*. What can the product accomplish, for whom, and under what circumstances? The salesperson must be armed with sufficient knowledge about what the product is capable of accomplishing and under what circumstances it can provide these beneficial returns. Lack of sufficient product knowledge has torpedoed many potential sales.

Potential Customers

The model also calls for a *definition of potential customers* for the product. The definition of the product potential helps in identifying the potential customers for such a product. For instance, the makers of economy automobiles are unlikely to be good potential customers for a new engine component planned to increase speed, horsepower, and racing ability.

For too many years, the pat definition of a good salesperson was someone who could "sell refrigerators to Eskimos," meaning the salesperson could sell something to people who had no reason to buy and who would derive no use or satisfaction from the product. Some types of the sales operations still work that way, such as the boiler rooms for selling worthless or near-worthless stocks and magazine subscription salespeople who are interested only in the advance payment and not in whether the magazines ordered will be useful, appreciated, or, at times, even delivered.

These examples and the old view of the successful salesperson are not professional salesmanship. The successful salesperson is one who can make the sale, go back to the customer without fear, and, while checking on the success of the first sale, make a follow-up sale to an already satisfied customer.

Potential Customer Needs

Another element listed in the model is the *definition of potential customer needs*. As noted, the successful sale includes satisfaction on the part of the salesperson for having made the sale, but to derive that satisfaction, the salesperson must be sure of a potentially satisfied customer. Otherwise, returning for subsequent sales will be difficult.

People in business frequently hear of the salesperson who could "sell anybody anything once" but could not get repeat business. Businesses generally shy away from hiring such so-called salespeople because they know that even after the salesperson has left their employment, the problems caused by that individual may live on to haunt the company.

Price Related to Benefit

The fourth element in the sales process model is *price related to benefit*. This factor does not mean that only the cheapest products can be sold successfully. The opposite is more often true.

If the salesperson can contrast the benefits to be provided by the product in relation to the price, many times the product that on the surface looks to be the more expensive is shown to be the better value. John Ruskin, whose name adorned cigars for years, said it most clearly when he declared there was no product that someone could not make less worthwhile and thus cheaper. Ruskin added that those who bought on price alone were that person's fair game.

Lawn mowers are priced from around $100 to more than $2,000. Why pay more than the lowest price for a lawn mower when all of them will cut grass? The advantages of the higher-priced mowers can be demonstrated and the price related to benefit shown.

The same applies to automobiles and their prices. At its most basic level, the automobile is a transportation device intended to move people from one place to another. Yet prices of new automobiles range from about $4,000 to well over $100,000. Why pay more than the rock-bottom price for an automobile? Those who have bought automobiles (and many who have not) have ready answers. Again, the price related to benefit makes the higher-priced automobiles salable.

Remember Henry the bootmaker? Why spend two days hoeing corn for a pair of shoes made by Henry when Papa could make a leather covering resembling shoes at home and avoid those two days hoeing corn in the hot sun?

The answer to all the above questions is that a price-benefit relationship has been established in the mind of the customer. Product A costs more than Product B, but Product A offers more of the benefits needed or desired by the customer than does Product B. When these benefits are taken into account, higher-priced Product A becomes the better value.

Think back to the example of the extremes of prices for lawn mowers. The basic mower cuts grass, as does the most expensive one. As the customer moves up the price scale, quality, durability, and extra features are available at the higher prices. Unless salesmanship demonstrates to the customer why the higher-priced mower better fits his or her needs and why the price-benefit ratio is better in the higher-priced mower, why should anyone buy other than the cheapest mower?

Remember, however, good salesmanship is not simply moving the potential customer up the price ladder. Good salesmanship is placing the potential customer at the point on the product and price ladder that maximizes the benefits for both the customer and the salesperson.

THE SALES GRID®

In *The Grid for Sales Excellence*, Robert Blake and Jane Mouton explain the sales process in terms of a grid that shows the concern of the salesperson (1) for making the sale and (2) for the customer (see Figure 1-1).

Blake and Mouton declare:

> *The concern for making a sale and the way in which it is linked with the concern for the customer are at the foundation of this selling strategy. . . . A high concern for making the sale joined with a low concern for the customer results in a significantly different sales approach than that encountered when a high concern for the sale is joined with a high concern for the customer, or when a high concern for the customer is coupled with a low concern for the sale.*[2]

From their grid, Blake and Mouton predict high effectiveness for the salesperson who has both a high concern for the sale and a high concern for the customer in sales to customers of all types, from those with high concern for the salesperson and low concern against buying to those customers with low concern for the salesperson and a high concern against buying.[3]

To sum up the grid and its meaning, the effective salesperson must have at least a fairly high concern for making the sale. If not, the salesperson does not really care whether the sale is made, and the sales effort will demonstrate this. Furthermore, the professional salesperson also must have concern for the customer. The sale that is not good for the customer is not good for the salesperson, especially in the long run. The level of this concern affects the sales process also.

The customer's concern about agreeing to the sale is also reflected in the grid. If the customer has such a high concern about the sale that he or she intends to buy nothing, this will adversely affect the sales effort of any salesperson. At the other end of the grid line, the customer who is willing to buy anything makes the sale easy. Normally, neither salesperson nor customer occupies either extreme.

BROADCASTING AS A BUSINESS

The first step in studying broadcast sales is recognizing that the majority of broadcasting outlets—those designated as commercial radio and television and cable television operations—are businesses. The purpose of these businesses is to make money for their operators and investors—to show a return on investment, to build financial independence, to build capital for reinvestment in the business or investment in other businesses, or for personal investment and well-being. As businesses, these broadcasting outlets are expected to return a profit. This expectation of profit is the reason for and the

FIGURE 1-1
The Sales Grid

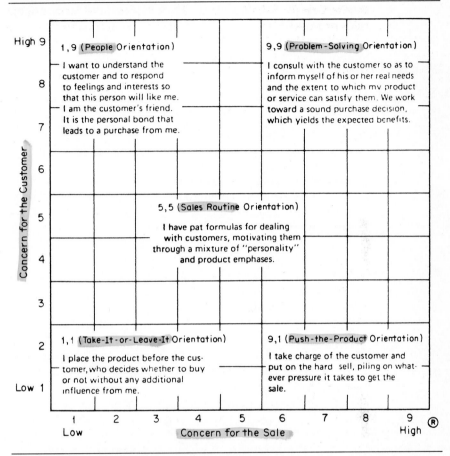

The Sales Grid figure from *The Grid for Sales Excellence* (2nd edition), by Robert R. Blake and Jane Srygley Mouton. New York: McGraw-Hill Book Company, Copyright © 1980, page 6. Reproduced by permission

responsibility of those charged with sale of the advertising time on these broadcasting outlets.

Product versus Service Orientation

Businesses usually are identified as either *product oriented* or *service oriented*. The business either makes a product for sale or it offers a service. Broadcasting should be approached on the basis that the underlying aim of the business is to make money by providing a service—access to the broadcast outlet's audience. This is not to say that one should concentrate totally on this aspect of the business, offering as little as possible for the highest price possible. Too many businesses have gone out of business by operating on that assumption.

Quality versus Low Price

The reputable business that wants to operate for the long term plans its operation to deliver as good a product or service as possible at a reasonable market price. The business plans on increases in sales of the product or service to allow it to increase its total revenues yearly. In broadcasting, however, the amount of product cannot be increased beyond the finite number of advertising availabilities within the station's time period of operation. Thus, when a sold-out or nearly sold-out condition exists at the broadcasting outlet, the price per availability can be expected to increase due to the popularity of the broadcast outlet as an advertising medium. Also, when the audience available at particular times increases, the broadcast outlet can be expected to raise prices for advertising availabilities within that time period because the benefit to the advertiser has increased.

Broadcasting—the radio and television station portions—operate on the basis of providing a service to the public and then selling to advertisers access to the public that consumes the provided service. Cable television outlets operate on the basis of selling a service—an expansion of the viewing channels available to the public—and of selling access to those viewing audiences to advertisers. This double-sales mode is similar to the operation of newspapers and magazines: the public pays a subscription or single-copy price for the newspaper or magazine, and advertisers are sold access to the audiences who purchase copies of the newspaper or magazine.

Broadcasting versus Print

Broadcasting differs from print media in that it is mandated by current communications law to operate "in the public interest, convenience and necessity." Each radio or television station is licensed by the Federal Communications Commission to utilize a particular portion of the broadcasting spectrum at stated power levels and under other particular conditions. Therefore, current deregulation efforts notwithstanding, the broadcaster offers a service to attract listeners or viewers in order to sell access to this audience to advertisers, but the broadcaster must also provide a public service function to the listeners and viewers as well. Due to the multiple signals available to the overwhelming majority of the public and the other competitive means of delivering signals, this public service function is not as predominant today as in earlier years when fewer radio and television stations were on the air. However, broadcasters still must be able to show that they serve their area and listeners or viewers with a needed service that is attuned to the peculiarities of the broadcaster's service area.

Broadcasters choose music or nonmusic formats for radio stations and networks and/or other programming sources for television stations, and they offer newscasts and public service programs and messages in order to be responsible broadcasters and hold their licenses as they attract and hold as large and as faithful an audience as possible.

Audience Access

The audience and potential advertisers' access to it provide the opportunity for the broadcaster to (1) go into business, (2) stay in business, and (3) make a profit in the business of broadcasting.

The beginning broadcast salesperson must keep in mind that the sale to be made is for time for the advertiser's message, but the audience accessible at the particular time sold is the essential component of success for the advertising message.

TANGIBLE VERSUS INTANGIBLE SELLING

The position of salesperson at a broadcasting operation is a vital one. Salespeople are charged with bringing in the revenue on which the broadcast outlet depends for its existence.

Selling is typically divided into tangible and intangible categories. *Tangible selling* is the sale of items that can be physically shown, displayed, or turned over to the customer to operate. Within this category are automobiles, shoes, clothing, and other products with which the customer may form a physical relationship by holding, touching, and operating the product.

The second category, *intangibles* or *nontangibles*, include such items as insurance policies, stocks, bonds, retirement programs, and broadcast advertising. In selling intangibles, the salesperson cannot build the physical relationship between customer and product that is possible with tangibles. Instead, the relationship must be built on a mental basis.

The beginning salesperson must learn the distinct differences between selling tangibles and selling intangibles to use them to advantage in the selling process.

Tangible Products

Many people feel that selling a tangible product is easier because it can be placed in the customer's possession to be looked at, tried, and enjoyed. Indeed, some salespeople believe that the sales process is half over when the customer agrees to accept the tangible product for try out.

When an individual looks at a new piece of clothing, the first step is to look at it on the rack to check texture, color, design, and perhaps price. The salesperson talks about the value of the material, the cut or design of the piece of clothing, the beautiful color, and perhaps the economy represented by the price of the article. Then the salesperson suggests that the individual try on the clothing to get the full effect of the special properties already pointed out. Getting the potential customer to try on the clothing is a major step in the sales process because the customer at that time is already thinking in terms of possible ownership of the article.

The same process works in the sale of an automobile. The customer on the sales lot is approached by the salesperson, who then begins to point out the features of the automobile in which the potential customer has expressed some interest. If no interest has been expressed in a particular automobile, the salesperson tries to get information from the potential customer to determine the automobile to which the potential customer should be steered.

After determining that the individual is interested in a particular automobile and really is a potential customer, the salesperson next wants to get that individual inside the automobile, to sit in it and try the controls, and to imagine himself or herself in control of the automobile. The next step for the salesperson is to get the individual behind the wheel of a demonstrator automobile to control the automobile on the street and further experience what ownership of the automobile would mean to the individual.

In simplest form, demonstration is the backbone of selling a tangible product: how it works, what features it has, what it can do for the customer, and the fact that it has a beneficial price-benefit ratio.

Intangible Sales

The salesperson selling intangibles, unlike the seller of tangible products, cannot establish a physical relationship between the potential customer and the intangible. In selling intangibles, the salesperson must build in the potential customer's imagination those benefits of ownership that are physically demonstrated in the selling of tangible products.

Despite the inability to establish a physical relationship between the potential customer and the item being sold, the seller of intangibles must conform to the same elements of the sales model. The salesperson must define the potential of the intangible product or service, the potential customers, potential customer needs, and a favorable price-benefit relationship.

The salesperson selling a life insurance policy to a potential customer does not make the sale by placing a policy in the hands of the potential customer. The broadcast salesperson likewise does not make a sale by placing a

Selling an intangible product

contract for a certain number of spots, or advertising availabilities, in the hands of a potential customer. Sellers of intangibles must build the advantages of ownership with ideas that create the benefits of the projected purchase within the potential customer's mind.

Some sales managers have compared the sale of intangibles to selling "not the steak but the sizzle." The demonstration of the intangible must be done in the mind of the customer because it cannot be carried out physically before the customer's eyes.

The advantage of possessing a number of radio or television (or cable television) spots does not lie in the physical possession of these advertising availabilities; it lies in what these advertising availabilities are intended to accomplish for the person or company purchasing them. People who sell intangibles build within the customer's mind the images of the same benefits that the seller of tangible products displays before the customer's eyes.

The seller of intangibles must be able to build this mental image based on the future action of the intangible, the benefits of its features, and the future favorable price-benefit ratio. Buying an intangible takes more faith in the salesperson and the salesperson's company on the part of the customer than does buying a tangible product that the customer can see, touch, feel, and/or operate.

In selling broadcasting, the salesperson must demonstrate to the potential customer that the proposed purchase of commercial time for advertising will bring the benefits the businessperson desires from advertising: increased business and increased revenue.

CREATING THE NEED

Some cynics describe the sales approach in mass production economies, such as that of the United States, as (1) creating a product, (2) creating a need for the product, (3) showing that the product fulfills that created need, and (4) selling the product to customers to fulfill the need they didn't know they had until the salesperson pointed it out and then proceeded to fulfill it with the product for sale.

This view of the selling and marketing of products is both cynical and simplistic. No one knew electric lights were needed before they were invented, yet Edison did not create the need for electric lights. Anyone who had suffered through the poor light of oil burning in shallow vessels, candles, kerosene lamps, or gas jets already had a need for better light. Each of these light-producing devices had come along to satisfy that need better than did its predecessor.

No one knew about the need for automobiles before the first horseless carriage was invented. However, many people had felt the need for a faster, more comfortable means of transportation than sitting astride a horse for days or traveling in a horse-drawn coach for long trips. Certainly no one said, "What we need is an airplane to satisfy our need for faster travel" until after the Wright brothers showed that people could fly in machines.

Filling a Need

The marketers of electric lights, automobiles, and airplanes did not create a need in their customers; all of them filled a need that had not been met adequately by preceding products. They succeeded by *identifying* this inadequately met need and then building a product that could better satisfy it.

Sponsors—that is, purchasers of advertising time on radio, television, or cable television who thereby sponsor or make available to the listener or viewer the program material—typically do not know they have a need for what the broadcast salesperson is selling, which is broadcast time in which they can advertise. The broadcast salesperson perceives how advertising time can benefit the potential sponsor. Then the broadcast salesperson plans a detailed campaign to convince the potential advertiser that the purchase of time on the salesperson's particular outlet can help the advertiser achieve goals.

The potential advertiser may not know—or may not admit to knowing—a need to advertise on the salesperson's particular broadcasting outlet or, indeed, in any advertising medium. The job of the salesperson may not be the single one of convincing the potential advertiser to buy advertising time on the salesperson's broadcast outlet. Instead, it may be the multiple task of first convincing the potential advertiser that advertising in some medium is needed to help the business meet its goals; second, convincing the potential advertiser that the advertising, or some part of it, should be placed in broadcasting; and third, that the salesperson's own broadcast outlet is the proper place for the broadcast advertising.

Note that in this process no need has been created; rather, the broadcast salesperson has identified a need that may not have been apparent to the potential advertiser.

MASS MEDIA AND ADVERTISING

A return to the story of Henry, the part-time bootmaker who became Henry the boot factory owner, is in order. As the economy of the nation grew along with Henry and others like him, hiring enough salespeople to individually contact each potential customer became uneconomical for Henry (or his successors at the factory).

Advertising Begins

About this time, some entrepreneurs were deciding they could make money by printing weekly newspapers or monthly magazines filled with items of interest to the public. At first, these publishers might have relied on meeting the costs of running the business and providing a profit for the owner through the price paid by the people who bought copies of the newspaper or magazine.

However, the publisher-owner of the newspaper or magazine might have had trouble meeting expenses and realizing a profit from the price paid by subscribers and decided to inform people of products and businesses as well as about the topics printed as news. This enterprising publisher would then seek out manufacturers and merchants and offer to inform readers about their products or businesses, provided the publication was paid to do so. On the other hand, some enterprising merchants or manufacturers, realizing how people looked forward to and read the publication, might have decided they might get more customers by spreading word of their wares to potential buyers through the publication.

Either way, advertising in mass media began.

Early mass media advertising

Mass Media Defined

Any medium that can deliver a message, including an advertising message, to a large number of people at the same time is a *mass medium*. This definition can include the person with an advertising sandwich board walking down a busy street in a large city as well as the airplane flying above the city trailing a banner.

For the purposes of this book, the definition of *mass media* is limited to radio, television, newspapers, magazines, and other periodicals, direct mail, and the newest electronic medium, cable television. These media are divided into two major segments: print advertising media and electronic advertising media. *Print advertising media* include newspapers, magazines, periodicals, and direct mail. *Electronic advertising media* include radio, television, and cable television. (Newer electronic services, including direct-broadcast satellites, are not included because of lack of establishment in the marketplace.)

The basic concept of advertising is that if mass media are used to show the identification of a need and how a particular product or service fills that now-identified need, then the sales job for that product or service becomes easier. Advertising preconditions the customer somewhat to be more receptive to the product or service.

Advertising and Mass Production

Many economic leaders profess that without advertising our economy could not operate at mass production levels and employ the number of workers necessary for our society. Most economists agree that without advertising to aid in the expansion of markets, which results in mass production, the products would be much more expensive, perhaps prohibitively so, for the potential customer or consumer.

When Henry Ford put into effect his method of producing large numbers of automobiles at a lower cost per automobile, the result was that more customers had to be found to buy this larger output of automobiles. Otherwise, the output of automobiles would have had to be cut and the price of each made higher so the company could stay in business.

The job of mass media advertising thus becomes helping to sell the products of mass production so that mass production can continue and grow. This growth allows the unit cost of the product to be lowered and thus the price to consumers to be lower.

Advertising and Lower Prices

The first digital watches introduced to the marketplace were priced at about $500 each. Today, digital watches are available at prices lower than $10 each. In the chain of events leading to drastically lower prices, all the best marketing aids were at work. Increased production of the components that go into digital watches brought down the unit cost of these components. Increased production of the watches took place because of increased availability of components at lower cost. The movement of more lower-priced digital watches to consumers through mass media advertising created more demand for the watches, thus refueling the entire cycle.

The same process happened in the case of hand-held calculators. The first small calculators were very expensive, but today similar models sell for less than $10. Again, mass media advertising helped the sales job of moving the merchandise into the hands of consumers, and more calculators could be built from components that became cheaper as more were manufactured. So, the price of the final product dropped precipitately.

The same process has been at work in the personal computer field, although it still takes much more than $10 to buy one. The small, inexpensive computers of today contain computing power beyond that of the earlier generation of computers that occupied large rooms, required massive air conditioning units, and represented major capital expenditures.

In all of this process, mass media advertising did not create a need. From Henry the bootmaker's first advertisement in the newspaper of his day to today's television advertisements for many different products, no one has created a need. What they have done is identify a need the customer had or stirred a latent need unknown to the consumer until the advertising triggered it.

Active and Passive Media

Newspapers, magazines, other periodicals, and direct mail are classified as *active media*, which means that the consumer must exert an effort to be exposed to the advertising messages contained in them. The consumer must turn the pages or open the direct mail piece and then must read in order to understand the advertising message and its intent.

Radio, television, and cable television are classified as *passive media*, which means the consumer is required to do nothing in order to absorb the advertising beyond turning on the radio or television. While the consumer is listening to a radio program or watching a television program, the commercial begins, with no effort on the part of the consumer. Thus, the commercial may be absorbed with no effort by the consumer other than to remain passive and keep eyes and ears open.

Early in our society, the newspaper became the dominant mass medium for advertising. Magazines followed, with direct mail trailing. Newspaper advertising was feasible for both national and local advertisers, but advertising in a nationally distributed magazine was not feasible for local firms. Direct mail was more expensive, but it could be targeted to a particular group of potential customers. The newspaper of this period also was the primary source of information and news for the society's citizens. This mass media mix prevailed until the 1920s, when radio first came onto the scene.

Electronic Advertising Begins

If Herbert Hoover, then secretary of commerce and later president, and others had had their way, our broadcast system in the United States would have developed along the lines of the British system, in which advertising was not allowed on radio (until the advent of television, when advertising was allowed on non-BBC stations).

Instead, electronic media advertising began in the United States on radio station WEAF in New York City in 1922, with a successful advertising promotion by a local real estate firm. Since then, as radio grew as an advertising medium, it was joined by television in the 1940s and by cable television in recent years.

As radio and television advertising revenues have grown, the total amount of money spent on advertising also has grown. In 1987, advertisers spent more than $88 billion on all forms of advertising. In 1988, that figure is predicted to rise to $95 billion.[4]

Today, television is recognized as the most influential mass medium by mass media analysts; newspapers are second and then radio, magazines, direct mail, and other forms of advertising. When advertising volume alone is considered, newspapers still rank first, with television second.

THE ELECTRONIC MEDIA

The electronic media are very young compared to the print media. In terms of influence as advertising media, the electronic media have grown rapidly in their relatively short lives and are strong competitors for the advertising dollar. This rapid growth has come about because of the unique characteristics of these newer media.

Radio

Radio, which was the first national advertising and entertainment medium in the electronic field, grew from being a novelty to being the mainstay of home entertainment. In what have been the "Golden Years" of radio, programs featured performances by top entertainers as well as commentary on news issues of the day, and the programs were supported by big national advertisers.

By the early 1950s, the newer medium of television was flexing its muscles and had lured radio's national network shows and personalities to the developing medium. Along with these entertainment shows and personalities went the national advertisers by the scores. As both an entertainment medium and an advertising medium, radio was predicted to be dead. Had the radio industry been incapable of change, it might have ceased to exist.

As the national programs and national advertisers deserted to television, radio changed its format to offer musical or news and information programs and then sold the advertising time in these programs to local businesses. Salesmanship took the place of taking orders, the lost national advertising revenue was replaced, the number of radio stations increased, and the amount of advertising revenue for radio as a whole increased greatly.

Thus, radio changed from a predominantly national advertising medium to a predominantly local advertising medium during the 1950s. In the years since, radio as an industry has prospered as a local advertising medium. In recent years, however, national advertising has been returning to radio as a major advertising vehicle, largely because of the rising cost of television advertising.

Television

Television combines sight and sound and generally is considered the premier advertising medium for most types of products and services. It is the medium with which the average person in this country spends almost as much time as is spent sleeping, and it is the medium that influences the buying habits of practically every family.

Television began in the late 1930s, but its expansion was delayed by World War II. Television experienced an explosion of growth in the late 1940s and 1950s, and VHF television stations became very profitable.

UHF television stations were most successful in those few markets where all the television stations were ultrahigh frequency. Independent television stations (those not affiliated with networks) had rough times; they did not have the payments from the networks for carrying network programs, did not have the audiences built by the popular network programs, and had to purchase syndicated programming and movies that would attract viewers away from the network programs shown by their local competitors.

In recent years, many of these independent television stations have grown greatly in profitability along with the UHF and VHF network-affiliated television stations. A number of UHF frequencies, which lay dormant for years, now have successful independent television stations in operation. However, these independent television stations as a class are still not profitable. The average independent television station lost almost half a million dollars in 1986, while the average network-affiliated television station showed a profit of almost $4.5 million.

One of the major factors in this downturn in profitability was reported to be the high and rising cost of programming, as more independent stations attempted to lock up or warehouse programming to keep it from their competitors.

LPTV In recent years the Federal Communications Commission has authorized a new class of television stations. These low-power television (LPTV) stations operate at very low power (in the manner of translator stations) but are allowed to originate programming and sell advertising rather than merely retransmitting the signal of an existing station. The LPTV stations have small coverage areas, generally the community of license.

Where the LPTV stations will fit in the advertising pattern remains to be decided as more of them are constructed and seek advertising revenue to sustain themselves.

Cable Television

Cable television began as a means of providing television station signals to homes whose residents otherwise could not receive viewable television. An enterprising businessman in Pennsylvania erected an antenna on a high tower on an elevation allowing reception of available television stations. The television signals were fed down wire cables to homes, and cable was first named community antenna television (CATV).

Cable remained primarily a relayer of broadcast television signals in the manner described for a number of years. The equipment became better and more sophisticated, with better and more selective antennas, better head-end equipment to process signals received by the antennas, better cable to carry the signals to the homes, and better amplifiers to enhance the signals periodically on their way to the consumers.

Community Antenna Relay System The first outreach by these local CATV systems came with the development of community antenna relay systems (CARS). Through cooperative effort, they developed microwave systems to transmit signals from more distant television stations and added these stations to their local area offerings.

Satellites The development and proliferation of communications satellites in orbit led to new opportunities for importation of signals by CATV systems. Satellites placed in geostationary orbit some 22,000 miles above the earth matched the earth's rotation and enabled the satellite to have a stable, large *footprint*, that is, coverage or reception area. Addition of a satellite-receiving antenna was another way for the community antenna television systems, rapidly changing into today's cable television systems, to receive additional signals to offer to their customers.

The Superstations With the addition of satellites, the signals that could be made available for cable systems proliferated. Ted Turner purchased a failing UHF television station in Atlanta and arranged for a satellite uplink company to place the station's television signal on a satellite transponder. The station's programming then was offered to cable television companies. Thus was born Superstation WTBS.

In order to receive the new offerings available on the satellites, the cable television systems had only to install a satellite receiving antenna or dish at the cable system head-end. Other enterprising businesspeople saw the opportunity for programming cable television services, and a variety of cable networks emerged. USA Network was one of the first. Later additions have included Lifetime, the Nashville Network, Cable News Network, the Weather Channel, and ESPN. These networks depended on advertising for their livelihood, although some of them, especially in earlier days, charged cable systems a small fee per cable system subscriber. (A number of cable networks now pay cable systems for carrying their signals.)

Home Box Office was among the leaders in cable networking but on a different basis. It did not accept advertising and thus relied on fees paid by cable system subscribers. It became a "premium" channel on cable systems, sold to cable subscribers for an additional fee above the basic charge. Other premium channels that soon joined in offering wares to cable systems included Showtime, the Movie Channel, Cinemax, and the Disney Channel.

Other television stations have attempted to follow the superstation route of WTBS, including WGN from Chicago and WOR in Secacus, New Jersey (New York City area). Shopping channels have also proliferated following the success of Home Shopping Network.

The cable television system of today is a far cry from the community antenna television systems that began the industry. Many more channels of programming come to the cable system subscriber's television set, and the signals of area television stations are but a small part of the overall cable offerings.

Although the cable system subscriber fee has continued to provide the lion's share of revenue for local cable systems, many of them have gone into local advertising sales. The advertising availabilities come in one of two ways: (1) through selling availabilities provided to the local systems by cable network operators within their programming or (2) through the programming of one or more channels by local systems themselves, and the sale of availabilities within that programming.

SUMMARY

The mass production economy of the United States, evolved from earlier self-sufficiency and barter systems that did not allow easy, free movement of goods from the producer to consumer. Production at the optimum level is necessary for the mass production economy to operate at its best.

Today's large businesses began with entrepreneurs who had the vision to see the possibility of lowering costs and prices through large-scale production.

Salesmanship is the process of moving the output of mass production from the producer to the consumer. Sales success depends on several factors: what the product can accomplish (definition of product potential); who is likely to need or desire it (definition of potential customers); why these people should need or desire it (potential customer needs); and how the cost of the product compares with the benefits to be gained (price related to benefits).

The effective salesperson is one who cares about both making the sale and benefiting the customer. This type of salesperson also cultivates a relationship in which the customer's regard for the salesperson outweighs customer resistance to the cost of the sale (see Figure 1-1, the Sales Grid).

Broadcasting is a business; its product is a service—access to an audience who has gathered for a purpose other than that of being exposed to broadcast advertising.

Tangible selling is selling a product that can be demonstrated, shown, or placed within the control of the customer. Intangible selling deals with selling something that cannot be placed in the hands of, or control of, the customer. The benefits of the sale must be created within the customer's mind.

No one sells a product or service by creating a need. The sale takes place through the identification of a need not adequately met by products already on the market.

Advertising is a necessity in the process of moving products from the producer to the customer. Mass media advertising includes those advertising media that reach mass audiences at one time.

Print media are classified as active media; broadcast media are classified as passive media.

Electronic advertising in the United States dates from the placement of an advertisement on WEAF in New York in 1922. Radio, the only electronic medium for decades, was joined and severely hurt by television in the late 1940s and early 1950s. Television went on to become the premier electronic medium, but radio changed from a nationally oriented to a locally oriented medium and found renewed success.

Television has grown as a dominant advertising medium and proliferated through the addition of independent television stations, low-power television, and cable television, with its many channels of viewing.

NOTES

1. U. Grant Marsh, *Salesmanship: Modern Principles and Practices* © 1972, p. 43. Reprinted by permission of Prentice-Hall, Inc., Englewood Cliffs, New Jersey.

2. Robert Blake and Jane Mouton, *The Grid for Sales Excellence*, 2nd ed. (New York: McGraw-Hill, 1980), pp. 2–6.

3. Ibid.

4. Warren K. Agee, Phillip H. Ault, and Edwin Emery, *Introduction to Mass Communications*, 9th ed. (New York: Harper & Row, 1988), p. 347.

Chapter 2

SALESMANSHIP

IN BROADCASTING

Before beginning to sell broadcasting, the salesperson needs a broad understanding of the overall concept of advertising. The sale of broadcasting—marketing the time availabilities on broadcast outlets for the placement of advertising messages—is one phase of the much larger field of advertising, and this sales effort needs to be viewed in terms of that much larger field.

ADVERTISING ASSUMPTIONS

Advertising is the conscious effort to spread information about a particular event, cause, or entity. Advertising is generally differentiated from public information, public relations, or public service messages in that advertisers pay for the time or space used to present their messages and the spread of information by the other means does not involve such a payment.

Under the above definition, any spread of knowledge or information for which payment of some kind is made becomes a form of advertisement. The sign that calls attention to the name or kind of business occupying a building is a form of advertising, as are placards and other public notices or enticements placed in the display window of the business. The firm's listing among other businesses and its own display listing, if it has one, in the telephone book are forms of advertising. Flyers and other printed matter distributed to the public and any other means of calling public attention to the business are forms of advertising.

Some basic assumptions may be made about advertising. The first is that advertising is a basic and needed commodity for any business that must interact with the public, segments of the public, or segments of the business community for its business success. Some business operators may profess they do not need advertising even while they are constantly engaging in some form of advertising as it has been defined.

The sign on the company building is a basic form of advertising because the sign is intended to let the public know that the firm is ready to engage in business. Placing goods in the window, perhaps with signs alongside, takes the firm a further step into the field of advertising. This is oftentimes called *merchandising* or *marketing*, but both are extensions of advertising in its broadest form.

When the firm goes beyond listing its company name to purchase a display ad in the telephone book, it has gone beyond passive advertising to an active form of advertising. They are more diligently seeking to spread word of their readiness to do business.

Even the packaging of a product is a form of advertising. Note the difference in packaging of the generic forms of products and the packing of the name brands of those same types of products. The generic packages state what is inside, such as paper towels or cigarettes. The name-brand product is usually a more attractive color, with artwork intended to capture the eye and whet the appetite for that particular brand over its competitors.

MASS MEDIA ADVERTISING

The preceding is not intended to imply that advertising is vital for every firm in order for it to stay in business. If an individual or firm sells a product that is indistinguishable to the general public when the public buys it, the seller has little need to use mass media to attempt to sell that product to the general public. An example is a farmer or farm concern that sells wheat to be made into flour. Because that particular farmer's wheat is indistinguishable from other farmers' wheat when they are mixed together to make the flour, farmers have no reason for advertising their wheat to the eventual consumer. However, that wheat is made into flour by a manufacturer who blends varieties of wheat in a certain manner and advertises the resulting flour to be "the one to use" or "like your mother used." Consumers who try it and like it continue to buy it on the basis that it is their preferred brand of flour.

Take the example of a miller who buys the wheat crops of numbers of farmers to blend a special flour mix to be sold to cookie bakeries that then bag the cookies and label them with the baker's brand name. This flour manufacturer does not advertise to the general public, of course, but does use some form of advertising to reach cookie bakers and convince them to use the company's special flour mix rather than the others available. The cookie baker, however, is taking the flour and other ingredients, putting them together, packaging the results as a product to be sold on the market, and, if the intended customer is the public, using mass media advertising to reach that public and condition them for acceptance and trial of the product.

One of the largest candy manufacturers professed for years that it had no need to advertise its principal product to the public. The rationale was that the candy in question was the premier candy of its type, and its name

Packaging as advertising

was so well known that advertising would be wasteful and only increase its cost. The manufacturer, however, was already using some forms of advertising, such as the distinctive wrapper for the candy—without acknowledging them as such. When competitors began to make inroads into the traditional market of the large candy company through the introduction and advertising of competitive candies, the manufacturer reluctantly decided to advertise to the public.

During World War II, sugar rationing limited the amount of syrup the soft drink companies could produce, and the Coca-Cola company found it could not meet even a fraction of the demand of its product. However, during the wartime shortage, Coca-Cola continued advertising in mass media, not to increase sales, but to apprise the public that the shortage of Coca-Cola was caused by the war, that Coca-Cola was cooperating in the national effort, and that when the war was over the company would do its utmost to satisfy the public demand for Coca-Cola.

When company management was asked why the company wasted money advertising when they had demand far above what could be supplied, the company management replied in effect that the day would come when the shortage would be over and all soft drinks would be plentiful. The management wanted people to remember Coca-Cola, retain their loyalty to the brand, and continue to be consumers of the extra production that would come with the end of rationing.

Another basic assumption about advertising is that practically all media are helpful in the advertising process if they are used properly to take advantage of their distinctive capabilities. This assumption does not mean that all are *equally* effective in any particular situation.

What's in a wheat?

An individual walking down a busy city street with a sandwich board can attract customers. An airplane flying overhead and trailing a banner advertising some event can bring patrons to that event. A direct mail solicitation letter can gain the interest of potential or real customers. An insertion in the Yellow Pages can yield inquiries, as can a newspaper ad, either classified or display. The same is true of a radio or television commercial, or one placed on a cable television channel.

In its simplest form, advertising tells people of the products and services the business has and is willing to sell to the public. This was the basic form of those first broadcast commercials on New York City radio station WEAF, which stated that a realty firm had two buildings for sale. Advertising today generally is much more sophisticated than that basic announcement, but all advertising is an extension of the concept that one party has something available for delivery to another party in exchange for something of value (money). The key to getting the best value for advertising dollars lies in determining which of the available media offers the advantages and prospects for success desired by the advertiser.

A third advertising assumption is that the larger the business (or the advertising budget for that business), the more likely that several advertising media (or a mix of the media) will be used to accomplish the advertising mission for the company.

A large company, with its large advertising budget, has (or should have) people in its management who are knowledgeable in advertising and employs an advertising agency (or agencies) to accomplish the aims determined by the company management. A firm that has a multimillion dollar advertising budget is not likely to spend it haphazardly or on the basis of a whim or hunch.

Although this large corporation may spend a large percentage of its advertising budget in one particular advertising medium, it most likely places some advertising in other media to expand the advertising impact, to take advantage of the particular abilities of the other media, or just to hedge its bet. Rather than putting all their advertising dollars in one basket, Ford, General Motors, and Chrysler all use a media mix, as do Xerox, IBM, AT&T, and the other giants of the corporate world.

Although each media salesperson feels that his/her particular medium is the best, each knows that that particular advertising medium is not the only one and that the salesperson's dream of having all of a company's advertising dollars spent in one place is unlikely.

A fourth advertising assumption is that a good advertising campaign has predetermined objectives to be met in order to determine its success. Even an *image campaign*—a campaign to improve the public image of the company or product—has goals, although they may not be as concrete as those in a product sales advertising campaign.

The successful large corporation sets its sales goals well in advance and then calls on its advertising management people and its advertising agency to devise advertising and advertising strategies to meet the projected sales goals. These advertising people within the company work with advertising agency personnel to divide the company's advertising budget among the campaigns planned and to divide the individual campaign budgets among the media in a way calculated to achieve the desired results. As in the case of any properly drawn budget, funds are set aside for contingencies, but the broadcast salesperson must remember that regular advertisers set advertising budgets for a year at a time. These budgets are not set in concrete, but the enterprising broadcast salesperson makes sure that his/her medium is included in the overall planning rather than attempting to break into an established advertising budget.

The fifth assumption is that the smaller the advertiser, the more likely it is that the advertiser will use only one medium or use any media on a haphazard basis without establishing what results it desires from the advertising campaign.

In every market some potential advertisers act on impulse in purchasing advertising, and others fear the unknown and stick year after year with the same advertising medium. For years getting department stores to advertise in the electronic media was difficult, and a good part of the cause was their lack of familiarity with the electronic media's advertising capability combined with their familiarity with their tried and true newspaper advertising. The stores may not have always achieved the results desired, but overall, they got results and felt they knew how to deal with that advertising medium. The Radio Advertising Bureau and the Television Advertising Bureau waged intensive educational campaigns to show department store advertising personnel how to use the electronic media effectively.

The smaller the local firm, the less likely it is to plan an advertising budget as fully as the larger, regular advertisers do and the more likely the firm is to act haphazardly or on impulse in purchasing advertising. Ideally, a business ought to advertise when business is poor. Realistically, downturns are when many firms decide to cut down or eliminate advertising.

A final basic assumption is that mass media advertising is a very large industry because it works. It gains attention for products and services and aids in the selling process.

BROADCAST ADVERTISING

The broadcast salesperson is involved in one aspect of mass media advertising, the selling of advertising time on broadcast outlets. The salesperson's product comprises the available times when advertising messages may be inserted in the broadcast program schedule. Because no additional hours can be added to the hours during which the broadcast outlet is licensed to operate, for practical purposes, the salesperson has a finite number of these availabilities to sell. For years, subscribing radio and television stations were limited by the National Association of Broadcasters Code that defined the amount of commercial time allowable. Since the U.S. Supreme Court overturned a portion of the code, the NAB has not enforced its other provisions. However, radio and television stations are limited in the amount of advertising time allowable by the performance plans they submit to the Federal Communications Commission showing their percentage of commercial time or advertising and by their need to show they operate "in the public interest, convenience and necessity" as required under the Communications Act.

Newspapers and magazines add extra pages when the request for advertising is higher. Direct mail advertising may be sent out in whatever bulk or with whatever frequency is desired. No additional time may be added to a particular time segment in radio or television: 9 P.M. until 10 P.M. is always 60 minutes and the afternoon radio station drive time of 4 P.M. to 6 P.M. remains two hours long. In both instances, only the advertising that logically can be included within those time periods can be inserted. Unlike print media page counts, the time periods cannot be stretched.

What Broadcast Advertising Can and Cannot Do

Salespeople for broadcast advertising outlets must not oversell the capabilities of their advertising medium. Advertising is a vital part of the overall strategy of selling goods and services, but it is not a panacea. No broadcast advertising schedule can solve every problem a client has, double the client's business in a few weeks on a spot-a-day basis, or guarantee the client immunity from slow business days, unsold inventory, or inflation. Any electronic medium chosen for advertising becomes just one of the ingredients of an overall plan for business success.

In *Advertising Pure and Simple*, Hank Seiden notes that "a good practitioner of advertising can convince a logical prospect for a product to try it one time." What more can advertising do? It cannot twist the arms of the public to buy a product or service; it can only convince them through "a rational appeal to . . . their intelligence."[1] Seiden also notes that the person being convinced needs to be a logical prospect, "one who is at that moment in time in the market for such a product, has a need for it (or can be shown that he has a need) and can afford to buy it."[2]

If a good advertising program motivates a logical prospect to try a product or service one time, then it has done its job. From that point on, the product or service is on its own. The buyer either likes it, in which case the prospect becomes a customer and advocate of the product or service, or does not like it, in which case the individual is unlikely to buy it again or recommend it to others.

> *Advertising has done all it can do. It convinced someone to try. Advertising does not make customers. Only products make customers.*[3]

As significant as what advertising can do is the understanding of what advertising cannot do. According to Seiden, his eight years of reviewing hundreds of advertisements and writing columns about them for an advertising magazine taught what advertising cannot do:

- *It can't sell a product to someone who has no basic need for it.*
- *It can't sell a product to someone out of the market for it.*
- *It can't sell a product to someone who can't afford it.*
- *It can't make a satisfied customer.*
- *It can't save a bad product.*

> *If anything, good advertising for a poor product . . . will put a manufacturer out of business. Why? Because the better the advertising, the more people who will try the product. The more people who try the product, the more people who will reject it. The more who reject it, the faster the product will fold.*[4]

Radio   Radio can be a primary or sole advertising vehicle for preselling or aiding in the sales process of products, services, or ideas. One of its principal advantages is the low cost of a radio commercial, which allows repetition to reinforce its message. This factor makes radio an excellent advertising medium by itself or a valuable adjunct in an advertising campaign that uses newspaper, television, or direct mail advertising, or any combination of these other media. The potential radio advertiser does not (or should not) buy one radio commercial on a local station and expect customers to mob the store to buy the advertised products. However, a flight (a series of commercials within the same advertising campaign) of radio commercials for a sale at a local store can have people lined up waiting for the store to open.

Radio as a sales aid is at its best when its repetitive selling ability is put to work selling a known product or service. People already have a mental image of the product, and the radio commercials can concentrate on selling advantages, features, or price. This is not to say that radio advertising cannot be used effectively for a new store, because the audience knows what stores are and what they are like. The same is true for a new brand of a product. If the product is a soft drink, the audience is familiar with soft drinks. Radio's job is to persuade the audience to try this new brand.

The selling job becomes more difficult when radio is called on to do the introductory advertising job for a product totally unknown to the radio audience. The job can be done by radio, but not as easily or as well as in the previous instance. If we wish to sell "wognets" through radio advertising, we first must spend time describing the wognet and familiarizing the audience with what a wognet is before we can create the mental image necessary to allow the sales message to come across.

Another thing that radio does not do well is to move merchandise off dusty shelves at its regular price when that merchandise obviously did not sell well originally at the regular price. Almost every salesperson who has sold commercial time for a radio station has encountered that local business that decides to test whether radio is any good by challenging the salesperson to move stale merchandise. Radio is not magical. If a product is hard to sell and has taken up shelf space for years, simply advertising it on radio is not going to bring phenomenal sales results.

Finally, radio does not effectively handle advertising that is just a long list of products and prices. Throwing all those prices at the audience presupposes that listeners are intently tuned to the radio to catch every word, assimilate it quickly, attach it to the next word, and then remember everything. The listening pattern for the radio audience does not support such a presupposition. Such price-list advertising may not be a complete failure. The radio listener may perceive some of the products and prices and the sponsor's name and location, and thus the impression of very low prices at the sponsor's business may get through. However, this type of advertising does not utilize radio's unique ability to be with the listener at practically any and all times: a companion in the automobile, a wake-up friend, a diversion while doing housework, and a pleasant entertainer in the office.

Thus, radio is an excellent, low-cost advertising medium when its advantages are well utilized, whether as the only advertising medium or in conjunction with any other mass advertising media.

Television Television is like radio in that it functions best when it transmits one idea or product in one commercial. It provides excellent recall capability in consumer minds for well-produced commercials. Most people can readily cite television commercials seen some time ago when asked to recall commercials they liked. (Many of us can also recall commercials that irritated us!)

Television, with its sight and sound capability, is an excellent introductory medium for new products or models. It can show and tell, display, and demonstrate. It can arouse the senses in a way that other advertising media may not. Looking at a steaming cup of coffee, or a succulent dessert followed by the action of drinking or dipping into that dessert can produce a reinforcement reaction with which other media have trouble competing.

Like radio (or any other advertising medium), television is not a magic genie. It cannot take an otherwise unsalable product and make the public buy it at high prices. Purchase of a television advertising schedule cannot guarantee a business instant success. Television does not cause the public to continue to buy an obviously bad product. As Seiden pointed out, it may help the manufacturer of a bad product to go out of business faster.

One of television advertising's biggest handicaps is its cost. The television time for the commercial is expensive, and the production of the commercial itself is also expensive, especially when compared to the cost of producing a radio commercial. This expense factor is responsible for the replacement of the standard 60-second television commercial with the present 30-second commercial. Advertisers wanting more advertising exposure for their money forced standardization of the 30-second format, and a number of large advertisers currently are attempting to force a further shortening of the standard television commercial to 15 seconds. These shortened commercials have produced one of television's largest drawbacks, the clutter of so many different advertising messages thrown at the viewer within relatively short periods of viewing. This clutter concerns advertisers, especially the larger advertisers, but it has not caused any downturn in the overall expenditures for television advertising. On the contrary, television advertising revenues increase each year.

Cable Television Cable television is television with a multiplicity of available channels. It largely does what ordinary television does. The many channels fragment the audience for each channel, but this fragmentation becomes an advantage, since it allows pinpointing of the audience type desired.

Guidelines for Broadcast Salespeople

The successful broadcast salesperson incorporates into the sales process several principles that guide him or her in selling advertising to be placed in the broadcast media.

1. Selling broadcast advertising time is honorable work that demands professionalism on the part of the salesperson.

2. Broadcast sales is not a banker's-hours position that pays well for little effort (although it can pay very handsomely for the real professional). The potential broadcast salesperson can look forward to working long hours at times and working early or late in order to deal with clients' time needs or to prepare presentations. Nevertheless, the professional broadcast salespeople enjoy accomplishments, but find time for the rest of their lives.

3. Professional broadcast salespeople never know it all but continue learning and trying to improve throughout their professional lives. The person who is interested in people and constantly learning from life is the person who grows.

4. The broadcast salesperson researches potential clients' businesses in order to counsel the potential advertiser on the effective use of broadcast advertising. Understanding the client's business, how it operates, and its particular needs is essential to professionalism.

5. The broadcast salesperson prepares in advance for a call on a potential client. Very few sales are made on a first call on a client. Research and a well-planned presentation are necessities.

6. A bad buy for an advertiser is a bad sale for the broadcast salesperson. Broadcast salespeople rely not on single sales but on repeat business built on confidence and trust.

7. The broadcast salesperson constantly works toward becoming the broadcast advertising counselor for the advertiser, earning the client's confidence and trust, and planning advertising campaigns to accomplish the client's aims.

The beginning broadcast salesperson who lives up to these seven principles is well on the way to being a professional, worthwhile representative of the broadcast media. These guidelines are not unique to broadcast selling. They exist in basic form, but expressed in different words, in other marketplaces. Salespeople for corporate giants such as IBM, Xerox, and Hewlett-Packard utilize professional consultant sales skills in representing their companies.

Professional salespeople from all fields have noted that regardless of what is sold the selling concepts used are the major ingredients in making the sale. The challenge to beginning salespeople is to learn the concepts and principles of professional selling that make themselves assets to their clients, regardless of the field in which they sell.

THE STRUCTURE OF BROADCAST SALES

The beginning broadcast salesperson must look at the overall structure of broadcast sales to understand his or her function in relation to that of others in the process of sales in the broadcast media. Although the titles may vary from medium to medium, from market to market, or from station to station, all these functions are the same.

At the top of the sales process in radio and television is the function of the general sales manager (or sales director or similar title). The function of this position is to control the station's inventory, that is, all available advertising time of the station, including program and spot announcement availabilities. This individual is charged with setting the selling price (developing the *rates*) under which this advertising time will be sold—often in concert with the station's general management—and approval or disapproval of clients and client advertising messages. This general sales management function is carried out by the general manager or station manager in most smaller-market radio stations and in some smaller-market television stations. The function more clearly emerges as the job of the top individual in sales in larger markets and in stations with more advertising revenues.

Directly beneath the general sales manager are three other management positions in sales. The national sales manager is responsible for dealing with the station's national representative firm, which, in turn, represents the station in dealings with national advertising agencies and accounts. If the station is network affiliated, this individual also deals with the station's network on sales matters. The national sales manager may work in concert with the station's rep to sell to large, national clients or at other times may function independently. Again, radio stations in small markets may have no well-defined national sales management position and no appreciable national client business. What national business such stations have comes from group representation of numbers of radio stations by firms that attempt to add national business to the affiliated stations. The responsibility for national sales management may also be in the hands of the station general manager if the market size does not necessitate full-time guidance.

A second management position subordinate to the general sales manager is that of the regional sales manager, who takes charge of sales and development of advertising on a regional basis. Again, in small radio markets, this function is the responsibility of the general manager, but emerges as a separate, distinct function as radio market size and station coverage area increase, and is common in smaller television stations.

The third management function under the guidance of the general sales manager is that of the local sales manager. This position deals with the advertising revenue from local clients and is a necessity at every radio and television station. Although the title may vary, the function is the development and sale of local advertising. At most radio and television stations, this position has many salespeople reporting to it. Being a member of this local sales force is the likely starting point of the broadcast salesperson.

Two types of selling will take place under the guidance of the local sales manager depending on the size of the market: local and retail. The term *local sales* usually refers to local sales that are made through local offices of advertising agencies that manage advertising budgets for their clients. *Retail sales* or *direct sales* is generally used to describe the face-to-face selling of advertising to a client without the aid of an advertising agency. Retail advertising sales comprise almost 100 percent of the sales at the smallest radio stations, but, as the market size increases, this percentage decreases. In the largest markets, a preponderance of local sales comes through the local (or agency sale) side.

The broadcast salesperson who works under the guidance of either of these sales managers is often called an account executive, meaning that he/she is the person in charge (for that station) of that account's (client's) advertising. Again, the use of the account executive title is more common in larger markets. We call this person a *broadcast salesperson* in this book to emphasize the function for which this person is employed—the sale of broadcast advertising time.

THE PROFESSIONAL BROADCAST SALESPERSON

Client-Centered Attitude

Basic concepts of successful selling have their roots in the time-honored realization that the overall approach and attitude must be client-focused rather than self-focused. All sales professionals are, by necessity, client-focused. They have relegated the pronouns *I* and *me* to the backs of their minds in the realization that doing so is the first step toward developing the client-centered attitude necessary for their success.

Failing to place the client at the focal point gives rise to an attitude that centers on "How can I get as deeply into this person's pocket as possible, so that I can receive the biggest commission on the package, program, or idea I am selling?" Such a self-centered attitude interferes with the salesperson's ability to understand the client's business, and thus the salesperson cannot be an effective problem-solver for the client.

Unfortunately, this attitude is encountered too often in today's marketplace. Admittedly, the natural tendency of untrained salespeople (and some supposedly trained ones) is to get what you can get for today, and let tomorrow take care of itself. However, by selling in this manner, the salesperson will develop the reputation of being either a huckster, a pitch artist, a high-pressure unloader of goods, or a clerk ready to take orders for anything in the briefcase that he or she can get the client to buy. The person who sells the electronic media in any of these ways will never earn the client's respect. Neither can he or she be of true value to clients, who must still cope by themselves with the business-related problems that a good salesperson could help solve.

Putting the Client First

A true professional realizes that putting the client first puts the salesperson first. The more done for the clients—the more goods they are helped to move, the more people the station brings into their stores, and so on—the more the salesperson benefits. Successful selling is much more likely as soon as the salesperson learns that the client is ultimately more important than the salesperson—at least during regular business hours!

Selling the electronic media should be no less professional than selling business computers or industrial chemicals. A Xerox salesperson does not just walk into a place of business, having done no prior research and knowing next to nothing about that business, and attempt to sell the president or the manager a copy machine that might retail for several thousand dollars. The idea is ludicrous. It's just as naive to believe that a person can just walk into a place of business and, through force of personality alone, sell an advertising campaign to a stranger who is running a business the fundamental concepts of which are foreign to the media representative.

Qualifications

Any discussion of the qualifications of people hired to present an industry's products or services to potential clients is guaranteed to elicit a variety of responses, with the proponent of each group of qualifications strongly defending the need for that particular list. The debate may be even hotter when the topic is the qualifications of broadcast media sales personnel because the only qualifications within the industry are those imposed by individual sales managers or station managers. As managers defend people they have hired and critics argue that no hiring standards exist, the lack of consensus becomes apparent.

Certified Radio Marketing Consultants (CRMCs)

No concrete qualifications exist for sales representatives in the electronic media. Some radio stations require their people to become certified radio marketing consultants (CRMCs) through the Radio Advertising Bureau (RAB), but the simple fact remains that no criteria exists that can be applied to the hiring of media salespeople nationwide.

It appears that anyone in reasonably good health who seems halfway willing to make a few calls can be hired as a sales representative at the majority of the nation's 8,500 commercial radio stations and 900 television stations.

Attrition

Some of these people succeed and become credits to the industry. Of course, these few are among the 15 percent of salespeople hired who actually enter their second year of employment. The attrition rate in radio is 85 percent—higher than that for the life insurance industry. In no other business that can be reasonably defined as a profession is the turnover rate as high. Anybody can be hired into the industry—and often is. Merchants can't be blamed for thinking they know as much about advertising as the two or three people from the same station who service the store's account each year. The same merchant would rarely question the advice of a lawyer, physician, accountant, or banker. He or she may obtain a second opinion on occasion but still respects the information initially given, continues to have a certain level of trust in the initial opinion, continues to consult with the first professional, and, in most cases, follows the original counsel.

Rare is the media salesperson who is looked upon by the total market with that degree of respect and trust. Granted, all salespeople have their buddy clients who let no one else handle their business, but these relationships have usually been cultivated through friendship rather than through respect and competence.

Gaining Trust and Respect

The intent here is not to condemn the manner in which a media salesperson cultivates trust and respect, but to point out that the industry as a whole is not looked upon with a high degree of trust and respect. To gain the level of trust and respect enjoyed by accountants, bankers, and other professionals, media sales representatives need to work that much harder, be that much more prepared, be a bit more articulate, and make sure their conduct is totally professional. Other professions have to gain their clients' trust too, just as you do when selling advertising; however, if a person is a lawyer, it is implicit that he or she has had a certain number of years of training. Your prospect has no idea what preparation you have had when you initially visit. You may be a sixth-grade dropout or hold a doctorate in marketing. What sells you to the prospect is your ability to consult on a professional level about real needs, your ability to assist in solving business-related problems, and your human relations skills.

We are now back to the initial argument about the qualifications necessary to be a media sales representative. Anybody can be an electronic media salesperson, we have noted, but not just anybody can be a *successful* media salesperson. Let's break down successful media salesmanship to its bottom-line components that can be analyzed, quantified, and discussed.

A Liberal Arts Education

Those aspiring to be successful in selling the electronic media need to understand the importance of a liberal arts education. What is learned in college is essential to the repertoire of those who have been successful in selling radio, television, or cable time, or in selling anything else, for that matter.

Many young people often have difficulty grasping the rationale behind the study of required courses such as history, social sciences, natural sciences, and humanities. Mastery of these courses connects students with the thoughts and experiences of other people and gives students a sense of the "other." Such a sense is called upon daily in selling a product or service to a prospective buyer, as empathy and understanding are critical to finding solutions to the client's problems or needs. Selling something or even communicating your point of view is difficult when you yourself can see only your point of view and that of no one else.

Therefore, in any ideal list of qualifications for electronic media salespeople, a liberal arts education would figure prominently. Complementing this more formal requirement would be the informal training one receives by merely coming into contact with people on a daily basis. Familiarity with human nature can be gained on the streets as well as from reading and studying. Although the two types of experience are different in nature, they both generate the sensitivity necessary to meet the needs of another human being.

Self-Image

A second qualification, less precise but no less important, is the salesperson's concept of self. Such a concept includes the salesperson's self-image, maturity in relation to self-motivation and ability to handle rejection, and willingness and skill in dealing honestly with himself or herself when success is elusive and the chips are down.

Success lies in the salesperson's overall attitude toward self (mental positioning), other people, and the service he or she is selling. There is no substitute for a positive self-image, especially on those days when you, as a salesperson, become convinced that the chips are not only down, but you are actually under the table looking for them while everyone else is kicking you. A person with a positive self-image tries again and again, analyzing mistakes and perfecting skills. Then, the person goes out to sell again and succeeds, not only because of the will to do so, but also because the salesperson has studied mistakes and learned from them and is now prepared to succeed. A salesperson wrapped in self-doubt and dreading each day programs self-defeat.

Self-Motivation

The concept of self-motivation is a favorite of banquet speakers, book publishers, and sales managers all over the world. With so many readily available sources on this subject, only some general comments on how the topic relates to the daily needs of the media salesperson need be made.

Motivation Involves People Motivation involves people, either yourself or others you are responsible for motivating to perform. Motivation implies an understanding of basic human needs, wants, and desires. Although similar in many ways, each person is an individual pursuing personal goals. Consequently, people have different motivators based on their needs as they perceive them, not as they are perceived by others. Determining an individual's needs as the individual perceives them is the first step toward successful motivation. To make it personal, you need to know what is important to you so that you may motivate yourself toward achieving meaningful goals. If peer recognition is more important than financial independence, different factors motivate you than motivate the salesperson who places monetary success above all other needs. Therefore, understanding what you want is crucial to understanding how to motivate yourself.

✳ MASLOW'S HIERARCHY OF NEEDS AND THE MARKETPLACE

The psychologist Abraham Maslow theorized that all human beings have basic needs that must be satisfied but that certain needs take priority over others. Maslow devised a *hierarchy of needs* postulating that all human beings are active at one of five levels (see Figure 2-1). Satisfaction of the lower-level need must occur before the higher level can be pursued.

Level One

The first human need is to survive and to take care of basic physiological needs. Matters of peer acceptance and self-esteem are inconsequential for

FIGURE 2-1
Maslow's hierarchy of needs

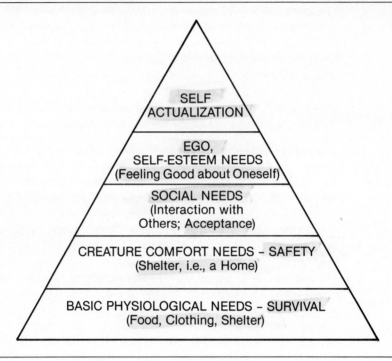

those whose next meal is uncertain. Our earliest ancestors operated and survived (or didn't survive) mostly at this level, and too many people throughout the world have to function at this level today.

Level Two

After the basic need to survive has been satisfied, Maslow asserts that the individual can then move to the next level, which involves satisfaction of safety or creature comfort needs. People who are no longer hungry or thirsty tend to focus on securing and on attaining protection from crime, fire, weather elements, and other dangers.

Most of us need not worry about these first two levels; they are generally not an issue in our lives. The affluence of our country allows the majority of people to operate on levels three, four, and five. Most of you and most of the people with whom you deal begin operation on level three.

Level Three

Maslow's third level concerns itself with social needs. Many people never leave this level, and their lives are a search for a continuous party. However, this basic need is much more complex than socializing as it is usually defined. Level three concerns itself with the human need for love, affection, and acceptance. Peer pressure causes many human deeds, both negative and positive. Many of us operate primarily on this level, where our goals center on our needs for belonging and friendship. However, others perceive their true motivators as being on one of the next two levels of Maslow's scale.

Level Four

At level four Maslow claims people seek self-respect, achievement, and power. Having satisfied physiological needs, security requirements, and desires to be part of a group, people seek self-esteem and want to be able to evaluate their contribution to the common good in a positive way. When people feel comfortable with themselves they can perform at optimum levels, thus setting the stage for advancement to the highest possible level, that of self-realization.

Level Five

On this final plateau—which few people reach—Maslow contends that people are at their most creative. Free from worry about survival, security, having lots of friends, and success, people can become creative, self-fulfilled, and capable of painting a Sistine Chapel, composing a symphony, or simply functioning creatively in whatever they choose to do.

Understanding motivation, then, begins with understanding on what level a person is currently operating and how advancement to the next level can occur. Success in sales just might be the factor that gives peace of mind and allows operation on higher levels. Remember that success is defined according to one's own needs: financial security, recognition from the boss or colleagues, or an altruistic feeling that comes from truly helping one's clients.

Electronic media salespeople may be motivated by the need for personal success, to be financially independent, to become an officer in the state broadcast association, to have a good track record for a future political career, or for any number of other reasons. The point here is to tap that individual motivation and make it work for you. Whatever the goal, however, success is the result of plain hard work and a commitment to following an organized system for successfully selling the electronic media. As H.L. Mencken recognized, "Most people don't recognize opportunity when it comes along, because usually it is disguised as hard work."

OTHER COMPONENTS OF THE SELF-CONCEPT

Handling Rejection

Being able to handle rejection is an important indicator of a person's self-concept. The most polished, professional media representative is sometimes flatly turned down. However, the organized, trained salesperson encounters rejection less often and is more capable of turning rejection into sales. Professional salespeople cannot allow a rejection of the sales proposal to send them out defeated. "No" is not an indication of the lack of ability of the salesperson, or of the client's personal feeling toward the salesperson, or of a major character flaw previously undiscovered. It is a challenge to be met, overcome, and turned into a sale down the road. A positive-thinking, successful media salesperson handles rejection as a problem to be analyzed so that it can be solved. The salesperson discusses with the sales manager what went wrong and why or researches the client in a way that will help the salesperson genuinely be of service to the client during the next meeting.

Nevertheless, fear of rejection is entirely normal and predictable. We have been born into a society where success is supposed to be the norm, not the exception. No other society in the world places so much pressure on people to succeed as does ours here in America.

The Success Ethic

In discussing the theories of Robert K. Merton, the sociologist Elbert W. Stewart writes, "In many poor parts of the world, poverty is the expected way of life of the majority, who were born into the lower class and . . . should be willing to remain there. No one is condemned for being poor. In the United States . . . the hard work and success ethic is very strong. People who are poor throughout their lives are viewed as failures. When old friends meet after many years, they try in subtle ways to find out how the other is doing and parents often play a status game of comparing their children's achievements with those of the neighbor's children. Given these attitudes, the failure to succeed brings humiliation as well as material poverty. Under such circumstances, people become success-oriented, subordinating means to ends. Driven by the pressure to succeed, many people stretch the rules. They cheat at least a little to gain their goals."[5] Merton's thesis rests on the societal pressures that demand that we succeed. Moreover, everyone is expected to succeed regardless of status at birth.

Need for Acceptance

All of us, media salespeople included, feel a certain obligation to ourselves to succeed at each task we undertake. From the earliest years on, we are involved in competition. We compete for affection from our parents, our peers, and our teachers. We are given verbal and written feedback, praise, condemnation, and grades on report cards that constantly reinforce our feelings that we are either doing well or not living up to expectations and tell us we are accepted or rejected by the society in which we find ourselves. All of us desire positive reinforcement, good grades on report cards, and the feeling that we are doing all right in an obviously competitive environment.

Fear of Rejection

The fear of rejection, of not being accepted, and of not adjusting to new situations (such as the first years at college) is a constant, ever-present reality. We are urged to succeed and expected to succeed. Such a feeling follows us like a shadow as we mature and becomes an ingrained part of our psyches. How many young people stare at the phone for hours, afraid to pick it up to call for a date? They are afraid of rejection. Others sit at home, hoping their phone will ring and bring them an invitation for a date on Saturday night. The fear of being the "only one" without a date can cause tremendous feelings of inadequacy. Constantly wondering what other people think of us can lead to some very strong emotions.

So now, after years of social adjustments and personal investments of time and money in formal and informal educational pursuits, the salesperson is sitting across from a client who will either accept or reject the salesperson's offering. Despite the level of personal adjustment and maturity, the fear of rejection is still present and always will be, to some degree. Fearing rejection is natural, and facing rejection never becomes an easy matter.

Intimidation by "Mr. Big" Perhaps, as Si Willing has claimed in *How to Sell Radio Advertising*, "The biggest enemy you have is yourself. You are afraid of what the sponsor will think of you. . . . Isn't that the reason you hesitate to make certain calls? To the President of the Might Bank. To the Chairman of the Board who sits in the decision making chair? . . . To the man who looks like he's all business, no heart and no soul? You are afraid not so much of him as you are of yourself and what MR. BIG will do to you. You're afraid that he will chew you up and spit you out. So you naturally find dozens of reasons to delay making those calls. You rationalize. You agree that the time is not ripe to make the call, etc."[6]

Such a feeling can extend to clients whose commercials are already on the air. Some salespeople are so relieved to have sold Mr. Tough that they are afraid to service the account for fear he might cancel his schedule.

Fear and rejection are difficult emotions to contend with. However, we must learn to deal with them sensibly and maturely in our lives, whether we choose sales or any other career.

Emotional Stress   According to W. Clement Stone, "If you take the time to develop the habit of controlling your own reactions, you will instinctively sense the signals and employ the principles in controling the acts of others."[7]

Stone told the story of an emotional young salesman who called on the owner of a shoe store and was determined to make the sale to impress his boss, who was accompanying him. When the prospect finally indicated that he was not interested in the service being sold, in desperation the salesman blurted, "I would never come to your store to buy a pair of shoes!"

The young salesman took the rejection personally and wanted to strike back at someone who had put him in a bad light in front of his sales manager. He was under such emotional stress, Stone says, that he made no more sales calls that day, until the sales manager directed his attention to the fact that the prospect had given his time, for which the salesman should have been grateful. He further explained to the salesman that if he left each place of business making the prospect feel good and happy, even though the prospect may have refused the sales presentation, then the salesman would be in a relatively happy mood and thus better able to direct the next prospect's thinking in the proper channel.

Stone's analysis of the scenario is worth noting. He writes, "When you are selling, do your feelings get hurt easily? If they do, you are the person who frequently hurts the feelings of others. Your own negative thoughts cause an intensified negative force by changing the direction of your prospect's thinking in line with your own negative attitude. If your feelings are very seldom or never hurt, then your positive, optimistic thinking and depth of understanding of the feelings of others will control their reaction in the same direction."[8]

THE THREE LEVELS OF BROADCAST SALES SKILLS

Each semester the students in sales classes at Western Kentucky University are asked to name several adjectives that describe a salesperson. The answers they supply invariably describe a pushy, obnoxious, pressure-oriented, sleazy, self-serving, commission-oriented person. Then the students are asked how many of them have fathers or mothers in sales. Usually, a half dozen or more hands are raised. When asked if these adjectives apply to their parents, the answers are an emphatic "No!" "Oh," we respond, "you mean there are different types of salespeople? How are your parents different from the common perception of salespeople?" So begins the discussion that terminates with the understanding that there are different levels of salespeople. Some are highly trained career professionals, and others have no training at all and are selling just to have a job or until they find something they consider better.

Common Perceptions of Salespeople

The reason young people always answer the question on common perceptions of salespeople in a negative manner is because that type of salesperson is the only one to which they have ever really been exposed. Each has had encounters with untrained door-to-door salespeople, the used-car dealer who wants to unload a problem car on a first-time buyer, or the high-pressure life insurance seller who wants to sign them up early "while the rates are low." This type of exposure to sales produces negative impressions, and most young people would rather not be involved in sales. Few high school or college students have a preconceived notion that they would like to be salespeople upon graduation. In any telecommunications program, students want to be on-air personalities, newspeople, floor directors, technical directors, production people, creative writers—anything but salespeople! They view salespeople as having no professional respect, whereas anchor people and creative people are looked upon with a great deal of admiration and respect, if for no other reason than their job title alone. They feel their parents didn't help them through college to have them become salespeople; after all, one doesn't need an education to be a salesperson!

Indeed, no formal education is required to be a salesperson in many companies. Although some products and services that are technical or professional in nature require the best-educated, most professionally qualified salespeople possible, other products and services geared toward different demographics do not require much skill to present and may not even require service after the sale. Those thinking of media sales as a career and those who have already made that career decision need to understand the various levels of broadcast sales skills that are present in the market today so that they can achieve the highest possible level of sales professionalism.

One of the foremost sales trainers of the eighties is Don Beveridge. In his seminars, tape programs, and book, *Notice . . . If You Want to Sell*, he outlines his perceptions of the four "generations" or categories of sales approaches. Beveridge classifies the unskilled salesperson who has received little or no training as a "Commercial Visitor." This salesperson wants to be liked, tries to develop close emotional ties to the client, and always gives holiday gifts, such as radios and pens with call-letter inscriptions, to clients. The commercial visitor believes sales are made because clients eventually feel they owe the sales rep some business.[9]

The seller with an overwhelming inventory of product (time availabilities) is Beveridge's "Peddler." He is pressured to sell the whole product line and must take action . . . he'll go through the motions, he'll detail product after product, service after service, feature after feature and then almost in a daring manner . . . ask . . . "Do you need any?"[10]

This book refers most often to Beveridge's third level of salesperson, the "Consultant" who sees business problems from the customer's point of view and attempts to fulfill genuine customer needs. Beveridge's ultimate salesperson, who clients will actually call to avoid business problems they may see on the horizon, is known as the "Sustaining Resource." This person serves and is viewed as an unsalaried member of the business's staff—an enviable position, to be sure.

Using the Beveridge model, we have combined the last two categories into one and present the three levels of broadcast sales skills as we have perceived them over a 20-year period.

The Order Taker

This skill level is the most often seen or encountered by the average person. Salespeople who operate on this bottom plane of knowledge and skill are likely involved in sales for the following generalized reasons:

1. No other job was available at the time they were job hunting.
2. They were unsuccessful in other jobs and thought they might as well try sales.
3. A relative or close friend, who owned or managed a company, convinced them to try sales.
4. They wanted to work in a particular business, like telecommunications, and sales was the only way they could enter that field.
5. They thought they would make a lot of money because they have always been the life of the party and everybody loves their jokes, stories, and general cutting up.

As a group, these order takers never planned on making careers of sales. They just fell into the job because of conditions at the moment. Such people are usually hired by companies or stations that provide little or no training. They are merely handed account lists and, after a few days on the streets with someone who has been taking orders for the station for the past 15 years, given account lists of their own and told to go sell.

Personality Kids   With no professional training, the newly hired salesperson acts and reacts in a predictable fashion by using the only sales tool in their possession—their personality. They glad-hand potential clients, attempt to buddy up to them as much as possible, know all the latest jokes, stories, and community gossip, and attempt to sell some spots only after they have ingratiated themselves ad nauseum. Having little regard for prospects' business needs and little knowledge of their own products and services, they expect potential customers to buy from them because they are likable.

The order taker

Occasionally, they sell a program or a sponsorship to a merchant, most likely one who has bought the same program for the last decade, so that all the order taker has to do is fill out the order form. The client receives no new factual or demographic information from the salesperson, who probably knows nothing more about electronic media advertising than does the merchant. Furthermore these order takers call on only those businesses they feel comfortable with, which tend to be contacts with plenty of time to shoot the breeze rather than dynamic managers too busy building successful companies to take the time to chat about the weather.

The personality kid's entire sales presentation, given only after 10 minutes or so of happy talk, consists of, "Well, I hear you're having a big sale this weekend. Would you like to buy some spots to promote it?" Sometimes they make a sale, but most of the time they do not. If you operated on this level, would you make the kind of money you would like to make and gain the respect you would like to receive as a member of your business community?

Unfortunately, most media salespeople in today's commercial radio and TV stations are reported to function on this order taker level. Some blame for this lack of professionalism falls on the rural location of many stations, particularly radio stations who serve communities of only a few thousand in population. Small communities do not have a population base large enough to provide a highly skilled or educated labor force. However, small markets (and any size market, for that matter) can have salespeople who are more than mere order takers or clerks if managers understand that they must pay for a training program to have an effective sales force.

The Spot and Program Peddler

The media salesperson at the second level has the personality and order-taking skills of those who operate on the first level. As door-to-door peddlers hawking their briefcases full of spots and program availabilities, however, they have managed to add an ingredient to their repertoire: an overwhelming selection of time availabilities, sponsorships, sports, general programs, and D.J. shows from which the client can choose a sponsorship or ad time.

Like the brush salesperson who always had an endless supply of brushes to fill every housewife's needs, this media salesperson offers program after program to prospects in hopes that they may actually like one and want to advertise on or near it.

Peddlers don't understand that businesspeople have unique needs that cannot be homogenized to the point that one "brush" can handle all of their needs. One furniture store's problems may not be another furniture store's problem, and telling every merchant to run a few spots here and a few spots there on this program or that shows no understanding of the particular needs of the merchant on whom this second level of salesperson is calling.

Prospects Can't Relate to "Stuff"   The salesperson who tailors nothing for clients and offers only an endless selection of "stuff" that probably means nothing to the client hopes that the merchant who sees enough inventory will eventually like something.

After ten minutes of happy talk, instead of just asking the businessperson to buy some spots, the peddler says: "Listen, I know you have a sale coming up this weekend. We're broadcasting the Little League finals on Saturday, so how about buying a sponsorship that will start Friday and give you promotional announcements as well? If you don't want Little League, I have some drive-time slots available. If that won't work, I have the noon news and farm report segments. I also have a Paul Harvey and some ABC news sponsorships. We have a remote early Saturday morning from the county fair. Or, how about a safety tip or two to remind drivers to slow down around school zones? Oh, you do know we're the exclusive carriers of state university football, don't you? Well, about that package . . ." And on and on and on. The prospect who hasn't fallen asleep by the time the salesperson runs out of breath may buy something that sounds appealing, but more likely expresses no interest in anything at the moment and hopes that the peddler does not return soon.

Even though a peddler can make a living by offering an overwhelming selection to clients, the client is not involved with the sale beyond reacting to an array of possible sponsorships and programs, like looking over so much

The peddler

merchandise at a flea market or pawn shop. The media representative has not bothered to learn about the client's business nor has any knowledge about what business or merchandising problems are faced in the marketplace, what makes this store different from the rest, or how the salesperson's station, with its unique demographics, can help the merchant bring in more customers to buy more merchandise.

The salesperson at level two is interested only in presenting what he or she wants to present to the client and in telling the client what the salesperson wants to tell about the station. The client's interests and concerns are of little value to this media rep, whose only concern is to sell as much as possible to whomever it can be sold for the sole purpose of collecting that commission check at the end of the month.

Management pressure can be blamed in part for this type of behavior, but salespeople should never forget that they are ultimately accountable for the decisions they make. They alone determine what level of sales skills they will be known for practicing.

Is It the Fault of Management?   Together, the first two levels of salespeople comprise more than three-quarters of the personnel selling radio, TV, or cable advertising today. Despite the high industry-wide turnover rate, professional sales training has not been a priority on the local level. Salespeople succeed on a hit-or-miss basis in many markets, while management, fearing that the worst won't succeed anyway and that the best will be hired away, is reluctant to invest in training.

Because of the seeming lack of professionalism in media sales, telecommunications students often feel that such a career path is lacking in glamor and prestige or that calling on clients demands little effort and even less training and therefore does not call on their formal education. Nevertheless, because a limited number of personality, production, writing, and technical jobs are available, some entry-level professionals take sales jobs because they are the available positions in broadcasting.

If local training is minimal (which is usually the case), once on the job these new salespeople will speak with and attempt to sell to their clients from one of the first two levels of selling skills. In the absence of training, the new sales reps rely on the assets they do have: a personality and an inventory of products. In media, the product list includes an inventory of time availabilities, program and promotional sponsorships, and other items sales managers want sold.

Media salespeople would be hard pressed to operate any differently than they currently do, given these circumstances. The pressures are present to sell all of these availabilities, which from a business and managerial standpoint must be sold. The problem arises when salespeople are not instructed in how to become effective media consultants.

The Consultant and Problem Solver

The highest level of media sales excellence is practiced by an estimated 10 percent of active sales personnel. These people have strong personalities and inventories of ideas and promotions, but they demonstrate a major conceptual difference. Media consultants, with the exclusion of five defined exceptions (see p. 54), never attempt to close a sale on the initial visit with a client; the order takers and peddlers always attempt to make a sale whenever they call on a client. What they continually forget is their obligation to learn as much as possible about the merchant's business to enable the station to tailor an effective media campaign based on the uniqueness of that particular business and its indigenous needs and problems. Media consultants channel their achievement drive into learning about the client rather than into overwhelming the client with personality and inventory.

Client-Centered Attitude   Learning as much as possible about clients and their needs is the heart of this third tier of sales expertise. The focus is on the needs of the customer and not on the personal commission needs of the salesperson. A media consultant realizes that the job, and the station for that matter, exists only because of the client. The media consultant's responsibility is to produce tangible, accountable results via a unique and creative ad campaign designed to reach the demographics the business wants to reach, the bottom line being that products and services are sold as a direct

The consultant—a cut above the rest

result of the campaign. This result rarely occurs with trite, stock copy written with the scant information that a level one or two salesperson brings back to the creative department. Copy information that results in commercials that sell can be developed only by an initial client interview. This interview is undertaken when a salesperson first sees a client and is referred to (initially by the Radio Advertising Bureau) as the *consultant call* (see Appendix I for a full discussion of this concept). The good news is that many stations now require this approach of all personnel on their sales staffs and, once it is implemented, salespeople discover that consulting is the most effective way to relate to and to serve an increasingly sophisticated and educated clientele.

Once a salesperson has operated at this level for a period of time and established a relationship of trust with the client, the Beveridge concept of sustaining resource begins to take form. The salesperson's expertise and credibility expand to the extent that clients ask for advice about their goals and forecasts and even about matters unrelated to sales and advertising. The sustaining resource's position with the advertiser at this point looks nearly invincible to competitors.[11]

All professionals, then, do everything they can to reach this level of expertise and be viewed with this type of respect by their clients. Only by forgoing the temptation to close a sale on the first visit before information for a media campaign can be gathered can this third and highest level be achieved.

Exceptions to the Two-Call Consultant Approach   The consultant approach of first interviewing the client to gather information and then preparing a media campaign with that information to be presented to the client during a second meeting is not appropriate in five types of situations.

1. *Calling on a "Smaller" Client.* When the salesperson is calling on a client whose business volume and store square footage is small, an in-depth interview is not worth the salesperson's or the merchant's time. The amount of advertising money that could be spent would not equal the value of the time it would take to put together an effective campaign, and enough commercials could not be run on a shoestring budget to solve existing problems effectively. Small mall stores of a few hundred square feet or less selling specialty items at low margin are examples of this kind of client because high overhead plus low margin equals small gross and a very small ad budget. This type of account should never be forgotten, however. It is an ideal candidate for station promotions.

2. *Selling Special Promotions.* Some special promotions need to be sold as soon as possible and are pitched to all merchants on each salesperson's client list. When the manager has ordered 40 six-foot, crushed-velvet Easter bunnies, they need to be moved as soon as possible or the station is stuck with them. Therefore, the promotional package should be sold in one call. Calling on merchants whose traffic would be high during Easter season is essential, as is effective and creative copy designed to get the station's listeners to consider the store for their Easter purchases. The bunny the merchant bought to be given away does not have to be included in the store's commercials on the station, but could be mentioned on separate promotional announcements.

Although we consider the consultant approach ideal, many stations are heavily promotion oriented; there is room for both, as long as promotions are secondary to the regular retail advertising generated by consultant interviews designed to solve identified business-related problems.

3. *Servicing an Existing Account.* When a store is running a schedule of announcements and its needs are already very familiar to the salesperson, he or she may want to increase the seasonal schedule with a promotion or a new idea to generate more impressions in the marketplace. A two-call sales approach is typically unnecessary in such situations.

4. *Certain Cold Calls.* A *cold call* is an unplanned and unscheduled sales call, made either because time permits or because a salesperson passes by an unknown business that would be a good addition to an account list. Depending on the nature of the business, it may be suited for a one-time promotion call, or an appointment can be made for a future interview, thus employing the consultative approach.

5. *When Your Competition "Out-Hustles" You.* When a salesperson is driving down the street and hears a commercial on a competing station for one of his or her clients or prospects and the advertising is for a sale for the upcoming weekend, there is no time for interviews. The salesperson must get to the client, realizing that not enough knowledge exists about the client's business to know that there is, indeed, a sale scheduled for the weekend. Attempting to get the client on the air for the weekend sale is the best that can be done at the moment.

Other than these five exceptions, the consultant call should be employed at all times. This third-level approach to sales is used at least 75 to 80 percent of the time by sales professionals. Only by becoming a true consultant does the media salesperson have hopes of becoming a sustaining resource to any of the accounts on his or her list.

SALES AS A CAREER

Over the years, salespeople have been cast in a negative light, sometimes rightly so and sometimes wrongly. As Miller and Heiman report in the first paragraph of their new book, *Strategic Selling*, "Selling is the largest profession in North America, perhaps the world. Yet it has one of the worst reputations of any profession—second only to that of politics."[12]

Of course, we in the media are all familiar with the plaid suit and equally plaid personality of WKRP's Herb Tarlec but, as with so many other images, TV has stereotyped salespeople with this overconfident, obnoxious character. Miller and Heiman put it this way: "This stereotype is so pervasive that men and women who sell are rarely called salesmen and saleswomen any more. To disguise their true function, their companies give them high-toned euphemistic titles: marketing consultant, account representative, field engineer, account manager, customer service consultant, marketing specialist and occasionally sales consultant or sales engineer. They're called anything but what they are."[13]

Misconceptions about Selling

Sales in general has traditionally been seen as a job rather than a career. The public's distorted view of those involved in sales will change in time, as more and more students study professional salesmanship in college curricula and enter the marketplace ready and willing to be further trained by the professionals at the station level, but for the time being many misconceptions persist. A 1972 study for *Harvard Business Review* by Donald L. Thompson found several misconceptions perceived as fact by a large percentage of the population.

- Selling is a job—not a profession or a career.
- Salespeople must lie and be deceitful to succeed.
- Sales brings out the worst in people.
- To be a good salesperson, you must be psychologically maladjusted.
- One must be arrogant and overbearing to succeed in sales.
- Salespeople lead degrading and disgusting lives because they must be pretending all the time.
- The personal relations involved in selling are repulsive.
- Selling benefits only the seller.
- Salespeople are prostitutes because they sell all their values for money.
- Selling is no job for a person with talent or brains.[14]

None of these statements is true, but we deal with a world of perceptions more than we deal with reality.

Career-Oriented Students

Our technological society, engulfed in a new age of information, places a great deal of emphasis on education and career training. Students are no longer satisfied with understanding the liberal arts; they want to know how they can apply the principles of their education in the marketplace. In short, they want to know how they can pursue a career after graduation, be productive in that career, and prepare financially for an uncertain future. However, our impression is that students, whether they enter the marketplace after high school or after college, are thinking strategically rather than for the short term. They are concerned about what they will be doing 20 years from now and are preparing specifically for that career path by studying telecommunications, journalism, computer science, and so on.

Today's students are more career oriented. Psychologists and researchers have noted that college was once a time for preparation in which young adults could search for truth, broaden their intellectual and cultural horizons in multiple directions, and decide what vocations best suited their talents. Today, students seem more interested in studies they think will give them the best chance of securing entrance to a career-path job after graduation. Some begin seriously thinking about personal career choices as early as high school. They often juggle jobs and school and thereafter are eager to begin a career, something with meaning and relevance. A job is found at McDonald's. A career is something thought about at an early age and prepared for after high school.

Sales as a Career Path

Despite public perceptions, sales, with its inherent intellectual and organizational demands, is most definitely a career path, in fact one of the most financially and personally rewarding careers available today. Sales cannot be classified as a job in which one does not normally become involved in personal planning or organizing and hence controlling the results of such efforts. Sales involves intense personal organization and detailed goal-setting, elements of professional careers that are rarely found in jobs.

Respect   A commitment to a sales career is no more demeaning than a commitment to accounting, education, or law. Sales, and especially electronic media sales, is a specific discipline that takes preparation and personal commitment and, when properly done, brings one professional and personal respect within the community. The common element that every professional strives for and ultimately demands is respect for what one does in relation to the total community. Such respect is closely tied to self-image, and receiving respect for what one does in a particular community enhances self-respect, which causes the salesperson to do an even better job in serving the business community. This cyclical concept is particularly interesting as it applies to electronic media salespeople, as community involvement on the part of any media outlet is the key to achieving high annual sales and eventual financial success within any given media market. Successful media salespeople are always at the heart of community involvement, simply because a career involves the practitioner with that local community, whereas a job usually does not.

Visibility   Media sales is therefore a visible occupation, unlike other career paths in sales. As Barbara Pletcher, Executive Director of the National Association for Professional Saleswomen in Sacramento, has noted in *On the Right Track*, "Professional selling is one of the least visible and most misunderstood careers. Very few people carry the title 'Salesman or Saleswoman' on their business cards, although it's estimated that one out of every ten workers in America is involved in selling."[15] She points out that one cause of misperceptions is statisticians who don't draw the line between sales activity and professional selling. Sales activity, like the "lump teenager standing behind the candy counter in a dime store,"[16] is a job. Professional selling is the highly trained sales representative who is pursuing a career. "Professional selling is a challenging career. If you are capable, it will provide you continuing opportunities to serve the needs of your customers, while benefiting yourself. Professional sales bears little resemblance to routine over-the-counter retail sales or high-pressure, fast-buck operations.

"Professional sales means that you actively investigate customers' needs to determine the best ways to satisfy those needs on a continuing basis. Often, these are needs which the customers themselves are not yet aware of. As a professional sales representative, you will serve as a helpful intermediary between your company and your customers."[17] In addition, the successful pursuit of a career in sales may well lead to higher management responsibilities within the local facility or the parent company.

SUMMARY

From understanding what advertising can realistically be expected to accomplish, to thinking about exactly what a professional broadcast salesperson is, those engaged in or about to enter the arena of broadcast sales can determine for themselves their level of selling. Those who choose the selling of broadcasting as a career will understand the inherent time and organizational commitment (see chapter 4) involved in becoming a consultant and problem solver. Those whose instincts tell them that they can get by with a lesser commitment or who engage in sales only until a better opportunity to their liking presents itself will become order takers or peddlers.

Involvement at any level produces subsistence income, but genuine professional satisfaction and higher-level incomes can occur only with the choice to become a consultant and do more for the client than anyone else in the marketplace is doing. The choice of how professional you wish to be and how you want to be perceived by your clients, your community, and your peers is in your hands.

NOTES

1. Hank Seiden, *Advertising Pure and Simple* (New York: AMACOM, 1976), p. 11.

2. Ibid.

3. Ibid., p. 12.

4. Ibid., p. 13.

5. Elbert W. Stewart, *Sociology: The Human Science* (New York: McGraw-Hill, 1978), p. 248.

6. Si Willing, *How to Sell Radio Advertising* (Blue Ridge, PA: Tab Books, 1970), p. 63.

7. Og Mandino, ed., *A Treasury of Success Unlimited* (Chicago: Success Unlimited, Inc., 1966) p. 188.

8. Ibid.

9. Don Beveridge, *Notice . . . If You Want to Sell* (Barrington, IL: D.W. Beveridge and Associates, 1982), pp. 76–78.

10. Ibid., p. 59.

11. Ibid., pp. 75–78.

12. Robert Miller and Steven E. Heiman with Tad Tuleja, *Strategic Selling* (New York: Warner Books, 1985), p. 9. © 1985 by Miller Herman & Associates. By permission of William Morrow & Company.

13. Ibid.

14. Reprinted by permission of the *Harvard Business Review*. Excerpts from "Stereotype of a Salesman," by Donald L. Thompson (January/February 1972). Copyright © 1972 by the President and Fellows of Harvard College; all rights reserved.

15. Barbara Pletcher, *On the Right Track* (Dubuque, IA: Kendall/Hunt Publishing Company, 1984), p. 2.

16. Ibid.

17. Ibid., p. 3.

Chapter 3

RESEARCH AND PROSPECTING

Enthusiasm, willingness to charge ahead, and knowledge of some basic fundamentals and guidelines of broadcast selling do not assure success in sales. All of these are needed, but preparation is necessary before the salesperson meets the prospective client with the completed sale as the goal.

One important preparatory step is *research*; another is *prospecting*. These two steps go hand in hand because much of the information on research applies not only to the process of getting started, but also to the continuing process of prospecting, which is vital to the continued growth of the salesperson.

RESEARCH

Pre-sales call research, as opposed to the qualitative client research discussed in Chapter 6, arms the salesperson with the information needed to prepare the sales presentation, carry it through to its logical conclusion, and win the sales order. Inadequate research is one of the major causes of failure to complete the sale. This preparatory research step is built on the five *P*s: *product* knowledge plus *prospect* knowledge plus *psychology* knowledge plus *perseverance* equals sales *productivity*.

Product Knowledge

Obviously, the salesperson (broadcast or otherwise) must represent a product or service that is salable, that is, one for which a need can be demonstrated and for which beneficial results from its use can be projected to the potential client. Assuming that the salesperson's broadcast medium is salable, the beginning broadcast salesperson's responsibility then is becoming educated as to the peculiar advantages of that particular broadcast medium.

No advertising medium exists in a vacuum. Potential advertisers can always find other ways to spend their money to gain recognition of their businesses, or they can elect not to spend money on advertising at all and instead rely on word of mouth, customer goodwill, or their business sign to let people know they wish to do business.

In gaining this product knowledge, which is vital as the background for all other parts of the selling process, the broadcast salesperson must get factual answers to some basic questions. The first of these questions is, How long has this broadcast outlet been operating as an advertising medium? The longer the broadcast outlet has been in business, the more likely it is to have a continuing relationship with clients and a collection of advertising success stories.

A broadcast outlet that is very new and has no such history is not unsalable, however. In this case, product knowledge does not focus on past successful client-medium relationships, but instead on why this new station has been established and the apparent need for such an enterprise. Perhaps the market was underserved by the existing advertising media, with the potential advertising greater than the capability of existing media to adequately serve it, thus driving up the pricing structure of available advertising.

In the instance of an outlet that has existed for some time, the salesperson finds one of several types of backgrounds: (1) The medium has a solid history of serving the advertising needs of clients well and has good relations with previous clients (or most of them). (2) The medium has a mixed history, with examples of good results for clients at times, good relations with previous clients at times, and not-so-good results and relationships with clients at other times. This type of history can be caused by bad management at some point: in the case of a radio station, an ill-advised change of format; in the case of a television station, a weakened programming schedule; or in the case of a cable television system, possible overselling. (3) The medium has a bad history and bad relations with previous clients.

Some media (both broadcast and print) make profits year after year while continuing to build bad histories in terms of results obtained versus results projected and with regard to their relationships with clients. In the earlier years of broadcasting as an advertising medium, some outlets built such reputations by overselling their capabilities with an "anything to get the sale" technique, by quoting one price and then billing the client at another, higher price, or sometimes by not bothering to broadcast all the advertising that was sold. Increased competition in recent years has made continuing these practices more difficult for such outlets, but some still exist.

Although the broadcast outlet's history forms an important first step for the beginning salesperson's research, it is not the most important part of this product knowledge. More important than what the outlet has been in the past or why a new broadcast operation has been started is what this particular broadcast advertising medium can now offer to its potential clients.

What *reach*, that is, potential audience coverage, does the medium have?

In broadcasting stations, this reach relies on the station's power and frequency in AM radio (as well as operating hours for daytime or restricted stations), on power and antenna height for FM stations, and on channel, power, and antenna height for television stations. For cable television systems, the reach is determined by the area of franchise wired and number of subscribers from the *home passed*, or those who could subscribe if they wished to do so. Therefore, the reach of the medium is the total number of homes or people who can tune in or sample that outlet if they want. (By comparison, the reach of a newspaper is the circulation, the number of papers delivered, plus those sold at newsstands and other locations.)

Knowing your product well does not mean understanding only the positive aspects of your station and attempting to sugarcoat or pass off any aspect you might not consider in your best interests. Take the example of an AM daytime directional radio station with a frequency around 1550 or 1600. The salesperson can be sure that the competition is presenting arguments to potential advertisers that allude to the station's coverage pattern.

A salesperson representing a station like this cannot pretend that these so-called weaknesses of frequency location and directional coverage pattern do not exist. For the salesperson of such a station, confronting the obvious is imperative. Find out the area the station does cover, along with the demographics of those who listen to the station in that area. The potential client will be interested if the salesperson can show that real people of the type the client wants to reach listen to the station.

Although the station is daytime only, the daytime is the peak listening time for all radio stations. In fact, RAB figures show that more people listen to radio between 6 A.M. and 6 P.M. than watch television or read a newspaper.[1] Granted, the station does not have a favorable location on the dial, but only an engineer would be able to detect the difference in signal quality between this station and a similarly powered station at a low dial position.

After determining the reach of the broadcast outlet, whether radio station, television station, or cable system, the broadcast salesperson needs to know how much of that reach is deliverable as an audience for the advertising client. This deliverable audience varies according to time of day, programming choice, broadcast outlet preference, and habit. The deliverable audience at different times of day and night (and a comparison to the deliverable audiences of other broadcast outlets) is available in reports from ratings services or from the outlet's own research.

As mentioned earlier, any advertising medium that is properly operated has enough audience to deliver results to a potential advertiser. The variables are the kind of audience, the audience loyalty, and the price at which that audience can be delivered.

In the instance of radio stations, each station has a core of listeners who are loyal to that station for whatever reason. With the proliferation of signals (added radio stations, cable television, low-power television stations), electronic media—especially radio—have fully entered an area of what might be called broadcast _narrowcasting._ Each radio station tailors its programming to reach a special, distinct portion of the total available audience.

In this search for a sizable, definable audience, independent television stations counterprogram against the network offerings of the network affiliates, and cable television networks specialize even further, to the 24-hour news-and-information format of CNN and CNN Headline News, the 24-hour all-weather programming of the Weather Channel, the all-sports format of ESPN, and even the all-religion formats of some channels.

The salesperson then studies the broadcast outlet's rate card, along with the rate cards of every potential competitor for the advertiser's dollar. This portion of the research gives the broadcast salesperson the overall cost per thousand (CPM) of members of the _circulation,_ that is, the theoretically deliverable audience of the broadcast outlet and its competitors.

The broadcast salesperson also must study the _immediate product,_ the programs within and around which the advertising will be placed. In radio, this means the format employed by the station, whether it is country, top 40, adult contemporary, or any of the other variations available. In television, the immediate product is the network programming offered by the medium and the local or syndicated programming that fills the gaps left beyond the network programming; in the case of independent television stations, it is the overall programming plan and the offerings that fill in that plan. In cable television, the salesperson studies the channels on which advertising may be placed and the programming fare offered, as well as the possibility of combining channels in a particular advertising sale.

The broadcast salesperson must also study the competition, including any source of advertising that can siphon off dollars from overall advertising expenditures. In local market sales, these competitors include newspapers, shoppers' guides, radio stations, television stations, cable television systems that sell local advertising (and the numbers of these are increasing yearly as cable system operators see an attractive source of revenue to add to subscriber fees), billboards, and special publications such as Yellow Pages and other telephone books, direct mail, and packaged delivery programs wherein a firm delivers ads from several businesses in one common group or enclosure.

Even school papers, annuals, and theater and special events programs should be recognized as potential siphoners of the advertising dollars. How much effort the broadcast salesperson should spend in combating these other competitors for the advertising dollar should be based on the importance of the competition in each market or situation. Too much effort to combat each of the potential competitors in each sales attempt classifies the salesperson as defensive and takes too much time from the positive aspects of the sales call.

However, don't make the mistake of writing off any of the competitors as not important enough to combat. In the case of a radio station serving a largely rural six-county area with ten high schools, the overall amount spent by one advertiser who bought ads in each school newspaper, annual, sports game program, and theater or other event program added up to a considerable sum spent principally for goodwill or public relations.

The broadcast salesperson needs to do this basic research to be able to point out advantages and show the prospective client why this particular system satisfies a need, projects potential benefits, and is economically justifiable. Note that we say "justifiable economically," which is not necessarily cheaper. Remember the earlier discussion on relative cost.

Prospect Knowledge

When the broadcast salesperson knows the product to be sold, the next step in research is learning as much as possible about the people to whom the desired sales should be made. In researching for prospect knowledge, the salesperson starts with the basics. The client list assigned to the new salesperson is a listing of the salesperson's *territory*, the clients from whom that salesperson is expected to derive business. The salesperson is not free to call on any and all possible clients, except in the increasingly rare case in which the station has only one salesperson.

The salesperson's client list is assigned by the sales manager (or in some markets, the general manager or other titled officer who functions as sales manager). Sales calls are made to businesses on this client list, unless the salesperson finds a business not included on any other client list and seeks permission from the sales manager to call on this business. This could be a new business that has opened without fanfare, one the sales manager has not noticed, a business tried by every other salesperson at the station with no success and thus dropped as a prospective advertiser, or an undesirable business with a bad payment record.

The broadcast salesperson then divides the client list into categories: Which are department stores? Which are speciality shops for women's clothing? Which are men's clothing stores? Which are hardware stores? Which are supermarkets? Which are other food stores? Which are automobile dealers? Which businesses provide legal, medical, or financial services?

The type of business indicates to the salesperson the important traditional seasons for advertising the business and the type of audience to which the particular business most likely wishes to appeal.

After separating the businesses on the client list into categories by type of business, the salesperson needs to research a history of advertising for each advertiser that is as complete as possible. The salesperson should find out if the client is a current advertiser on the broadcast outlet or has been an advertiser and, if so, how much the advertiser has spent yearly on the particular outlet, at what times of the year, for what types of program availability, and in what amounts per campaign.

Many salespeople undersell clients because they lack confidence that the client can and should spend more on particular campaigns. Some clients go along with this. They know they need advertising, but if the campaign proposed by the salesperson is less than they were willing to spend, they feel they have "saved" money! The sales manager usually briefs new salespeople on which businesses are "active" advertisers on the broadcast outlet, what their spending range is or has been, and much of the other information above.

After determining what the client's history of spending for advertising on the particular outlet has been, the broadcast salesperson needs to broaden the scope of research for each client to find out the overall advertising strategy of each client on the list. Accomplishing this means asking—and answering to the fullest extent possible—several other questions.

1. Does the client advertise on any competitor in the salesperson's medium (for a radio station salesperson, does the client advertise on competing radio stations)?

2. If so, which, and to what extent?

3. If so, why does the client not advertise on the salesperson's particular outlet?

4. Does the client advertise on other types of media (for a radio salesperson, does the client advertise in newspapers, television, handbills, billboards, or elsewhere)?

5. If so, which medium and to what extent?

6. What seasons does the client use for advertising in these other media?

7. Does the client use an advertising agency to purchase advertising?

8. Who is the contact person for salespeople who attempt to sell advertising?

9. Can that person make a decision and buy, or simply refer a proposal to another person?

10. Who makes the final decision on the purchase of advertising?

11. Does the client operate under a strictly allocated advertising budget, with amounts and media specified at the start of the budget period, or is there flexibility in media, amounts, or accounting for special activity during the year?

12. What particular types or themes of advertising appeal to the particular client?

A separate client record for each business on the client list is desirable. The major consideration is that as much information about each client be gathered as early as possible and then data added as the salesperson-client relationship continues. The better the salesperson knows the client and his or her business, advertising needs, and likes and dislikes, the better the salesperson is prepared to help the client. Salespeople who help the client are those who are welcomed.

Another step in being able to help the client is using appropriate language about advertising and business problems. How does a salesperson become educated about the businesses of each potential client? Obviously, the salesperson cannot become expert in each of many diverse fields. However, the salesperson who desires success as an advertising consultant to various businesses must learn enough about those businesses or industries to be able to understand potential needs, "talk the language," and design advertising to aid in the business's aim of attracting potential customers.

One good way to gain part of this needed background information is from the Radio Advertising Bureau or Television Advertising Bureau Instant Background Books. These paperbacks are published each year and are always up-to-date. Information listed for each category includes size of the industry, best shopping days, characteristics of shoppers, seasonal trends, what items the business sells in total percentage of the businesses's sales, and best business months.

Another way to learn a great deal about the prospect's business is through station subscription to the major trade journals for the various types of businesses, from the automobile dealer's association journal to the journal for frozen food dealers. The number of subscriptions, of course, has to be kept within reasonable bounds.

Salespeople also can stay current on many business trends that affect their clients by reading various daily, weekly, or monthly publications such as the *Wall Street Journal, Barron's, Fortune,* or *U.S. News & World Report*. The salesperson desiring success is willing to make the effort to learn about and keep informed of prospective clients' businesses.

One often neglected way of gaining more prospect knowledge is simply asking the client about his or her business. Most people are willing to talk about themselves and the business they feel is important enough to be a major part of their lives. The salesperson who appears genuinely interested can gain volumes of information about the business.

Psychology Knowledge

Psychology knowledge, the third of the five Ps, also takes work on the part of the salesperson. A good part of the psychology of sales is understanding the positions of the two participants in the projected sale, the seller and the buyer.

The good salesperson can put himself or herself in the position of the buyer to get a feel for how the proposal sounds from the client's position. If the salesperson were charged with running the particular business, what reaction would he or she have to the projected sales proposal? What questions would the salesperson have about this proposal? What might be the determining factors in the success of such a proposal? The salesperson should project answers to these questions prior to the sales call.

Good media salespeople become familiar with human nature. They know that clients have certain predictable feelings about spending money, about advertising in general, and about receiving a sales pitch. The media salesperson takes these into account in planning the presentation for the particular client.

The client reaction to the salesperson's initial request for time to talk with the client is also largely predictable. Many prospective clients come up with almost any excuse to avoid having to listen to a sales pitch without ever admitting to the salesperson their reason for being "busy right now." Few professional salespeople have not heard something similar to "filled with appointments today—try me next Tuesday."

Many give this type of answer because they fear they might buy, or feel they should buy, if the salesperson is allowed to give the presentation. Some of them consider listening to any salesperson a waste of time because they don't earn money that way; in fact, they might even spend some!

Others feel they have no need to advertise because they have gotten along all right all these years without really advertising. The number of these types of businesses diminishes yearly.

Some prospective clients profess they have tried advertising in the electronic media in the past and may again someday, but in the meantime they get results that are good enough from their current advertising in whatever medium they employ. These prospects realize that businesses do advertise on radio, on television, and on cable television channels, and down deep they realize that the leading businesses in the country (and in the locality) would not advertise via radio, television, and cable if they were wasting money that did not return results. If prospective clients were to admit openly that they ought to be doing the same, they would have to learn much more about the electronic media and its advertising possibilities. With all the radio stations, television stations, and cable channels, and the constant all-day and all-night availability, prospects see a confusing jungle of more ways to lose than to win. Much more comfortable (and comforting) might be the sales flyer or print ad that comes out only once per period and gives the client a copy of the ad that can be held in the hand, admired, stuck up on the wall, and referred to continually.

The electronic media salesperson who takes the time to understand sales psychology can overcome many of these hidden, unspoken reasons for client avoidance. Handling the actual sales presentation is another subject that is dealt with at length later.

Perseverance

Perseverance is the fourth *P*. As Rome wasn't built in a day, neither is a salesperson's beginning account list built into a source of large commissions within a week, or two, or three. The beginning salesperson must have the perseverance to go through the product and prospect knowledge steps, work with the psychology knowledge, make the introductory calls to get acquainted, begin to build relationships with clients that will mean sales later, and work with the reluctant or hard-to-see client.

Sales records are not built without patience and perseverance. Successful salespeople learn to wait out those exasperating interruptions, the client who says "I really don't have the time today to see you," and their own tendency to push too hard and too fast to try to make the sale immediately.

Perseverance is made up of patience and persistence and must be practiced in conjunction with the psychology introduced earlier. The salesperson must have the patience at times to forgo the attempt to make the sale now but must also have the persistence to push through the client's sham attempts to avoid being sold. Learning when to use which of these characteristics is a major part of long-term sales success. Perseverance is an acquired trait but one that will serve the broadcast salesperson well over the long term.

Productivity

Productivity is the fifth element of our five *P*s. The ultimate goal of the salesperson is, of course, individual sales, but at the same time developing each account on the client list to its full potential. The beginning broadcast salesperson who masters the first four *P*s is well on the way to productivity in a sales career.

There is no guarantee of absolute success. However, the preparation of a good sales presentation cannot take place until the salesperson knows the product thoroughly, knows the potential client and client business as well as possible, and incorporates psychology and perseverance into the process. At this level, the beginning salesperson is ready for three additional steps: organizing for efficient, targeted sales calls, preparing well-planned, effective sales presentations, and delivering forceful, convincing presentations to receptive advertising clients.

PROSPECTING

The term *prospecting* may bring to mind a grizzled man with his faithful mule ceaselessly searching mountain and desert for the mother lode of gold. More generally it means searching, seeking, exploring, generally with hope of some reward. Salespeople view each potential client as a prospect whose cultivation may yield a reward in terms of commissions.

Practically all salespeople recognize the necessity of prospecting, but many confess they are much more comfortable serving their established clients than prospecting (digging) for new or additional sales possibilities.

Some broadcast salespeople reach a level of comfort in their sales commissions and decide either that they are making as much money as they need or desire or that searching for additional clients is too much trouble. Many of these salespeople are chagrined when an astute sales manager removes some prospective clients from their account lists and gives them to other salespeople to develop.

Prospecting is a necessary part of the salesperson's career, one that should never stop. In broadcasting, it makes the *billings* (that is, the amounts billed to clients) grow and makes the salesperson's commissions grow.

Prospecting can be divided into cold prospecting, developmental prospecting, upgrading prospecting and out-of-the-blue prospecting.

Cold Prospecting

Cold prospecting means visiting firms that are in business but about which the salesperson knows little or nothing except that the firms are in business. This type of prospecting is done with businesses that are not assigned to the salesperson's account list or to any other account list at the broadcast outlet. The firm may have been left off the account list inadvertently, someone may have made the assumption that the firm is not a potential prospect for the particular broadcast outlet, or the firm may be new or newly established in the particular market.

In cold prospecting, the salesperson is making an introductory call to gain beginning information, from which the basic research can be started toward the aim of qualifying the business firm through prospect knowledge research. The salesperson attempts to meet the owner, manager, or other head of the business, introduce himself or herself and the broadcast outlet, and try to gain background information about the business. Normally the salesperson does not expect an immediate sales reward, but the information gained can be valuable if it is followed up through the prospect knowledge step to possible sales presentation calls later.

Many salespeople detest cold prospecting because of the low likelihood of immediate or near-term return on the time spent. Some salespeople see cold prospecting as a challenge to turn that business into a customer, immediately or in the future.

All salespeople should recognize cold prospecting as a necessary part of successfully developing the sales territory. Like the prospector who follows up signs of possible minerals, the broadcast salesperson sees signs of possible advertising revenue in the fact that the business exists.

Developmental Prospecting

This type of prospecting is one step removed from cold prospecting in that the business is listed on the salesperson's account list, but it is similar to cold prospecting in that the business is not now an active customer and may never have been an active customer for the broadcast outlet. In developmental prospecting, the salesperson first checks with others at the broadcast outlet to find out if any problem exists with the business firm. Problems might include disputes over past advertising, lack of payment of bills, or very slow payment. A small business may have been sold a very large advertising campaign and become soured on the broadcast outlet as a result.

Through the prospect research phase, the salesperson can determine the present and past relationship of the business and the broadcast outlet. This research should include searches of recent newspapers to see if the business is a regular or frequent newspaper advertiser. By listening to the area radio stations, viewing the television stations, and keeping an eye on local advertising on the cable channels the salesperson can get an idea of the advertising, or lack of it, by the business.

Of course, the salesperson cannot spend days listening or watching for advertising by a particular firm. The research is an ongoing activity carried out when the salesperson is able to do it and for more than one business at a time. The salesperson stays alert for any and all of the clients on the account list to keep up-to-date on what all the account list clients are doing in advertising.

The developmental prospecting call can be made on a particular business when the salesperson has obtained all the information he or she reasonably can. Developmental calls focus on adding more information to that gained and on introducing the salesperson to the business decision makers. Often it resembles cold prospecting. In most instances, however, someone at the broadcast outlet is able to give at least some basic information about the businesses on the account lists, unless the broadcast outlet is new to the market.

Every firm on the account list is already a potential advertiser, but many need to be developed into actual clients. In the case of cold prospecting, the salesperson is attempting to see if the business firm should be placed on the account list and then developed.

Upgrading Prospecting

This third level of prospecting usually is the most rewarding. It entails the evolution of an existing client's present level of expenditure toward its optimum advertising expenditure.

Many sales consultants do not use the term prospecting in connection with clients who are advertising on the particular broadcast outlet. To return to the analogy of the prospecting miner, such clients are gold nuggets found along the way. Should the prospector be content with those few nuggets or should he continue trying to upgrade his return by searching that site?

Too many broadcast salespeople, having made a sale to a client that places regular advertising on the broadcast outlet, do not follow up to raise the advertising level of the client. Perhaps they fear that an attempt to raise the client advertising level may just shift present advertising expenditure to the newly offered advertising plan, with no net gain for the broadcast outlet or the salesperson, or even lead to cancellation of the present advertising.

The broadcast salesperson must realize that other salespeople are (or should be) constantly working to upgrade their clients in terms of use and purchase of the products or services they represent. A major part of becoming a professional consultant to the business firm lies in showing that firm how additional purchases of the salesperson's wares can bring additional dividends to the business.

Upgrading is not overselling the client. Overselling the client is worse than underselling because it tends to result in disgruntled ex-clients. However, the successful salesperson does not undersell. This salesperson knows the client's potential for the product or service and continues to work at upgrading that client for the client's own good.

Out-of-the-Blue Prospecting

Some business comes to the salesperson unsolicited from out of the blue. It is not expected, and the salesperson has made no specific effort to acquire the business or interview requested.

In the case of the broadcast salesperson, perhaps a call from a business comes into the outlet's office. The information from the call is passed along to the salesperson on whose account list the firm appears, if the firm is on any of the lists. If the business is not on any list, the sales manager designates a particular salesperson to respond to the call.

A business that does not appear on any list normally would be a cold prospect, but in this instance the business wants to purchase advertising time or at least get information about the salesperson's broadcast outlet and its offerings and rates. This interest makes the prospect very different from ones on which a cold prospecting call is undertaken. Likewise if the business in question appears on the salesperson's account list but has been inactive, it would normally be in the developmental prospecting area for the salesperson. The call from the business soliciting the sales effort makes the approach different from that of normal developmental prospecting.

The normal response to such out-of-the-blue invitations is to be overjoyed. The salesperson should call the potential client and set up an appointment as soon as possible. In the meantime, the salesperson bones up on the particular business to make the contact beneficial to the business and a fore-runner of much more business.

In some markets in the past, television salespeople received much business from out of the blue. Business leaders called and asked a television salesperson to come by so they could buy television advertising time. Those times are in the past now, but still calls come from out of the blue to brighten the broadcast salesperson's day and make the follow-up call on the potential client much easier than so much of the other necessary prospecting.

SUMMARY

Researching and prospecting are vital parts of the broadcast salesperson's work.

Research includes:

- Learning everything possible about the salesperson's broadcast outlet (product knowledge).
- Studying the background and advertising habits of firms on the salesperson's account list (prospect knowledge).
- Learning how to apply sales psychology in the management of contact with the businesses on the salesperson's account list (psychology knowledge).
- Becoming familiar with the attributes of patience and persistence in the sales process (perseverance).

The proper application of these four *P*s leads to productivity, which is the broadcast salesperson's goal for proper representation of the broadcast outlet and for increased personal remuneration.

Prospecting, a necessary part of the salesperson's career, is divided into four types:

- Cold prospecting involves calling on businesses with little or no information about them or their qualifications as potential broadcast advertising clients.
- Developmental prospecting is working with nonproductive businesses on the salesperson's account list to attempt to find proper ways to turn them into clients.
- Upgrading prospecting is developing a client's current advertising to its full potential.

- Out-of-the-blue prospecting involves calling on firms that have indicated their likelihood of becoming clients by contacting the broadcast outlet to purchase advertising time or to ask for a salesperson to call on them.

NOTE

1. Radio Advertising Bureau, New York.

Chapter 4
ORGANIZING
THE SALES
EFFORT

The information gained from study and research, as discussed in the previous chapter, has to be organized to make it meaningful and readily usable for the salesperson. Such organization includes arranging the client list, evaluating individual clients, and setting up and maintaining a record-keeping system. Other procedural necessities are sales projection goal setting and the establishment of daily and weekly agendas and priorities.

THE CLIENT ACCOUNT LIST

Most broadcast outlets (radio stations, television stations, and cable systems) keep a master account list that is used for assigning individual accounts to each salesperson. This list is fluid and alters frequently to reflect changes occurring in the marketplace, such as new businesses opening and others going out of business. Keeping such a master account list is management's way of knowing which salesperson is responsible for each account and therefore accountable for the billing of that account. *Billing* is the amount of advertising business contracted for by the client and thus billed by the station on a monthly basis. Another important term for salespeople is *collections* because many broadcast outlets base salespeople's pay not on the amount of business billed during a given month but on the amount of business collected or paid for by the client during that period.

Individual Account Lists

The sales manager of the broadcast outlet assigns accounts from the master list to the individual salesperson. The result is that salesperson's account list. However, even the individual account list is fluid in that an account presenting particular problems to one salesperson might be shifted by the sales manager to let someone else try the account. Moreover, account trading among the salespeople themselves (with the knowledge of the sales manager) can take place.

Each salesperson has his or her own individual account list at all times. No one else on the staff may call on or service that account except during times of vacation or illness. Each account on that list is the sole responsibility of the salesperson. The salesperson either makes a client of each account on the list or is unable to establish a sales relationship due to any number of personal or business reasons. If a business relationship cannot be established by the salesperson to whom the account is assigned, another member of the sales staff may be assigned the account in an attempt to build rapport with the prospect and therefore complete a sale.

Organizing the Client Account List

The salesperson's individual account list needs to be organized in a manner that assists the salesperson in planning sales calls. For example, the accounts spending very little money with the station (and with small advertising budgets) should not be called on several times a week. Conversely, accounts spending a great deal of money with the station need to be seen on a more regular basis for copy changes and other service. If you have sold Mr. Tough, you must not now avoid him in hopes that he will keep running his schedule without your going back to service the account, even if you fear that if you do return, he'll cancel the schedule. Cancellations and other serious problems occur only if you have not properly interviewed and qualified the client, as discussed in Chapter 6.

The client list can be organized in a number of ways. The salesperson should select the method that appears most appropriate and be open to change to another system if needed.

Monthly Breakdown of Accounts   The account list can be organized on the basis of the amount of money spent by the individual accounts each month or the salesperson's projections of amounts that could be spent in future months. Spending categories can be set up according to dollar figures that fit the station's market. At a small radio station, for example, those figures could be up to $250 a month, $250 to $750 per month, $750 to $1,000 per month, and over $1,000 per month. An account at the top of one category should be sorted into the next higher grouping on the assumption that the account billing meets the minimum and is likely to increase with the salesperson's efforts. Then sales can be projected into future months to forecast anticipated business in the coming six to twelve months and help the station in overall long-range planning and goal setting. (See Figure 4-1.)

FIGURE 4-1
Forecasting anticipated business on a 12-month basis

Sales Forecast 19 ___

Salesman ___

ADVERTISER	CONTRACT		DAYS OF WEEK	UNIT PRICE		JANUARY	FEBRUARY	MARCH	APRIL	MAY	JUNE	6 MONTHS TOTAL
	START	STOP		PROG.	SPOTS							
MONTHLY TOTAL												

ADVERTISER	CONTRACT		DAYS OF WEEK	UNIT PRICE		JULY	AUGUST	SEPTEMBER	OCTOBER	NOVEMBER	DECEMBER	6 MONTHS TOTAL
	START	STOP		PROG.	SPOTS							
MONTHLY TOTAL												
PAGE TOTAL												

These records can be kept in file folders with pages inserted for each account's information, on file cards large enough for a good amount of information, or in a computer database into which additional information can be inserted and periodic printouts obtained.

Segmenting Accounts by Type of Business   The account list can be organized on the basis of types of business so that all automobile dealers are together, all department stores are in another file, and so forth, with notes on which are active, which are dormant, and the advertising spending patterns of each with your own station and in competitive media. The account file should be updated whenever new information is available. Include data on when the account was last contacted, what sales idea, promotion, or plan was offered and the firm's response to it, when advertising budget planning takes place, who the contact person is, who makes the buying decision, seasonal advertising high points, whether an advertising agency is used, the salesperson's best guesstimate of the account's advertising budget, and how that budget is allocated among the advertising media.

Beware of Prejudging   Because evaluation of the accounts of clients and potential clients can begin by classifying the estimated dollar amount of the advertising budget for each, the temptation is to *qualify* accounts, that is, to prejudge them.

When doing so, however, understand that how much an account can spend is usually a guess on the part of the salesperson, who often must prejudge prospective clients with little or no knowledge of the actual businesses. Mistakes at this point are common and need to be corrected as more information is gained about the businesses on the client list.

In NAB's *Radio in Search of Excellence*, Donald H. Kirkley, Jr., states that "when we close our minds to alternatives or make up our minds before we have all the facts, we are guilty of prejudgment. Frequent prejudgment creates an image of closed-minded authoritarianism. Apart from the obvious impact on personal credibility, the manager also becomes cut off from fresh ideas and information that could improve the station's performance."[1]

Kirkley then relates the story of a young radio salesman who received a $4,000 order from a small advertising agency in 20 minutes. The client for whom the order was placed had never used radio. "Back at the station, the sales manager was astonished. 'They just don't buy radio,' he said. Had our young salesman been forewarned (thus prejudging the agency), he might well have fallen victim to the manager's self-fulfilling prophecy. Instead, he went into the agency assuming that they would be able to do business—a very different kind of self-fulfilling prophecy. Positive thinking really worked for him."[2]

Prejudging accounts can result in lost business that can never be regained. Although the beginning salesperson must make some judgments in evaluating clients, these judgments are preliminary and subject to change as more information is gained. Even with the best information, the salesperson can never be precise about the amount of advertising money that can be spent by any individual client. A flexible salesperson who is ready to offer clients more than their classifications warrant may find that many clients can afford to invest in good ideas that are tailored to their needs.

Effective Time Management   Most salespeople recognize that business vary in size and some of them cater to a different clientele than does the radio station or afternoon TV programming. Thus, the salesperson must invest the greatest effort in those clients who wish to reach the audience the station serves and who are capable of buying enough to return a respectable dividend for the effort expended. Deciding which clients deserve the greatest effort means effectively evaluating each client in every separate category and planning your time accordingly. Although such advice should not be interpreted as a green light to concentrate on only a few large accounts while totally neglecting the others on the list, keep in mind that some firms can make decisions to buy in thousands of dollars as quickly and easily as other businesses can make a decision to buy in hundreds of dollars.

The research information gained and organized for the salesperson's account list gives the salesperson the basis to evaluate the capability of each business on the list, plan what kinds of advertising to offer, determine what times of the year are best for a client to advertise, and enable a realistic appraisal of the prospect's potential sales value to the station.

WEEKLY SALES CALL PLANNERS

On a day-to-day basis, salespeople follow a weekly planner (Figure 4-2) that tells them exactly which accounts will be seen on which day of a given week and exactly what will be discussed with that account, for example, a new promotion or a copy change.

In order to reserve time for preparation, weekly planners should be filled out by the Wednesday of the previous business week. Such planners serve as guides and should not be intimidating to the salesperson. Should something come up at the last moment, changes can be made. However, plans are necessary to avoid random calling on the accounts with which the salesperson feels more comfortable and avoiding the accounts that demand more time and skill to handle. Given a choice, we all want to visit those who treat us best, but we cannot do business with only a small circle of friends. Visit all accounts on a planned and regular basis and use the weekly planner to monitor the number of times you call upon a particular account.

FIGURE 4-2
A weekly planner provides next week's schedule

REMEMBER! _____

WEEKLY PLANNER

TYPE

NAME _____   DATE _____ TO _____

P—Promotion   R—Regular Schedule   S—Sports

N—News   SP—Special Program   W—Other   O—Other

MONDAY					TUESDAY					WEDNESDAY					THURSDAY					FRIDAY			
Account	Type	Flip	Spec		Account	Type	Flip	Spec		Account	Type	Flip	Spec		Account	Type	Flip	Spec		Account	Type	Flip	Spec

DAILY SALES REPORTS

The discussion of weekly planners brings about the need to introduce the concept of daily sales reports, an example of which is illustrated in Figure 4-3. Most salespeople are intimidated when this topic arises because they view such exercises as providing the boss with something negative to "come down on them with."

Of course, when they are used by sales managers in this manner, the entire concept is being misused. Far from a tool to be used punitively by management, daily sales reports provide the salesperson with a written record of account progress over a period of time. Information from such forms can be transferred to the permanent file cards for productive use by the salesperson. Daily sales reports are a way for salespeople to monitor themselves and keep accurate notes of exactly what is happening during sales calls.

Many sales trainers claim that 75 percent of daily sales reports are fictitious, probably because most sales managers use them to intimidate their salespeople rather than as a positive tool that salespeople can use to monitor their own individual progress. Sales managers should help with that progress by consulting with each salesperson about the reports instead of using them as a threat to the survival of the sales force.

CLIENT RECORD-KEEPING SYSTEMS

The salesperson who has paid attention to organizing a client account list, evaluating and categorizing the individual clients on that list, and updating the list with the assistance of daily sales reports then has the base of a comprehensive client record-keeping system. Such a system serves the salesperson well as a continuing source of information for a successful sales relationship with the client if it is added to as business conditions change and kept up-to-date. Too many beginning salespeople work diligently in building a record-keeping system as they start the selling process and then feel they know their clients so well that they no longer need the records. They are telling themselves that paperwork is too much trouble and that they can remember everything important about their accounts, but they are kidding themselves unless they have very short account lists.

Too many people go into sales looking forward to being out every day making relaxing presentations to potential clients, selling them right and left, and not bothering with the mundane tasks that occupy other people. In reality, however, salespeople need to be better organized than most other people. Every hour of every day should be accounted for, and such organization involves keeping up with the paperwork a record-keeping system re-

FIGURE 4-3

Data from daily sales reports should be transferred to permanent files

DAILY SALES REPORT

REMEMBER! _____ _____ _____ _____ _____

NAME: _____   DATE: _____

Client	New	Call Back	Serv.	Type	Cold	
1						
2						
3						
4						
5						
6						
7						
8						
9						
10						
11						
12						
13						
14						
15						

quires. A salesperson does not have to like such paperwork; he or she just has to do it.

Client Record Keeping and Commissions

Picture for a moment how the salesperson and effective record-keeping tie in to the commission structure. To gain the best efforts of the individual salesperson, compensation usually is in the form of a salary plus commission or a commission matched against a "drawing account." In either arrangement, the value of the salesperson is readily apparent to management. If the station management perceives that the salesperson is costing the station X dollars per month and the salesperson is bringing in sales billings less than that amount, the salesperson is on shaky ground indeed. If the salesperson is bringing in a little more in sales billings than the individual is costing the company, the ground on which the salesperson stands is not really firm. Different companies weigh the cost of a salesperson differently, but a broadcast salesperson who is not bringing in billings well above his or her cost is a liability to the company.

Keeping good records on the potential clients on the account list is just one part of getting to be a "producer" as a salesperson. A permanent record of when and how often the client has been visited and what transpired during those meetings is important. What was the last amount spent with the station or outlet? What schedule was bought and run? What were the results of that buy? When are the client's special sales days? When is the client's birthday? For that matter, is the client contact a golfer, a basketball fan, or a bridge player?

This kind of information needs to be written down because carrying all this information about multiple clients around in one's head is too difficult. If such data is entered in the right file at the end of each business day, the salesperson will always have up-to-date information to stay several steps ahead of less diligent competitors.

Reviewing this information shortly before seeing a prospect makes the salesperson more like a consultant and less like a peddler. The more prospect knowledge the salesperson has, the better the aim of the sales presentation toward the particular prospect's needs and problems. Clients are impressed by salespeople who have a grasp of the problems and concerns at hand—the client's problems and concerns, not the salesperson's problems and concerns. The sales call can then concentrate on solving the client's business problems rather than on rehashing or gleaning information that was procured during a previous meeting.

Talking about the client's golf game the previous weekend can open the conversation. Getting from there to the serious business of getting the client to spend money for the right package of advertising requires the information contained in the salesperson's record-keeping system.

ORGANIZING YOUR DAY

As you begin to follow the guidelines set forth in your weekly planner, prepare to make your first call at 9 A.M. or before. You're fresh and the client is not yet bogged down with the day's details. The number of calls you make on a given day depends on the type of calls. If you plan nothing but formal presentations based on previous information-gathering meetings, two or three calls may be all you can make. If you are servicing accounts or selling a promotion that you want to begin on the air in a few weeks, ten or more calls may be appropriate. Plan to return to the station around 4 P.M. or so to have time to meet with other station personnel about copy, orders, and similar matters before they go home for the day.

A lot of salespeople think that working past 5 P.M. or over 40 hours a week is undesirable. In radio, TV, or cable sales, the successful pro realizes that the salesperson is not being paid for time put in but for expertise and ability to solve the problems of the clients. Forty hours a week is fine, and so is 50 or 60 hours a week. Either way, the salesperson is directly paid for the contribution made to others, which beats a 40-hour week anytime.

Making the Appointment

Making up a weekly sales planner requires making appointments in advance. Some clients are tough to see, and a day and time need to be arranged beforehand. These clients should be the most preferable, as you know when you come in the door that you'll have a fair forum with no distractions such as customers, phone calls, or other salespeople to bother your client while you are there. The client or prospect is expecting you and, excepting emergencies, you should have priority over whatever else happens during your visit.

Advantages of Appointments   Appointments are advantageous for several reasons. First, appointments may be the only way you will ever see a client alone without distraction. Second, a client may be difficult to find on a random drop-in basis. Furthermore, if the salesperson is attempting to gather as much prospect knowledge as possible via a client interview, at least a half hour of the client's time is needed. An appointment helps to ensure uninterrupted time.

Appointments are made in one of three basic ways.

1. By calling the client or the client's secretary
2. By sending the client a note on station letterhead
3. By seeing the client or prospect in person for a few moments when you find the client at the place of business

Appointment by Phone   If you elect to make a phone call, which is probably the easiest and most convenient way for you and for your prospect, know what you are going to say. Be prepared to talk about the benefits of an idea you have for the business.

Explain that you have a plan to increase traffic or make money for the business and that you'd like a chance to sit down and talk about it. If you have not yet established credibility and trust and do not know the business well enough to have come up with an idea to assist it, make the appointment to learn about the business.

Give the client a choice of two times that you have already determined are good for you: "Would you like to meet me for lunch this Wednesday or would Thursday morning around nine be better for you?" A forced-choice question such as this is preferable to saying, "May I see you tomorrow afternoon sometime?" Giving the client a choice of options lessens the chance of a flat rejection.

If your prospect is not in when you telephone, you can usually make an appointment through the secretary. When part of the secretary's job is protecting the boss from all salespeople, dropping by, being friendly, and asking the secretary's thoughts about the business's ad campaign may help you both understand the business and get to see the boss.

Appointment by Writing   If you elect to write to the client, suggest a future meeting and mention that you will call to confirm a suggested date, or one date of two possible choices. Because you cannot commit the client to a meeting without the client's approval, make your letter one that will encourage him or her to agree when you call to confirm the appointment. Again, as with the phone call, tie in a benefit that makes the client look forward to meeting with you. On p. 85 is a sample letter you can follow.

As RAB material and other sales literature has pointed out, you can always resort to gimmicks to get into the office of someone who never gives you an appointment. If you're imaginative, confident, and ready to show the prospect a presentation that is worthwhile when you get space on the client's calendar, send a pitch for an appointment on a cassette. RAB relates the story of a salesman who did exactly this, sending only the cassette with no cover letter and no cassette label. The prospect, naturally curious, played the cassette and called the salesman for an appointment.

Making the Appointment in Person   Usually the most effective of the three methods for obtaining an appointment, actually seeing the client allows you the greatest flexibility in setting a convenient time and place. Although the other two methods are indeed effective, being able to establish eye contact and interact with another person is the environment in which all salespeople thrive.

```
                                    DATE
WKKK


Big Prospect
2001 Peachtree Lane
Radio City, U.S.A.
00000


Dear Prospect:
     We've just received a copy of the latest radio ratings survey done in
our market, showing our station to have the highest number of female lis-
teners 18-49 during several time periods throughout the broadcast day. We
can translate this fact into dollars for you, as your store relies heavily
on the business of women who fall into this demographic group. May I please
make an appointment to meet with you either this Wednesday or Thursday at
9:00 A.M. to discuss this in more detail? I'll call to confirm the day.


Sincerely,


Media Consultant
```

Setting Daily and Weekly Agendas

As confusing as the concepts of sales organization may appear to novices as well as to veterans, the daily and/or weekly agenda helps to provide mental organization and confidence that all of this really can be accomplished within a specified time frame. The following suggested agenda can assist in your personal organization on a daily and weekly basis.

Daily Agenda

1. Check each day's planned schedule and note any changes.

2. Review the next business day's agenda to be sure a full day is planned. Call or write to confirm appointments or to make new appointments.

3. Note items that you told clients you would not forget and follow up immediately.

4. Send thank-you notes at the end of the day to new clients or contacts you may have seen.

5. Check the next day's log to be sure clients who are scheduled to begin are actually on the log.

6. Turn in orders from the day's sales to the traffic department and copy request forms to the creative area. Do all other paperwork required of you as an independent businessperson.

Weekly Agenda

1. On Monday of each week, review your weekly sales planner and make any appointment changes. If you are selling a promotion, for example, you will be making more one-stop calls than normally. During the summer months, note clients on vacation to avoid remembering the contact is gone only after having driven to the business and pulled into the parking lot.

2. On Wednesday of each week, make up the following week's sales agenda. List the clients you intend to see each day.

3. On Friday of each week, review the past week's planner and transfer any pertinent notes from it or from the daily sales call forms onto the client's card or folder file for future reference.

Establishing Priorities

In this process, the salesperson is establishing priorities to be sure that what needs to be accomplished on Monday is accomplished and so on throughout the week. As Howard Bonnell, author of *How To Give Yourself a Raise in Selling*, has noted, "Time is a precious commodity to a salesperson. . . . A salesperson should be very careful how he invests his time."[3] The agenda can help you establish priorities, and following priorities is a key to greater overall sales productivity.

GOAL SETTING

The importance of goal setting cannot be overemphasized to the beginning salesperson, nor can it be ignored by the veteran. Goals and goal setting receive much lip service in the corporate office, in the sales arena, and in radio, television, and cable stations. Most sales managers require each salesperson to set personal sales goals. Unfortunately, all too often the process ends at the point of setting the goal. Little good comes from an academic exercise of this nature unless constant follow-up is undertaken by each individual salesperson and the sales manager. In larger-market radio stations and most television stations, organized follow-up between the sales manager and each salesperson measures how well the salesperson is meeting the goals that were set in an earlier joint meeting. Projected sales goals are set for specific reasons. Constant monitoring gives the salesperson feedback on his or her performance, as compared to projections. For the station, goals become a measure of how effective the salesperson is for that company.

As salespeople begin to visualize the goals they have set, they can imagine themselves achieving these goals and thus turning visions into reality. As goals become reality, achievement drive is increased.

Motivating Factors

Tom Peters and Robert Waterman's *In Search of Excellence* made the point that employees of any organization must be made to feel part of the team. This means being given access to as much information as possible within a free-flowing and open communicative environment.

These findings parallel the writings of Frederick Herzberg, whose management studies on motivation have had a wide acceptance in management circles. Management needs to provide positive environmental or hygienic factors, such as acceptable working conditions, money, security, and policies under which to work. Once provided, these factors do not motivate employees because they soon become the norm. If these factors are not present, however, efforts to enrich the job with motivational or long-term factors do not work.

Factors like achievement, recognition, challenging work, advancement, and personal growth are the true motivators, as opposed to raises and environmental working conditions. Achievement in sales requires setting and achieving goals on a regular basis. Once this has become an ingrained part of each salesperson's day, positive attitudes result in the setting of realistic, achievable goals that translate into personal and business success.

Motivational Goals

According to Ron Willingham in *The Best Seller*, a necessary ingredient to sales success is the setting of motivational goals. He explains that a motivational goal is some tangible item like a car or clothes or something intangible like recognition or status. "The trick is to set motivational goals that you'll give yourself as rewards for reaching your sales goals. A motivational goal motivates us to go out and sell in order to earn enough money or recognition to get the things we want."[4]

Whatever the motivator happens to be, setting a motivational goal can increase your achievement power. Maybe you would like a new wardrobe or a vacation in Hawaii this year. By making your motivational goal something that excites you, you are likely to sell enough to achieve that goal sooner than you think.

Motivational goals can be either short or long term. Saving enough to fly to Hawaii may take time, but you can make smaller purchases if you sell enough in a week or a month to achieve your goal. Willingham suggests the following method:

> First, select the thing you want to have—the reward that you'll present to yourself when you reach a specific sales goal.
>
> Write it down. Get a picture of it in your mind. Get a real picture of it to look at each day.

Then select the sales volume goal that you'll have to reach before you reward your-self with the motivational goal. Write it down also. In fact, write out this statement on an index card: By July 30, I'll sell $20,000 (for example) of radio advertising.

Then continue by writing, "When I reach this goal, I'll reward myself by buying a new briefcase (or whatever you most want)."

Analyze this and you'll see you have set a:

1. *Sales volume goal*
2. *Target date*
3. *Motivational goal*

I can assure you that if the motivational goal is something you really want, it'll be a strong power in helping you reach your sales goal. Your mental computer, the mind within you, will be fueled by strong emotional desire. It'll work night and day for you—helping you figure out the most efficient ways to reach your sales-volume goal.[5]

Daily, Weekly, and Monthly Goals

The earlier discussion on organizing your sales effort was actually a session on goal setting. As you project what a particular account may bill over a period of a month, a quarter, or a year, sales volume goals are actually being set. An annual or a quarterly projection of each account can render a long-range goal to be achieved. Long-range sales goals can then be broken down into monthly, weekly, and even daily volumes.

One of the industry's most respected sales trainers, Ken Greenwood, has developed a "SMART" system of goal setting for salespeople:

*S*et performance, define it, establish it

*M*easurement method must be defined

*A*greement of performance of goal

*R*einforcement, reprimand, praise, coach

*T*rack performance, evaluate

Step one is to get the salesperson to set the goal and then jointly agree with the sales manager on the goal. The goal ought to be something that is simple, attainable, and measurable. The second step is to agree on measurement. Will the criterion be a dollar number, percentage, number of calls, or number of presentations? The next step is to agree on performance goals and set a time span for the goal to be achieved. The fourth step is monitoring the goal and checking indicators for progress. The last step is to evaluate the performance at the end of the time span.[6]

BEFORE MEETING WITH THE CLIENT

Once the media account executive has a firm command of the areas of product and prospect knowledge, has devised a personal record-keeping system, has organized client data in a manner that is understandable and meaningful, and has set realistic and attainable sales goals, the time to begin thinking about meeting with the client face to face is at hand. Before you march out the door to confront the client, however, the professional media salesperson must take care not to trip over untied shoelaces en route to the front lines.

In the early morning, you open that closet door revealing the real you in the clothes hung on those hangers. Move all of your fluorescent plaids to the back of the closet, along with your multicolored shoes or your high heels. These items do not project a serious business image. You are not working in business to make a fashion statement. Business is business and part of selling yourself to your clients is projecting a neat, professional business image. So, move your more conservative but attractive blues and grays to the front of the closet, and wear them with clean white, blue, or other appropriately colored shirts, blouses, and accessories. Do not perk up your outfit by adding a wide paisley tie with pink flamingos or a garish scarf. Men, leave your open-neck, no-tie look at home with your gold chains. You're not dressing to inform the world how cool you are. You're dressing as a serious, mature businessman who is not ashamed of the important role he is playing in the world of commerce. Women, make your avant-garde fashion statement outside business hours. You're projecting a neat, competent appearance that focuses attention on you as someone who can advise businesspeople.

First impressions can either make or lose a client. Make sure that your first impression is as positive as you are able to project—in dress, grooming, and overall attitude.

ONCE YOU LEAVE THE OFFICE—A POTPOURRI OF HELPFUL TIPS

Tip # 1 Hit the streets early! We mention this again for purposes of reinforcement. As most media advertising is sold in the morning, plan on seeing your best prospects before their days become too hectic to give your ideas priority.

Tip # 2 Call your station at least twice during the day to check on phone messages from clients, sales activity on the time slots you may be trying to sell, and other business matters. A salesperson who doesn't call in loses sales. For example, a client who is eager to buy your station for a big campaign may make other plans if you cannot be located. Pick up messages throughout the day, not at the end of the day. Those who fail to call in also risk selling a "hot" available time slot that another salesperson has already sold. A quick call to the station confirms the availability of the time slot and reserves the time.

Tip # 3 Check your equipment if you have a demonstration tape (spec spot or demo tape) prepared for a client on a cassette or if you are planning to have the client record some information for commercials. If your batteries are weak or dead, you are setting yourself up for exposure as unprofessional and certainly for an embarrassing meeting with the client.

Tip # 4 If you have to wait in the store or business for the client, wait no longer than 10 to 15 minutes and make use of your time by reading company literature if it is available. If not, rehearse your presentation or write copy—anything other than sitting in a chair looking bored. When 15 minutes expires, leave. Don't give the impression that you aren't busy and have nothing better to do. Who wants to do business with someone who isn't busy? A busy person obviously has a lot of business and therefore must be good.

Tip # 5 If your client is busy with a customer when you come in, even if you have an appointment, leave and phone later. One of the authors once made the mistake of saying, "Oh, that's all right. I'll be happy to wait," while the client was trying to sell an expensive piece of jewelry to a customer. When the customer said, "Well, I see someone is waiting to see you" and left, guess who was blamed for the lost sale?

Tip # 6 Avoid driving around aimlessly during the day. Schedule your calls in one area of the city to avoid wasting gas and time. You can park once and see a number of clients on foot.

Tip # 7 If you finish your day unusually early, avoid ducking into a coffee shop or the local real estate agent's hangout for a three-hour visitation. Make cold calls, prospect for new accounts, or service that account you've been avoiding for several weeks because you're afraid the client, with whom you don't get along especially well, might cancel the advertising upon seeing you.

Tip # 8 When you return to the station at the end of the day, take the time to send out notes thanking clients for their business or their time. Your clients and potential clients are going to support you and your family for a number of years, so you're running a daily public relations campaign with those on your account list. You have to build up long-term trust and confidence. You're not the traveling salesrep who sees your prospects only once, sells them hard, and then leaves town forever, never to see the client again.

Tip # 9 Don't oversell the service of radio, TV, or cable. Remember Hank Seiden's words on what advertising can and cannot be expected to do.

Tip # 10 Read this book carefully and patiently and do what it says!

With all of these last-minute helpful hints, you are just about ready to leave the station and meet with the client face to face. What you now need is the sales know-how, basic knowledge of a selling system, and an understanding of psychology and communications as they relate to the selling process, so that you know exactly what to say in your own words, when to say it, and how to phrase it. You also need to think about the type of salesperson you want to be.

SUMMARY

Perhaps more than any other profession, sales demands strict organizational control in the areas of personal planning and time management (daily, weekly, monthly, quarterly, and annual goals). Without organizational control, meaningful goal setting would not be possible and the salesperson could not monitor progress toward worthwhile, predetermined goals. By utilizing the elementary forms suggested, the salesperson is better able to control his or her time on a daily basis and thus can become successful in establishing priorities, categorizing accounts, and visiting those accounts on a routine basis determined by size and business volume.

NOTES

1. Donald H. Kirkley, "Communication: The Key to Productivity," in *Radio in Search of Excellence* (Washington DC: National Association of Broadcasters, 1985), p. 86.

2. Ibid.

3. Howard W. Bonnell, *How to Give Yourself a Raise in Selling* (New York: Bell Publishing Company, 1985), p. 97.

4. Ron Willingham, *The Best Seller!* (Englewood Cliffs, NJ: Prentice-Hall, 1984), p. 9. © 1984. Reprinted by permission of the publisher.

5. Ibid., p. 11.

6. Ken Greenwood, "Excellence in Managing and Motivating Salespeople," in *Radio in Search of Excellence*, p. 77.

Chapter 5
RATINGS
AND RATES

Broadcasting (commercial radio stations, commercial television stations, the networks) is a $20 billion industry that depends on ratings for its success. Decisions on whether programs continue or are cancelled are made on the basis of ratings for those programs. Whether an individual performer or executive retains a position or is fired and how advertising rates are calculated are influenced greatly by the ratings—on how many of what segments of the population are watching or listening at particular times.

The rise of just one rating point for a network evening television newscast can mean additional advertising revenues of almost $8 million per year brought in by that program alone. The market value of the radio station, the television station, or the network rises and falls with the ratings of its programs because the higher the programs are rated, the more advertising revenue comes in, and higher profits mean a higher value for the broadcast outlet.

The broadcast salesperson finds out quickly that ratings play an important part in the selling of broadcasting advertising, with the exception of the smallest radio markets, especially the few single-station markets. Thus, the salesperson must learn the terminology and the use of ratings in the sales process.

RATINGS AND RATINGS SERVICES

The first question that arises is, Why ratings for broadcast media when print advertising is sold on the basis of *circulation*, or the numbers of newspapers or magazines sold and delivered to the public? Everyone who has a radio can tune to programs on the radio stations in a particular market. Everyone who has a television receiver can tune to the television programs on stations in the market.

While circulation figures are the vital ones for print media, the differences in delivery constitute the reason for the different measuring methods. Broadcast programs and their advertising reach potential consumers without any provable record of the purchase of the broadcast service by the consumer (except for cable television service, in which the services containing advertising are billed on a monthly basis according to the number of subscribers). The broadcast programs and the advertising are there and available within the reach of the potential consumer. To know whether and when these programs and advertising are being chosen by the consumer, something else is needed.

A subscription or individual purchase of a newspaper or magazine indicates that whoever has bought that advertising medium will presumably read it and thus be exposed to the advertising that surrounds the reading material. The assumption that the purchaser has read or been exposed to all of the advertising in the print publication is a fallacious one that will be dealt with later.

With the broadcast media, listeners or viewers are free to tune in to any available channel or frequency and to change that choice at any moment. The radio and television sets are present and the programs are available, whether the potential consumer is at the location or not. Without some form of measurement of how many of these potential consumers are watching or listening during some particular time segment, broadcasters would be selling advertising time on radio and television based on their reach. This *reach* is the theoretical maximum number of persons able to receive the broadcast station. It does not show listener or viewer use or preference among all the broadcast signals receivable. To answer this need, the concept of ratings was devised.

Ratings and ratings services came into being when early advertisers on radio felt they needed some measurement of the size of the audience that could be reached through radio stations or networks. These early advertisers began the Cooperative Analysis of Broadcasting (CAB) in 1930 to provide additional information on which to make advertising decisions. The CAB featured telephone recall surveys, in which people were called and asked about their recollection of programs or advertising that had been aired. From this limited research sample, projections could be made on the size of the audience that had listened to a particular program and thus heard the advertising.

In 1934, a group of magazine publishers who felt the CAB technique overestimated the size of radio audiences began a second rating service. This group commissioned C. E. Hooper, a well-known pollster, to begin a new rating service that featured telephone calls made while the radio program was on the air to determine what percentage of the sample population was actually listening. This sample figure was then projected to the population as a whole. Since those early efforts, the ratings field has developed into a $100 million business, with a small number of independent research firms providing ratings reports and other research information on broadcast audience size and composition.[1]

Each of these research firms may use its own procedures, but all aim for the same goal: precise estimates of the audience and the demographics of that audience. _Demographics_ may be defined as the segregation of a group of people into various segments according to like characteristics. A simple demographic segregation would measure the estimated numbers of males and females in the audience. A second step would be to break these gender divisions by age groupings, such as males 12 and over, females 12 and over, and so forth. Today's ratings research firms go well beyond these simple breakdowns of the audience to provide information on radio audiences away from home, working women, ethnic groups, and other aspects of the audience.

The ratings research firms measure audiences in the categories of network television, network radio, local television, and local radio. Some firms have now begun specialized local cable ratings for cable television systems. Two of the largest and best-known firms in the ratings research business are the Arbitron Company, a subsidiary of Control Data Corporation, and A. C. Nielsen. The oldest of the ratings services is the Nielsen Television Index (NTI), which measures network television viewing (see Figure 5-1). It uses meters for household viewing data and diaries for personal viewing.

Figure 5-1

The Nielsen Television Index, which measures network television viewing

Courtesy, A. C. Nielsen Company

Both Nielsen and Arbitron provide ratings services for individual television markets across the country. They use diaries (as illustrated in Figure 5-2) in more than 200 television markets and household viewing meters in a number of major television markets.[2]

The household meters Nielson and Arbitron use in larger television markets add to the information gathered by the ratings survey diaries. These meters report when a television set is on, the channel to which the set is tuned, and how long the television set is tuned to a particular channel. This is accomplished through a television meter attached to the television set, a household collector to gather and store information from the meter, and a data retrieval system that operates from a firm's research headquarters to collect the information from all the household collectors early each morning through dial-up lines.[3] Figure 5-3 shows data from household meters.

PeopleMeters

In 1985, a new participant entered the ratings business in the United States with a new type of meter to measure television viewing. AGB Research was established as a U.S. company by AGB Research, PLC of London. The parent firm described itself as Europe's largest research company, one that does

Figure 5-2
Arbitron television diary

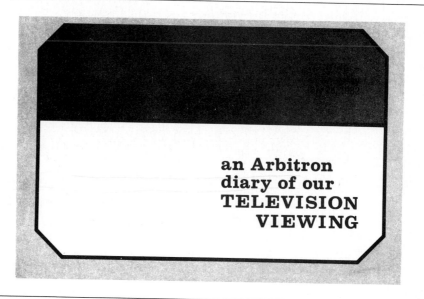

an Arbitron
diary of our
**TELEVISION
VIEWING**

Courtesy, Arbitron Ratings Company

Figure 5-3
The Arbitron weekly meter report

Time Period Estimates

Program Audience Estimates

Courtesy, Arbitron Ratings Company

Figure 5-4
AGB's People Meter (lower left), a remote-controlled portable handset with eight buttons, and the People Monitor (upper left), which sits on top of the TV set and at periodic intervals provides a flashing reminder to people to record their viewing with the handset

4,000 Nielsen Homes

Works because of Statistics

business in more than 20 countries including television research in 12 countries.[4] In its U.S. debut, the company introduced the PeopleMeter, an electronic device through which individuals record their viewing by touching numbered buttons on a portable handset similar to the units used with remote control television sets. Figure 5-4 shows PeopleMeter equipment. AGB Research said in the 1985 introduction that versions of the PeopleMeter were in operation in five countries and that in some instances the PeopleMeters had been in use for eight years.[5]

The remote handset unit has eight pushbutton numbers. Each individual within a household is assigned a specific number to push to indicate that person's viewing. A small monitor atop the television set provides a flashing reminder at periodic intervals to remind the individuals to record their viewing. When the individual stops viewing, he or she pushes the assigned pushbutton, which turns off the lighted monitor on the television set.[6] AGB Research claimed that its PeopleMeter is easier to use and more accurate than a diary, brief channel changes are automatically recorded, and measuring the same individuals' viewing for an extended period allows much more sophisticated analysis than was previously possible.[7]

Both Nielsen and Arbitron began testing similar meters to measure individual viewing as an alternate to their household meters that indicated when the television set was on and what channel was in use but not who was watching the television set at that time. AGB then announced its plans to establish a national rating service to compete head-on with the Nielsen Television Index.

Since its introduction, the PeopleMeter concept has excited many people in the advertising industry and caused some consternation. *USA Today* reporter Brian Donion, in a 1987 article subtitled "Sophisticated people meters are pushing some wrong buttons at the networks," wrote that the system promises more information for programmers and advertisers, but that "the technology and a test audience that tilts to younger, college-educated viewers has the networks in an uproar and could threaten some shows."[8] Ad people looked forward to knowing what they were getting for their money.[9] A Nielsen initial test of a thousand homes showed that some of the television hits under the older systems of measurement (household meter and diary) did not rate as well under the people-metered system and that some shows that had been cancelled because of poor ratings might have remained on the air because of increased audience and very good demographics.[10]

Fortune, Broadcasting, and other specialized and general publications carried stories on the new ratings concept. In a 1987 *Fortune* article, writer Brian Dumaine pointed to the problems as well as promise of the new system.

> *According to the newfangled meters, some prime-time shows are drawing audiences as much as 15% smaller than what the networks thought they were reaching. For target groups like women ages 18 to 49, the shortfalls of certain shows are even larger, as much as 18%. Advertisers, who spend $9 billion a year to hawk their wares on network shows, are up in arms. The networks are on the defensive.[11]*

Dumaine pointed out that the promise of the new system included correction of what has been a criticism of the diary method.

> *With the rise of cable and independent stations, advertisers began to complain bitterly that the diaries inflated network viewing. In the 1960s and 1970s, when the three networks dominated the airwaves, it was fairly easy for people to remember which shows they had watched. But today, with 30, 40, or more channels to choose from, keeping a diary becomes dauntingly confusing. Diary keepers tend to remember the smash hit network series like "The Cosby Show" and "Cheers" and to forget whether Junior watched the water polo match on, say ESPN or the Sports Channel.[12]*

The concept of metering people's individual viewing practices, with modifications to improve the reliability of the data provided as the system matures, is here to stay. Nielsen began installation of its national people-metering system in 1985 and began releasing ratings from this system in January 1987. AGB ran tests of its system in Boston and elsewhere and set its system to debut nationally for the 1987–88 television season.

Nielsen announced a change in its system to overcome the problem of people not pushing the button. Its passive meters "emit constant waves, either of invisible infra-red light or of sound. As long as somebody is interrupting the waves by sitting in front of the tube, Nielsen's latest meters signal that the broadcaster has hooked a live one."[13]

In 1987 R. D. Percy, a small Seattle company, entered the market with its Voxbox, a passive meter designed to measure whether people are watching commercials. "When its infrared beam fails to sense a body, the meter sends a message to the TV screen that asks 'Who is in the room?' If no one responds by pushing a button, the Voxbox reports that the commercial is playing to an empty house."[14] Some large national advertisers who have signed up for the R. D. Percy service are watching the outcome of this further metering of people.

National Radio Measurement

RADAR, from Statistical Research, Inc., is the only radio network measurement service. This system estimates audience measurements through telephone recall methods in which each person in the sample population is called daily for a week and asked questions to seek listening recall over the previous 24-hour period. Arbitron offers local radio ratings services using a diary technique that measures 12 weeks at a time rather than the four-week sweeps for television. In addition to Arbitron, several other research firms operate in more limited market areas or perform specialized research for radio stations on a market-by-market basis. Some of these firms also provide research services for television stations.

Away-from-Home Ratings

Television ratings are confined to in-home viewing, which omits viewing by people in hotels and motels, bars, waiting rooms, dormitories, and hospitals, as well as viewing outside the home on portable television sets, which have gained popularity in recent years. However, radio audience measurement includes listening by individuals wherever they may be because radio has such a significant out-of-home audience.[15]

Ratings Use

Anyone who plans to use ratings information must keep in mind that the ratings figures provided by the research firms are approximations of the audience listening or viewing patterns. Although the research is conducted with the best sampling techniques possible, the ratings should be taken as a guide rather than considered as a completely accurate projection of the audience. Broadcast Rating Council, an independent organization composed not of ratings services but of broadcasting entities that represent rate users, monitors the operations and performance of accredited broadcast ratings services and thus adds to the confidence users have in the projections of audience characteristics by the ratings services. However, the council itself states that "a prudent approach is that used by one veteran agency media executive who accepts no rating change as actionable without confirmation from another service or a subsequent report."[16] The major ratings firms also note in their audience reports to subscribers that the figures presented are estimates and should be treated as such. Users of ratings information should also remember that the figures are quantitative estimates that are not intended to judge the quality of programs or to predict any future behavior of the audience.

Ratings Methodology

Ratings research firms use five basic methodologies today.

Know a few.

1. Instantaneous electronic meters that automatically record when a set is turned on and the channel to which it is tuned
2. Diaries kept by respondents for one week and then sent to the research firm
3. Telephone interviews using questions to ascertain audience recall
4. Telephone interviews conducted coincidentally with the broadcast
5. People-metering devices that measure when television is watched, who is watching, and the changes in viewing over any time period measured

The time relationship of broadcasting makes measurement easier and more valid than in the print field. In broadcasting, the audience is assembled at a particular point in time to listen to or view a particular program, although continuing expanded use of video recorders to time-shift television programs will have an impact on this relationship. Use of the electronic meters to determine when the television set is turned on and to what channel and how long the set remains on or on a particular channel eliminates the need for the audience to remember what was watched at particular times. The new people meters enhance measurement because recall is eliminated and each viewer's presence is recorded. Coincidental telephone interviewing also takes away the need to remember what was viewed or listened to at times in the recent past. Diaries and daily telephone recall interviews rely more on the individual's memory. Television people and especially radio listening are habitual for most people, and this regularity contributes to accurate recall over the short term. Almost all viewers and listeners habitually tune more often to certain favorite stations and channels than to the other available stations or channels.

All of the methodologies used by the ratings services have their plusses and minuses. The meter services used by Nielsen and Arbitron use a form of semi-instantaneous meters that automatically record each minute showing the time, whether the television set is off or on, and if the set is on, the station to which it is tuned. This electronic information is stored in the unit within the household for 24 hours or less until it is read by a central computer, which can then provide station rating results overnight. According to the Broadcast Rating Council, "Strictly as a tuning measurement device, this type of meter is perhaps the most accurate instrument in all survey research. Nevertheless, the meter has limitations, the most significant of which is the lack of data on who, if anyone, is viewing."[17] The new people-metering system attempts to answer this limitation.

Metered services, however, are fairly expensive to operate and maintain and in the past were restricted to relatively small panels of sample households. Nielsen's National Television Index used some 1,200 household meters; from 300 to 500 such meters were used for local service measurements in New York, Los Angeles, and Chicago.[18] (By contrast, Nielsen began tests of its people-metering devices with 1,000, had 2,000 in place in 1987, and projected 4,000 for 1988. AGB planned to have 5,000 of its PeopleMeters in operation by the same time.

Diaries include the local market television diaries used by Arbitron and Nielsen NSI, the local market Arbitron diaries for radio, and the television Audiolog used by Nielsen NAC. For television diaries, each diary is designed to show the viewing of each and every household member as a composite during the week's time. A separate diary is furnished for each television set in the household. A sample of such a television diary is shown in Figure 5-5.

For local market radio information, Arbitron respondents use open end diaries for a week, with each member of a household keeping a separate diary.[19]

A third diary form is used by Nielsen for its National Audience Composition (NAC), which is used to supplement the metered measurements of the National Television Index. This audiolog service has respondents selected by area probability sampling parallel to the NTI Audimeter Service,

Figure 5-5
Arbitron television diary page

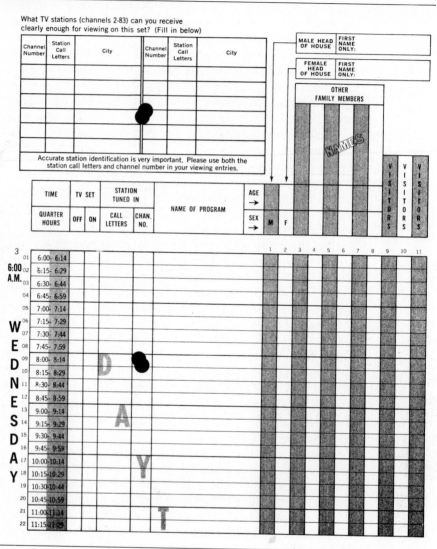

Courtesy, Arbitron Ratings Company

and its television sets are equipped with recordimeters that have a reminder feature and count the number of hours the sets are used during the week.[20]

The use of the telephone recall interview method, which was an early measure of radio listening, has developed largely for radio. As the Broadcast Rating Council points out, "One procedure, employed by RADAR for network ratings, involved recruitment of a panel of respondents who agree to be interviewed about their previous day's listening every day for a week. RADAR also used random digit dialing as a sample mechanism so as to produce a probability sample of all telephone households."[21]

Research information shows that the American people spend a lot of time each day with radio and television. Radio listening is three hours per day for the average American; in the average home, the television set is on seven hours per day, and the average person watches about three hours of that time.[22]

Ratings Terms

Learning the meanings of common terms is the first step in understanding the wealth of information provided by ratings reports. Although some of the terms are the same from one broadcast medium to another, we will consider radio and television (including cable television) separately.

Radio Ratings   In radio and television audience measurement, a *rating point* represents one percent of the *population*, that is, the audience being measured, whether the measurement is of the metro survey area or the total survey area. Radio ratings usually are based on the population in the metro survey area. Sometimes radio measurement is conducted in a larger area, the *area of dominant influence* (ADI), which is Arbitron's term for a television survey area.

The number of listeners is another important factor for radio. The rating for the time period in question is given as follows:

$$\frac{\text{Listeners}}{\text{Population}} = \text{Rating Point}$$

For example, if the population is 400,000 in the area being surveyed and the estimate of listeners to a station at a particular time is 20,000, then the rating for that time period is 5, indicating that 5 percent of the area population listened to the station at that time.

If the rating and the population are known, then listeners can be calculated thusly:

$$\frac{\text{Population} \times \text{Rating (\%)}}{\text{Listeners}}$$

Using the same figures as before, 400,000 multiplied by 0.05 percent equals 20,000 listeners at that time.

Radio Facts, published by the Radio Advertising Bureau (RAB), lists the most common terms needed to understand audience research for radio.

Average quarter-hour audience (AQH persons): An average of the number of people listening for at least five minutes in each quarter hour over a specified period of time. RAB says that in today's radio, the average quarter-hour measurement should be considered a measure of total time spent listening.

Average quarter-hour rating (AQH rating): The average quarter-hour audience expressed as a percentage of the population measured. AQH persons divided by the population equals AQH rating.

Share of audience (share): The percentage of those listening to radio in the AQH that are listening to a particular station. AQH persons for one station divided by the AQH persons listening to radio in that market at that time equals the station share.

Cumulative audience (cume persons): Also called *unduplicated audience*, this is the number of different people listening at least five minutes during a particular time segment. Cume persons is the potential group that can be exposed to an advertising message on the radio station, just as readership is the potential exposure for print media.

Cumulative rating (cume rating): Cumulative audience expressed as a percentage of the population being measured. Cume persons divided by the population being measured equals cume rating.

Total time spent listening (TTSL): The number of quarter hours of listening to radio, or to a particular station, by the population group being measured. AQH persons multiplied by the quarter hours in the time period equals TTSL in quarter hours.

Average time spent listening (TSL): The time spent listening by the average person who listens to radio or to a particular station. TTSL divided by the cume persons equals TSL.

Audience turnover (T/O): The number of times the average quarter hour audience (AQH persons) is replaced by new listeners in a specified period of time. Cume persons divided by the AQH persons equals T/O. T/O is also the number of announcements needed to reach approximately 50 percent of the station's cumulative audience or cume persons in the time period.[23]

Reach: The number of different people who are exposed to a schedule of announcements; those listening during a quarter hour when the announcements are broadcast. Reach also can be expressed as a rating or a percentage of the population being measured. Persons reached divided by the population equals reach rating.

Gross impressions: The total number of exposures to a schedule of announcements, not the number of *different* people exposed to the announcement. AQH persons multiplied by the number of the announcements equals the gross impressions.

Frequency: The average number of times the audience reached by an advertising schedule is exposed to a commercial. Gross impressions divided by reach equals frequency.

Gross rating points (GRPs): The gross impressions expressed as a percentage of the population being measured, as one rating point is equal to one percent of the population. Gross impressions divided by the population equals GRPs; it is also calculated by AQH rating multiplied by the number of announcements equals gross rating points.

Cost per thousand (CPM): The basic term for determining unit cost of an announcement or schedule. It is often used to compare different schedules and stations. Schedule cost divided by the gross impressions expressed in thousands equals CPM.

Big Markets **Cost per rating point (CPP):** The unit cost of one rating point or 1 percent of the population being measured. Schedule cost divided by the gross rating points equals CPP.[24]

The share of a radio station is an important figure because it is relatively stable and not affected to any great extent by the seasonal and other factors that affect the ratings of stations. The share provides a good rough comparison of the popularity of a particular program or station at a particular time.

Having a consistently higher share of the total available listening audience or of a particular demographic group for certain time periods can be important selling points for the broadcast salesperson. One station in the market may claim to be number one on the basis of highest total ratings, and another station may successfully counter that claim by showing it has a consistently higher share of adults aged 18 to 24 or some other demographic grouping.

The larger the radio market, the more the ratings data are needed and used. However, in any radio market where such information is available, the salesperson should be able to use it to advantage, even though the information is less often quoted in prepared sales presentations to retail clients in smaller radio markets.

In any market of any size with competition from one or more other radio stations, from within or without the market, the good businessperson wants to know how the product of the radio station—its programs, time periods, advertising availabilities—compares with competing stations. How the station rates against its competition influences commitment of advertising dollars. Thus, most (if not all) radio stations need ratings information of some type, even if it is not as sophisticated and thorough as that commonly furnished by the ratings services for every television market.

As an example of the ratings research information for a particular radio market, Figure 5-6 shows a portion of the Arbitron radio audience estimates for Mobile, Alabama, which is not a particularly large or small metropolitan market. Mobile is in Mobile County, but Baldwin County is also included in the metropolitan market, which has a population of 453,700. Mobile is part of the Mobile-Pensacola television market, ranked as the 61st television market, with 401,700 television homes in the area of dominant influence and 625,300 television homes in the television survey area.[25]

Figure 5-6
Arbitron radio audience estimates for Mobile

MOBILE
APRIL/MAY 1980

TOTAL PERSONS 12+

MON-SUN 6:00 AM-MID

STATION CALL LETTERS	A/M 78	O/N 78	A/M 79	O/N 79	A/M 80
STN. A	10.3	6.0	5.1	5.1	4.1
STN. B	6.5	14.3	10.2	16.8	13.3
STN. C	7.5	6.8	11.3	7.4	8.4
STN. D	5.1	4.9	5.9	6.9	6.5
STN. E	5.1	...	...	2.1	1.4
STN. F	1.0	.4	1.4	.4	1.2
STN. G	5.1	8.6	6.8	10.6	10.0
STN. H	20.8	18.4	14.1	15.8	17.2
STN. I	1.8	.9	1.6	1.2	3.5
STN. J	9.1	5.6	10.7	8.8	15.5
STN. K	7.1	10.7	10.5	7.6	6.3
STN. L	3.6	5.1	3.7	2.1	1.6
STN. M	2.8	2.3	1.4	.5	.8
STN. N	10.3	8.3	9.4	4.2	2.0
STN. O	...	.8	...	...	.4
METRO TOTALS	15.0	15.6	15.0	15.9	13.8

MON-FRI 6:00 AM-10:00 AM

STATION CALL LETTERS	A/M 78	O/N 78	A/M 79	O/N 79	A/M 80
STN. A	11.5	7.3	6.1	6.4	5.4
STN. B	7.3	11.2	7.4	13.9	11.3
STN. C	7.5	6.8	9.0	4.9	5.5
STN. D	3.7	3.2	2.4	3.1	2.0
STN. E	...	...	...		
STN. F	.8	.3	1.8	1.2	1.1
STN. G	10.3	12.5	10.8	15.3	14.8
STN. H	15.9	17.8	13.5	13.5	15.6
STN. I	1.4	.5	.8	1.5	2.5
STN. J	10.6	7.2	12.8	12.6	17.3
STN. K	5.3	11.0	9.7	7.9	5.9
STN. L	3.4	3.9	3.1	1.4	.7
STN. M	1.9	1.8	1.5	.5	.6
STN. N	12.6	9.6	12.6	5.9	2.5
STN. O	...	1.2	...	...	.4
METRO TOTALS	22.4	22.8	21.1	20.6	22.6

MON-FRI 10:00 AM-3:00 PM

STATION CALL LETTERS	A/M 78	O/N 78	A/M 79	O/N 79	A/M 80
STN. A	11.7	4.6	5.3	4.4	5.3
STN. B	3.5	10.2	4.9	15.8	7.7
STN. C	5.2	4.9	7.1	6.1	5.5
STN. D	2.5	4.1	7.6	5.6	4.2
STN. E	...	...	...	1.2	.9
STN. F	.4	.9	1.4	.5	1.8
STN. G	2.5	9.2	6.5	9.7	13.1
STN. H	17.1	17.7	11.8	16.8	16.0
STN. I	2.7	.9	1.4	.6	4.2
STN. J	13.0	6.8	13.8	9.4	19.3
STN. K	8.2	12.2	16.1	9.7	9.0
STN. L	4.3	6.0	4.1	2.4	2.2
STN. M	2.3	3.1	1.4	.9	.9
STN. N	12.8	8.5	9.9	4.6	1.5
STN. O	...	.3	...	...	
METRO TOTALS	15.6	17.2	16.6	18.5	15.3

MON-FRI 3:00 PM-7:00 PM

STATION CALL LETTERS	A/M 78	O/N 78	A/M 79	O/N 79	A/M 80
STN. A	9.0	5.5	6.1	6.3	5.2
STN. B	5.0	16.1	12.9	19.2	14.0
STN. C	10.0	6.7	12.7	10.8	9.3
STN. D	2.4	2.2	4.1	...	5.4
STN. E	...	...	...	1.0	.4
STN. F	...	.5	1.6	.5	1.3
STN. G	4.2	5.9	4.9	9.6	5.8
STN. H	25.1	22.8	14.5	18.3	19.2
STN. I	2.0	1.0	.8	.9	2.8
STN. J	8.8	6.4	9.4	8.0	15.7
STN. K	9.0	9.8	11.7	8.2	7.3
STN. L	1.2	2.1	2.9	1.6	1.3
STN. M	5.4	3.1	1.6	.3	1.5
STN. N	9.6	9.7	10.4	4.9	2.4
STN. O	...	1.6	...	...	.9
METRO TOTALS	15.2	17.0	14.3	16.1	13.1

MON-FRI 7:00 PM-MID

STATION CALL LETTERS	A/M 78	O/N 78	A/M 79	O/N 79	A/M 80
STN. A	6.6	3.1	3.6	2.7	2.2
STN. B	10.1	24.1	18.8	25.5	24.9
STN. C	9.7	12.1	16.0	13.7	10.5
STN. D					
STN. E	...	...	...		
STN. F					.6
STN. G	2.2	1.3	1.6	.4	.6
STN. H	4.8	5.8	5.6	12.5	7.7
STN. I	32.2	23.7	22.8	16.9	23.2
STN. J	11.9	12.1	6.8	6.8	6.1
STN. K	7.5	2.2	2.2	7.6	9.4
STN. L					
STN. M					
STN. N	7.5	7.6	8.4	3.1	1.1
STN. O	...	1.3	...	...	
METRO TOTALS	6.9	6.6	7.3	7.2	5.1

Courtesy, Arbitron Ratings Company

The Arbitron survey of the Mobile radio market for April–May 1980 measured listening in the Mobile metro service area of Mobile and Baldwin Counties (Alabama) and in the total service area, which consists of the metro service area, plus the counties of Washington, Clarke, Monroe, Conecuh, and Escambia in Alabama and the counties of Santa Rosa and Escambia (which includes Pensacola) in Florida. Arbitron used a total of 1,628 diaries in the TSA, with a total of 199 MSA telephone retrievals to add to the diary information. Ethnic weighting was applied in the MSA to project the sample proportionately to represent the black population at 28.2 percent.[26]

The Arbitron demographic breakdown for Mobile showed estimated total persons 12 years old or over at 785,200, with adults 18 years old or over comprising 673,100 of that number. Of these adults, 321,000 were men, and 351,400 were women. Total adults 18 and over estimated for the metro service area were 303,900, with men accounting for 141,900 of these and women totaling 162,000.[27]

Fourteen radio stations were listed in the metro service area, and one radio station outside the MSA was included in the tabulation of Arbitron estimates of audience. Figure 5-6 shows a portion of the average share trends from the Arbitron report with the station call letters replaced by alphabetical designations.

The information on average share trends shows that Station H held a 20.8 share of the total audience for Monday through Sunday from 6 A.M. to midnight in the 1978 survey, decreased its share in 1979, and reclaimed part of that loss to show a 17.2 share in the April–May 1980 report. Station A's share declined from 10.3 in 1978 to a 4.1 share in the 1980 report, while Station B more than doubled its average share during the same period. The Arbitron report also details estimates of average share trends for the other demographic groupings of adult men, adult women, and teens.

Further in the report, average quarter hour and cume listening estimates are given not only for Monday to Sunday from 6 A.M. to midnight, but also for each part of the day: weekdays 6 A.M. to 10 A.M., 10 A.M. to 3 P.M., 3 P.M. to 7 P.M., and 7 P.M. to midnight, the same time periods for Saturday, and the same time periods for Sunday. In each of these, the audience is broken by age and sex into men 18 and over, 18 to 34, 18 to 49, 25 to 54, and 35 to 64 and women divided into the same age groupings. The same age groupings are shown for adults for the same day parts, and the estimated listening by teens is shown according to the same breakdown of day parts. Average quarter hour listening estimates and cume listening estimates are shown for teens and the different age groupings in men and women. The report also includes average quarter hour listening estimates on an hour-by-hour basis.[28] Average quarter hour and cume listening estimates for adults during one time period are shown in Figure 5-7. In analyzing the drive-time period (3 P.M. to 7 P.M.) and looking at the average quarter hour and cume listening estimates for adults by age grouping, one can see that Stations H and J are

Figure 5-7
Arbitron AQH and cume listening estimates

MOBILE
APRIL/MAY 1980

MONDAY–FRIDAY
3:00PM–7:00PM

STATION CALL LETTERS	ADULTS 18+ TOTAL AREA AVG. PERS. (00)	CUME PERS. (00)	METRO SURVEY AREA AVG. PERS. (00)	CUME PERS. (00)	AVG. PERS. RTG.	AVG. PERS. SHR.	ADULTS 18-34 TOTAL AREA AVG. PERS. (00)	CUME PERS. (00)	METRO SURVEY AREA AVG. PERS. (00)	CUME PERS. (00)	AVG. PERS. RTG.	AVG. PERS. SHR.	ADULTS 18-49 TOTAL AREA AVG. PERS. (00)	CUME PERS. (00)	METRO SURVEY AREA AVG. PERS. (00)	CUME PERS. (00)	AVG. PERS. RTG.	AVG. PERS. SHR.
STN. A	21	193	21	189	.7	5.8	16	137	16	137	1.3	8.4	18	167	18	163	9	6.8
STN. B	60	449	35	306	1.2	9.6	52	385	30	252	2.4	15.8	58	430	34	291	1.7	12.8
STN. C	43	355	29	257	1.0	8.0	37	258	24	176	1.9	12.6	42	335	28	243	1.4	10.5
STN. D	11	143	11	137	.4	3.0	8	105	8	99	.6	4.2	10	133	10	127	5	3.8
STN. E	2	25	2	25	.1	.6	1	7	1	7	.1	.5	1	7	1	7	1	.4
STN. F	6	37	6	37	.2	1.7	1	18	1	18	1	.5	6	32	5	32	3	1.9
STN. G	27	271	27	262	.9	7.4	3	57	3	54	2	1.6	6	106	6	101	3	2.3
STN. H	104	818	62	468	2.0	17.1	77	583	43	296	3.4	22.6	94	736	58	416	2.9	21.8
STN. I	12	111	12	101	.4	3.3	6	53	6	53	.5	3.2	11	82	11	75	6	4.1
STN. J	101	629	70	434	2.3	19.3	46	273	30	177	2.4	15.8	77	489	47	313	2.4	17.7
STN. K	37	270	34	250	1.1	9.4	7	66	7	66	6	3.7	17	147	17	140	9	6.4
STN. L	5	33	5	33	.2	1.4	3	14	3	14	2	1.6	3	17	3	17	2	1.1
STN. M	7	39	7	39	.2	1.9	6	23	6	23	5	3.2	6	23	6	23	3	2.3
STN. N	13	139	11	129	.4	3.0	6	70	6	68	5	3.2	9	94	9	92	5	3.4
STN. O	38	288	3	39	1	8	30	224	2	28	2	1.1	35	274	2	34	1	8
METRO TOTALS			363	1973	11.9				190	969	15.2				266	1430	13.5	

STATION CALL LETTERS	ADULTS 25-49 TOTAL AREA AVG. PERS. (00)	CUME PERS. (00)	METRO SURVEY AREA AVG. PERS. (00)	CUME PERS. (00)	AVG. PERS. RTG.	AVG. PERS. SHR.	ADULTS 25-54 TOTAL AREA AVG. PERS. (00)	CUME PERS. (00)	METRO SURVEY AREA AVG. PERS. (00)	CUME PERS. (00)	AVG. PERS. RTG.	AVG. PERS. SHR.	ADULTS 35-64 TOTAL AREA AVG. PERS. (00)	CUME PERS. (00)	METRO SURVEY AREA AVG. PERS. (00)	CUME PERS. (00)	AVG. PERS. RTG.	AVG. PERS. SHR.
STN. A	15	136	15	132	1.1	8.4	16	141	16	137	1.0	8.0	4	50	4	46	3	2.9
STN. B	31	235	21	167	1.5	11.7	31	235	21	167	1.3	10.6	8	59	5	49	4	3.6
STN. C	15	129	11	96	8	6.1	15	132	11	96	7	5.5	6	92	5	76	4	3.6
STN. D	2	38	2	38	1	1.1	3	43	3	43	2	1.5	3	38	3	38	2	2.2
STN. E	1	7	1	7	1	.6	1	7	1	7	1	.5		6		6		
STN. F	5	32	5	32	4	2.8	5	32	5	32	3	2.5	5	19	5	19	4	3.6
STN. G	6	96	6	91	4	3.4	6	105	6	100	4	3.0	13	129	13	123	1.0	9.4
STN. H	53	411	35	262	2.5	19.6	56	429	36	270	2.2	18.1	26	222	19	162	1.4	13.7
STN. I	10	74	10	67	7	5.6	10	75	10	67	6	5.0	6	52	6	42	4	4.3
STN. J	64	393	39	244	2.7	21.8	71	421	46	270	2.8	23.1	51	310	36	215	2.7	25.9
STN. K	17	147	17	140	1.2	9.5	21	166	21	156	1.3	10.6	18	138	18	128	1.3	12.9
STN. L		3		3				3		3				8		8		
STN. M	1	13	1	13	1	.6	1	13	1	13	1	.5		5		5		
STN. N	6	71	6	69	4	3.4	7	83	7	81	4	3.5	5	46	5	46	4	3.6
STN. O	21	173	2	26	1	1.1	21	175	2	26	1	1.0	7	59		6		
METRO TOTALS			179	993	12.6				199	1082	12.1				139	778	10.3	

Adults

Courtesy, Arbitron Ratings Company

the most popular among average persons for the total service area, with figures of 10,400 and 10,100, respectively and cumes of 81,800 and 62,900, respectively. In the metro service area, however, Station J tops Station H by 7,000 average persons to 6,200 average persons. Station H moves back into a lead in the metro service area when cume persons for all adults are considered. Station J moves ahead when cume persons in the 35 to 64 age group is the figure to be considered, but Station H leads in cume persons in the 25 to 49 and 25 to 54 age groupings.[29]

Figure 5-8, a portion of the average quarter hour listening estimates for a weekday hour, further demonstrates the completeness of the audience estimates. Station H apparently has a broad-based format that appeals to several demographic groupings, at least during this hour of drive time. Note that in the metro survey area the station is second in the market in adult men, first in adult women, and second in teens in the average quarter hour persons. It has the highest metro share in the total 12 and older audience (although by a small margin), the highest share of adult women, the second highest share of adult men, and the second highest share of teens.

An important part of the radio audience estimates is the measurement of the away-from-home listening estimates. In Figure 5-9, away-from-home listening estimates for Mobile show Station H second in audience estimates in the metro survey area in total persons aged 12 and older, tied for third in adult men, and first in adult women. The percentage figure is the diarist's estimate of the amount of listening done away from home.

Nevertheless, as the research firms and the Broadcast Rating Council point out, ratings are only estimates. No one knows at any particular moment how many people are actually listening to which radio program or how many people are actually watching what television program. No one can tell exactly how many people are reading newspapers or magazines at a particular time, nor can anyone tell exactly how many people actually read any particular page of a newspaper or magazine. However, the ratings research firms have refined their sampling techniques for radio and television to the point where the estimates are reasonably reliable figures that can be relied on to show trends and relationships between stations, programs, and day or night time parts.

Ratings information for other markets is similar in design and breakdown to the sample figures presented for the Mobile market. Fewer pages of information are presented for smaller markets, and larger market reports cover many more pages of research information.

An Arbitron radio report for Winter 1982 for the Philadelphia market was 162 pages in length, compared to the 69 pages in the 1980 report for Mobile. In the Philadelphia report, 27 radio stations were shown as home stations in the metro area, 19 other stations were outside the metro area but home to the Philadelphia ADI, and two more stations were outside the metro area and the ADI. Information on the 46 home stations is contained in

Figure 5-8
Arbitron AQH listening estimates for a weekday hour

MONDAY–FRIDAY
3:00PM–4:00PM

SURVEY AREA, IN HUNDREDS

	WOMEN					TNS 12-17	STATION CALL LETTERS
	18-34	25-49	35-44	45-54	18+		
STN. A	14	18/20	3	6	24	6	STN. A
STN. B	34/41	21/20	6	1	41	50	STN. B
STN. C	17/23	12	8	2/4	23	28	STN. C
STN. D	5/7	2	2	2	7	17	STN. D
STN. E					4		STN. E
STN. F	1/6	6	5		6		STN. F
STN. G	3/3	3	3		12		STN. G
STN. H	62/77	37	32	10/9	87	60	STN. H
I & J	3/3				5	4	I & J
	22/38	32/28	12	1/12	60	6	
TOTAL	25/41	34/30	12	13	65	10	TOTAL
STN. K	9/15	15	13	4/7	37		STN. K
STN. L	3/3				5	1	STN. L
STN. M	1/1	1	1		3		STN. M
STN. N	3/5	3	1	2	7		STN. N
STN. O	23/28	11	11	5	30	6	STN. O
TOTAL LISTENING IN METRO SURVEY AREA							

AVERAGE PERSONS—METRO SURVEY AREA, IN HUNDREDS

STATION CALL LETTERS	TOT. PERS. 12+	MEN							WOMEN						TNS 12-17
		18-34	18-49	25-49	25-44	35-44	45-54	18+	18-34	18-49	25-49	25-44	35-44	45-54	
STN. A	36	6	6	6	6		6	6	14	20	18	15	3	6	24	6
STN. B	83	21	21	6	6		1	21	18	23	14	13	4	1	23	39
STN. C	47	13	13	2	2			13	13	17	8	5	1	3	17	17
STN. D	29	6	6	1	1			6	4	6	2	2			6	17
STN. E	5							1							4	
STN. F	10	4	4	4	4			4	1						6	
STN. G	29	4	4	2	2			17	6	6	3	3			12	
STN. H	127	30	39	25	25	9	7	40	41	41	23	19	7		48	39
I & J	23	7	14	14	8	1	6	15	3	3	2	2	11	9	4	4
	98	25	34	32	32	9		49	26	26	22	21	11	9	47	2
TOTAL	121	32	48	46	40	10	7	64	29	29	24	23			51	6
STN. K	56	1	8	8	2	1	13	21	9	15	15	13	4	7	35	35
STN. L	7	1	1					1	3	3					5	5
STN. M	3		1	1				1	1	1	1	1				3
STN. N	16	4	7	7	7	3	2	11	3	5	3		1	2	5	
STN. O	3	1	1	1	1	1		2	2	1	1				1	
TOTAL	633	128	166	114	100	24	26	233	116	179	124	107	46	43	266	134

METRO SHARES

STATION CALL LETTERS	TOT 12+ %	MEN 18+ %	WM 18+ %	TNS 12-17 %
STN. A	5.7	2.6	9.0	4.5
STN. B	13.1	9.0	8.6	29.1
STN. C	7.4	5.6	6.4	12.7
STN. D	4.6	2.6	2.3	12.7
STN. E	.8		.4	1.5
STN. F	1.6	1.7	2.3	
STN. G	4.6	7.3	4.5	
STN. H	20.1	17	18.0	29.1
I & J	3.6	6.4	4.1	3.0
	15.5	21.0	17.7	1.5
TOTAL	19.1	27	19.2	4.5
STN. K	8.8	8.9	13.2	
STN. L	1.1	1.1	4.1	9
STN. M	2.5	1.1		
STN. N	4.7	1.9		
STN. O	5	9	4	

Courtesy, Arbitron Ratings Company

Figure 5-9
Arbitron away-from-home radio listening estimates

	AVERAGE PERSONS AWAY-FROM-HOME—TOTAL SURVEY AREA								AVERAGE PERSONS AWAY-FROM-HOME—METRO SURVEY AREA							
MOBILE APRIL/MAY 1980	TOT. PERS 12+		MEN 18+		WOMEN 18+		TEENS 12-17		TOT. PERS 12+		MEN 18+		WOMEN 18+		TEENS 12-17	
	NO AWAY (00)	% AWAY	NO AWAY (00)	% AWAY	NO AWAY (00)	% AWAY	NO AWAY (00)	% AWAY	NO AWAY (00)	% AWAY	NO AWAY (00)	% AWAY	NO AWAY (00)	% AWAY	NO AWAY (00)	% AWAY
STN. A	17	53	7	70	8	44	2	50	17	53	7	70	8	44	2	50
STN. B	38	34	20	56	10	27	8	21	29	38	15	56	7	30	7	26
STN. C	22	31	9	45	10	31	3	17	16	31	6	38	7	29	3	27
STN. D	4	12	1	8	2	20	1	8	4	12	1	8	2	20	1	8
STN. E	1	10	1	25					1	10	1	25				
STN. F	3	43	2	100	1	20			3	43	2	100	1	20		
STN. G	11	15	8	21	3	9			10	14	7	18	3	9		
STN. H	61	34	27	53	24	32	10	18	34	31	13	41	15	33	6	20
STN. I	14	78	13	93			1	100	14	78	13	93			1	100
STN. J	54	39	39	65	15	20			36	34	26	60	10	17		
STN. K	18	41	10	71	8	27			18	45	10	71	8	31		
STN. L	1	20			1	25			1	20			1	25		
STN. M	1	17			1	25			1	17			1	25		
STN. N	7	44	5	63	2	25			7	44	5	63	2	25		
STN. O	20	43	7	58	13	52			2	67	2	67				
TOTAL LISTENING IN METRO SURVEY AREA									209	33	118	47	71	24	20	21

Courtesy, Arbitron Ratings Company

the ADI section of the report, and more extensive information is presented on 30 of the stations that figure more prominently in metro area listening. The portion of the Philadelphia report shown in Figure 5-10 details the average quarter hour listening estimates for 6 A.M. to midnight.

The Spring 1982 Arbitron report for New York covered 275 pages with detailed information on 47 radio stations, 46 of which were listed as home stations within the metro area. A portion of that report is shown in Figure 5-11.

At this point, the implications of so much data may be overwhelming, especially with the realization that only a small portion of the 69-page Mobile report (and even less of the larger Philadelphia and New York reports) is shown here. The estimate data are immense, but the broadcast salesperson has to learn to extract the data that are important for his or her broadcast outlet and be able to compare these data with that of competing outlets to see how the particular station rates, what the strong selling points are for the station, and how good a job the station is doing of delivering the desired audience segments for the advertisers using the station.

Our brief analysis of the Mobile report shown suggests how each station

Figure 5-10

Arbitron cume listening estimates for Philadelphia

PHILADELPHIA
WINTER 1982

MONDAY-FRIDAY
6:00AM-MIDNIGHT

AVERAGE PERSONS—TOTAL SURVEY AREA, IN HUNDREDS

TOT. PERS. 12+	MEN 18-24	MEN 25-34	MEN 35-44	MEN 45-54	MEN 55-64	WOMEN 18-24	WOMEN 25-34	WOMEN 35-44	WOMEN 45-54	WOMEN 55-64	TNS. 12-17	STATION CALL LETTERS
984	21	76	74	81	101	23	60	78	88	99	14	KYW
31		2	2		2	2	2	5	4	10		WBCB
338	10	16	32	20	21	5	15	9	25	65	5	WCAU
677	62	69	37	19	9	78	87	55	19	7	222	WCAU FM
50		1	7		1		6	4		3		WCOJ
90	2	4	2	1	4	3	9	7	12	18	6	WDAS
650	121	87	43	10	4	108	106	47	17	4	98	WDAS FM
540	4	20	18	57	72	20	15	41	66	86	2	WEAZ
210	6	16	30	11	17	16	24	10	22	18	4	WFIL
31			1	3	3			4	2	1		*WFLN
153	2	20	19	33	15	1	7	21	14	2		WFLN FM
184	2	20	20	36	18	1	7	25	16	3		TOTAL
141	4	7	7	3	4	3	12	24	11	16	16	WHAT
234	29	20	14	2	1	41	22	37	2	4	59	WIFI
328	50	84	32	2	1	59	51	17	14	1	16	WIOQ
442	23	32	39	36	44	15	40	62	60	32	8	WIP
679	91	132	46	19	7	103	154	52	48	10	13	WMGK
612	174	99	19	1	5	99	59	25	9	3	119	WMMR
405	9	10	18	47	51	5	12	34	83	77		WPEN
30		2	2		6	5	3	3	6			*WRCP
190	18	12	23	4	3	33	37	19	15	6	9	WSNI
64	10	5	5			4	15	6	1		15	WSSJ
278	11	26	39	28	20	21	19	36	32	23	3	WUSL
494	7	33	33	44	60	6	9	13	11	92	3	WWDB
404	1	12	35	53	45	4	19	33	38	52	1	WWSH
455	161	79	4	9	3	60	24	4	1		110	WYSP
54		2	12	2	3	2	14	4	5	2	3	WZZD
169	1	9	6	20	16	11	5	27	21	20		WJBR FM
134	21	5	3	1		16	6	4	3	6	69	WPST
153	19	42	6	3		19	22	19	3		19	WSTW
143		4	6	11	1		3	7	12	17		WOR

AVERAGE PERSONS—METRO SURVEY AREA, IN HUNDREDS

STATION CALL LETTERS	TOT. PERS. 12+	MEN 18-24	MEN 25-34	MEN 35-44	MEN 45-54	MEN 55-64	WOMEN 18-24	WOMEN 25-34	WOMEN 35-44	WOMEN 45-54	WOMEN 55-64	TNS. 12-17
KYW	881	20	58	71	71	92	22	57	75	85	92	13
WBCB	31		2	2		2	2	2	5	4	10	
WCAU	288	10	15	30	16	18	2	15	8	23	52	5
WCAU FM	581	48	62	23	19	9	69	80	37	17	7	200
WCOJ	50		1	7		1		6	4		3	
WDAS	89	1	4	2	1	4	3	9	7	12	18	6
WDAS FM	621	113	84	42	10	4	104	101	47	17	4	90
WEAZ	461	4	20	10	53	65	19	14	33	52	73	2
WFIL	191	5	11	27	9	15	16	21	9	21	17	4
*WFLN	27			1	3				4	1	1	
WFLN FM	110	2	15	16	29	8	1	3	10	10	1	
TOTAL	137	2	15	17	32	8	1	3	14	11	2	
WHAT	139	4	7	7	3	4	3	12	24	11	16	16
WIFI	160	23	17	10	1		25	16	31	2	4	31
WIOQ	280	37	77	27	1	1	58	44	11	13	1	9
WIP	402	23	24	38	23	44	15	36	57	54	32	7
WMGK	615	88	117	43	19	6	90	136	49	45	8	11
WMMR	417	123	63	11	1		71	25	22	8	3	90
WPEN	379	9	10	16	47	44	5	12	33	81	64	
*WRCP	30		2	2		6	5	3	3	6		
WSNI	163	18	10	21	4	2	27	27	17	15	5	8
WSSJ	64	10	5	5			4	15	6	1		15
WUSL	216	11	10	37	20	10	18	17	28	24	21	2
WWDB	388	6	19	31	32	36	6	8	13	11	68	2
WWSH	310	1	11	25	38	37	4	10	21	26	45	1
WYSP	326	109	54	2	9	3	47	14	4	1		83
WZZD	51		2	12	2	3	2	12	4	4	2	3
WJBR FM	71		8	2	3	10		3	17	4	12	
WPST	71	16	5	2			4	3	1		6	34
WSTW	36	12	7		3		3	4	5			2
WOR	35			1	3				3	3	7	
TOTAL LISTENING IN METRO SURVEY AREA	8022	727	791	580	470	451	655	756	633	597	594	644

SHARES—METRO SURVEY AREA

STATION CALL LETTERS	TOT. PERS. 12+ %	MEN 18-24 %	MEN 25-34 %	MEN 35-44 %	MEN 45-54 %	MEN 55-64 %	WOMEN 18-24 %	WOMEN 25-34 %	WOMEN 35-44 %	WOMEN 45-54 %	WOMEN 55-64 %	TNS. 12-17 %
KYW	11.0	2.8	7.3	12.2	15.1	20.4	3.4	7.5	11.8	14.2	15.5	2.0
WBCB	.4		.3	.3		.4	.3	.3	.8	.7	1.7	
WCAU	3.6	1.4	1.9	5.2	3.4	4.0	.3	2.0	1.3	3.9	8.8	.8
WCAU FM	7.2	6.6	7.8	4.0	4.0	2.0	10.5	10.6	5.8	2.8	1.2	31.1
WCOJ	.6		.1	1.2		.2		.8	.6		.5	
WDAS	1.1	.1	.5	.3	.2	.9	.5	1.2	1.1	2.0	3.0	.9
WDAS FM	7.7	15.5	10.6	7.2	2.1	.9	15.9	13.4	7.4	2.8	.7	14.0
WEAZ	5.7	.6	2.5	1.7	11.3	14.4	2.9	1.9	5.2	8.7	12.3	.3
WFIL	2.4	.7	1.4	4.7	1.9	3.3	2.4	2.8	1.4	3.5	2.9	.6
*WFLN	.3			.2	.6				.6	.2	.2	
WFLN FM	1.4	.3	1.9	2.8	6.2	1.8	.2	.4	1.6	1.7	.2	
TOTAL	1.7	.3	1.9	3.0	6.8	1.8	.2	.4	2.2	1.9	.4	
WHAT	1.7	.6	.9	1.2	.6	.9	.5	1.6	3.8	1.8	2.7	2.5
WIFI	2.0	3.2	2.1	1.7	.2		3.8	2.1	4.9	.3	.7	4.8
WIOQ	3.5	5.1	9.7	4.7	.2	.2	8.9	5.8	1.7	2.2	.2	1.4
WIP	5.0	3.2	3.0	6.6	4.9	9.8	2.3	4.8	9.0	9.0	5.4	1.1
WMGK	7.7	12.1	14.8	7.4	4.0	1.3	13.7	18.0	7.7	7.5	1.3	1.7
WMMR	5.2	16.9	8.0	1.9	.2		10.8	3.3	3.5	1.3	.5	14.0
WPEN	4.7	1.2	1.3	2.8	10.0	9.8	.8	1.6	5.2	13.6	10.8	
*WRCP	.4		.3	.3		1.3	.8	.4	.5	1.0		
WSNI	2.0	2.5	1.3	3.6	.9	.4	4.1	3.6	2.7	2.5	.8	1.2
WSSJ	.8	1.4	.6	.9			.6	2.0	.9	.2		2.3
WUSL	2.7	1.5	1.3	6.4	4.3	2.2	2.7	2.2	4.4	4.0	3.5	.3
WWDB	4.8	.8	2.4	5.3	6.8	8.0	.9	1.1	2.1	1.8	11.4	.3
WWSH	3.9	.1	1.4	4.3	8.1	8.2	.6	1.3	3.3	4.4	7.6	.2
WYSP	4.1	15.0	6.8	.3	1.9	.7	7.2	1.9	.6	.2		12.9
WZZD	.6		.3	2.1	.4	.7	.3	1.6	.6	.7	.3	.5
WJBR FM	.9		1.0	.3	.6	2.2		.4	2.7	.7	2.0	
WPST	.9	2.2	.6	.3			.6	.4	.2		1.0	5.3
WSTW	.4	1.7	.9		.6		.5	.5	.8			.3
WOR	.4			.2	.6				.5	.5	1.2	

Footnote Symbols: (*) means audience estimates adjusted for actual broadcast schedule.

ARBITRON

Courtesy, Arbitron Ratings Company

Figure 5-11
Arbitron radio report for New York City

Facilities of Stations Listed in This Report

Information below is obtained from the stations and/or recent industry publications. (For an explanation of the criteria for reporting stations, see Pars. 30-32 in the back of this report.) Stations that broadcast on the FM portion of the broadcast frequency spectrum are identified on this page with an FM suffix after the call letters. This suffix is used regardless of whether or not it is included in the official FCC license designation for the station.

Station	Power (Watts) Day	Night	Frequency (AM in kHz) (FM in mHz)	Network Affiliation	City	County	State
HOME TO ARBITRON RADIO METRO AREA							
(S) WABC	50,000	5,000	770	ABC C	NEW YORK	NEW YORK	NY
WADO	5,000	5,000	1280	IND	NEW YORK	NEW YORK	NY
WALK		500	1370	IND	PATCHOGUE	SUFFOLK	NY
(S) WALK-FM	18,000		97.5	IND	PATCHOGUE	SUFFOLK	NY
(S) WAPP-FM	50,000		103.5	IND	LAKE SUCCESS	NASSAU	NY
WBAB-FM	3,000		102.3	IND	BABYLON	SUFFOLK	NY
(S) WBLI-FM	10,000		106.1	IND	PATCHOGUE	SUFFOLK	NY
(S) WBLS-FM	50,000		107.5	IND	NEW YORK	NEW YORK	NY
WBNX	5,000		1380	IND	NEW YORK	NEW YORK	NY
(S) WCBS	50,000	50,000	880	CBS	NEW YORK	NEW YORK	NY
(S) WCBS-FM	7,200		101.1	IND	NEW YORK	NEW YORK	NY
WCTC	1,000	250	1450	IND	NEW BRUNSWICK	MIDDLESEX	NJ
* WCSP	25,000		740	IND	HUNTINGTON	SUFFOLK	NY
WHLI	10,000		1100	MBS	HEMPSTEAD	NASSAU	NY
WHN	50,000	50,000	1050	IND	NEW YORK	NEW YORK	NY
WHUC-FM	50,000		100.7	ABC I	NEW YORK	NEW YORK	NY
(S) WHUD-FM	50,000		1010	IND	PEEKSKILL	WESTCHESTER	NY
(S) WINS	50,000		1010	IND	NEW YORK	NEW YORK	NY
(S) WJIT	5,000		1480	IND	NEW YORK	NEW YORK	NY
WJLK	1,000		1310	IND	ASBURY PARK	MONMOUTH	NJ
(S) WKHK-FM	3,000		106.7	IND	NEW YORK	NEW YORK	NY
(S) WKJY-FM	50,000		98.3	IND	HEMPSTEAD	NASSAU	NY
WKTU-FM	3,000		92.3	IND	NEW YORK	NEW YORK	NY
WLIB	10,000		1190	IND	NEW YORK	NEW YORK	NY
* WLIR-FM	3,000		92.7	IND	GARDEN CITY	NASSAU	NY
WMCA	5,000	5,000	570	APP	NEW YORK	NEW YORK	NY
* WMGQ-FM	1,000		98.3	SBN	NEW BRUNSWICK	MIDDLESEX	NJ
(S) WNBC	50,000	50,000	660	NBC	NEW YORK	NEW YORK	NY
WNCN-FM	50,000		104.3	IND	NEW YORK	NEW YORK	NY
(S) WNEW	50,000		1130	IND	NEW YORK	NEW YORK	NY
WNEW-FM	5,000		102.7	IND	NEW YORK	NEW YORK	NY
WNJR	5,000		1430	IND	NEWARK	ESSEX	NJ
WOR	50,000	50,000	710	ABC E RKO-II	NEW YORK	NEW YORK	NY
(S) WPAT	12,000		930	IND	PATERSON	PASSAIC	NJ
WPAT-FM	12,500		93.1	IND	PATERSON	PASSAIC	NJ
* WPIX-FM	5,400		101.9	IND	NEW YORK	NEW YORK	NY
(S) WPLJ-FM	7,200		95.5	ABC R	NEW YORK	NEW YORK	NY
WQXR	50,000		1560	IND	NEW YORK	NEW YORK	NY
WQXR-FM	50,000		96.3	IND	NEW YORK	NEW YORK	NY
WRFM	9,200		98.7	RKO-I	NEW YORK	NEW YORK	NY
WRKS-FM	5,000		620	IND	NEW YORK	NEW YORK	NY
WVNJ	24,000		100.3	IND	NEWARK	ESSEX	NJ
WVNJ-FM	5,000		970	IND	NEWARK	ESSEX	NJ
WWDJ	5,000		970	IND	HACKENSACK	BERGEN	NJ
WWRL	5,000		1600	ABC FM	NEW YORK	NEW YORK	NY
(S) WYNY-FM	50,000		97.1	IND	NEW YORK	NEW YORK	NY
OUTSIDE ARBITRON RADIO METRO AREA BUT HOME TO ADI							
OUTSIDE ARBITRON RADIO METRO AREA AND ADI							
* WARF-FM	3,000		95.9	IND	POINT PLEASANT	OCEAN	NJ
* WBZN-FM	25,000		49.9	IND	BRIDGEPORT	FAIRFIELD	CT
* WICC	1,000	500	600	IND	BRIDGEPORT	FAIRFIELD	CT
* WPDH-FM	50,000		101.5	ABC FM	POUGHKEEPSIE	DUTCHESS	NY
(S) WPPI-FM	50,000		95.1	IND	BROOKFIELD	FAIRFIELD	CT

Note: This report is furnished for the exclusive use of network, advertiser, and advertising agency clients, plus subscribing stations.

Footnote Symbols:
( ) Listed only in Metro and Total Survey Area
(+) Listed only in Area of Dominant Influence
(S) Subscribing stations   Deadline: two days prior to market report publication.

Network Affiliation Abbreviations

ABC C — American Contemporary Radio Network	IND — (Denotes Independent Stations)
ABC D — American Direction Network	MBS — Mutual Broadcasting System Radio Network
ABC E — American Entertainment Network	NBC — National Broadcasting Company Radio Network
ABC I — American Information Radio Network	RBN — National Black Network
ABC R — American Rock Radio Network	RKO — RKO Radio Network
ABR — American Black Information Network	RKO-II — RKO II Radio Network
ABS — Associated Press Radio Network	SBN — Sheridan Broadcasting Network
CBS — Columbia Broadcasting System Radio Network	NBC — The Source
RADRAD — CBS Radio Radio Network	UPI — United Press International Radio Network

Courtesy, Arbitron Ratings Company

in the market can look for and find the areas, time periods, or demographic groupings in which the station fares best in the report estimates and use those particular instances to aid selling efforts. A principal use for the ratings research should be to determine how well the station is doing what its management set out to do—to appeal to a particular segment of the overall available listening audience.

No radio station can be all things to all people in the audience. Each station management must determine what the station will be, to whom it will appeal, and how it will go about achieving that aim, in other words, what the placement of the station will be in its market.

One station may choose to appeal primarily to the teen market, another may choose to appeal to young adults, and yet another may decide to appeal to that segment of the audience seeking news, weather, sports, and other informational programming. Still another station may decide to go for a talk or listener phone-in format.

Each management wants a unique station or the best (most popular) station among those utilizing the same or similar formats. The ratings research estimates reinforce the rightness of the management decisions or indicate that adjustments are needed to bring the station's delivery of audience to the projected level. Stations sometimes make format changes as a direct result of continued audience estimates in the ratings reports that are lower than management projected as needed to stay with the existing format.

Radio stations are businesses and as such must make a profit over the long term to stay in business (public noncommercial radio stations excepted). Therefore, the station's management chooses to appeal to a certain segment of the audience—perhaps women aged 25 to 49—for which the station desires to be first or dominant and concentrates on programming aimed at delivering a major portion for that market segment to advertisers better than any other station in the market. This becomes the station's market placement. And if another station in the market delivers a larger share of the teen market, it is not of concern to management, because its station is not aiming at teens.

Simmons Market Research Bureau compiled a summary of profiles of radio stations by program format that was reviewed by the RAB Research Department in December 1984.[30] The distribution of listeners of each format was compared to the distribution of the same demographic group to the U.S. population. The demographic groupings included adult men and women further refined by age, education, household income, occupation, marital status, race, and size of household.

The Simmons research report showed the adult contemporary music format to be the most popular among adult men and women; it was favored by 20.9 percent of adult men and 19.7 percent of adult women. The second most popular format among adult women and men was the country format, favored by 17.6 percent of adult men and 15.1 percent of adult women. A station management has to look beyond these surface observations, however, to decide to cast the station's destiny with either format. The question is not that either would be bad—both have been winning formats for numbers of stations across the country—but, is this the correct format for this particular station in this particular market? Does it address the segment of the population that the station and its advertisers want to reach?

A closer look at the demographic features of these audience profiles points out major differences. First, adult males aged 25 to 44 accounted for 42.3 percent of the U.S. population in 1984 and for 49.2 percent of the listeners for the adult contemporary format in 1984. Adult women of the same two age groupings (25 to 34 and 35 to 44) accounted for 39.5 percent of the U.S. population and 46.6 percent of the listeners to the adult contemporary format. Thus, a station studying a switch to this format would see that it could appeal to a considerable segment of the adult men and women from 25 to 44 years of age.

However, a radio station staking its future on a format change would want to know more about the people it would aim to serve by this change. As illustrated in Table 5-1 the Simmons Market Research Bureau report provides such information.

The 1984 report shows that of the listeners to that type of format in 1984, 41.8 percent of the adult male listeners had either attended or completed college, as compared to 37.4 percent of the general adult male segment of the U.S. population. This format's listeners seem to be a little better educated than the general adult male population.

The fact that 49.2 percent of adult male listeners to the adult contemporary format are 25 to 44 years old would impress some stations (the 25-to-34 group is largest at 27.4 percent, and the 35-to-44 group is next at 21.8 percent). Again, this percentage is higher than that age group's percentage of the total population.

In the female portion of the summary, the largest segment is also aged 25 to 44, who comprise 46.6 percent of the format listeners. Of the female listeners to this format, more than 36 percent have attended or graduated from college.

In household income, 56.2 percent of adult males favoring this listening format are from households with annual incomes of $25,000 or above and 24.6 percent are from households with annual incomes above $40,000. The adult female figures are lower for annual household income; 48.2 percent from households with incomes of $25,000 or more and 20.5 percent from households with annual incomes of at least $40,000.[31] Clearly, such demographic information can help a station management better target its audience and better position what the station management desires as the market placement.

Table 5-1

Adult contemporary profile

| Format Average Daily Cume (M–F, 6AM–MID.) | Adult Men | | | Adult Women | | |
| | 20.9% | | | 19.7% | | |
	% Of Pop.	% Of Format Listeners	Index	% Of Pop.	% Of Format Listeners	Index
Age						
18–24	17.6%	15.2%	86	16.6%	14.8%	89
25–34	24.4	27.4	112	22.8	27.5	120
35–44	17.9	21.8	122	16.7	19.1	114
45–54	13.7	14.4	105	12.9	36.6	105
55–64	13.1	11.4	87	13.4	12.6	94
65+	13.3	9.8	74	17.5	12.4	71
35–49	24.7%	28.4%	115	22.8%	25.8%	113
Education						
Graduated College	20.2%	22.5%	111	13.7%	15.8%	115
Attended College	17.2	19.3	113	17.3	20.6	119
Graduated High School	36.1	37.5	104	41.7	43.7	105
Did Not Grad. H.S.	26.6	20.7	78	27.3	19.9	73
Household income						
$40,000+	22.7%	24.6%	108	17.2%	20.5%	119
$25,000+	50.3	56.2	112	41.2	48.2	117
$20,000–24,999	10.9	9.9	91	11.2	11.3	101
$15,000–19,999	10.0	11.8	117	10.4	10.6	102
$10,000–14,999	14.0	10.9	78	15.2	12.9	85
Under $10,000	14.7	11.3	76	22.0	16.9	77
Occupation						
Prof'l./Mgr'l.	19.0%	23.5%	123	12.2%	14.9%	122
Technical/Clerical/Sales	14.2	14.7	103	22.2	29.0	130
Other Employed	38.0	38.5	101	15.3	15.3	100
Marital status						
Single	24.7%	23.2%	94	18.1%	17.1%	94
Married	65.5	67.3	103	58.4	61.3	105
Div./Wid./Sep.	9.8	9.4	96	23.5	21.7	92
Race						
White	87.9%	91.0%	104	86.4%	91.9%	106
Black	10.0	7.3	73	11.4	6.8	59
Other	2.1	1.6	76	2.2	1.3	60**
Spanish Speaking	7.0	5.0	72	7.0	6.1	87

Table 5-1
Adult contemporary profile (cont.)

Format Average Daily Cume (M–F, 6AM–MID.)	Adult Men 20.9%			Adult Women 19.7%		
	% Of Pop.	% Of Format Listeners	Index	% Of Pop.	% Of Format Listeners	Index
Size of Household						
1 Person	9.4%	8.7%	92	13.6%	12.0%	89
2 People	31.2	26.2	84	30.6	28.1	92
3–4 People	41.2	44.7	108	38.7	42.2	109
5 Or More	18.1	20.4	113	17.2	17.6	103

*Projection relatively unstable because of small base—use with caution.
**Number of cases too small for reliability. Shown for consistency only.
  Source: 1984 SMRB. Courtesy, Radio Advertising Bureau.

As part of a comparison, the country music format information for 1984 from the same report (Table 5-2) showed lower education levels among adult males, 31.3 percent of whom had attended college or were college graduates. The comparison also shows lower annual income: 46.9 percent of adult male listeners from households with incomes of $25,000 or more and 17.3 percent from households with at least $40,000.[32]

The Kassof research report for the National Association of Broadcasters suggests that profitable stations establish unique identities and unprofitable stations tend to be copycats that spend a lot of money trying to catch up to the market leader.

> *Finding your niche means having an* edge *over the competition . . . one that can be perceived by listeners. At a minimum, that means capitalizing on your competitors' vulnerabilities. At best, it means serving an out-and-out 'hole' in the market—needs that aren't being served by ANY other station.*[33]

Station managers who want to change formats are encouraged to look for listeners whose needs are not being satisfied by any station in the market in sufficient numbers to make the format economically viable.[34] The Kassof report goes on to recommend *multidimensional scaling*, a mapping of the market that spatially represents where listeners position each station in the market and where they position themselves in the markets.[35]

Table 5-2

Country profile

Format Average Daily Cume (M–F, 6AM–MID.)	Adult Men 17.6%			Adult Women 15.1%		
	% Of Pop.	% Of Format Listeners	Index	% Of Pop.	% Of Format Listeners	Index
Age						
18–24	17.6%	11.9%	68	16.6%	14.0%	84
25–34	24.4	26.2	107	22.8	23.2	101
35–44	17.9	20.6	115	16.7	22.4	134
45–54	13.7	17.7	129	12.9	13.2	102
55–64	13.1	12.1	93	13.4	12.2	91
65+	13.3	11.4	86	17.5	15.1	86
35–49	24.7%	29.4%	119	22.8%	28.8%	126
Education						
Graduated College	20.2%	16.4%	81	13.7%	11.1%	81
Attended College	17.2	14.9	87	17.3	15.4	89
Graduated High School	36.1	40.6	113	41.7	46.8	112
Did Not Grad. H.S.	26.6	28.1	106	27.3	26.7	98
Household income						
$40,000+	22.7%	17.3%	76	17.2%	14.1%	82
$25,000+	50.3	46.9	93	41.2	38.6	94
$20,000–24,999	10.9	13.5	123	11.2	12.0	107
$15,000–19,999	10.0	10.8	108	10.4	10.9	105
$10,000–14,999	14.0	14.2	101	15.2	16.8	110
Under $10,000	14.7	14.6	99	22.0	21.7	99
Occupation						
Prof'l./Mgr'l.	19.0%	16.5%	87	12.2%	10.9%	89
Technical/Clerical/Sales	14.2	12.9	91	22.2	24.4	110
Other Employed	38.0	46.7	122	15.3	16.4	107
Marital status						
Single	24.7%	16.3%	66	18.1%	12.3%	68
Married	65.5	74.0	113	58.4	64.9	111
Div./Wid./Sep.	9.8	9.8	100	23.5	22.9	97
Race						
White	87.9%	91.6%	104	86.4%	91.7%	106
Black	10.0	7.2	72	11.4	7.3	65
Other	2.1	1.2	58*	2.2	1.0	44**
Spanish Speaking	7.0	5.2	74	7.0	5.0	71

Table 5-2
Country profile (cont.)

	Adult Men			Adult Women		
Format Average Daily Cume }	17.6%			15.1%		
(M–F, 6AM–MID.) }	*% Of Pop.*	*% Of Format Listeners*	*Index*	*% Of Pop.*	*% Of Format Listeners*	*Index*
Size of Household						
1 Person	9.4%	7.6%	80	13.6%	12.2%	90
2 People	31.2	32.3	104	30.6	29.9	98
3–4 People	41.2	41.1	100	38.7	40.7	105
5 Or More	18.1	19.1	105	17.2	17.2	100

*Projection relatively unstable because of small base—use with caution.
**Number of cases too small for reliability. Shown for consistency only.
Source: 1984 SMRB. Courtesy, Radio Advertising Bureau.

Television Ratings In *Everything You've Always Wanted to Know about TV Ratings*, the A. C. Nielsen Company answers the question, Why have ratings?:

> Simply because the networks and stations are in the business of entertainment. They couldn't survive very long without being responsible to people's likes and dislikes. You'll ·find all kinds of parallels to this: the theatre which keeps tabs on the box office receipts; the newspaper which closely follows circulation trends; the manufacturer who can tell from sales figures if his product is acceptable. . . . The act of tuning in and watching a TV program is, quite literally, a vote for that program. A vote in preference to other programs being aired at the same hour. Ratings represent a tally of these votes.[36]

The authors also point out that ratings are quantitative and not qualitative and that the ratings information does not attempt to make judgments about program quality but simply tallies the votes of the sample population.

The discussion of these television ratings and their use in selling advertising time must begin, as in radio, with the terminology used by the ratings research firms. Some of this terminology is the same as that used in the radio ratings section. The definitions are courtesy of Arbitron.

Rating: The estimated percentage of television households or persons within those households tuned to a particular station for five minutes or more during an average quarter hour of the reported time period for the ADI, metro, or home county. One rating point indicates 1 percent but 1 percent of the *television households* of the area being surveyed (not 1 percent of the total population as for radio). *whether on or off*

Television households (TVHH): The estimate of the number of households (including those on military installations) having one or more television sets. Seasonally or periodically occupied housing units are not included.

Total households: An estimate based on 1980 census figures provided by market statistics.

Total survey area (TSA): A geographic area comprising those counties in which, by Arbitron estimates, about 98 percent of the net weekly circulation of the home stations occurs.

Net weekly circulation: An estimate of the number of unduplicated television households that viewed a television station for at least five minutes at least once during the week.

Households using television (HUT): The estimated percent of television households with at least one television set turned on for five minutes or more during an average quarter hour, as reported for the ADI, metro, or home county.

Area of dominant influence (ADI): A geographical area consisting of all counties in which the home market commercial stations and satellite stations reported in combination with them received a preponderance of total viewing hours.

Home county: The county in which a station's city of license is located.

Metro (or home county): Metros generally correspond to metropolitan statistical areas (MSA) as defined by the federal Office of Management and Budget.

Average quarter hour audience: Same as quarter hour audience.

Quarter hour audience: An estimate of the unduplicated audience that viewed a station for a minimum of five minutes within a specific quarter hour. These quarter hour total audiences when combined into larger time periods become average quarter hour audiences.

Cume: For each reported home market station (or for all viewing in the case of total market cumes), an estimate of the number of different television households or different resident persons within those households that view at least once during the average week for five minutes or more during the reported day part. This is an unduplicated or cumulative estimate of circulation.

Share: The percentage of the total HUT (households using television) and persons viewing television reached by a station during a specified time. Arbitron notes that shares of 100 appear in the reports as 99.[37]

In its station index, Nielsen produces viewer in profile reports for the various markets and uses some terminology that is slightly different from the terms listed above from the Arbitron glossary.[38] Nielsen's major viewer in profile terms and definitions are listed so that the similarities and differences can be assessed. Of course, the rating carries the same definition regardless of the company measuring the audience: in television, one rating point is 1 percent of the television homes in the area being surveyed, whether it is the metro area or the entire area being surveyed.

Some other terms as defined by Nielsen follow.

Metro Area (or central area): The central city area of the market, which usually correspond to the standard metropolitan statistical area as defined by the U.S. Office of Management and Budget. It is the most densely populated portion of the market.

Designated market area (DMA): Generally a group of counties in which stations located in the metro area achieve the largest audience share. This is a nonoverlapping area used for planning, buying, and evaluating television audiences.

NSI area: A group of counties reflecting the primary (typically 95 percent) source of audience to the local stations.[39]

The Nielsen station index reports also use the following terms for reported data in the viewers in profile reports for individual markets:

Weekly cumulative audiences (by day part): The total number of different TV households and/or persons (excluding visitors) in TV households reached one or more quarter hours during the average measured week. Metro area estimates are shown for the current measurement period. Station total estimates are for the latest all-market measurement cycle (November, February, or May) as well as July.

Average quarter hour audiences (by day part and/or quarter hour or half hour): Reported in viewer in profile reports in terms of the following:

Households using television (HUT): Television households in the metro/ DMA area with a TV set turned on as a percentage of the Metro/DMA Area TV households.

Persons using television (PUT): Persons in television households in the DMA that are viewing any station or cable service as a percentage of persons in DMA households.

Metro/DMA area rating: Television households in the metro/DMA tuned to a specific station or cable service as a percent of the metro/DMA television households.

Metro/DMA share: Television households in the metro/DMA area tuned to a specific station or cable service as a percent of the metro/DMA area TV households with a set turned on.[40]

In addition to the above television terms (and a number of others defined by Arbitron in its glossary), several cable television terms should be understood.

Cable-originated programming service: A service that provides to local cable systems programming that is not broadcast or transmitted over the air.

Cable subscribers: The estimate of the number of television households receiving one or more cable services.

Cable system: A distribution system for delivering, via cable connection to television households, programming from specified television stations and other originating services. Arbitron considers each distinct carriage of a station or services to be a separate system.[41]

Both Nielsen and Arbitron provide publications to help the beginner learn to read and understand the ratings information contained in each of the television market reports. Nielsen's *Nielsen Station Index INSIDE for the Mid 1980's* and Arbitron's *Inside the New Television Market Report* should be in the libraries of each television station sales department.

To contrast the measurement areas of the Nielsen and Arbitron reports and show their similarities and minor differences, we will explore the Arbitron and Nielsen reports of November 1984 for Peoria. Figure 5-12 shows the Peoria market area map used in the Arbitron ratings television market report for November 1984.[42] Figure 5-13 shows the Peoria market area map used in the Nielsen viewer in profile report for November 1984.[43]

In comparing the two maps, Arbitron shows the metro area of Peoria and the counties of Peoria, Woodford, and Tazewell in darker shading. Nielsen shows the same metro area without shading, in white.

In the next designation, the areas are the same, but the terminology differs slightly. On the Nielsen map, the DMA (designated market area) is shown as the metro area plus the darker shaded counties of McLean, Mason, Fulton, Stark, Marshall, and Putnam. On the Arbitron map, the ADI (area of dominant influence) is shown by coarse cross-hatching outside the metro area. The Arbitron ADI includes the metro area plus the counties of McLean, Mason, Fulton, Stark, Marshall, and Putnam, the same area as the Nielsen DMA.

Arbitron shows a group of counties in white (Lee, LaSalle, Livingston, DeWitt, Logan, Sangamon, Morgan, Menard, Cass, McDonough, Knox, Henry, and Bureau) that, included with the ADI area listed above, makes up the Arbitron TSA (total survey area). Nielsen refers the reader to a Table 5 (Figure 5-14) for their NSI area county lists, which include six counties beyond the DMA (Bureau, Knox, LaSalle, Livingston, Logan, and Menard). The two ratings services are measuring the same areas through the DMA and ADI level but differ in the outlying territory. The Arbitron TSA is substantially larger than the Nielsen NSI.

The Arbitron ratings television report for Peoria shows 485,100 total households in the total survey area; 475,300 of those are television households. Total households in the ADI are 221,000, of which 216,700 are televi-

Figure 5-12
Arbitron TV ratings map of Peoria

ARBITRON RATINGS

TELEVISION

© 1984 Arbitron Ratings Company

Audience Estimates in the Arbitron Market of

Peoria

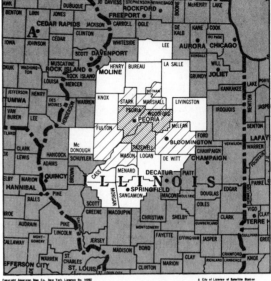

Copyright American Map Co., New York, License No. 14882   A City of License of Satellite Station

The "Total Survey Area" of this market is shown in white on the accompanying map. Where appropriate, the "Area of Dominant Influence" is indicated by coarse cross-hatching and the Arbitron "Metro (or Home County) Rating Area" by fine cross-hatching.

Survey Period: OCT 31–NOV 27   1984

Survey Months:
NOV FEB MAY JUL

This report is furnished for the exclusive use of network, advertiser, advertising agency, and film company clients, plus these subscribing stations-

WRAU WEEK WMBD

Schedule of Survey Dates 1984–85

October	September 26 - October 23, 1984
November	October 31 - November 27, 1984
January	January 2 - January 29, 1985
February	January 30 - February 26, 1985
March	February 27 - March 26, 1985
May	May 1 - May 28, 1985
July	July 10 - August 6, 1985

Estimates of Households in Market

	TSA	Pct TV HH	ADI	Pct TV HH	Metro Rating Area	Pct TV HH
TOTAL HOUSEHOLDS	485,100		221,000		139,700	
TV HOUSEHOLDS	475,300	100	216,700	100	137,200	100
MULTI-SET TV HH	262,400	55	125,100	58	81,100	59
CABLE SUBSCRIBERS	273,000	57	126,900	59	82,000	60

Television Stations

Call Letters	Channel Number	Affiliation	Home Home Non-ADI Outside	City of Identification Authorized by FCC	
WRAU-TV	19	ABC	H	PEORIA, IL	
WEEK-TV	25	NBC	H	PEORIA, IL	
WMBD-TV	31	CBS	H	PEORIA, IL	
WBLN	43	IND	HN	BLOOMINGTON, IL	
WTVP	47	PTV	H	PEORIA, IL	
WGN -TV	9	IND	O	CHICAGO, IL	
WTBS	17	TBS	O	ATLANTA, GA	
VHBO				HOME BOX OFFICE	ESTIMATED TO BE ON 26 CABLE SYSTEMS

NOVEMBER 1984   INT-1   PEORIA

Courtesy, Arbitron Ratings Company

Figure 5-13
Nielsen TV ratings map of Peoria

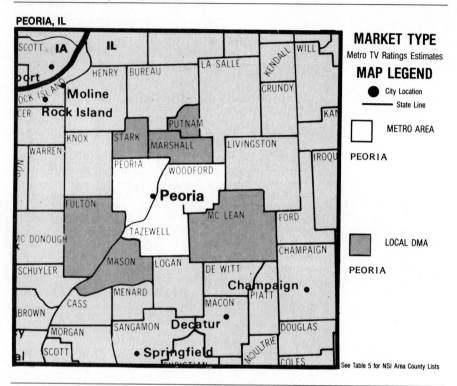

Courtesy, A. C. Nielsen Company

sion households. The metro rating area has 139,700 total households; 137,200 of them are television households. Fifty-five percent of the television households in the TSA are multiset households; 58 percent of the TVHH in the ADI are multiset households; and 59 percent of the TVHH in the metro area are multiset households. Sixty percent of the television households in the metro area are cable subscribers; 59 percent of the television households in the ADI and 57 percent of the television households in the TSA are cable subscribers.

Arbitron lists four television stations as home television signals for the area: WRAU-TV (ABC affiliate); WEEK-TV (NBC affiliate); WMBD-TV (CBS affiliate); and WTVP (PTV station). In addition, viewers in the market receive and view in measurable form WBNL, an independent station from Bloomington, Illinois; WGN-TV, an independent station from Chicago (via cable); WTBS, an independent superstation from Atlanta (via cable); and HBO (Home Box Office, also via cable, estimated by Arbitron to be on 26 cable television systems within the market area).[44]

Figure 5-14
Nielsen Peoria area county list

MARKET DATA

PEORIA, IL
DMA RANK #101
NOVEMBER 1—NOVEMBER 28, 1984

TABLE 5-TV HOUSEHOLDS AND IN-TAB DIARY HOUSEHOLDS
BY SAMPLING AREA

ADJ DMA CNTY		COUNTY & STATE		MRS TERRI- TORY!	EST. TV HHLDS JAN. 1985	CNTY SIZE!	IN-TAB DIARY HHLDS
#1		BUREAU	IL	WC	14,970	D	23
	D	FULTON	IL	WC	16,690	C	35
#1		KNOX	IL	WC	23,590	C	29
#2		LA SALLE	IL	WC	43,070	C	25
#2		LIVINGSTON	IL	WC	14,410	C	6
#3		LOGAN	IL	WC	11,600	D	24
	D	MCLEAN	IL	WC	45,240	C	86
	D	MARSHALL	IL	WC	5,520	D	12
	D	MASON	IL	WC	7,620	D	12
#3		MENARD	IL	WC	4,660	B	11
	MD	PEORIA	IL	WC	75,530	B	164
	D	PUTNAM	IL	WC	2,260	D	6
	D	STARK	IL	WC	2,780	D	7
	MD	TAZEWELL	IL	WC	49,740	B	108
	MD	WOODFORD	IL	WC	12,050	B	23
		METRO TOTAL			137,320		295
		DMA TOTAL			217,430		453
		NSI AREA TOTAL			329,730		571

#1 = DAVENPORT-R. ISLAND-MOLINE #2 = CHICAGO
#3 = CHAMPAIGN&SPRNGFLD-DECATUR
NOTE: VIEWING IN ADJACENT DMA'S IS NOT LIMITED TO NSI AREA COUNTIES IN
TABLE 5. THE ABOVE LIST OF COUNTIES DOES NOT NECESSARILY REPRESENT
ENTIRE AREA FOR WHICH VIEWING OCCURS TO STATIONS IN THIS MARKET.
SEE INSIDE BACK COVER FOR FURTHER STATION TOTAL AREA DESCRIPTION.

Courtesy, A. C. Nielsen Company

Inside the 113 pages of statistical information for the Peoria market report of November 1984, the information is broken down by day part audience estimates summary, network day part estimates summary, weekly program estimates, time period average estimates, station break average estimates (the latter three done both for all weekdays and by individual days), the ADI people share trend estimates, weekly program estimates, program audience estimates, program title index, and ADI trend estimates. All in all, it is a volume of information for the individual station and its sales (and other) departments to study in order to ascertain the market position of the station in relation to all other competitive television signals.

Beginning broadcast salespersons need to know that such voluminous information is available and provided to subscriber stations. It can be used to calculate the station's receptivity in the market and the popularity of the station's local programming, that received from its network affiliation, and that obtained from its syndication suppliers. To a great extent, it helps calculate the value of the station's principal salable product—the advertising availabilities it can offer to advertisers in local, syndicated, or network programming.

Local news is one of the major local products supplied by television stations. Figure 5-15 contrasts news audiences in the Arbitron report for Peoria in November 1984. (Remember that these estimates are a frozen slice of time

Figure 5-15
Arbitron Monday news ratings in Peoria

Weekly Program Estimates   **Time Period Average Estimates**

DAY AND TIME / STATION / PROGRAM	WK 1 10/31	WK 2 11/7	WK 3 11/14	WK 4 11/21	RTG	SHR	JUL 84	MAY 84	FEB 84	NOV 83	RTG	SHR	TV HH	18+	12-24	12-34	TOT 18+	18-49	12-24	18-34	25-49	25-54	WKG WMN 18+	TOT 18+	18-49	18-34	25-49	25-54
col#	1	2	3	4	5	6	58	59	60	61	8	9	11	13	15	16	18	19	20	21	22	23	24	25	26	27	28	29
RELATIVE STD-ERR 25% THRESHOLDS (1 σ) 50%	16 4	15 4	14 4	13 3	4 1						6 1		10 2	15 4	15 4	15 3	12 3	10 2	15 4	12 3	9 2	9 2	10 2	12 3	11 3	14 3	10 2	10 2
MONDAY																												
3:30P- 4:00P																												
WRAU DALLAS-S	5	5	10	5	6	20	18	19	19	23	7	22	13	12	3	7	8	6	1	4	6	6	1	3	2	2	1	2
WEEK DUKE HAZRD-S	3	5	2	4	3	12	13	13	14	16	5	14	8	4	2	3	3	1			1	1	1	2	1	1	1	1
WMBD HOUR MAG	6	8	4	10	7	24	25	28	28	23	10	30	16	18	1	2	15	3		1	3	5	1	3				
WBLN SCOOBY DOO-S	3	3	–	4	3	9	4	5	6		3	9	7	3	1	3	2	2	1	2	1	1		1	1	1	1	1
WTVP PTV	–	4	3	1	2	7	4	4	4	5	3	8	5	2		1	2	1		1	1	2						
HUT/TOTAL	29	33	28	28	29		27	25	33	26	34		49	39	7	16	30	13	2	8	12	15	3	9	4	4	3	4
4:00P- 4:30P																												
WRAU FAMILY FEUD	2	5	11	7	6	20	17	13	13	22	6	19	15	20	3	6	13	6	2	3	5	6	2	7	2	2	1	2
WEEK DUKE HAZRD-S	3	5	1	4	3	10	10	15	21	18	4	13	7	4	3	4	2	1		1	1	1	1	2	1	1	1	1
WMBD PEOPLES CRT	8	9	5	7	7	23	25	27	20	19	10	28	16	18	3	6	13	5	2	3	4	4	1	5	3	1	3	3
WBLN SUPERFRNDS-S	3	2	–	6	3	9	7	8	11	3	2	6	8	3	2	4	2	2	1	2	1	1		1	1	1	1	1
WTVP PTV	1	5	2	4	3	10	7	3	7	7	5	14	8	3		2	3	2		2	2	3	1					
HUT/TOTAL	26	32	31	35	31		25	27	33	28	34		54	48	11	22	33	16	6	10	13	15	5	15	7	5	6	7
4:30P- 5:00P																												
WRAU NEWLYWED GME	12	3	14	8	9	29	15	16	12	19	9	27	22	29	7	16	18	11	5	8	8	9	4	11	6	5	5	5
WEEK TAXI-S	2	3	2	6	3	10	22	19	26	30	3	10	7	8	2	5	3	3		2	3	3	2	5	2	2	2	2
WMBD HPY DAYS AGN	2	9	2	5	5	15	21	24	16	15	7	21	11	11	5	6	7	3	2	2	2	2	1	5	3	2	1	1
WBLN HE-MAN UNVRS	2	2	1	6	3	9	7	5	9	2	2	6	7	3	2	3	2	2	1	2	1	1		1	1	1	1	1
WTVP PTV	–	5	2	4	3	8	5	3	5	7	4	11	7	3		1	1	1		1	1	1	1	1	1	1	1	1
HUT/TOTAL	27	29	34	37	32		27	29	35	30	33		54	54	16	31	31	20	8	15	15	16	8	23	13	10	10	10
5:00P- 5:30P																												
WRAU JEOPARDY-S	7	7	17	10	10	26	20	25	20	27	12	28	23	29	4	12	16	7	2	5	6	7	4	13	8	5	7	8
WEEK LIVE AT FIVE	9	13	7	13	10	26	25	23	23	30	10	25	23	38	1	7	19	7		2	7	8	2	19	7	4	7	8
WMBD THREES CMPNY	4	11	6	10	8	20	20	16	21	12	9	23	19	23	13	17	14	8	6	6	3	4	4	9	6	5	3	3
WBLN DRM JEANNIE	1	1	2	3	2	5	5		3	3	1	3	5	4	2	4	2	2	2	2	1	1		1	1	1	1	1
WTVP PTV	–	1	1	1	1	2	3	2	2	4	1	3	1	1			1							1	1		1	1
HUT/TOTAL	34	39	42	43	39		33	34	46	39	41		71	95	20	40	51	24	10	15	17	20	10	43	23	15	19	21
5:30P- 6:00P																												
WRAU 19 E NWS 530	3	8	17	8	9	20	19	18	16	24	10	22	21	29	5	8	18	7	2	5	5	6	2	10	5	2	4	5
WEEK NBC NGHT NWS	14	19	9	22	16	35	30	28	28	30	14	32	38	57	2	17	28	12		7	12	15	6	29	15	9	14	15
WMBD CBS EVE NEWS	10	11	4	4	7	16	17	18	20	13	10	22	18	25	2	5	15	6	1	3	5	6	3	10	5	1	4	6
WBLN MAYBERRY RFD	1	–	1	4	1	3	4	8	8	6			3	3	4	5	3	3	2	3	1	1						
WTVP PTV	–	2	–	–			3			3	1	1	1	1		1	1	1						1	1	1	1	1
HUT/TOTAL	42	47	43	47	45		37	42	53	48	45		81	115	13	36	64	28	5	18	23	28	11	50	26	13	24	27
6:00P- 6:30P																												
WRAU ABC WRLD NWS	6	7	20	10	11	20	27	17	15	20	10	19	24	32	3	6	20	7	2	3	6	7	4	12	5	2	5	7
WEEK 6 PM NEWS	17	25	13	26	20	37	29	32	31	31	19	35	48	75	3	21	36	15	1	8	14	17	9	38	19	12	18	20
WMBD NWCNT 31 6P	6	11	8	12	9	16	19	21	22	19	13	23	20	26	5	7	16	7	3	3	5	6	2	10	5	1	5	5
WBLN NW D V DYKE	1	2	1	4	2	4	8	5	6	2	3	4	5	3	4	4	3	2	3	1	1		1				1
WTVP PTV	3	2	–	1	1	2	3				1	3	4		1	1	1							1	1	1	1	1
HUT/TOTAL	47	56	55	62	55		45	47	60	56	54		99	142	14	39	79	32	8	17	26	31	16	62	30	16	29	34
6:30P- 7:00P																												

Courtesy, Arbitron Ratings Company

that indicates the best estimate of what the particular programs were doing in terms of viewer attention at that particular time. These estimates are not intended to imply qualitative judgments or be predictors of what the particular programs may do in the future.) The weekly program estimates for the Monday 5:30 to 6:00 P.M. and 6:00 to 6:30 P.M. time periods for the Peoria market area in November 1984 show that the ABC affiliate, WRAU-TV, ran its local news at 5:30, the same time as the network newscasts were broadcasting on the NBC and CBS affiliates.

The first four columns of the figure shows the week-by-week ADI television households ratings for the stations. The NBC newscast on WEEK-TV led the ADI ratings comfortably for three of the four weeks. In the third week of the ratings sweep, the local newscast on WRAU-TV came in with a 17 rating, beating both of the network newscasts on the other network affiliates. On the four-week average, however, the NBC newscast on WEEK-TV led the ADI ratings (garnering a 35 share) with an average rating of 16. The NBC newscast also was the leading program of this time period in the metro ratings but not by as large a difference (rating of 14, compared to 10 for both the CBS News and the local newcast on the ABC affiliate). Although the NBC news had the highest share of the metro audience (32 percent and 22 percent for the ABC and CBS affiliates, respectively), its lead was not quite as strong as in the ADI.

At the 6:00 to 6:30 P.M. time period on Mondays, the CBS and NBC affiliates programmed their own local newscasts while the ABC affiliate was airing the ABC network newscast. Again, the NBC affiliate, WEEK-TV, led the ADI ratings with ratings ranging from 13 to 26 (losing the third week again to WRAU-TV, the ABC affiliate), an average ADI rating of 20, and a 37 share in the ADI. It also led the metro with a 19 rating and a 35 share.

Figure 5-16 shows the same time periods for Tuesday from the weekly program estimates of the Arbitron report for Peoria. Those figures show basically the same data as the Monday evening numbers: leadership in the 5:30 P.M. period by the NBC network newscast and leadership in the 6 P.M. period by the local newscast of the NBC affiliate, WEEK-TV, in both the ADI and the metro area. Average ratings and share for the ADI and for the metro area show similar leadership in weekly program estimate figures for the 5:30 and 6:00 half hours on Wednesday, Thursday, and Friday of the ratings period.[45]

In the Nielsen viewers in profile for the same Peoria market for November 1984, the WEEK-TV lead over the other stations in the 5:30 and 6:00 half hours is shown as similar to the Arbitron report. In Figure 5-17, a portion of the NSI average week estimates of the November 1984 Nielsen report is reproduced. This information shows WEEK-TV's NBC newscast at 5:30 had an average Monday rating of 17 and an average metro share of 37 (compared to the average 14 metro rating and average 32 share for Mondays assigned it in the Arbitron estimates). The DMA average rating for the NBC newscast was 17, with a DMA share of 37 (compared with the Arbitron ADI average rating of 16 and share of 35).

Figure 5-16
Arbitron Tuesday news ratings in Peoria

TUESDAY

3:30P- 4:00P																													
WRAU DALLAS-S	3	3	8	4	4	17	16	19	15	20	6	20	10	9	3	6	7	6	2	4	5	5	2	2	1	1	1	1
WEEK DUKE HAZRD-S	2	3	2	5	3	12	14	9	13	13	4	16	8	9	6	7	4	2	2	2	1	1	1	1	5	4	3	2	2
WMBD HOUR MAG	1	6	5	9	5	19	20	24	30	32	7	24	11	11	1	2	8	2	1	1	2	2	1	5	3
WBLN SCOOBY DOO-S	2	2	3	4	3	10	7	7	4		3	12	6	2		1	2	2		1	2	2	1
WTVP PTV	-	4	3	1	2	7	2	5		5	2	8	5	2			1	1			1	1
HUT/TOTAL	18	28	29	31	26		31	25	31	26	28		40	33	10	16	22	13	5	8	11	11	5	10	5	4	3	3

4:00P- 4:30P																													
WRAU FAMILY FEUD	-	5	8	8	5	19	15	8	18	20	4	14	11	12	1	4	8	4	1	2	4	4	2	4	1		1	1
WEEK DUKE HAZRD-S	3	3	2	4	3	11	12	17	16	18	5	17	9	9	8	9	4	3	2	2	1	1	1	5	5	4	2	2
WMBD PEOPLES CRT	3	4	5	9	5	18	26	23	18	25	8	25	11	13	3	4	9	2	2	1	2	3	1	4	1		1	2
WBLN SUPERFRNDS-S	1	3	2	4	3	9	6	14	4	2	8	7	3	3	4	3	1	3	2	2	1
WTVP PTV	1	6	2	2	3	11	2	6	5	6	4	13	7	2		1	2	2		1	2	2
HUT/TOTAL	22	28	27	36	28		33	26	31	27	30		45	39	15	22	26	14	6	9	11	12	5	13	7	4	4	5

4:30P- 5:00P																													
WRAU NEWLYWED GME	2	3	12	10	7	24	14	9	17	19	7	27	17	19	4	10	13	7	2	6	6	7	4	6	2	2	2	3
WEEK TAXI-S	3	4	2	4	3	12	18	22	25	31	4	13	9	11	7	9	3	3	1	1	2	2	1	7	5	4	3	3
WMBD HPY DAYS AGN	3	6	2	6	4	15	21	22	17	16	7	23	11	10	5	8	7	4	3	3	4	4	2	3	3	2	1	1
WBLN HE-MAN UNVRS	3	4	3	4	4	13	10	8	10		4	13	10	4	1	3	3	3	1	3	2	1	1	1	1	1	1
WTVP PTV	-	3	1	1	1	5	2	5	4	7	2	6	4	1				1
HUT/TOTAL	21	29	27	35	28		34	30	31	29	28		51	45	17	30	27	17	7	13	14	16	8	17	11	9	7	8

5:00P- 5:30P																													
WRAU 19 E NWS 530	4				4	12							11	13		5	9							3
JEOPARDY-S		12	16	10	12	32					13	32	28	35	6	16	22	13	5	9	10	11	6	12	7	5	7	8
--4 WK AVG--					10	27	22	17	24	23	10	28	23	29	5	13	19	11	4	7	9	9	6	10	6	3	5	6
WEEK LIVE AT FIVE	14	10	6	13	11	29	22	29	25	29	12	31	25	34	4	9	20	8	3	3	7	9	3	14	7	3	7	7
WMBD THREES CMPNY	5	10	4	10	7	19	14	15	19	15	9	24	18	20	10	14	12	5	4	4	4	4	2	8	5	4	2	2
WBLN DRM JEANNIE	2	2	1		2	5					2	6	5	4	1	4	2	2		2	2	2	1	2	2	2	2	2
SNOWTIME					3	7							7	1		2								1
--4 WK AVG--					2	5	5	5	7	3	2	6	6	3	1	4	2	2		2	2	2	1	2	1	1	1	2
WTVP PTV	-	-	-	-			5	2	3	3				1
HUT/TOTAL	33	39	32	47	38		36	33	45	39	38		72	86	20	40	53	26	11	16	22	24	12	34	19	11	15	17

5:30P- 6:00P																													
WRAU ABC WRLD NWS	3					3	7						10	17		2	10							7
19 E NWS 530		9	15	8	11	24					12	27	24	34	9	14	23	11	4	6	9	9	5	11	6	5	2	5
--4 WK AVG--					9	20	20	21	16	19	9	21	21	30	7	11	20	10	3	5	8	8	5	10	5	4	2	4
WEEK NBC NGHT NWS	17	15	7	24	16	35	28	32	26	32	15	35	35	49	6	15	27	11	4	5	9	12	4	22	11	6	11	12
WMBD CBS EVE NEWS	10	8	8	5	8	18	15	19	22	15	10	22	19	24	2	6	15	5	2	3	5	5	3	9	4	1	4	4

PEORIA   25   MON/TUE   NOVEMBER 1984 TIME PERIOD AVERAGES

Weekly Program Estimates   **Time Period Average Estimates**

DAY AND TIME	WEEK-BY-WEEK ADI TV HH RATINGS				ADI TV HH		ADI TV HH SHARE/HUT TRENDS				METRO TV HH			TV HH	TOTAL SURVEY AREA, IN THOUSANDS (000's)													
															PERSONS			WOMEN							WKG WMN 18+	MEN				
STATION PROGRAM	WK 1	WK 2	WK 3	WK 4	R T G	S H R	JUL 84	MAY 84	FEB 84	NOV 83	R T G	S H R	TV HH	18+	12-24	12-34	TOT 18+	18-49	12-24	18-34	25-49	25-54		TOT 18+	18-49	18-34	25-49	25-54
	10/31	11/7	11/14	11/21																								
	1	2	3	4	5	6	58	59	60	61	8	9	11	13	15	16	18	19	20	21	22	23	24	25	26	27	28	29
RELATIVE STD-ERR 25% THRESHOLDS (1 σ) 50%	16 / 4	15 / 4	14 / 4	13 / 3	4 / 1						6 / 1		10 / 2	15 / 4	15 / 4	15 / 3	12 / 3	10 / 2	15 / 4	12 / 3	9 / 2	9 / 2	10 / 2	12 / 3	11 / 3	14 / 3	10 / 2	10 / ?

TUESDAY 5:30P- 6:00P (CNTD)																												
WBLN MAYBERRY RFD	2	1	1		1	3					1	3	3	5	3	4	3	3	1	2	2	2		2	2	1	1	1
DRM JEANNIE				4	4	8							9	2		10	3							2	2	1	1	1
--4 WK AVG--					2	5	3	7	6	7	2	4	4	5	4	5	3	3	1	2	2	2		2	2	1	1	1
WTVP PTV	1	-	-	-	1	2						2
HUT/TOTAL	40	43	42	53	45		37	40	51	42	44		79	107	20	37	65	29	10	15	24	27	12	43	22	12	18	21

6:00P- 6:30P																												
WRAU 84VOTE-700P	8				8	15							17	24		4	14							10
ABC WRLD NWS		6	19	12	12	22					13	24	17	42	9	14	25	10	3	4	8	10	4	17	8	6	5	7
--4 WK AVG--					11	21	22	12	17	21	11	21	24	37	8	11	22	9	3	3	8	10	5	15	7	5	4	7
WEEK 6 PM NEWS	18	24	12	25	20	36	27	33	29	30	19	35	46	69	2	16	38	14	1	7	14	17	6	31	15	8	15	17
WMBD NWCN1 31 6P	6	14	9	5	9	16	17	20	22	20	12	22	21	27	2	6	18	6	1	4	6	7	6	9	4	1	4	4
WBLN NW D V DYKE	2	3	3	5	3	6	6	10	7	6	3	5	7	10	6	7	6	6	4	5	2	2	1	4	3	1	2	2
WTVP PTV	-	-	-	-		1				1		1	1	3			2
HUT/TOTAL	52	54	53	57	54		46	45	57	50	53		99	146	18	40	86	35	9	19	30	36	16	59	29	15	25	30
6:30P- 7:00P																												

Courtesy, Arbitron Ratings Company

The different figures are presented not to show that they are different
but to show that when compared with the figures for other stations and
services the research by two different firms, using two different samples and
perhaps accomplished at slightly different time periods, is still remarkably
similar *in the differences* shown between services available to the television
households. The ratings research firms may be different in methodology, in

Figure 5-17
Nielsen NSI average week estimates

METRO HH		STATION DAY PROGRAM		DMA HH											
				RATINGS WEEKS				MULTI-WEEK AVG.		SHARE TREND II			HUT
R T G	S H R			1	2	3	4	RTG	SHR	MAY '84	FEB '84	NOV '83	
1	2			3	4	5	6	7	8	10	11	12	13
5		*R.S.E. THRESHOLDS 25•%*		*13*	*13*	*13*	*13*	*3*					
7		*(1 S.E.) < WK AVG 50•%*		*3*	*3*	*3*	*3*	*1*					
		5.30PM											
20	38	WEEK	MON NBC NITELY NWS	12	20	19	22	18	36	29X	23	30	51
18	37		TUE NBC NITELY NWS	13	17	18	16	16	36	32X	26	26	44
19	41		WED NBC NITELY NWS	12	21	16	13	16	37	32X	26	28	43
22	43		THU NBC NITELY NWS	17	22	19		19	39	30	27	29	49
16	39		FRI NBC NITELY NWS	12	19	15	12	15	36	32X	28	30	41
19	*40*		*AVS NBC NITELY NWS*	*13*	*20*	*17*	*16*	*17*	*37*	*31*	*26*	*29*	*45*
19	*49*		SAT NBC-NWS SAT	14	19	21	10	16	43	28	36	38	38
<			SUN NBC-NWS SUN		10			10	23	34	20	16	45
13	*24*	WMBD	MON CBS EVE NWS	11	14	11	8	11	22	22X	15	18	51
8	18		TUE CBS EVE NWS	9	8	12	6	9	20	19X	20	16	44
7	15		WED CBS EVE NWS	6	10	8	4	7	16	24X	16	19	43
9	18		THU CBS EVE NWS	7	10	10	5	8	18	20X	15	20	45
9	*22*		FRI CBS EVE NWS	9	6	10	8	8	21	19X	15	16	41
9	*20*		*AVS CBS EVE NWS*	*9*	*10*	*10*	*6*	*9*	*19*	*21X*	*16*	*18*	*45*
<			SAT NWSCENTER 31	4				4	12	21	14	15	34
<			SUN HEALTHBEAT			3		3	7	11	27	30	45
9	17	WRAU	MON 19 EYEWIT NWS	6	3	11	13	8	16	20	21	19	51
9	20		TUE 19 EYEWIT NWS	3	5	6	10	7	16				42
10	*22*		*WOR 19 EYEWIT NWS*		*5*	*8*	*10*	*8*	*18*	*17*	*20*	*21*	*44*
8	17		WED 19 EYEWIT NWS	4	7	10	8	7	17	19	17	20	43
6	14		THU 19 EYEWIT NWS	6	3	7	4	5	11	20	22	20	45
7	18		FRI 19 EYEWIT NWS	6	4	8	9	7	17	16	17	19	41
8	*17*		*AVS 19 EYEWIT NWS*	*5*	*5*	*9*	*9*	*7*	*15*				*44*
8	*17*		*WOR 19 EYEWIT NWS*	*6*	*5*	*9*	*9*	*7*	*16*	*19*	*19*	*20*	*45*
6	14		SUN ALL IN FAMILY	5	7	5	3	5	12	10	13	16	41
		6.00PM											
2	3	WBLN	MON NEW D VAN DYKE	1	4	2	1	2	3	5	7	4	55
2	5		TUE NEW D VAN DYKE	1	4	2	4	3	5	7	5	5	53
2	3		WED NEW D VAN DYKE	1	3	3	1	2	4	5	7	2	48
1	1		THU NEW D VAN DYKE	1	2	1	2	1	3				50
<<			*WOR NEW D VAN DYKE*	*1*		*1*	*2*	*1*	*2*	*8*	*6*	*3*	*52*
1	*3*		FRI NEW D VAN DYKE	<<	3	1	2	1	3	3	6	2	46
2	*3*		*AVS NEW D VAN DYKE*	*1*	*3*	*2*	*2*	*2*	*3*				*50*
2	*3*		*WOR NEW D VAN DYKE*	*1*	*3*	*2*	*2*	*2*	*3*	*6*	*6*	*3*	*51*
3	6		SAT MOVIN' ON	3		1	3	3	6	4	3	2	43
3	5		SUN LIFESTYLES	3	1	3	2	2	3	3	2	3	58
20	37	WEEK	MON 6 PM NWS	20	16	19	20	19	34	29X	28	32	55
20	36		TUE 6 PM NWS	19	17	17	18	18	33	35X	29	33	53
20	39		WED 6 PM NWS	16	20	17	12	16	34	29X	27	33	48
24	43		THU 6 PM NWS	21	20	20		20	36	38	31	31	56
15	35		FRI 6 PM NWS	13	17	16	13	15	33	33X	35	34	46
20	*38*		*AVS 6 PM NWS*	*18*	*18*	*18*	*16*	*17*	*34*	*33*	*30*	*33*	*51*
23	48		SAT NWS 25	15	22	25	18	20	46	29	29	33	44
14	25	WMBD	MON NWSCNTR 31-6PM	11	14	15	12	13	23	23X	18	18	55
11	20		TUE NWSCNTR 31-6PM	9	10	12	13	11	21	14X	18	17	53
8	16		WED NWSCNTR 31-6PM	9	10	8	8	9	18	23X	16	18	48
13	25		THU NWSCNTR 31-6PM	12	13	11	10	12	22	16X	16	18	52
10	23		FRI NWSCNTR 31-6PM	11	13	9	9	10	23	16X	17	18	46
11	*22*		*AVS NWSCNTR 31-6PM*	*11*	*12*	*11*	*10*	*11*	*21*	*18X*	*17*	*18*	*51*
7	*15*		SAT SOLID GOLD	8	3	4	7	5	13	32	25	27	43
27	46		SUN 60 MINUTES	18	33	21	26	25	42				59
28	*47*		*WOR 60 MINUTES*	*18*	*33*	*21*	*26*	*26*	*43*	*42*	*43*	*44*	*60*
9	17	WRAU	MON ABC-WORLD NWS	6	10	8	11	9	15	19X	18	20	55
<			TUE '84 VOTE	10				10	18	29	26	25	54
11	21		TUE ABC-WORLD NWS	6	11	10	7	8	17				49
11	*21*		*WOR ABC-WORLD NWS*		*11*	*10*	*7*	*9*	*18*	*20*	*21*	*17*	*51*
12	25		WED ABC-WORLD NWS	9	10	11	9	10	20	21X	20	19	48
9	17		THU ABC-WORLD NWS	8	8	10	5	8	15	18X	20	19	52
9	21		FRI ABC-WORLD NWS	8	5	10	8	8	17	17X	14	17	46
10	*20*		*AVS ABC-WORLD NWS*	*8*	*9*	*10*	*8*	*8*	*17*				*50*
10	*20*		*WOR ABC-WORLD NWS*	*8*	*9*	*10*	*8*	*9*	*17*	*19*	*18*	*18*	*50*
10	23		SAT 2 CLOSE-COMFRT	8	16	7	3	8	20				42
6	*14*		*WOR 2 CLOSE-COMFRT*			*7*	*3*	*5*	*11*	*17*	*22*	*16*	*43*
14	25		SUN BELIEVE IT-NOT	10	13	13	14	13	22	17X	25	24	58

(Left margin, vertical: PROGRAM AVERAGES)

Courtesy, A. C. Nielsen Company

sample individuals, and in the estimate figures, but they are remarkably similar in most instances in the differences between television choices they show and in the implications of their research information.

Ratings research figures are only estimates. Any suspected trend spotted in one rating sweep should be followed up in subsequent rating periods before station management conceded it to be a real trend. As in radio, one station may be ahead of another in total numbers at a certain time period, but one of the stations not leading in total numbers may be able to show advertisers that the station does a better job of delivering the demographic breakdown audience the advertiser wants or desires. Furthermore, rates differ from station to station and from time period to time period, and a station without the highest figures may be the better buy.

Theoretically there are no bad buys in advertising. However, there are those that are better than other available buys for the time period and the advertiser need.

The beginning broadcast salesperson should not despair at the voluminous information provided by the ratings research firms for his or her market. Likewise, the salesperson should not attempt to turn into a research director to be able to absorb and properly store all this information in the best place for maximum use in client presentations. In larger stations, the research director or staff (and these are becoming more and more common in television and radio stations) extracts the material and aids the salespeople in the use of the data.

Once again, the capabilities of the knowledge contained in good research material about the product of the radio or television station point out the need for management in markets not regularly surveyed by the major ratings firms to find a way to gain the best research information possible for their market. The station can arrange with a research firm to do so or sponsor their own efforts to gather research information. Properly used, such information is not only an excellent sales tool, but also is an excellent planning tool for management in assessing where the station is in terms of where management wants it to be and in pointing out possible future planning decisions for the best operation of the company.

The information introduced in this chapter on ratings research and audience estimates is but a small portion of the research capability offered by the ratings research organizations. Both Arbitron and A. C. Nielsen Company offer many other audience-related studies and publications. AGB Research, through its PeopleMeter system, promises more in-depth research on trends over time, and several other firms undertake specific research projects for particular markets. These firms can be found in the latest issue of *Broadcasting/Cablecasting Yearbook*.[46]

Cable Television Ratings   One of the major problems of selling advertising on cable television has been the lack of solid ratings research information on the specialized cable service networks and the independent television stations (superstations) brought into cable subscribers' homes via the cable connection. The very factor that has helped cable television sell its services better to individual subscribers—the multiplicity of cable channels available—works against the cable television organization in ratings and audience estimates material. When the television signals for the Peoria market were listed, WGN-TV in Chicago, WTBS in Atlanta, and Home Box Office were listed among the eight television stations received in the Peoria survey area.

Cable television has made any signal carried on the cable a local signal in terms of reception. Cable receives no credit for viewers to broadcast stations that are native to the area, such as the three network-affiliate television stations or the public television station, all located within the home Peoria market. If cable subscribers were not on cable, they would still be able to receive these stations, just as those who do not subscribe to cable do.

Some cable-delivered television services, such as WGN-TV, might or might not be receivable in parts of the Peoria market without cable; certainly, HBO and WTBS would not be receivable as a broadcast signal without cable. Satellite receivers would serve as substitute cable television systems for dish owners.

With the rapid "cable-ization" of much of the country in the recent past and the increasing numbers of cable networks available, the research organizations have begun issuing special reports on the cable-available services. These services normally do not garner audience estimates large enough to be listed among the television stations in the market audience estimates of the major research firms.

As an example, if one fourth of the 20,000 subscribers of a particular cable television system were tuned at some time to one of the cable television services, that would be 5,000 viewers. In an ADI of 216,700 homes such as the Peoria market, the rating would be 2 (2 percent of the television households). Note that the Peoria report showed that HBO was estimated to be on 26 cable television systems. On each cable system, it was one of many available channels, yet did not have sufficient audience estimates to show, at least in the time periods at which we looked. However, the share figures added up for a time period show that a portion of this share figure is not attributed to any of the listed television stations. The research organizations do not list those television stations that elicit less than 1 percent (one rating point) in responses (or a fraction large enough to round off to 1).

Although the cable television system services did not show up in the weekly program estimates of the Arbitron television ratings report for Peoria discussed earlier, two did show up at times in the day part audiences estimate summary of that report. The highest ADI rating shown for WGN-TV in the Monday to Friday day parts was a 4 in the 6:30 to 7:00 P.M. period. The highest ADI rating shown in the same section for HBO was a 3 in the 7 to 10

P.M. period. The highest ADI rating for WTBS was a 1, recorded in a number of time periods.[47] A similar Arbitron television ratings report for Dayton for the same period shows WTBS receiving a rating of 1 in a number of the day part segments of the Monday to Friday day part audience estimates summary.

RATES AND USING RATINGS WITH RATES

Audience estimates information, such as that discussed in the first part of this chapter, forms an important part of the process of establishing and changing the rates at which radio and television advertising time is sold.

Radio Rates and Ratings

In earlier years, radio stations began selling advertising time based on rate cards that in most instances actually were cards—multiplefold cards that showed the beginning cost of a program sponsorship for each time length available: 60 minutes, 30 minutes, 15 minutes, 10 minutes, and 5 minutes. From this beginning cost for sponsoring one such program, these early rate cards projected discounts based on the frequency of sponsorship of the program, with the discounted price generally coming at frequencies of 13, 26, and 52 up to 312, which would translate to program sponsorship six days a week, Monday through Saturday, for 52 weeks.

These early rate cards generally quoted prices on 60-second spot announcements in the same manner, with the same frequency breaks up to a 312 time rate for the spot announcements. Later additions to the spot rate for radio stations brought some rate cards up to frequency discounts for 1,000 and 2,000 spots. The emphasis then was on selling a yearly contract for a certain number of spot announcements, with the advertiser using those spot announcements in whatever quantity in the segments desired or coaxed from the sponsor by the radio salesperson who serviced the account. Table 5-3 shows such a rate card for a hypothetical radio station.

With the change of radio after the advent of television, program sponsorship (at least of the longer times) became less common, and different prices for different times of the day, according to the change in audience habits, became more common. In this process, with television becoming established as the new star, especially in the evening, the times in the early morning and afternoon became more important to radio and thus more valuable than nighttime, when television competed more fiercely for the audience. For most radio stations, 6 to 10 A.M. became prime time, and the afternoon drive time became the next most important in terms of listeners. Categories of time-price relationships were established with different beginning prices for spot announcements according to the time of day and the

Table 5-3
Early rate card structure

| | **Announcements** | | | | | | |
| | | | *Frequency* | | | | |
	1	**13**	**26**	**52**	**104**	**156**	**312**
60 Seconds	15.00	13.00	12.00	11.00	10.00	9.00	8.00
30 Seconds	9.00	8.25	7.50	6.75	6.00	5.50	5.00
10 Seconds	4.50	4.00	3.75	3.50	3.00	2.75	2.50

Contract Packages

60 Second Announcements.... 1,000   Times........................ 6.00
30 Second Announcements.... 1,000   Times........................ 3.75

length of the spot announcement, with the frequency discounts shown in tables on the rate card.

Television rate cards initially followed the pattern that had prevailed in radio for years but soon began charging for time periods according to the audience size as shown by the ratings surveys. Radio in the ensuing years has moved toward the television practice of selling spot announcement availabilities more on the basis of what is being delivered (the audience estimates) than on the basis of a fixed, printed rate card with little relationship to the audience listening characteristics. Modern radio, especially in the larger markets, is sold on the basis of delivery of audience for the advertiser. Radio stations today generally sell on the basis of a rate schedule that reflects seasonal and audience changes and may or may not be in the form of a card.

Two major characteristics mark the modern radio station schedule. The first is that stations normally divide the broadcast day into parts based on audience availability, such as AAA, AA, A, and perhaps further designations. At one time, station rate cards showed B, C, and perhaps D designations for different times of the day, but, perhaps understandably, A time sells better than C time, even if both are the same period of the day! You can expect as many of the time periods as possible to be some variation of *A*. Morning drive time would certainly be the AAA (or AAAA for some stations) period and thus higher priced. Next on the price scale would be the AA time, most likely the afternoon drive time. The other designations would be for the other portions of the broadcast day.

Assume 6 to 10 A.M. as the AAA time, 3 to 7 P.M. as the AA time, and 10 A.M. to 3 P.M. as the A time period. Evenings 7 P.M. to midnight then would be B time, and the period from midnight until 6 A.M. would be classified as C time. The price differential between the top time and the bottom time can be very large. A station that charges $250 for a spot announcement in AAA times may charge as little as $30 for a spot run in the early morning around 3 A.M.

The second major characteristic of radio schedules is that many radio stations divide the rate card prices into *grids*. These grids establish prices that are effective during different portions of the year or as determined by the station. The lower the grid used to calculate the rate for the advertiser, the less protection or guarantee the advertiser has of the particular time purchased. Grid I prices are highest and operative at the peak selling periods of the year or when the station advertising availabilities are very well sold. Grid II prices are lower, and the station with more inventory offers the discounted price to advertisers. Many stations establish four such grids. As an example, an advertiser purchasing spot announcements at Grid IV price levels (the grid level at which the spot availabilities are sold is determined by the station and not by the advertiser) may have a spot preempted without notice if that availability is sold at a higher grid price.

In addition to these two basic ways of establishing rate card prices, some radio stations offer a best time available price within each grid. The advertiser then receives the best time the station can offer after the higher priority spots have been scheduled.

The radio rate card normally also contains feature rates for such things as sponsorship of or spot availability in weather reports, sports, newscasts, traffic reports, and the like. Many of the rate cards list conditions of acceptance of advertising, billing and payment, and regulations regarding copy and copy deadlines, along with any discounts that apply on longer-term buys of whatever packages of announcements or features are sold. These discounts normally reduce the price per spot on a package of spots that is bought for 26 or 52 weeks.

The radio rate card is a planning tool for the broadcast salesperson rather than an item to be left for the advertiser to pick and choose from the available prices and schedules. Most radio today is sold on the basis of *impact schedules*, that is, schedules that achieve the impact the advertiser needs to accomplish the desired effect with the advertising. This is a job for the salesperson who is knowledgeable about the station's product and about the client's business.

The impact schedule of spot announcements based on gross impressions, cost per thousand, and frequency of impression delivers the audience calculated to be needed and affordable for the advertiser's purpose, whether it be a better recognition of the company name or the upcoming giant sale of the year. It requires listing some ways of using the audience estimate information in a productive mix with the rates and format or demographic focus of the radio station. The beginner needs some equations to calculate how these come together as a beneficial schedule for the advertiser and a good sale for the station.

As noted in the Mobile radio market report, to calculate a rating, you first need to know the population and the number of listeners. To derive a rating, divide the listeners by the population. If a station shows 20,000 listeners in a market with a population of 400,000, then

20,000 ÷ 400,000 = 0.05, or 5%

In this instance a rating of 5 (5 percent) results. Given the population of the area measured and the rating (in this case, a population of 400,000 and a rating of 5), translate the rating into a decimal figure (5 represents 5 percent or 0.05) and multiply the population by the rating:

400,000 × 0.05 = 20,000

This yield 20,000 listeners at the particular time period.

According to Arbitron's *Understanding and Using Radio Audience Estimates*, calculating gross rating points (GRPs) for a spot schedule requires the average rating for a time period and the number of spots to be run on the station in the time period. Multiplying the average rating by the number of spots yields the gross rating points of the schedule.[49]

Calculating the station's share of the audience requires two numbers: the total listening audience (average persons tuned to all radio stations added together) and the listeners to the individual station (average persons). If the average persons figure for the station is divided by the total of the metro average persons (all persons listening to radio on all stations in the metro area), then the station's share of the audience at that time period is the result.

To develop the CPM (Cost per thousand or cost of reaching one thousand people with an ad impression), the total cost of all spots in the package (expressed in thousands) is divided by the gross impressions. Similarly, the cost per rating point can be determined by dividing the cost for the schedule of spots by the gross rating points.[50]

To sell the impact of the radio station, the salesperson must have information on what audience is being delivered during what time periods. The rule of thumb is that the larger the radio market, the more precise is the information available and the more the advertising time is related to the amount and kinds of audiences delivered during the time in question. The demographic sections of the ratings reports give valuable information for spot campaigns aimed at particular demographic segments.

Taking the roughest calculation of what is being delivered, the gross impressions, begin with a 24-spot campaign run during a time period when the total audience is estimated to be 20,700 total persons, including teens and adults. To find the gross impressions:

AQH Persons × Number of Announcements = Gross Impressions

In this instance, 20,700 (AQH persons) multiplied by 24 spot announcements equals 496,800 gross impressions. In other words, the 24-spot campaign should be heard 496,800 times by people.

One of the next things the advertiser might want to know is the cost of reaching one thousand of these people. The CPM is derived by dividing the schedule cost by the number of gross impressions. If the cost is $30 per spot announcement, the total 24-spot campaign costs $720. Multiply the dollar figure by 1,000 or divide the gross impressions by 1,000 because you are looking for a cost for each thousand impressions delivered and not for a unit cost. Dividing 720,000 ($720 campaign cost times 1,000) by the 496,000 (the extra 800 impressions can be dropped) gross impressions yields $1.45 CPM, or $1.45 for the cost of reaching a thousand people with the radio spot announcement.

The CPM also can be calculated by an alternate method. Find the average cost of a spot by dividing the total campaign cost by the number of spots, in this instance, $720 divided by 24, or $30. Then divide this average cost per spot by the average quarter hour persons (the average of the AQHs delivered by all 24 spots expressed in thousands, so that the average AQH of 20,700 is expressed as 20.7). In this case, divide $30.00 by 20.7 and arrive at a $1.45 CPM.

The names and types of plans available for commercial schedules vary from market to market and from station to station. Nevertheless, all should be based on one reality: the delivery of a certain amount of audience (of a certain type) at a rate that shows a fair CPM (cost per thousand) for the exposure of that audience to the advertiser's commercial.

Just as the question, How much does a house cost? has a nearly infinite number of answers, so does the question, How much does it cost to advertise on radio? Broadcast salespeople must be planners and consultants who work with the advertiser to devise an advertising plan that accomplishes the aims of the advertising campaign, not order takers who present a menu (that is, a rate card or schedule) to the advertiser for selection of items.

The salesperson can calculate the gross rating points achieved by an advertising schedule or package of spots and determine the per-rating-point cost of the campaign. Because each rating point represents 1 percent of the audience in the survey area (for radio, normally the metro service area), adding the average rating for the time periods in which each commercial will be placed determines the gross rating points or the percentage of the overall survey area population that the campaign schedule is planned to deliver.

As an example, assume an average rating of 1.5 for 30 commercials sold at $50 per spot on a 30-spot plan. First find the cost of the campaign.

$50 (per spot) × 30 (spots) = $1,500

Then determine the rating points achieved.

1.5 (average rating) × 30 (spots) = 45 Gross Rating Points

Given the cost of the campaign and the gross rating points, the cost per rating point can be calculated.

$$\frac{\$1,500 \text{ (Total Schedule Cost)}}{45 \text{ (Gross Rating Points)}} = \$33.33 \text{ Cost Per Rating Point}[51]$$

In the above instance, the schedule planned delivers to the advertiser an audience equivalent to slightly less than half of the survey population area for the $1,500 spent, or a unit rate of $33.33 for delivery of an audience equivalent to 1 percent of the survey population area. Thus, multiplying this 1 percent cost by 100 for delivery of an audience equivalent to the total population of the survey area (100 gross rating points), the campaign cost would be $3,333.33. Note that there is no intention to convey the impression that *every person* over 12 years of age in the survey area would be exposed to the advertiser's commercials in a 100 gross rating points schedule. The intention is that the estimated total impressions would equal the area population, without any attempt to delineate how many times some people were exposed to the commercials or how many people were not exposed to them because they were listening to another station or not listening at all when the commercials appeared.

Because the population of the survey area was not given in the example used above, we have no way of calculating the CPM. In a real sales call, the salesperson has that information and can calculate the CPM, but usually this figure is not necessary. When the cost per rating point is used, the interest is in the cost of impressions equal to a percentage of the market rather than the actual number of impressions.

A quicker method of calculating cost per rating point is given below.

$$\frac{\$50 \text{ (Average Cost Per Spot)}}{1.5 \text{ (Average Rating)}} = \$33.33 \text{ Cost Per Rating Point}$$

At times the salesperson needs to know the reach or the frequency of an advertiser's campaign. Reach, frequency, and gross rating points are interrelated, and any two of the factors predict the third factor.

Reach × Frequency = GRPs

$$\frac{\text{GRPs}}{\text{Frequency}} = \text{Reach}$$

$$\frac{\text{GRPs}}{\text{Reach}} = \text{Frequency}$$

If 100 GRPs are purchased and the advertiser has determined that a frequency of 4 is necessary, the reach is 25.[52] The effective frequency in any given campaign varies with the campaign aims and the product or service. The following relates the terms and information to a planned schedule for a salesperson to offer to a prospective client: If a 24-spot campaign is projected with half the spots in the 6 to 10 A.M. period and half the spots in the 10 A.M. to 3 P.M. period at a cost of $28 per spot, the campaign will cost the advertiser $672.

Suppose average audience estimates for the 6 to 10 A.M. period were 17,000 adults and average audience estimates for adults in the 10 A.M. to 3 P.M. period were 13,000. Then the average adult audience per spot is 15,000. Multiplying 15,000 by the 24 spots equals 360,000 gross impressions. Dividing the average spot price of $28 by the average audience figure of 15,000 (expressed in thousands as 15) yields a CPM (cost per thousand) of $1.87, a very efficient figure.

If the average persons rating in the metro survey area shows an average rating of 4.1 for the earlier period and 3.2 for the later period, the average rating per spot for the MSA is 3.65. The gross rating points of 24 multiplied by 3.65 equals 87.6. The cost per rating point is then $672 divided by 87.6, or $7.67.

Another radio sales tool from the ratings research information is the amount of time spent listening to each station, which presumes more listener loyalty to the station listened to longer. This time spent listening (TSL) may be calculated by using a formula with the information supplied in the ratings report.

Multiplying the number of hours in the time period by 4 gives the number of quarter hours in each time period, and multiplying this answer by the number of days involved gives the total number of quarter hours. As an example, Monday to Sunday from 6 A.M. to midnight equals 18 hours per day times 4 to equal 72 quarter hours per day. The number of quarter hours in the time period each week is 72 quarter hours per day times 7 days, which equals 504.

The time periods Monday to Friday from 10 A.M. to 3 P.M. and from 7 P.M. to midnight have 100 quarter hours each. The time periods Monday to Friday from 6 to 10 A.M. and from 3 to 7 P.M. have 80 quarter hours each.

In an example used by Arbitron Radio, shown in Table 5-4, Stations 1 and 2 are in a virtual tie based on the average persons audience. However, when time spent listening to the stations is computed, the answer shows that the average listener to Station 2 listens 23.5 quarter hours and the average listener to Station 1 listens only 13.9 quarter hours. If the advertising goal is to reach as many different people as possible, then Station 1 might be best for the advertiser, but if the goal is to reach the same people over and over to deepen the advertising impression, then Station 2 might be the choice among the three stations.[53]

Table 5-4

Time spent listening

Station	No. Qtr.-Hours in Time Period		Avg. Persons Audience (00)		Gross Qtr.-Hrs. Of Listening		Cume Persons Audience (00)	Time Spent Listening
Stn. 1	100	×	142	=	14,200	÷	1,024	13.9 Q.-H.
Stn. 2	100	×	143	=	14,300	÷	610	23.4 Q.-H.
Stn. 3	100	×	193	=	19,800	÷	1,088	18.2 Q.-H.

Courtesy, Arbitron Ratings Company

Television Rates and Ratings

In the early years of television, television stations and networks emulated the older radio in terms of rate card construction. However, the television industry realized that the highly structured radio rate card common in those days was not usable or flexible enough.

As a result, television has evolved even more than radio (except in the largest radio markets) toward a rate structure that is based primarily on the amount of audience to be delivered and the popularity of the time period (or the competition for it). As an example, the head of sales at a television station in one of the nation's largest markets remarked in mid-1986 that the station was involved in the process of re-estimating its advertising availabilities on an almost weekly basis. The term *re-estimating* means management decisions on how much the station availabilities are worth in the marketplace and thus their offering or selling price.

The same sales director said that a syndicated television program placed in the time period between local news and the network-programmed prime time apparently had caught on with a lot of advertising agency people, who wanted to buy availabilities within that program. Ratings for the program were not way ahead of similar programs, but because of the demand the price for availabilities in the particular program had risen well above availabilities at similar times in other programs.

Like radio, television is sold in spot announcement packages. Television emphasizes individual spot availability, whereas radio emphasizes the overall spot package.

Under the advertising standards in the old National Association of Broadcasting program codes for television and radio, time limits were set for the amount of commercial time for radio and nonprogram time for television that was allowable for stations subscribing to the codes. The courts ruled that a portion of these codes was unenforceable, and so the NAB no longer publishes or attempts to enforce them. However, most television and radio stations continue to adhere, in the main, to the limits on advertising time set forth in those codes. For radio, the amount of commercial time per hour under the radio code was limited to 18 minutes per hour. Network-affiliated television stations in prime time were allowed $9^{1}/_{2}$ minutes of nonprogram time (commercials, promotional announcements, and the like) per hour. Independent (non-network-affiliated) stations could program up to 14 minutes of nonprogram time per hour during prime time. Both types of television stations could program up to 16 minutes of nonprogram time per hour in nonprime time.

Stations have two possible reasons to continue to recognize these commercial time limits: Too much commercialization brings a station under closer scrutiny from the Federal Communications Commission when a license is up for renewal, and several large national advertising agencies have initiated discussion about the clutter of advertising impressions, especially on television.

A television station has a finite number of advertising availabilities to sell. Some stations sell from rate schedules that list the beginning prices of their spot announcement availabilities, the time periods of the broadcast day (which may cover much or all of the 24-hour day), and grids as noted in the section on radio rate cards. During a period when sales are better and the number of availabilities for sale are down, higher grid prices are used for the offering price; during slower periods, the lower-price grid rates are used and the advertiser is warned of preemption.

In radio, the salesperson normally talks about selling spot announcements; when dealing with television, they talk about availabilities. In both cases, what is actually being sold is the time in which an advertiser's commercial may be placed.

Many advertisers have their commercials already produced and ready for insertion in the time period purchased. If an advertiser does not have a prepared commercial, a majority of the radio stations (especially in the smaller markets) prepare and produce the commercial for the advertiser at no additional cost beyond the cost of the airtime. Television commercials are far more expensive to produce, and most television stations apprise the advertiser that the purchase is of time for insertion of the commercial only and that the advertiser who desires preparation and production of a television commercial for use in the campaign can use an advertising agency, an outside production facility, or the station itself, but at extra cost and not as part of the availability sale package.

Some television stations produce computerized lists of the station's commercial availabilities with prices for the availabilities in each program half hour separately stated, as these availabilities are frequently re-estimated. Most television stations provide their sales force and national rep with updated lists of availabilities daily because a commercial slot once sold cannot be occupied by another commercial. Radio is more flexible, and spots are sold to be run within time parameters less rigid than the commercial positions fixed within the television programs.

Thus, a 30-second television commercial availability within the Super Bowl football game can command a price of $550,000 (the price for availabilities in 1986), or a 30-second television commercial availability may go for as little as $40 for a local client buying an availability in the CBS early morning news (between 6 and 7 A.M.) for the Miami market. In the same Miami market, an availability in the CBS "60 Minutes" program cost $5,500 in June 1986. A portion of rates and availabilities from WTVJ, Miami is shown in Figure 5-18. The summary shows the availability times, the price up to late June, the price after late June, the amount of inventory (the number of spot availabilities in that time period for sale), and the breakdown of this inventory by the number available each week.

Gross impressions for television spot announcements are calculated in the same manner as for radio. The average persons (the average number of persons viewing from the ratings report) is multiplied by the number of spot announcements. Determining the gross rating points also calls for the same calculation as for radio: Multiply the average rating of the spot announcements by the number of spot announcements.

The cost per rating point of a television spot announcement schedule also is computed the same way as it is in radio. For either one spot or several, add the rating points achieved by each spot availability, and divide the cost of the commercial(s) by the gross rating points.

Cable Rates and Ratings

Cable television advertising at the local level has been seen as television advertising that is sold like radio advertising. Although cable networks and services such as CNN, ESPN, USA, and others have been selling national advertising availabilities within their programming for years, local cable systems were slower to attempt to sell the availabilities provided for local sale within many of the cable networks.

As an example, some of the services have provided two minutes per hour for local systems to sell for local system revenue. Some local cable systems have had a form of advertising dating back to the 1960s, when they had a revolving time-and-weather set that focused on a clock, thermometer, humidity gauge, and printed cards with advertiser or sponsor messages. Some cable systems have sold similar cable channel advertising that focused on a news teletype that alternated with card advertising.

Some cable television systems have operated a local origination channel as a television mini-station. (As one cable pioneer says, "When it appears on

Figure 5-18
Miami availabilities and rates

WTVJ 30" Availabilities

Effective Selling Levels

** Indicates rate changes. All rates are effective immediately.
Indicates changes in programming, additional programming or new specials added this week.

Military Time/ Day Time	Program	Eff. Thru 6/22 L-/ Rate	Eff. 6/23– TFN L-/ Rate	Tot Inv	6/9	6/16	6/23	6/30	7/7	7/14
0558-0657 M-F 6-7AM	SSU# 0525 CBS Early Morning News	L-61 $ 40	L-61 $ 40	113	4	47	65	74	79	85
0658-0857 M-F 7-9AM	SSU# 0535 CBS Morning	L-54 $ 220	L-56 $ 160	125	1	13	29	43	53	49
0858-1156 M-F 9AM-12NN	SSU# 0540 AM Ros	L-53 $ 250	L-55 $ 190	255	0	40	41	57	128	160
0858-1227 M-F 9AM-1230P	SSU# 0542 AM Ros/News	L-51 $ 350	L-53 $ 250	330	0	53	50	82	164	203
1157-1227 M-F 12N-1230P	SSU# 0545 News 4	L-47 $ 550	L-49 $ 450	75	0	13	9	22	36	45
1228-1557 M-F 1230-4PM	SSU# 0600 CBS PM Ros	L-44 $ 700	L-46 $ 600	105	2	35	33	48	67	75
1158-1557 M-F 12N-4PM	SSU# 0550 PM Ros	L-45 $ 650	L-48 $ 500	180	2	48	42	70	103	120

a channel on your television set, it's a television station to many people.")
On these local origination channels, some of the cable systems have programmed as if the channel were a local television station by selling advertising and producing programming of interest to the locality. Some cable
systems sell advertising of a semiclassified type on particular channels
called *message channels* that allow people to purchase time for happy birthday
wishes, ads to sell things, and the like. Some systems have sold time in
terms of *infomercials*, an entire program that is one long commercial. Such
cable channels do not come under FCC scrutiny as do broadcast television
stations.

Cable systems have only in recent years begun to exploit the advertising
capability on their various channels. The selling of this advertising availability has been farmed out by some systems to organizations who do the selling
and scheduling for the local system. This type of arrangement has left these
system operators free to concentrate on the part of the business more familiar to them and the part that brings in the bulk of the revenue—adding subscribers and adding premium channel service to subscribers' cable
connections. Rate cards and schedules for many systems have simply been
figures on a sheet of paper that would serve as rates if someone wanted to
buy time availability.

To return to the similarity to radio, many systems sell the availabilities
on the nationally programmed channels on a rotation basis, and the advertiser's message appears on several of the channels several times a day or several times a week for a blanket price.

One of the problems in selling television advertising locally on the cable
channels has been the lack of viewer ratings information in the ratings research firms' market reports. As noted in the ratings section of this chapter,
some cable services and networks are beginning to show up in market ratings. Nielsen reports that 89 of the DMAs show reportable shares for WTBS,
99 show audience shares for HBO, and smaller numbers of DMAs show reportable audience shares for CBN, USA Network, WGN-TV, Showtime,
and some others. Fifty DMAs, seven of which are among the top ten market,
have no reportable shares for cable services or superstations.[54]

SUMMARY

Ratings are an important part of the business of radio and television and are
becoming more important to cable television systems as they sell local advertising. The larger the market size, the more important these ratings are to
radio station salespeople. Print publication advertising is sold on the basis of
circulation, the number of copies delivered by some means to potential consumers.

The two most prominent firms in ratings research for radio and television are A. C. Nielsen and Arbitron. In 1985, AGB Research was established as the American arm of the British company AGB Research, PLC, which is reported to be Europe's largest research firm.

Ratings information is gathered from individuals in the research company's sample by diaries filled out by household members and in the larger markets by household meters that register whether the television set is on and the channel to which it is tuned. AGB introduced the PeopleMeter, which has pushbuttons for individual family members to push to indicate not only the channel being watched but also the individual watching that channel for more complete demographic information. Nielsen also began testing a people-metering concept in 1985 and in early 1987 began issuing reports including information from these devices. Ratings form the basis for much of the rate structure used by television stations and radio stations in larger markets with regular ratings sweeps.

Radio rates once were largely based on the cost of a program or spot announcement price for a one-time airing, with discounts based on frequency intervals of 13, 26, 52, and so on. Modern radio is sold largely on the basis of impact schedules calculated to do the job the advertiser needs. The modern radio rate schedule most likely includes rates for several different grades of airtime and several grids applicable to teach of those grades.

Television rates began as an offshoot of the radio rate cards, but shifted to a delivered-audience base in which the rate is calculated largely by the estimated audience for the availability, the season of the year, and the amount of inventory or unsold availabilities the station has.

NOTES

1. *Understanding Broadcast Ratings* (New York: Broadcast Rating Council, 1981), p. 2.

2. Ibid., p. 3.

3. *Arbitron Meter Service* (New York: The Arbitron Company), p. 1.

4. *The PeopleMeter, Background and Overview* (Hicksville, NY: AGB Research, 1985), p. 6.

5. Ibid.

6. Ibid.

7. Ibid.

8. Brian Donion, "How Will TV's New Ratings System Rate?" (*USA Today*, July 15, 1987, Section D), pp. 1–2.

9. Ibid., p. 1.

10. Ibid., p. 2.

11. Brian Dumaine, "Who's Gyping Whom in TV Ads?" (*Fortune*, July 6, 1987), p. 78. © 1987 Time Inc. All rights reserved.

12. Ibid., p. 79.

13. Ibid.

14. Ibid.

15. *Understanding Broadcast Ratings*, p. 3.

16. Ibid., p. 4.

17. Ibid., p. 13.

18. Ibid.

19. Ibid., p. 14.

20. Ibid., pp. 14–15.

21. Ibid., p. 15.

22. Lynne Schafer Gross, *Telecommunications: An Introduction to Radio, Television and Other Electronic Media*, 2nd ed. (New York: Wm. C. Brown Publishers, 1986), p. 7.

23. *Radio Facts* (New York: Radio Advertising Bureau, 1984), pp. 38–41.

24. Ibid.

25. *Broadcasting/Cablecasting Yearbook 1984* (Washington, DC: Broadcasting Publications, 1984), p. C-169.

26. *Arbitron Radio Estimates in the Arbitron Market of Mobile* (New York: The Arbitron Company, 1980), p. 2.

27. Ibid., p. 3.

28. Ibid., pp. 10–61.

29. Ibid.

30. "Profiles of Radio Listeners by Format," in *RAB Research*, December, 1984.

31. Ibid., p. 1.

32. Ibid., p. 9.

33. *Research and Planning Information for Management* (Washington, DC: National Association of Broadcasters, 1985), p. 1.

34. Ibid., p. 2.

35. Ibid., p. 3.

36. *Everything You've Always Wanted to Know About TV Ratings* (Northbrook, IL: Nielsen Media Research, 1981), p. 6.

37. *Inside the New Television Market Report* (New York: The Arbitron Company, 1980), pp. 26–28.

38. *Viewers In Profile—Peoria, IL* (Northbrook, IL: The A. C. Nielsen Company, 1984).

39. Ibid.

40. Ibid.

41. *Terms to Keep You on the Right Road Through the Broadcast Ratings Jungle* (New York: The Arbitron Co.).

42. *Arbitron Ratings Television Peoria* (New York: The Arbitron Company, 1984), p. INT-1.

43. *Viewers in Profile—Peoria*, inside cover.

44. *Arbitron Ratings Television Peoria*, p. INT-1.

45. Ibid., pp. 33, 37–39, 43.

46. *Broadcasting/Cablecasting Yearbook 1984.*

47. *Arbitron Ratings Television Peoria.*

48. *Arbitron Ratings Television Dayton* (New York: The Arbitron Company, 1984).

49. *Understanding and Using Radio Audience Estimates* (New York: The Arbitron Company, 1982), p. 5.

50. Ibid., p. 12.

51. *Radio Memo* (New York: Radio Advertising Bureau, 1986).

52. Ibid.

53. *Understanding and Using Radio Audience Estimates*, p. 13.

54. *Broadcast Marketing and Technology News* (Washington, DC: National Association of Broadcasters, 1985), pp. 4–5.

FINAL
MON 10:30

Chapter 6

THE MEDIA SYSTEM
FOR SALES SUCCESS

The preceding chapters are preliminary to the principal function of the broadcast media salesperson, which is meeting with clients and selling the particular broadcast medium. However, skipping the earlier chapters to get right to the heart of the matter in this chapter is not a good idea. Although preliminary, the matters discussed in the earlier chapters are vital to the professional preparation of the media salesperson.

As should be apparent by now, selling is more than meeting face to face with the client, although everything a salesperson does is designed to lead to this all-important moment. Organizing, planning, dressing for your role as a successful businessperson are only parts of a complete sales training program. An explanation of this overall larger system of sales training is appropriate at this point.

DIRECT VERSUS AGENCY SELLING SITUATIONS

No matter the size of the market in which a broadcast salesperson works, be it a top 50 Arbitron ADI (area of dominant influence) market or a market in the remaining 150 + ADIs, that salesperson is involved in direct, face-to-face selling a certain percentage of each work day. In small- to medium-sized markets, broadcast salespeople will likely be involved in direct selling 100% of the time. In a top 50 market, perhaps less than half of each day will be devoted to direct selling. The remainder of the time will be spent in agency selling situations.

The essential difference between the two, as noted in a comprehensive study of electronic media salespeople and agency media buyers compiled by Professor Lauranell Scarfo of the University of Kentucky, is noteworthy. In direct selling, a station salesperson is presenting to a client who is less knowledgeable and sophisticated about the electronic media, has limited access to media evaluation information from ratings companies and/or advertising agencies, and essentially views the media in an emotional way based on increases in customer traffic or sales. To the average merchant or retailer, the electronic media is a totally intangible oddity that creates fleeting images and impressions that cannot be measured in any quantifiable way.

On the other hand, as Professor Scarfo notes, presenting to an agency media buyer is almost the opposite. A skilled buyer understands how the electronic media operates, possesses clear ideas about the target market, will not be persuaded to buy a station that does not reach the target market of the client, and engages in post-campaign analysis to determine the reach and effectiveness of the media campaign. Agency media buyers view broadcasting results as more tangible, since the product is perceived in terms of numbers that can be quantified.

This chapter addresses itself to direct selling, "consultant" situations where the salesperson must address client needs, problems and emotional perceptions—the selling situation where human relations skills and empathetic attention play a larger role in the sales process than the more aggressive, adversarial approach of traditional selling.

SALES TRAINING

Training helps salespeople become top producers. According to *Successful Sales Managing*,

> *"Training is successful when it helps people learn to do their jobs well . . . it is a day-to-day task . . . done properly, it means generating enthusiasm among salespeople about the importance of doing the job the way it should be done. Once your salespeople realize that earnings increases come with improved performance, they should regard training as the prime pathway to success."*[1]

Indeed, media salespeople need to understand all facets of the selling profession they have chosen. An overall training program can help them achieve peak performances as rapidly as possible and keep them producing at the highest attainable level. When implemented properly, it helps industry salespeople become masters of each selling situation they encounter and also insightful professionals who understand the present and future needs and problems of each individual client.

Proper Training Prepares for Performance

With the stage set for the first face-to-face meeting with the client, the curtain rises as you shake hands with your prospect. The word *stage* is an appropriate metaphor, not a cliché; the analogy to a play is an accurate comparison. What is done in the following 10 to 30 minutes with the client is a performance. All of the salesperson's professional skills and sensitivities are brought into play as this system of professional selling begins, much as the strengths of a quarterback are called upon at the moment he calls the audibles at the line of scrimmage to put his professional system into play.

The word *performance* describes what occurs between salesperson and client, as the salesperson wants to be better during a sales presentation than he or she is normally. Consciously behaving above the norm is a performance posture. At this point, the salesperson needs and wants to be totally alert, observant, a good listener, responsive, sensitive, and client-oriented. All these qualities demand in-depth concentration, an overall condition none of us consistently experiences in a so-called normal day. When we call all of these personal qualities into play at once, the result is a performance played for the benefit of the client.

Significance of a Selling System

Understanding the significance of a system is important. Every team, every group of people with a specific purpose operates under one sort of system or another. Professional athletic teams do not take the field and just pass the ball to whomever they wish. They each have a system of previously planned offensive plays and defensive formations, and they know the other team by name, position, and reputation. In other words, they go into competition with a system, a game plan that they believe will lead them to victory in the end.

Groups of civic-minded people like the Jaycees and the Rotarians do not get together regularly with no specific agenda. Meetings are planned ahead of time and a system is followed.

Systems are used and followed every day. They are necessary to ensure organization and a sense of order and to measure progress toward specific, predetermined goals. Why, then, would a salesperson ever leave the station to see a client without knowing how to structure a presentation in a manner that assists the client in making a favorable decision? Yet, every day salespeople leave the office with no idea of where they are going and even less of an idea of how they are going to sell what to a particular prospect. They are not using a sales system that has been designed to produce the results that they desire; they are not, in fact, using a system at all.

THE MEDIA SYSTEM

The personal selling system developed to meet the needs of electronic media salespeople is conveniently labeled the MEDIA system for sales success. This system consists of five time-proven ingredients that overcome the feelings that any prospective customer inevitably has when a salesperson walks in the door. As a mnemonic for its five steps, the MEDIA system is easily memorized by students and entry-level salespeople, as illustrated in Table 6-1.

Table 6-1
The MEDIA system for sales success outline

M (M)EETING THE CLIENT
 The Entrance
 The Four Types of Client Behavioral Styles
 Receiving the Client's Personal Attention
 Receiving the Client's Business Attention

E (E)XPRESSING INTEREST IN THE CLIENT VIA INTERVIEW

D (D)EVELOPING THE CAMPAIGN

I (I)NTERESTING THE CLIENT
 Stressing station and program benefits
 Stressing campaign benefits

A (A)SKING FOR THE ORDER/CONFIRMING THE SALE

Psychological Feelings Overcome by the System

The Dale Carnegie Institute sales course lists five negative emotions prospects feel about salespeople.

1. Rejection
2. Indifference
3. Skepticism
4. Put off or delay
5. Fear

Combining these five reactions with the five keys of the MEDIA system for sales success that are designed to overcome these negative feelings, we come to Table 6-2.

As noted by Miller and Heiman in their book, *Strategic Selling:*

> You probably don't like to think of your sales proposals as threats, but buyers can, and often do, see them in just this way. The strategic sales representative understands that anytime you ask someone to buy something, you're asking that person to make a change. . . . Since people react to change in different ways and since virtually every change can be viewed as threat or opportunity, there's always a chance that a buyer will perceive your sales proposal as threatening, even when it's "obvious" to you that it's not.[2]

Table 6-2
The MEDIA system interaction with prospect feelings

MEDIA System	Prospect Feelings
Meeting the client (overcomes)	Rejection, a client's initial feeling upon seeing a salesperson.
Expressing interest via interview (overcomes)	Indifference about what you will be able to do for the client.
Developing campaign (overcomes)	Skepticism that you can develop a solution for a genuine problem.
Interesting the client by stressing benefits (overcomes)	Put off or delay.
Asking for the order/confirming (overcomes)	Fear of buying and fear that a better or cheaper proposition may be secured elsewhere.

An effective selling system, then, helps the client overcome the real or perceived risk of change that results from considering a sales proposal. Each MEDIA step is essential to assisting the client in dealing with these emotions. As each step is learned and implemented, so is the process of assisting the client in dealing with the change that may take place if a sale is successfully concluded. The first step is meeting the client.

MEETING THE CLIENT

Any meeting anywhere between two people always begins with a greeting of some sort. Usually, such greetings are meaningless generalities along the lines of "Hey, how are you doing?" or "What's happening?" Such greetings elicit such equally banal responses as "OK, how are you doing?" or "Not much, how about you?" This habit, practiced several times a day for decades, is difficult to break when we become salespeople and need to attract the honest attention of a client.

Pointless greetings tend to degenerate into meaningless drivel, with little attention to the actual purpose of the call—selling your station—until the last possible moment, when the client needs to turn his attention elsewhere. Then the salesperson blurts out, "You wouldn't want to buy any spots for your sale this weekend, would you?" To avoid this distasteful situation, let's back up to the point where the media salesperson walks into the business.

The Entrance

Theories of nonverbal communication indicate that we accept or reject others, and are accepted or rejected by others, at first meeting and in a relatively short period of time, usually within the first minute of an initial introduction. The impact of first impressions is the main reason why dress is so important, but dress is not the only factor that sends messages about you to the prospective buyer you are greeting for the first time.

Other factors that influence first impressions, whether consciously or unconsciously, include eye contact, facial expression, posture, gestures or nervous movements, and overall attitude. These factors are examples of nonverbal communication.

If you think about it, *not* communicating is virtually impossible. Our bodies are constantly communicating our feelings, emotions, and attitudes. Thus, we should learn how to use and control nonverbal behavior by understanding what it is and its positive and negative uses in the sales process.

Figure 6-1 defines the various categories of nonverbal behavior and gives examples of each type of communication form. This information is vital to the first step of the selling process, as 65 percent of all communication involves nonverbal communication. The importance of nonverbal communication is outlined in Figure 6-2.

From this understanding of wordless communication, the salesperson can readily understand that there are positive uses of nonverbal communication, such as those in Figure 6-3. Conversely, some actions, such as those in Figure 6-4, can be considered negative nonverbal communication. The conscientious salesperson should be aware of these actions in order to avoid incorporating them into personal behavior.

Nonverbal communication is a large part of the salesperson's entrance. *Entrance* as a description of the primary meeting between salesperson and client was initially coined by Ken Delmar in *Winning Moves: The Body Language of Selling*:

> A smooth, confident entrance, unimpeded by self-conscious vacillation, instantly augments your stature in the prospect's eye . . . . as in most areas concerning the sales confrontation, the salesperson will be viewed and treated largely according to how he or she expects to be treated. And these expectations are communicated entirely in nonverbal signals.[3]

The Handshake   As the salesperson greets the prospect, social courtesies dictate that a handshake is always used, and that handshake is a strong nonverbal device. Delmar suggests that salespeople set aside briefcases so they can shake hands unencumbered. He recommends the two-handed handshake in which the left hand of the salesperson is placed on the forearm of the prospect.

Figure 6-1
Making a good first impression depends on your nonverbal communication

Categories of nonverbal communication	Examples
Kinesic Behavior—Communicative use of body motion including gestures, movement of the body, limbs, hands, feet and legs, facial expression, eye movement, and posture	Facial expression Eye contact Gestures Posture Distracting mannerisms Arms, legs, hands, feet movement Lateral movement
Proxemics—Communicative use of social and personal space	Intimate zone 0–1½ feet Personal zone 1½–4 feet Social zone 4–12 feet Public zone More than 12 feet
Paralanguage—Voice behavior that deals with how something is said, not with what is said *Don't use "... you know!"*	Pitch, rate, stress, loudness, enunciation, pronunciation Laughing, crying, sighing, yawning, coughing, clearing throat, vocalized pauses ("uh")
Object Language—Communicative use of artifacts—material ranging from clothing and costumes to furniture and visual aids	Clothes, hair-style, purse, jewelry, briefcase, note pads, pens, furniture arrangement, office decor
Time—Clock orientation	Time of day, amount of advance notice, timing, time spent waiting for an appointment
Tactile—Physical contact between people	Pat on back, arm around shoulders, handshake, red face of anger, blush of embarrassment, rash
Olfactory—Sense of smell	Body odor, mouth odor, perfumes, cologne

This gives you tremendous psychological control if you can bring it off fearlessly. Don't use it on a female prospect. . . . If you can, come at the prospect from the side of the desk—this means an easier, more comfortable reach for you both. Your body faces the prospect directly; do not turn to the side. Another little trick to gain control quickly: pull the prospect toward you a little as you shake. Just a bit. Men can do this with a female prospect also. It shows your lack of fear of the prospect, and your warmth. Don't be

Figure 6-2
How to communicate nonverbally

1. **Nonverbal and verbal messages sometimes contradict one another.**

   Nonverbal messages far outweigh verbal ones when these contradictions occur. Inconsistent messages occur more frequently in informal than in formal communication situations.

   For example, you may say "Let's get to work" while you are smiling. Your smile contradicts the seriousness of your verbal message, and some listeners will believe the smile rather than your words.

2. **Messages may be clear or unclear depending upon the number of pauses that occur, the frequency and placement of the pauses, and the overall "flow" of sound.**

   Jerky speech patterns convey a message of uncertainty. When many pauses occur, or when pauses last a long time, listeners become uneasy about what you are saying.

3. **Speakers/Communicators who make no facial changes while they are speaking will appear bored or apathetic.**

   The lack of facial changes will be accepted as a *negative* rather than a *neutral* message. In one-to-one and small-group communication situations, small changes in facial expression will be quite obvious to the receiver.

4. **Eye contact or "looking at" receivers of messages is very important in American society because it indicates the sender's interest in his receiver.**

   In public communication situations, speakers can look between, over, or "through" their audiences without appearing to do so.

   In informal situations, because of the closeness of the sender and receiver, you need to learn to look at the faces of your group. By picking up facial cues instantly, they can modify their own behavior to adapt to receiver behavior.

5. **Movement, in itself, is a message.**

   Movement gets our attention, particularly when it is contrasted to a lack of movement in surrounding objects and or people who feel that to move around would not be appropriate.

Figure 6-3
Reasons for using nonverbal communication

1. Gain the attention of your listeners.
2. Show a genuine interest in your listeners.
3. Open the lines of communication between you and your listeners.
4. Monitor the listeners' understanding of your message.
5. Express your trustworthiness and honesty.
6. Establish your credibility.
7. Clarify your main points and message.
8. Express your attitude toward yourself, your message, and your listeners.
9. Start, control, and end the communication process.
10. Express your confidence and expertise in a given area.
11. Express your emotions.
12. Reinforce your message.
13. Appease your listeners (especially important with a hostile or apathetic group).
14. Indicate transitions within a message.
15. Control and dictate crowd behavior.
16. Direct attention to visual aids or to other people.

---

surprised if you feel the prospect pulling back slightly. Now he knows you are not afraid. . . . Let the prospect decide when to end the handshake. If he attempts to terminate it with undue haste, hold on a beat longer. Don't let him get away from you so soon. If you are male and the prospect is female, however, you must end the handshake immediately when she signals she wants it to end.[4]

Do not pump the prospective buyer's hand, as this gesture signals that you're afraid you'll lose control if you let go. Always give a firm grip while maintaining eye contact. Be sure that your hand is dry before you offer it to a prospect, but never wipe your hands on your clothing.

Eye Contact   The eyes reflect overall character and personality as well as at-the-moment attitudes and feelings. Eye contact is the most effective way to hold a prospect's attention directly on you and your message, and proper eye contact conveys confidence and trust. If you maintain constant eye contact, you telegraph personal interest in your client, who intuitively believes more of what you have to say about your prepared campaign and

Figure 6-4
Nonverbal communication behaviors to avoid

1. Indirect eye contact
2. Nervous body mannerisms (e.g., clicking a pen)
3. Poor posture (standing or sitting)
4. Inappropriate dress
5. Inattention to listener
6. Gestures that contradict oral message
7. Any action that calls attention to the action instead of the message
8. Intruding on another person's personal space
9. Leaning away from the speaker/listener
10. Closing your arms in front of your body
11. Shifting eyes
12. Inappropriate body scent

your station. Looking at the bridge of the other person's nose establishes "eye contact" yet avoids a glazed stare.

Learn to be natural with your eyes. Don't stare a prospect down in an attempt to gain some false, psychological edge. Use them warmly, as you would with your friends or your children. Delmar suggests that you use your eyes as your principal instruments to:

- *Underline and accentuate your verbal material*
- *Show concentration, especially in listening—your ears may hear, but they can show no sign of comprehension*
- *Show enthusiasm, wonder, awe, surprise, and delight*
- *Evince fearlessness and courage*
- *Display agreement or disagreement*
- *Show understanding and empathy or withhold it*
- *Point or direct the prospect's attention elsewhere*
- *Reassure; add sincerity to a promise; guarantee or verify*
- *Show deep willpower, strength under fire, and pertinacity*
- *Establish a sense of humor, personal warmth, and charisma.*[5]

The entrance is your first and most important winning move. Make the best impression you are capable of making. To see how you score nonverbally at this point, take the quiz in Figure 6.5 and compute your own score.

Figure 6-5
Test how good a first impression you make

Check yes, usually, or no for each question in the quiz.

YES   USUALLY   NO

_____ _____ _____ My facial expression matches my words

_____ _____ _____ I avoid using "and uh," "um," "like," and "you know" when I talk

_____ _____ _____ When I talk, I sound like I know what I'm talking about

_____ _____ _____ I use a lot of facial expressions when I talk

_____ _____ _____ I look people in the eye when talking to them

_____ _____ _____ I use my hands and move my body when I talk

_____ _____ _____ My posture is erect but not stiff (standing and sitting)

_____ _____ _____ I dress to fit the occasion

_____ _____ _____ I pay close attention when people speak to me

_____ _____ _____ I don't touch people until I get to know them well

_____ _____ _____ I lean toward people when I talk to them

_____ _____ _____ I avoid crossing my arms during a conversation

_____ _____ _____ I am often complimented on my grooming

_____ _____ _____ I am often complimented on the neatness of my clothing

_____ _____ _____ I am often told that I know how to dress

_____ _____ _____ I bathe and wash my hair daily

_____ _____ _____ I avoid biting my fingernails

_____ _____ _____ I am enthusiastic

_____ _____ _____ I am sincere

_____ _____ _____ I am honest

_____ _____ _____ I am modest

_____ _____ _____ I avoid playing with my glasses, hair, tie, rings, watch, keys, etc.

_____ _____ _____ I avoid scratching in public, even if I itch

_____ _____ _____ I avoid chewing gum when I talk with people

_____ _____ _____ I avoid rubbing my ear, nose, chin, etc. when I am talking

cont.

Figure 6-5
Test how good a first impression you make (cont.)

Check yes, usually, or no for each question in the quiz.

YES   USUALLY   NO

_____ _____ _____ I know how much cologne or perfume is too much

_____ _____ _____ I avoid slumping when I sit or stand

_____ _____ _____ I think about what I say before I say it

_____ _____ _____ I dress stylishly but not trendy or faddish

_____ _____ _____ I am on time for meetings and appointments

_____ _____ _____ My handshake is firm and vigorous

_____ _____ _____ I am polite

_____ _____ _____ I am well mannered

_____ _____ _____ I take good care of my skin

_____ _____ _____ I use deodorant or antiperspirant each time I bathe

_____ _____ _____ My parents tell me that I do a good job taking care of my room

_____ _____ _____ I wear a minimum of jewelry

_____ _____ _____ Smiles are a big part of my day-to-day communication

_____ _____ _____ My shoes are always clean or polished

_____ _____ _____ I make sure that my nonverbal communication matches what I say with words

How to Score the Nonverbal Communication Quiz:

Count 2 points for each YES
Count 1 point for each USUALLY
Count 0 points for each NO

Total each column.

Add the three column totals to get your score.

EXCELLENT   70–80
GOOD   60–69
FAIR   50–59
POOR   49 or below

Source: Evan E. Rudolph and Barbara R. Johnson, *How to Find and Get the Job You Want* (Stone Mountain, GA: Linton Day Publishing Co., 1988), pp. 52–54. Used with permission of the authors

All Clients Are Not Alike

All clients that you begin to interact with are not the same. Not all display the same personalities or behavior styles. Learning to identify the various behavioral styles of prospects can greatly enhance the salesperson's skills.

After the first several minutes of conversation, the alert salesperson has observed the prospect's nonverbal characteristics and personal mannerisms on his or her own territory, the place of business or office. The salesperson begins to gain insight into that client's personal and business personality. Personal attributes such as drive, motivation, degree of self-confidence, and responsiveness to ideas, other people, and general business conditions begin to surface. The prospect's degree of receptivity—how open and receptive he or she is to the actual presence of the salesperson—is also apparent.

Openness   In *Non-Manipulative Selling*, Alessandra and Wexler note that when people act and react in social situations they display verbal, vocal, and visual actions. By observing the two personal dimensions of *openness* and *directness* in these actions, the salesperson can define the prospect's behavioral style.

> *Openness is the ease with which a person shows emotions and is accessible to others. It also encompasses a person's readiness to develop new relationships. It determines whether a person jumps in and gets involved interpersonally or remains aloof.*[6]

An open person is the opposite of the closed or self-contained individual who shows minimal nonverbal feedback, does not smile often, and is basically an introvert. Self-contained people are hard to read, as their faces tend to be expressionless and they prefer a physical and mental distance, that is, sitting behind a desk or table and showing very little feeling or emotion. A self-contained person wants to learn the reason a salesperson is calling as soon as possible and is impressed with facts and figures. Contrast that with the animation of an open person who gets excited, shows emotions, and talks about a myriad of topics before finally getting to the point.

Directness

> *Directness refers to the amount of control and forcefulness a person attempts to exercise over situations or other people. It is also about how people make decisions or approach risk or change.*[7]

According to Alessandra and Wexler, indirect people are less willing to contribute to group situations and approach change and risk with extreme caution. Body language is minimized, with a maximum display of patience, diplomacy, and cooperativeness. They tend to reserve their opinions and go along with the group unless strong conviction dictates otherwise. Eye contact is intermittent, and the guarded nature of indirect people prohibits them from initiating a social introduction or even from demonstrating a firm hand-shake. Indirect people follow established rules and policies by the book, as they fear being the one who goes against the grain. These low-key people would rather avoid conflict than directly deal with it.

The direct person, in contrast, is forceful, demonstrative, and control oriented, with an outward display of confidence that causes them to voice opinions and constantly argue or present their point of view. Rules are guidelines, and flexibility provides them the opportunity to do things without permission. Their attitude is that it's "easier to beg forgiveness than seek permission."[8]

Each salesperson is also somewhere between direct and indirect, and between open and self-contained according to individual behavioral style. Understanding each style and where you and your clients fit is the next challenge to meet.

Prospect Behavioral Styles

People are motivated by very real needs, as we learned in discussing Maslow's hierarchy of needs. Motivating needs are such things as the need for safety and security, belonging and acceptance into a peer group, status and recognition, and personal self-esteem. Prospects buy, in large part, to satisfy these motivating needs. Thus, instead of buying radio, TV, or cable solely for what the service will do for a prospect's business, prospects become buyers to satisfy basic, inner needs.

Ken Greenwood teaches that prospects generally have one of four categories of behavioral styles. Not each client fits neatly into one particular style, but people can be generally classified as favoring or leaning toward one style over the other three. He divides prospective buyers into analytical, driving, amiable, and expressive categories. Alessandra and Wexler teach that clients are either socializers, directors, thinkers, or relaters. In *Integrity Selling*, Ron Willingham divides potential buyers and clients into the talkers who are social types, doers (achievers), plodders who are content with the routine, and logical, rational controllers. Learning to recognize each style and how to relate effectively to the behavior each presents is part of your challenge as a salesperson.

The suggested questions in this section for each personality type are not necessarily designed to be asked of a client during a first meeting. Rather, they are given to provide you with a means of gaining rapport over a period of time, maybe several weeks or months after you have identified a personality style.

The Socializer   The socializer is an exquisite talker who loves to see salespeople. They get the socializer's mind off the routine of business and onto what they enjoy most—socializing. Such client types are perhaps the most open and direct of all four behavioral styles. They are quick and persuasive and avoid details. Facts aren't interesting enough to be bothered with, and they operate on a best-guesstimate basis. Socializers are open, gregarious, talkative, and stimulating. At parties they are born entertainers, which stems from their need for approval and an ego need for feedback.

> *Talkers (Socializers) love people. They love to visit and socialize. They like block parties, family reunions, bowling leagues. They're easy to gain rapport with—easy to approach. After ten minutes you'll think you've been friends for life . . . they like to tell jokes . . . enjoy chit-chat. They're friendly and affable. They often have a cluttered environment. Their automobile interiors usually need cleaning. They like pictures and things that bring them recognition. They're often more daring with their dress and jewelry.*[9]

As "good ole' boys," socializers are usually nonthreatening. Should they reject you, such rejection will involve your business proposal, not you as a person.

At the second step, the interview, dealing with the socializer is a matter of understanding his or her style and of knowing which questions to ask. First of all, don't rush an interview or meeting with a socializer. Get to know the person. When you're making a presentation, offer creative solutions in a lively, entertaining manner. They'll want to know who else is using your station, so have your testimonials ready. Don't get bogged down in details with lots of ratings facts and statistics. Socializers love to hear their commercials and often like to be their own talent. Give them the opportunity to be a star and the chances of confirming the sale become greater.

Because socializers love to talk, ask questions like:

- *Where are you going on vacation?*
- *What do you do for recreation or hobbies?*
- *Tell me about your children (or family).*
- *Where will you spend the holidays?*[10]

Relationships with these optimistic, emotional people can be fun, but don't spend the entire morning with them telling jokes. You'll be wasting the time of both of you, and you may later be resented for wasting such time.

The Achiever   Less open and direct than the enthusiastic socializer, the achiever is proud of his or her accomplishments in life. Often taking over family-owned businesses from their fathers, these prospects often display a certain arrogance about their status that places them "above" other people (like media salespeople).

Not all achievers are arrogant, but this seems to be a common characteristic. They are businesslike and bottom-line oriented and love to remain in control of all situations. Those who cannot keep up with them are resented and looked on as incompetent, which explains their disdain toward those who don't have high-status jobs or country club memberships.

Achievers tend to display their success with material goods such as new, expensive cars, jewelry, and taking people to lunch at the club. These are symbols that often come with an "I have it and you don't" attitude. Because their objective is to accomplish tasks and get them finished, they resent anyone who tries to slow them down.

> *They like you to get to the point. They're impulsive and will make decisions based on gut feelings. They're very decisive and will make quick decisions once they think they have a grasp of the necessary facts and information . . . they are often surrounded by trophies, awards, plaques. They exhibit and talk about goals and rewards for achievement. They're restless and have nervous mannerisms.*[11]

Terry

In dealing with achievers, then, get to the point by selling benefits with facts and logic. Be professional and prepared and offer solutions to genuine problems that he or she has discussed with you. Ask these Type A personalities questions like:

- *How do you manage to get so much done?*
- *What are some of your secrets about time management?*
- *What does it take to be successful in your position?*
- *How are you able to juggle so many different responsibilities?*
- *What advice would you give to someone who wants to achieve your level of success?*
- *What are some things that have helped you get where you are today?*[12]

These types of questions get achievers talking, even though time is precious to them. When you return for the presentation, make sure your prepared copy, scripts, or storyboards tout the business as successful, well managed, and prestigious.

The Pleasant Person   We all know people who are genuinely warm, friendly, and open. They are soft-hearted types who would do anything to avoid hurting others' feelings.

Joanne

They are, however, somewhat difficult to sell to, as they want to know what others think before they make decisions. Even if they possess the positional authority for decision making, they want to double-check with an accountant, the staff, or the family simply because they don't want to do something that might upset others. They want to be liked, so they're good listeners and great team players, but to them decisions mean change and change could disrupt a comfortable routine.

Because these personality types are sensitive and people oriented, be informal. Listen well and show your interest in them and their businesses. Reveal your feelings and your human side. These people are very empathetic, make good counselors and teachers, and are the most genuinely open and direct, as contrasted to the sometimes boisterous, false bravado of the very open and direct socializers. Pleasant personas buy from people they trust. They may need prompting to make a decision, as they often procrastinate, but they appreciate a creative, image-oriented campaign that talks about people and the role they play in the success of the business.

Some good questions for the pleasant personas are:

■ *Tell me about your people and your relationship with your staff.*

■ *How do you stay so calm and in control?*

■ *Your store (business) looks so clean and neat. How do you keep it that way?*

■ *What are the qualities you look for in a salesperson?*[13]

The Intellectual/Analytical Person In total control, the intellectual can philosophize about general or specific business conditions, politics, sports, community affairs, literature, and his or her business and how it interrelates to the greater economy. Analytical people are organized and make decisions based on research, facts, and figures; they do not make decisions based on emotion. Analytical people seem aloof and less open and direct than any of the other three behavioral styles, and they enjoy problem solving. They love charts, facts and figures, and computer printouts, and they ask lots of questions of salespeople.

They may work late at night on minute details in a structured and organized environment. Basically loners, they don't particularly enjoy involvement with others, and those who report to them must be businesslike, professional, and able to justify their thinking and their work. Analytical people are the most organized of all personality types, have the neatest desks (even if work is piled all over it), and talk about methods, conditions and functions.[14]

Some good interview questions for the intellectual are:

■ *What's your secret for being so well organized?*

■ *How do you keep up with so many facts and so much information?*

■ *How are you able to obtain information so quickly?*

■ *What are the most important elements that keep your organization functioning?*

■ *How are you able to use your time so well?*

■ *What are some problem-solving techniques that work for you?*[15]

A presentation to this individual should be like making a proposal to one of your more demanding college professors. The intellectual won't go for the cheerleader presentation that appeals to the socializer. The media proposal must be highly organized, substantiated with facts, and articulated well with logical, well-thought-out solutions. The more proof and evidence backing up your plan, the better. Because this prospect is perceptive and analytical, present both the advantages and disadvantages of your proposal; don't be perceived as holding back on points that may be interpreted as weaknesses. A buying decision here is not made in your favor by chance but only by your showing the analytical person the logic of using your station to accomplish his or her predetermined goals.

Summarizing Human Behavioral Styles   In summary, the analytical people and achievers are much less direct and open than are the gregarious socializers and the people-oriented pleasant personnas. A person can be open or closed and direct or indirect in any of the four behavioral styles presented, but in general terms the more extroverted the personality, the more open and direct it is.

No one behavioral or personality style is superior to another. Each style is generally descriptive of a grouping of human beings, and each style boasts an equal number of successes and failures in the business community. Many of us can recognize something of ourselves in each style. However, all of us fit into or lean more toward one style than another.

Value Conflict

Problems between people develop when personalities of different behavioral styles meet and tension begins to emerge. This value conflict cannot be avoided. Your personal value structure—what is really important to you as a human being such as wealth, altruism, or honesty—is certainly not an exact parallel to the value structure of most people you meet. For example, if you are detail oriented, you must adapt your style to that of the client. Otherwise, you will never connect with a socializer who doesn't care about facts or details.

Learning to recognize your style and being able to relate to others of differing styles is a tremendous challenge to you as a salesperson. You have to learn to treat your prospects as they wish to be treated and sell to them as they want to be sold.

You need to learn how to meet each person's behavioral style needs by letting them take the lead; you then follow. If they want to move fast, you move fast. If they want to get to know you, allow more time for the interview. When you begin meeting their needs in this manner, trust eventually develops and an open, productive relationship begins.

Behavioral Flexibility

Remember that you are the salesperson. The prospect won't change his or her style to conform to your style; you must adapt your style to conform to that displayed by the prospective buyer. When you conform your style to that of the prospect, you're practicing behavioral flexibility. The more flexible you become, the faster you establish rapport and begin building a long-term client relationship that is mutually beneficial.

Receiving the Client's Personal Attention

As earlier mentioned, any media salesperson begins a visit to a prospect with a greeting. Such a greeting may even be as basic as "How are you doing?" but what is said immediately thereafter is the crucial element in successfully opening a sales call. Your goal, at this point, is to gain the attention of the client and to get his or her mind off current priorities and focused onto you.

Knowing how to open a conversation when you are on a sales call is essential in enabling you to employ your system of helping the client solve problems and move merchandise. Immediately following a handshake, the salesperson may comment on a recent civic event, sports event, or local event of mutual interest. The purpose is to establish a friendly atmosphere and erase as much as possible of the natural tension that exists when a businessperson is called on by any salesperson selling anything.

Establishing Common Ground What the salesperson is doing is what the successful speaker does to gain immediate favor with an audience or what interpersonal communication theory tells us we should do if we wish to be effective communicators with others—establish a common ground. Communication is always easier among peers than it is from higher-status individuals to lower-status individuals or vice versa. Politicians roll up their sleeves and help dig a ditch in front of the news media because they wish to be perceived as common people rather than as highly educated, wealthy members of an elite aristocracy. Establishing a common ground puts them on a level with the voting electorate.

Because a salesperson is generally perceived as pushy and obnoxious, you have to make an effort to circumvent that perception and establish a common ground with the prospect. After this has been accomplished with a short comment, the salesperson can then move on to the real reason he or she is there, to discuss media advertising or to obtain a client interview that may eventually lead to such advertising.

The Compliment One of the best and most effective ways to establish this common ground and to open your sales call is a method so simple that many of us never think of it at all. How do you feel when someone tells you that he or she likes your new car, the landcaping around your home that you worked on all weekend, or the color combination on your new suit? All of us like to be recognized, to be accepted, and to be complimented on something that represents us, the work we do, or the business we run.

The businessperson you call on as a media salesperson is no different and may have more problems and fewer compliments than we could guess. That's why such a prospect is likely to respond positively to you if you begin your sales call with a genuine compliment. That compliment lets the client know you notice and appreciate something he or she has done or is doing with the business or the store, in the community, or whatever. This kind of approach is the best way to get a businessperson's mind off the pressing problems of the moment and focus personal attention onto you.

Here's an example of a simulated conversation of this nature. Assume the salesperson is selling in the summer months.

Salesperson:	Good morning, Mr. Jones. Nice to see you today. Wow, that humidity is already getting me down and it's only nine o'clock!
Prospect:	Yeah, it's gonna be another one of those scorchers of a day, for sure.
Salesperson:	You know, as I drove by your store the other day, I noticed you working in the display window and then yesterday when I walked by, I saw that you completely changed your earlier scene to a new summer scene with lots of green and white. Boy, that new display sure accents those athletic and running shoes that you have displayed there. It's really attractive. Who on your staff comes up with the ideas for these display windows? [Notice that the compliment ends with an open-ended question.]

No matter how the compliment is worded, if what you say relates to something you know the person has worked hard on or is proud of and you deliver your compliment with sincerity, it will always make the businessperson feel good. In what better way could you cause that person to forget the immediate problems of the moment?

Open-Ended Questions   The compliment must end with an open-ended question that draws the client into the conversation and gets him or her to brag a bit about whatever you have pointed out. "Did you think of the window display idea?" requires only a nod for an answer and does not draw a preoccupied client into your conversation.

Genuine Sincerity   Your compliment must be sincere. Don't be phony and tell people you like their ties or something trite that pegs you as a smooth-talking pitchman. The store, civic affairs, family, church activities, children's accomplishments in Little League, spouse's new job, the mannerisms of salesclerks, the service given customers, and other substantial areas give you plenty of room to find something to compliment. The prospect's office provides wall plaques, certificates, and paintings on which you can hang a compliment. Just be naturally curious and interested in the client as a person, and you'll find plenty of genuine compliments that can effectively open up a conversation.

Then don't talk forever on the subject. Be polite and move on to the reasons you came. Clients appreciate a salesperson who does not waste their time.

Receiving the Client's Business Attention

You now know about the compliment designed to win the client's personal attention and about the four types of client behavioral styles. Now you need to learn to move from the compliment to the real reason that you came to see the businessperson. In other words, how do you get the client's *business* attention? The two ways are the direct approach method and the leading question method.

Direct Approach Method   To illustrate this method, let's improvise a conversation using the direct approach. The conversation begins after the compliment or ice-breaking phase of the initial meeting, when the prospect has answered a question such as "Who designed that attractive display window?"

Salesperson: Well, I enjoy working with someone who can come up with all your ideas and keep a store looking fresh and new every month. You're obviously interested in keeping the attention of your current customers and attracting new ones, as well. But obviously, I didn't come here to steal your ideas on store windows, but to talk with you about your business.

I'm excited about the new information our market's latest media survey shows about our station. If our audience profile fits the profile of your customers, I'd like to share these figures with you and maybe we can help you.

The Leading Question Method   The transition from the complimentary question to this method is the same as before, but then we progress to a leading question rather than to a direct approach.

Salesperson:	Well, I enjoy working with someone who can come up with all your ideas and keep a store looking fresh and new every month. You're obviously interested in keeping the attention of your current customers and attracting new ones, as well. But obviously, I didn't come here to steal your ideas on store windows, but to talk with you about your business.
	Tell me, if you could attract more potential customers into your store with fresh new ideas—like the ones you came up with for your store windows, for example—and these ideas could generate more traffic and more sales—without making you readjust your current monthly ad budget—would you be interested in hearing about them?

In this example of a leading question, the conversation shifted from the ice-breaking phase to the business attention phase in just a few sentences, and you gave the prospect reason to listen to you by speaking directly about something you know is interesting: the business and how to generate more traffic and more sales. All businesspeople are interested in a healthy return on investment, and a question related to these matters always elicits favorable business attention.

Not all salespeople agree with the leading question method that solicits answers they know in advance will be affirmative. That is because some salespeople turn them into leading *manipulative* questions. Leading questions that confirm to a prospect that you may be able to help are ethical. Leading manipulative questions that are designed to get a prospect to answer "yes" to any and every question are not.

The prospect has no choice but to answer a leading manipulative question in the affirmative. This method of pushing the prospect into a corner makes that person feel uneasy, and this pressure can hinder or terminate honest communication between salesperson and prospect. Ask yourself, "How would I feel if someone were to ask this of me?"

No businesspeople we've ever met have admitted that they don't desire more customer traffic, more sales, more business, and more profits—the prospects' predictable but very real needs. By responding positively to your question of whether or not they would be interested in discovering how more business can be done, traffic can be increased, and so on, clients have shown interest in at least wanting to know more about what the salesperson has to say. You have targeted a real need that has caused the prospect to want to listen and you have overcome an initial negative reaction of partial if not total rejection. The prospect is now saying between the lines, "Go ahead, give me some more information! I'm still skeptical, of course, but I'm willing to listen."

To this point, all you have done is arouse prospect interest. Without further qualifying the "suspect" and conducting a client-oriented interview, you have yet to determine whether your station can be helpful or turn the "suspect" into a genuine prospect and eventual buyer. You qualify your prospective buyer by listening very carefully to the information given during the second step of the interview.

Summarizing the Direct and Leading Question Approaches   In the direct approach example, you moved smoothly from personal to business attention by making a flat statement that you could help the client if he or she had a target customer who matched your target listener. In the leading question method, you accomplished the same thing by asking questions that received an affirmative answer. In both cases, you received permission to continue by stating that you needed to know more about the business before you could help.

You have now received the business attention of the person you are calling on and have overcome an initial negative reaction. The first step of meeting the client is now complete. Here, you must move from this step into the second step of Expressing interest in the client via interview.

Moving toward the Interview

Regardless of whether you choose the direct approach or prefer asking leading questions, the transition into step two of the MEDIA system would sound something like this:

> **Salesperson:**   Well, the reason I said that our station may be able to help you is because I believe there *might* be a way that you can increase your traffic at a surprisingly low cost. But before we get around to discussing this possibility, I need to know a little bit more about your business [or business represented if you are interviewing a media buyer at an advertising agency]. I think we'll be able to work well with each other, but I want to be sure that my station can, indeed, be of service to you. Would it be all right if I could get your opinion on a few questions?

What you actually say to a client depends, of course, upon what question you initially ask a client to win business attention. By stating that you might be able to assist, you have confirmed your earlier and perhaps surprising statement to the client that you may be able to help his or her business.

Now is *not* the time to plunge into your rap about how well your station did in the last ratings. You have confirmed that you may (not that you *do*, but that you *may*) have a way for the prospect to increase traffic; you do not yet have enough prospect knowledge to know that you can help, and you have not erased feelings of skepticism toward you and your station. You can erase that skepticism and develop a good working knowledge of the business by completing the interview step of the MEDIA system for sales success, the step when you actually present the questions about which you want the prospect's opinion.

Keep in mind that you ought not to request permission to ask questions. A natural response to questions is defense. Rather, request "your opinion on some questions" to eliminate that defensiveness. Prospects give you opinions whether you ask for them or not. Making yourself receptive to these opinions can help you get the client to tell you what you want to know.

As complicated as this step may seem thus far, getting to this point can and should be accomplished within the first five minutes of conversation. Now that you've made a favorable impression and know to some extent the type of personality you're dealing with, you're ready to develop a customer needs analysis by asking questions. Besides providing you with the information you need to make certain business decisions and giving you needed knowledge of your prospect's business, asking questions here can be beneficial in other ways.

Asking permission to ask questions is the transitional method to the second step of the MEDIA sales system. You express interest in somebody by asking questions. When you meet someone you like, you are initially curious and want to know where they work, what their interests are, and where they went to school, and the only way to ellicit information of this sort is to ask questions or, in a business sense, to conduct a client-oriented interview.

In other words, you need to find out what a potential client wants or needs to buy. In *What They Don't Teach You at Harvard Business School*, Mark McCormack writes:

> First, find out what they want to buy. If you don't know, ask, and let them tell you. Find out a company's problems, then show them how "we can work together" to solve them. It is so much easier to sell someone what they want to buy than it is to (persuade) them to buy what you are selling.
>
> Second, find out who does the buying. Every company has its system, procedures, and pecking order for making decisions. Don't always buck it.[16]

EXPRESSING INTEREST IN THE CLIENT VIA INTERVIEW

When the client gives you permission to ask questions, begin with a series of questions that can uncover the information needed to determine whether your station can help the client. In short, you wish to determine whether your station can produce results for this business; if not, recommend a station that can better meet the client's needs. Then proceed to locate an account that meets the qualifying criteria discussed in this chapter. This sequence is the reason why you cannot say earlier that you definitely have a plan for the prospect. How can you have a plan to assist the businessperson to solve business-related problems or to move recently purchased merchandise without an interview? How else would you find out about the store, how it operates, what the best months are, and why people shop elsewhere? You can research such information *before* initially seeing the client, and prior research will increase in importance to the profession in the 1990s. Nevertheless, you will always have to interview prospects to learn the specific information about the particular business that enables you to determine if and how you can help the business.

Having established with the prospect the need for an interview, the salesperson continues the presentation by asking questions in an interview fashion. The more that is learned about a business *before* a sales call is made, the better the interview will go and the fewer questions need to be asked. The salesperson can use questions from the RAB consultant sell interview in Appendix I or ask natural questions of curiosity that provide needed information.

In responding to your questions, the client is participating in the interview process and begins to open up. As this participation unfolds, you also discover your prospect's main interests and achievement needs. If all goes well, at the conclusion of this step you know the client's primary interest in operating a business and the client knows the depth of your interest as well. You also know if they do, will, or can advertise, and you will have uncovered more useful information about your prospect than you ever believed possible. Such knowledge is the first step toward in-depth or progressive selling, as knowledge of a person's true motivators helps you become the client's ally in goal achievement, not just another peddler trying to pick pockets.

Interview Questions

All types of clients need to be asked certain questions so you may gather sufficient information to construct an appropriate media campaign. Combine these questions with those appropriate for your client's behavior style. If you already know the answer to one or several questions due to prior client research, don't ask. The important questions deal with what the client feels the strengths of the business are and the advertising goals of that business, so get ready to become a good in-depth listener. Questions relating to your own curiosity should also be added as the interview unfolds and you feel more comfortable in beginning to learn from the client.

All questions should be asked in a casual, conversational manner that shows your genuine desire to learn. Word each question so it sounds like you and not a memorized pitch that could be given by a computer.

Questions to Elicit Client Participation

1. Now, you're the manager [or whatever], correct?

2. And one of your responsibilities here is handling advertising for the business? [If they don't advertise, ask if they would be willing to do so in the future under the right circumstances.]

3. Does anyone else share in this endeavor, or do you yourself decide your store's advertising direction?

4. If you don't make the decision, do you make recommendations and, if so, to whom do you recommend a media buy?

These first four questions provide information on whether you are speaking with the right person, the person who actually makes the buying decision. If another person is involved, you may have to schedule a second meeting with the two of you. If you're not speaking with the person who can actually make the advertising buying decision, politely leave and arrange to see the person you ought to be seeing. You also discover whether the business does advertise (question 2) and therefore if it is a prospect for your station.

5. You seem to have a successful operation here. How does this business actually run? In what areas does your profit lie? What are your biggest challenges?

These questions involve the businessperson in discussing the business while you are also beginning to learn about the client.

6. I see. Well, what is it about your store that makes people want to shop here? Who exactly is your average customer? Demographically, who are you trying to reach?

7. OK. Then, taking all this into consideration, why do you feel people shop your competition?

Question 6 is a central question because it provides information the client would like to hear on the spec copy* you should later provide. It also

---

*"Spec" copy or tape: common industry term for prepared commercials on a cassette tape, prepared as speculation with no advance input from client. Clients usually love "spec tapes," and they make the chances of closing greater. Even commercials prepared after the interview are "spec" in nature as the client has not heard them.

informs you about things of which the client is most proud. You may learn what perceived shortcomings exist in the question about the competition; in well-written copy, these qualities could be turned into strengths. For example, if the businessperson feels potential customers shop at the competition's business due to a more attractive or accessible location, well-written, humorous copy giving directions to the store could be successful in the media marketplace. In other words, a positive commercial can overcome a perceived weakness and make it seem to be a strong point.

8. What is your opinion of your competitor's advertising?

9. What did you like about your last (radio, TV, or cable) ad campaign? What didn't you like?

10. What have other stations done for you that you liked? That you didn't like? (Be careful not to defend what you are selling here. You're gathering information, not selling or defending your station.)

11. I see. Well, then, in respect to any advertising your store does, what do you want this advertising to do? In other words, what are the goals of any advertising or PR program you may run?

12. Is anything keeping you from accomplishing these goals?

13. If you did do business with us, how could we help you accomplish these goals?

What you are doing here is asking for opinions, a gesture much less threatening to a prospect than direct questions. Prospects begin speaking more freely and opening up when they speak on something they are certain about—their opinions. Asking for opinions also shows your interest in the prospect and allows you to develop trust by focusing on extremely relevant information, thus making the prospect feel comfortable in the presence of someone who really cares about doing a professional job.

14. If I understand you correctly, you obviously would like your advertising to increase store traffic [promote a positive image, or whatever], right? Or, I noticed you've advertised your new line of sofa sleepers. Has this line been good for you? Have they moved well?

With these questions, you can discover what your prospect expects from advertising and which media he or she feels works best. If radio is being sold and the prospect feels that newspapers are the best bet, you know you'll have to sell "against" newspaper during your return visit when you present your media campaign to the client. If TV is preferred, you know where your competition for the total advertising dollar lies.

Suggested Questions Leading to the Dominant Buying Motive

15. What does more traffic mean to your store? (The client will probably say something similar to "more sales" or "more business.")

16. OK, well, what does more business mean to you as a manager here? (If the client is still with you, a phrase like "more profits" or "more money" will be the likely answer.)

17. Fine. I guess that's why we're all in business, right? But, what does more money mean to *you* personally? (If he or she is noncommittal or wishy-washy on this one, go on to the next question.)

18. What I mean is, if you get more money or make more sales and thus have better business because of your effective media program, what will this mean to you? Do you want to open a second store someday? (Or move up the ladder to the company's main office or own your own store or achieve financial independence for yourself or whatever?)

The Dominant Buying Motive

By answering this series of questions, your client reveals exactly why he or she bothers to get out of bed and come to work each morning, why there might be any interest at all in buying from you, why the prospect does anything. In each case, the answer is what has just been revealed to you—financial independence, early retirement, a second store, or whatever. This is the client's primary interest in working and the dominant buying motive (DBM). The client buys *now* to achieve these long-range goals. There are many different motives, but the client is not always outwardly conscious of that fact. Now that you are aware of this inner motive for buying, you are in a unique position to become the prospect's ally in the pursuit of long-term goals.

The behavioral system described here is what researchers refer to as *positional behavior* or the motivation one has to better one's position within the company. A buyer's motive to do business with a salesperson is prompted by that desire to advance one's career.

Identifying a Business Problem

During this question-and-answer period, the salesperson learns a great deal about the business. Areas that concerned the businessperson, such as location, competition, a prime demographic group slipping away, customer flow, or reduced volume, may have surfaced during the course of the interview.

However, what the salesperson really needs to discover is whether the prospective buyer has a genuine business problem or need that can be addressed or solved by the salesperson's station. Solving specific and identified areas of concern for the client produces long-term business, as opposed to running generic ads that all the other media are running. If "everybody" runs the same type of ads, all share in the success or failure of a business campaign. Salespeople who are consultants rather the peddlers want credit for developing a campaign and producing results. They know that failures are few when they sell to clients who are right for the station's audience or demographics.

To propose solutions for clients, specific problems need to be identified. A good salesperson does not leave until a specific area has been identified that he or she knows can be properly addressed by the station. If no particular problem or marketing need surfaced by the time the consultant was ready to leave, a naive question dealing with things an effective media campaign might change for the business could bring such concerns to the surface.

The Naive Question If an area of concern has not been confirmed by the close of the meeting, the consultant might try another approach:

Salesperson:	We've been talking for a while here and it's time I leave. But, before I do, I'd like to ask you one further question. If I could grant you one wish that could change anything about your business that you'd like to change or cause anything to happen, what would that be?

This fanciful question usually elicits initial amusement about your role as the genie in the bottle or a suggestion that you reroute the freeway to end at the store. After you muse that you doubt that you could get city permits to divert a major thoroughfare, the businessperson usually divulges a nagging area of concern or perceived problem that has been present for a period of time. Such a problem or worry is likely to deal with one of four areas of concern:

1. Perceptions of traffic flow or of the type of traffic in terms of the quality or demographics desired

2. The economic conditions of the moment that are perceived as directly affecting cash flow

3. A specific merchandising or inventory problem that has built up in the store, such as a room full of reclining chairs that have not sold

4. A specific buy recently made, such as a truckload of tires at a bargain price, which now has to be sold

Such information, gathered by that naive question, tells the consultant if the businessperson can be helped by advertising on the station. Remember that no station can solve every problem and every problem confessed by a client should not be addressed. Only problems that the station's listening audience is likely to respond to should be accepted.

Order takers and peddlers, of course, take any concern revealed by the prospect and promise immediate results, but the chances are that the problem is the wrong one and that the campaign is doomed to failure before it begins. After it does run, the businessperson probably has encountered another unsuccessful venture with radio or TV and reverts to the habitual response of putting most of the annual budget into the newspaper.

Turning Down Business   As a consultant, the salesperson has to learn to resist the temptation to take anything he or she can get just to return to the station with an order. Miller and Heiman in *Strategic Selling* word it this way:

> All of us who make our living in sales are under constant pressure to sell; pressure from managers, from colleagues, from family and friends and from ourselves. Because of this pressure, most of us are constantly tempted to take on marginal or potentially troublesome business that we really ought to stay away from . . . this means that you have to turn some business down. To many people in sales—especially those who were trained by tradition-conscious managers and trainers—this is simply unthinkable. "Any sale is a good sale," they tell themselves. Or, "all dollars are alike."[17]

What the radio-TV salesperson has to turn down are businesses that cannot be helped: businesses that do not meet certain, specific, predetermined criteria, businesses that will eventually become a liability because the station won't be able to produce effective advertising results. "*No* single product or service is made for everybody and . . . you prosper in today's selling environment by finding the matches that serve the self-interest of every one of your customers."[18] The bottom line is that if you can't assist the prospective buyer turn the business down and recommend a station in town that can help the client—a station that has the demographics and/or the features the prospective buyer needs.

Identifying a Marketing Need You Can Handle   How does a media salesperson find this fit so that his or her station can become a primary media buy? How can he or she effectively identify a problem, concern, or area of need that the station can handle in a results-oriented media campaign? Media consultant Jason Jennings has suggested three specific criteria that a problem must meet before a salesperson should accept it as something the station can solve through an intense and effective ad campaign. Any identified problem must be:

1. Advertised on a station whose demographics match those of the client's target customer
2. Solvable in a reasonable amount of time

3. Large enough to justify an advertising campaign designed to address the problem area

First, the demographics that the businessperson is attempting to reach must match the demographics of the station. No businessperson's problem can be solved by a station whose audience is different from the demographics comprising the client's main customer group or desired main customer group. For example, if you are a radio salesperson for a beautiful music station, you would not have a demographic match if you were attempting to solve the business problem of a record store's overstock of heavy metal music.

Secondary Markets   A prospect may be interested, however, in your demographics as a secondary market. His or her prime market may be served by another station. In this case, you may be able to become a secondary buy, running a lesser schedule that would expose your audience to the products or services offered by the client. Product awareness is sometimes a goal of an advertiser whose target customer may listen to another station, but whose business "fringes" into your demographic. If this is recommended, make sure the client knows that such a buy is, indeed, a secondary buy.

No problem can be effectively solved if the demographics of the station and the business do not match or if the client is not interested in the audience delivered by the station. (TV stations have less of a problem, as station demographics change from program to program; computerized systems such as Sell-a-Vision keep track of who views which programs, and the consultant can suggest programs based on these demographic printouts.)

Second, the problem or area of concern related by the client must be solvable relative to time. Your naive question may elicit this sort of response.

Prospect: Well, I'm not pleased with the type of neighborhood this is turning into around here. I mean, years ago, I had a high grade of clientele in here. Now, they all live in suburbs and won't come near here. Today, I get a lot of bad credit risks. I just don't know what to do.

Even though a demographic match may be present in this case, the consultant would not take on this concern. The key words are *years ago*. If the problem has been developing over a period of years, how long will it take to solve? It might be solvable over time, but the client is probably not willing to commit to a three-year campaign to attain measurable results. The consultant should look for a more immediate problem or concern to solve.

Third, the client problem or area of concern should be large enough to encourage substantial investment to get rid of it. The merchant who has $1,000 worth of unsold shoes won't want to spend much to get rid of them. The problem must be large enough for the merchant to spend part of the margin or markup on it and still make a profit if the merchandise moves. As Jennings points out, such a prospect is probably willing to spend 10 percent of the value of the problem to sell it. Ten percent of $1,000 is only $100, but 10 percent of $10,000 or $50,000 is another matter altogether.

More than general information of the Yellow Page variety is needed to tailor a results-oriented campaign for the client. Although general information can paint a nice image for the store in the mind of the listener, it does not give potential customers a reason to shop at the store and spend money. Creativity without reason is copy that does not sell. Find a reason for the businessperson to advertise on your station, make sure it fits the three criteria discussed, and then creatively inform your audience why they should go to that store or business. They will, if the copy is right and the client's target customer is in your audience.

Knowing a businessperson's dominant buying motive is not enough. That can't be advertised. You should advertise only real reasons why people should do business with your client.

After Identifying the Problem   When the problem area has been identified according to the discussed criteria, you want to say, "I think we at the station might be able to help you [do whatever]. I know that may be presuming a lot, but let me think about what you have said for a few days and then get back with you."

You have now completed Step 2, the interview step. Many salespeople ignore this crucial step in their rush to present their facts and brag about their ratings. The client's feelings may indeed be skeptical at this point, as you have yet to prove anything by offering a solution to a genuine business need, but at least the feelings of rejection and indifference have turned to toleration.

By leaving at this point, you position yourself apart from the clerks who attempt a close on the first visit. No solution can be proposed until the information just gathered can be studied and turned into a workable campaign to be presented to the prospect within four to six business days.

Note that if you are on a one-stop call, one of the five exceptions to conducting a consultant call, the next step of developing the campaign would have already been completed. Before the sales call, you would have decided to present a particular promotion or available program or time slot to the prospect, and you would have no need to return to the station. Instead, proceed to the fourth step of interesting the client by stressing the benefits of the station and the promotion.

DEVELOPING THE CAMPAIGN

When enough information has been gathered to put together a creative campaign that addresses whatever problem or reason the businessperson may have to use your station as an advertising outlet, the consultant leaves to embark on the single most difficult mission in electronic media sales: developing an advertising campaign or presentation based on the information gathered during the interview phase.

An order taker or peddler would not give much thought to campaign development or the presentation and would mindlessly construct a haphazard schedule based on current available time slots without consideration of station demographics at the time of scheduling. Then this salesperson would return to the prospect with stock copy that sounds like everything else in the market. A consultant, however, knows that whatever is presented to the prospect during the second meeting must be fundamentally different and better than whatever was used before because whatever was previously used did not effectively address the very real concerns that are still present. Maybe the business person was not targeting the message to the right potential customers via the correct radio or TV station, the frequency of commercials run was not heavy enough to produce results, the schedule did not run long enough, or the copy was poor. The current problem was probably addressed by advertising somewhere at some time, and yet the problem still persists. Therefore, it was not effectively solved. Whatever the consultant puts together now had better work because the consultant knows that he or she will be held accountable for the effectiveness and scheduling of the campaign.

Client Research

A campaign that can be taken back to the client is usually the product of the hard work and creative cooperation of many of the station's staff. The creative department is charged with the responsibility of developing copy that is creative enough to sell the listening audience. This effort presents a potential problem in smaller markets where the number of staff members is kept at a minimum to hold costs down, and the salesperson is also the copywriter, with everyone else too busy to help brainstorm ideas for copy or scheduling. In this instance, the salesperson can only do the best possible job at the time. Sales managers should understand that professional selling on the consultant level demands more staff time than if only order takers were on the payroll.

The salesperson also needs to engage in further client research in order to produce an effective schedule that targets the right listener at the right time. In *Sound Management*, Andrew Giangola and Daniel Flamberg write:

> At the heart of any discussion about research lies the retailer's query, "Why should I care about your audience?" Searching for a reason to believe that a station's listeners are primary qualified prospects for a particular establishment, many [media] salespeople are

turning to product use data to answer objections and make the link between a retailer's cash register and their [media outlets].

In many instances retailers have a vague or stereotypical idea about whom their customers are. Even large chain stores often rely more on a generalized "feel" for their customers rather than on survey data. Providing product use and psychographic information which qualifies and defines a store's most likely patrons is a genuine service to clients and positions [the consultant] as a marketing partner rather than a persistent vendor.

A greater understanding of who customers are and why they buy gives a [media] marketer new ways to work with retailers. Using this data, a . . . presentation can more directly offer a client a positioning campaign or suggest a particular brand, service, area, audience or product line that should be a core of the campaign. Better data about listeners/customers can direct [media] copywriters and producers to create spots that a client's core shoppers can relate to.[19]

A Threefold Challenge

If retailers lack access to such needed information, stations, too, can be faced with serious obstacles and may be underequipped in their war of numbers to sell the quality of their audiences to skeptical prospects. The challenge, at this point, to salespeople in small, medium, and large markets is threefold.

1. How to sell a prospective buyer on the value of advertising, as many business people are skeptical about advertising in general, often due to past experiences with unprofessional sales representatives

2. How to overcome skeptical feelings the prospect may have about the medium and the station

3. How to define, confirm, and present to the businessperson those qualitative aspects of your station that can overcome such skeptical feelings

Selling the Value of Advertising   Selling electronic media advertising is difficult, especially to a prospect who is skeptical about any form of advertising. Preparation of a campaign to sell the prospect on the value of a particular station must therefore begin by selling the prospect on the merits of advertising. Most businesspeople do not fully understand what advertising can and cannot do.

All media salespeople should understand as much as they possibly can about advertising. In *Advertising*, William Bolen has written.

Advertising as a term is used by many to cover almost any topic in the promotional area of marketing. This usage of the term is incorrect. The term promotion includes personal selling and advertising along with sales promotion and publicity. But the term advertising does not include personal selling, sales promotion or publicity. Personal selling by its nature involves face-to-face contact with the customer. Advertising, on the other hand, is a marketing vehicle that is designed for the masses, whereas sales promotion, which includes such items as trading stamps and contests, is considered to be supplementary or complementary to the other elements of the promotional effort. Finally, publicity is concerned with the development and placement of information before the public in a non-promotional format (e.g. a news story). It is important to note that advertising should be developed in conjunction with personal selling, sales promotion and publicity when appropriate, but it should not be confused with any of these other promotional approaches. . . . Advertising is any controlled form of impersonal presentation and promotion of ideas, goods or services by an identified sponsor that is used to inform and persuade the selected market.[20]

According to *Advertising Age:*

A company is in business to do two things: To make a product—or provide a service—and sell it at a profit. In making a product, the company is a manufacturer; in selling it, it is a marketer. As a marketer, it uses advertising to inform people of the product's existence and availability and to persuade them to buy it.

Advertising is a sales tool, a substitute for personal selling; a quick and relatively inexpensive way to reach millions of people at one time. It is one element of something called the marketing mix, which also includes such activities as distribution and pricing. As a selling tool, advertising is used in one form or another by nearly every business establishment in the nation.[21]

The Power of the Electronic Media

In terms of understanding *advertising*, radio and TV are arguably more effective in delivering customers to an advertiser's door than are newspapers. To understand this, consider how it is that you have knowledge of *anything* at this point in your lifetime? Why do you know, for example, that 9 times 6 equals 54 or that 8 times 6 equals 48?

The simple answer is because of repeated exposure (repetition) to new information until it became memorized and, hence, a part your continuing knowledge base. You know that 9 times 6 equals 54 because you were exposed to the multiplication tables, probably via the flash card routine, in grade school. Continued exposure (repetition) soon becomes knowledge that you carry with you for life. (However, you never think about this process that caused you to *learn* this information initially.)

The electronic media works in the same way. Radio and TV are affordable enough (have a low enough cost per minute) for merchants to play their message over and over again until the mind of the consumer has been imprinted with the message of the ad, which becomes "old" knowledge or a part of the consumer's own data base. Where do all children want to eat when they go out? McDonald's. When you go to a drive-in, you order a hamburger and a _____. Can you finish it? A Coke. Name five automobiles you see everyday on the streets.

Now, does this "knowledge" become a part of your brain's data base due to the viewing of a newspaper ad? Clearly not. A newspaper ad, no matter how large, represents *one* exposure to a product message; there is no repetition. And you read it only if you choose to. The electronic media exposes you to ads without any action on your part. Their intrusiveness is a plus. Most of the time, you watch or listen to them even though they interrupt your program. You can't selectively pass over these ads as you do the ones in the newspaper, so you are exposed to messages multiple times. If the ads are creative, you might enjoy seeing or hearing them again. How many times do you read a newspaper ad over and over again because it's so cute, creative or attractive to the eye? Do kids want to go to McDonald's because they've read a newspaper ad over and over again? No. McDonald's doesn't use the newspaper for obvious reasons. Newspapers provide price-item, non-image building advertisements designed to appeal to the "now" buyer—the person in the market to whom the merchant wants to appeal with price alone at that immediate moment. No lasting images are built. No new "knowledge" is imparted via repetition. For just one of these print images, newspapers charge an amount that would buy dozens if not hundreds of radio or TV commercials (depending on rates and market size) that could work themselves into the "data base" of the consumer's mind and become permanent knowledge.

Merchants need "price-item" advertising occasionally; but not to the extent that print outbills radio (in some markets, by as much as 10 times). Merchants must be made to realize that radio and TV can more cost-effectively deliver customers to them than can newspapers. The cost per minute of an ad in the electronic media is low enough to enable merchants to afford continual repetition of their messages, which is the only way that particular message will ever become old or permanent knowledge in the minds of the majority of potential customers in their marketplace.

Overcoming Skeptics with Qualitative Information

After helping a prospect understand the merits of advertising, your second area of concern is to assist them in understanding how your station can help. You can do this partly through the presentation of qualitative information, which is the third challenge. How do you define, confirm, and present those qualitative aspects of your station to the prospect? Potential solutions to these problems can come from syndicated or custom research, which *Sound Management* defines as follows:

> *Syndicated research tends to be broad-based surveys, often encompassing other stations and other media. Crosstabulations are made between product and media use, by dayparts and other variables. Data is displayed as indices broken down by age, sex, income, education or geography.*

Syndicated research encompasses national and/or local data available from Simmons, Scarborough, Arbitron (Target AID), Birch Qualitative, International Demographics and Mediamark (MRI). Syndicated research can range from showing station indexes for "Working Women 18–54" listening to drivetime radio, to female homemaker college graduates who buy canned moist dog food.

Customized proprietary research breaks out local survey data specifically for your station and crosstabulates it against local stores. Some services also can reflect psychographic factors and account for geography. The client-specific data determines consumer purchase patterns for local products and services, expands demographics covered and segments the market psychologically. Local samples and in-depth questions supposedly make [customized] research an accurate "reality" representation that easily identifies marketing opportunities for clients.[21]

Normally, such research is not done by small market stations with few employees. However, the more research you can do, regardless of market size, the better you will be able to serve your clients.

Both approaches to localized, retail research have their proponents. Those who favor the syndicated, broad-based approach argue that basic products and services have similar customer profiles regardless of region or market size. The demographic profile (age, sex, income) of a person in Denver buying a high-quality cherry dining room suite, for example, are not dissimilar from those of a buyer in Boston, Houston, or Seattle. The differences that exist are not in the buyer's profile but in the size of the market for the product or service being purchased in that particular city.

Those favoring the customized approach believe that national averages fall short of providing accurate statistics in individual markets. They feel clients are concerned only about data reflecting trends and events occurring locally, not on a nationwide scale.

Research that profiles markets can be contracted out to such service firms as Impact Resource, CHIPS (Consumer Household Intent to Purchase Survey), Leigh Stowell, Management Horizons, or Great Empire Research. Local retail research can also be done by stations and salespeople themselves. Many stations engage in successful research of this nature by encouraging listeners to fill out surveys probing demographics, financial status, and product usage. The difficult part is mixing such research results into literature, facts, and statistics on a station's positioning in the market and then tying the overall presentation into the needs and concerns of the client. Again, such a challenge is lessened in direct proportion to the amount of prospect knowledge a salesperson has, and additional *client* research may be required to understand the marketplace niche.

Whatever approach is taken, the consultant realizes that the client and market research done between visits is perhaps the most difficult part of being a consultant. The order takers and peddlers, however, involve themselves in nothing more than the writing of commercials based on scant information provided by the client. As can be seen, the preparation of copy is only one aspect of campaign preparation.

Devising Commercial Schedules

After completion of the necessary research, the salesperson must devise several commercial schedules of sufficient frequency to reach the target customer desired by the prospect. Several schedules give the client a choice of options, as does the presentation of two distinctly different campaigns. The salesperson could devise a large, medium, and small schedule, but experience tells us that a client given this range of options inevitably chooses the least expensive schedule. Therefore, be sure that the smallest schedule is still large enough to do the job that both you and the client expect.

One technique is to present three schedules of the same dollar amount but structured differently. Such a three-tier proposal causes the client to concentrate on scheduling and store sales goals, rather than on the price of the schedule. For example, one schedule might be for 1 week, the other for 2 weeks, and the third for 3 weeks but all would be for $2,000. If the dollar amount seems high, the client could be split-billed, that is billed half the amount in one month, the other half in the following month.

How to Determine Schedule Size If you have only one recommended schedule for the client, you will need a highly organized presentation that will persuade the client that this is the one and only way to go. The dollar amount of this single schedule, or of the smallest schedule, should be equal to 10% of the value of the identified problem area you are attempting to solve. If the "problem" is intangible (e.g., moving of the store location), sell impact by devising a "double-truck" 13-week radio or TV schedule equivalent to several thousand dollars or the price of a "double-truck" newspaper ad run once per week for 13 weeks. Merchants readily identify with newspaper terminology, so this gives you a chance to explain the power of the electronic media—low CPM and intrusiveness through repetition—by showing how this can be accomplished for the same investment as *one* newspaper impression (ad) per week for the length of the schedule. Moreover, the budget will be sufficient to accomplish the goals of the campaign.

Presenting the Various Schedules The main focus of the presentation should be the largest of the three schedules as the one designed to provide maximum benefits and accomplish the desired campaign goals with the greatest efficiency. This schedule should have the lowest spot rate and provide total audience coverage in all day parts in radio, including prime drive time as well as midday and evening slots. The heaviest concentration of commercials should be scheduled when the most target listeners are tuned in and run with enough frequency to provide maximum reach. If TV, all programs catering to the prospect's desired demographics should be covered.

Schedule the length of the promotional effort for up to 13 weeks or even longer, depending on the needs of the client. Clients usually expect measurable results in less than 13 weeks, and a campaign that meets the proper criteria should produce expected results within that time frame. Gross impressions are crucial at this point, so the schedule must run long enough to produce the desired results. Just make sure that your schedule sells two of the top strengths of the electronic media—impact and intrusiveness.

The medium and small schedules provide fewer commercials at a spot rate higher than the heaviest schedule as determined by the station's printed rate card. A lighter schedule offers a corresponding loss of benefits (for example, fewer commercials targeted to the "heavy user"), with the end result being that a longer time frame is needed to solve the problems or address the needs of the client. This difference should be made clear in the presentation, as it may be more cost-efficient in the long run for the client to confirm the top schedule in order to reap maximum results as soon as possible.

Making the Campaign Creative

The recommended campaign, program, or promotion for which the copy has been written must be creative enough to stand above the airwave clutter that is present in every media market today. The stock copy formula that homogenizes most copy in many markets and that is written for all clients by the same person(s) does not stand out and should not be accepted by the consultant who is truly interested in solving the client's business-related problems that were uncovered during the interview process. The consultant wants a program that he or she can be held accountable for when it produces results because this is the only way long-term relationships are established and a station's business and reputation are built.

Avoiding Stock Copy Of the hundreds of commercials run daily on most stations, only a few are memorable creative productions. The remainder are written and produced as quickly as possible to avoid backlogs, especially at stations with smaller staffs, with little thought given to the overall quality of writing or production. After 30 or so minutes of answering questions for the salesperson during the initial meeting, the businessperson is presented with commercials that essentially sound alike, with the same announcer doing most of them from unexciting, predictable, formula scripts. The information will reach the listening audience in a quasi-professional manner, but it has little chance of registering in the minds of potential customers, much less being remembered. Therefore, the consultant should not be willing to accept the typical commercial production standards that prevail in the industry, but instead strive for the best at all times.

Many TV markets are also notorious for marginal writing and production. Almost inevitably, when compared to network standards, the local commercial appears amateur. Of course, comparing a $500,000 network ad for McDonald's with a $250 local ad for a car dealer is not fair, but the commercials you produce should have as much visual appeal as possible, regardless of budget. Local production houses that work on a small-market budget can often take the creative burden off a small or underequipped TV station production staff.

The media campaign as finally written and produced should address itself to the specific business problem, concern, need, or area that was discussed during the question and answer period in the step of Expressing interest in the client via interview. A grouping of generalized stock-copy commercials cannot possibly address themselves to a specific problem or need. Further, such a pedestrian campaign cannot be traced or held accountable for producing results for the client. In fact, most salespeople worry about "accountable" advertising, as they fear their station will be blamed for the failure of a client's sale or retail promotion. Generalized copy gets them off the hook as they can easily spread the blame for lack of client performance by saying such copy was also in the newspaper and on other stations, as it probably was. Generalized copy does not give specific reasons for people to come to a particular store to spend money. Consultants know this and insist on copy that addresses the client's specific problem. If the campaign is correctly executed, the results are apparent and the salesperson is held accountable—for an advertising campaign that worked! If the interview has gone deep enough, the station's advertising solves a problem that has not been addressed by newspapers and competing stations and you are primarily responsible for producing a campaign that works and produces results.

Returning with the Campaign

The ideal follow-up to the interview process is to return to the client's place of business within four to six business days. You need time to put together a workable solution to the problems or needs uncovered during the interview, but too much time between visits results in the client forgetting about the initial visit. Generally, three to six business days are required for the station to finalize a campaign or a program and for the salesperson to properly research and construct a recommended schedule. Optimally the solution should be brought back to the client within three to four business days and absolutely no later than six business days later.

The solution itself should give the client a choice. The client presented with one "flavor" may not like it. Give an either-or option and present two different campaigns that represent a clear choice. Two different campaigns take time to write and produce or to storyboard, but closing the sale on a tailored program that produces results and brings long-term dollars into the station is surely worth the effort.

Psychology also comes into play here. Presenting two professional programs begins to erase the client's nagging feeling of skepticism. The client recognizes the amount of effort put into the campaign and is encouraged by the fact that a potential answer exists to some major business problem. Give the client a choice. Present two different commercial campaigns with different themes and production voices and allow him or her to choose the one that will do the best job.

The Value-Added Provision   The final campaign or recommended program(s) must be sold with a value-added provision, the service the client will receive after the sale. Many of the reasons we as consumers buy a particular big-ticket product deal more with the guarantee and the feeling of how we'll be treated after our money has been put down than with the actual product itself. The merchant needs to know that the copy will be changed on a regular basis and that the salesperson will call frequently to discuss the progress of the campaign, public responses to it, and the amount of merchandise sold. In fact, the letter S could be added to MEDIA, with the final S standing, of course, for service.

INTERESTING THE CLIENT BY STRESSING BENEFITS: THE PRESENTATION

Customize

May bring flip charts

Snaz it up

The presentation section of the MEDIA system for sales success has three basic objectives.

1. The presentation to your prospect of important or relevant facts about the station that back up your claims, demographics that specifically identify the characteristics of your listening audience, and testimonials from satisfied clients

2. Presentation and explanation of the problem-solving strategy, program, or idea to the client, including the research rationale and based on the information gathered during the initial interview

3. Presentation and explanation of the recommended schedule, including times and dates when all commercials will run, explanation of unit and overall costs, and clarification of all station billing procedures

If these objectives are successfully completed, you have allowed the prospect to see that your service is needed, that you can fulfill that need as well as provide adequate service, and that the problem-solving idea you have developed outweighs the required investment. Skepticism and a sense of risk are still present in the prospect's mind, and the sentiments of "maybe it won't really work" or "maybe I can get it cheaper at another station" may cause second thoughts. Your job as a consultant is to overcome these feelings through accomplishment of the stated objectives.

Returning for the Second Visit

Upon returning for this second visit, greet the prospect and remind him or her of your initial visit, some of the key points discussed, and that you have spent some time in an attempt to develop a results-oriented, customized program. Get the prospect to agree or to reaffirm what was told to you during the first meeting and then begin your presentation.

To accomplish the first objective, some station facts should be presented, as most people like to know something about any company with which they do business. Facts are only facts, however, unless the client is given a reason why those facts are beneficial to the business. A fact without a benefit elicits a "so what" response from the client, whether vocalized or not. Just don't overwhelm the client with too much information on your station. Clients are more interested in ideas that will solve problems and sell inventory or services than they are in hearing how many stations you beat in every daypart.

One way to present this type of information to the prospect is to present a fact to the client, tie in a resulting benefit, and confirm it by saying, "This is what you want, isn't it?" An example follows:

Salesperson: WFUN covers the entire metro area as well as the five major counties surrounding this shopping zone. Our latest survey shows us to be the dominant station in reaching woman 18 to 35, which means that you could target your commercials so a majority of these women could hear them at selected times. Now, your women's wear section is a big profit center for you, so this would be important to you, wouldn't it?

Present a Fact, Then Confirm   Here's the formula that was used: Presenting a fact, bridging it with a transitional phrase such as *which means*, tying in a resulting benefit to that fact, and then confirming the statement with a leading question.

You can't confirm all of the facts you present in this manner, or you'll sound like a broken record repeating "This would be important to you, wouldn't it?" five or six times in a few minutes. Use your common sense and confirm benefits at least twice during the time your station facts are being

Paint word Pictures

presented. Do not overwhelm the prospect with information that may be difficult to understand, and do not use industry language that may be unfamiliar. For example, don't talk about GRPs, cumes, or ADIs unless these terms are necessary and are explained in ordinary language. Remember that the prospect is more interested in results such as moving merchandise than in looking at your ratings book or discussing quarter-hour cumes. Make sure you don't ask the client to agree with any benefit that does not directly tie in with what you know your station can do to help the client. When this step is properly completed, the client believes that the station is credible, will produce the claimed results, and is worth the required investment.

The PAPA Approach   An alternative tactic is Ken Greenwood's PAPA system. The system begins with the salesperson offering a promise (*P*) that is converted to a benefit:

Salesperson: You will reach your target customer of females aged 18 to 24 with this creative and humorous campaign. The benefit of reaching them is selling your shipment of Jantzen swimsuits before the demand for them decreases.

The salesperson then amplifies (*A*) this statement; for example, a comment could be made on the fact that the merchant originally said this benefit would be the goal of any ad campaign he or she would run. Proof (*P*) of performance, that is, showing the client how and why this stated goal will occur, is then provided to the prospect in the form of station research and literature, and action (*A*) is generated by the client agreeing with the salesperson and then with the campaign itself.

The PAPA approach is perhaps more persuasive than the fact-bridge-benefit concept because it concentrates on benefits and proving that they will generate results. In today's competitive selling environment, salespeople need to back up all claims and statements with documentation and research.

Presenting the Campaign

Under this fourth step of interesting the client by stressing benefits, the second objective is to present the problem-solution idea or plan—the campaign prepared especially for this client based on the information gathered during the initial interview and that targets a specific business-related problem. The salesperson is taking the initial information gathered during the interview step and playing back the prospect's ideas:

> **Salesperson:**   As you have seen, our station has produced some impressive results in this market. Our idea, based on what you told me last week, to help you increase your customer traffic and your sales for the holiday period next month is. . .

Then explain the promotion or your idea and its benefits. Confirm some of the benefits, explain the investment required, and play a cassette tape (if you are selling radio) on which you have prepared the two different campaigns that directly address the problem or need you identified.

If you are selling TV, the cost of bringing a spec commercial on videotape would be prohibitive. Instead, bring two completed storyboards or video samples of commercials you have created for other clients. The objective is that the prospect will like one of your spec commercials or storyboards and will decide on one campaign or the other. Stress the benefits of both campaigns. If the prospect favors one, defend the other, and the client will be inclined to defend his or her choice and like it even more.

Those clients who are willing to put you off in lieu of a better or a cheaper idea from someone else are usually turned into believers when presented with logical, concrete solutions to dilemmas. As you stress the benefits of your campaign, you are allowing the prospect to imagine—by listening to your tape or viewing your storyboards—that he or she is already enjoying the benefits of advertising on your station, although no commitment has yet been made and the client may not be advertising on your station at the moment. You can further enhance this effect by drawing a word picture that allows the client to visualize the success of the promotion and all the customer traffic possible from it while the client also enjoys the great word picture drawn by your commercial that displays the business and the colorful products or services being offered.

The client's imagination can be stimulated by something like the following:

> **Salesperson:**   As you can see, this is an exciting promotion. Once we get your commercials on the air, our audience will hear about the great savings they can get and will want to come, look at your merchandise, and register for a chance at winning one of our major prizes. They can register right over here by the counter when they buy their merchandise. Your cash register will be ringing and lots of people will be in the store. . .

You have drawn a word picture that has helped the merchant to imagine the recommended campaign already in progress and the success it is bringing the business. The imagery encourages the merchant to want the promotion now and to give less thought to putting you off until tomorrow, next week, or indefinitely.

You then pause a second and say, "This is what you want, isn't it?" If the client has been straight and honest with you to this point, the answer is affirmative and you are ready for the confirmation. However, before we discuss this final step, we need to look more closely at stressing benefits.

Stressing Benefits   If you have ever purchased a car, what did the salesperson say as soon as you showed any interest at all in a particular unit on the lot? The salesperson might begin by asking you if you would like to sit in a car and see how it feels, but as soon as you seem to be a hot prospect, you are asked the killer question: "Would you like to take a test drive?" By sitting in the car and then driving it, you are imagining it is already your car. You fill your nostrils with that unique new car smell, rub your hands over the upholstery, turn on the radio, and accelerate at your own pace, all the while imagining the look on your friends' faces when they see you in this great new machine. You haven't paid a dime yet, but in your mind that car is yours. The salesperson is trying very hard to close and to get you to commit yourself on the basis of just one step in the selling process, when the benefits of owning this new machine are dancing like a chorus line in your mind.

When the salesclerk at your favorite clothing store spots you pulling items from the rack and holding them up for a better view, he or she asks, "Would you like to try them on?" When you do and then look at yourself in that three-way mirror, those clothes are yours. You have them on and are already imagining where you are going to wear them or how great you will look. You are being sold by the use of this one step in the selling process, the *I* step in MEDIA in which benefits are stressed and desires are built.

Presenting the Proposed Schedules

The last objective of this fourth step in the MEDIA system for sales success is to present the recommended commercial schedule to the prospect and explain the exact times and dates they will run, the total investment required for the campaign, and how it will be billed. (Many consultants present the price of the campaign first, so that the impact of the amount takes on less importance as the facts and benefits are explained.)

The presentation as a whole—station facts and statistics, the campaign idea, and the schedule—should be packaged in a six-to eight-page flip-chart. This makes a good visual aid during the meeting with the prospect. If the entire presentation is not in writing, at least the recommended commercial schedule should be. A listing of the number of commercials scheduled should be noted, on a calendar, for example, or a flip-chart page. The number scheduled per day, week, and month should be noted, with totals for each. The research prompting the commercial placement should be explained in terms of station and client demographics, the final investment (cost) to the prospect should be noted, and billing procedures should be fully explained.

When all of this has been successfully accomplished, you are ready for the fifth and final step of the MEDIA system for sales success, that of confirming or closing the sale. You can ask for the order with a great deal of confidence if you know that you have prepared a results-oriented program based on identified problems, needs, or concerns.

By this time, you certainly should have positioned yourself apart from order takers and peddlers. As a consultant, your credibility, genuine interest in the client, and overall integrity should be readily apparent. The client should be much more relaxed with you now than during your first visit. The client's defensive behavior should now be replaced with a genuine interest in discussing business concerns and solutions in an open atmosphere of trust and respect. In this positive selling environment, confirmation of your plan or idea to help the client's business should be the natural response of what the two of you have been discussing to this point.

ASKING FOR THE ORDER

This last step in the MEDIA process deals with what has traditionally been called the *closing* in the sales presentation. We prefer the term *confirming* the sale, as confirmation is the natural result of the presentation when the salesperson has developed a logical and well-researched proposal based on information gathered during the interview and on meeting the honest needs of the prospect. As a mutual agreement on solutions develops, confirmation is the logical result; as Alessandra and Wexler note, "the separation between proposing and closing is barely perceptible."[23]

Closing sounds like a calculated, manipulative process, something done in lieu of a well-thought-out media plan and client proposal. If the initial interview questions are answered accurately, the prospect is qualified properly, and a professional proposal is made, a salesperson won't have to close; the prospect will have changed his or her mind to agree with what is being presented by the salesperson. A natural progression to the commitment will have transpired.

This last step should take the least amount of time, even though salespeople have traditionally been taught that most of their time should be spent closing. You want a convinced buyer, not a pressured one, and a sale that is a mutual commitment in that the client agrees to do certain things (provide you with copy, pay a monthly statement, and the like) and you in turn produce results while providing good service and open communications from this point on. A consultant eliminates the canned closes and those that rely on pressure rather than logic.

Alessandra and Wexler note that in confirming the sale "radical, complicated or tricky closing techniques are unnecessary. Therein lies the difference between confirming and closing. It is primarily a qualitative distinction that embodies both attitude and behavior."[24]

Confirming by using the MEDIA system is essentially bringing the prospect back to what he or she told you in the initial interview. Remember, you were told the nature of the business problem or need, that the prospect wished to address that area of concern, and was willing to make an investment for doing so. You can therefore remind the person, if there is hesitation, that he or she expressed such concerns and wanted them addressed. You have properly qualified the prospect, have developed a solution, and wish to implement it to produce desired results.

The Difficulty of Confirming

Despite all the literature that has been produced on closing, it is a weak area for some salespeople. Asking for the order is so difficult because this is the point when, after all the hard work that has been invested, the consultant puts everything on the line and risks being rejected. Even if one knows the prospect has been interviewed properly, qualified, and given a professional presentation, the feeling of not wanting to be turned down is most powerful at this point. Many salespeople hesitate for fear of being rejected, just as the client may hesitate for fear of making the wrong decision for his or her business.

But, you cannot blindly hope that the sale will confirm itself with you standing there saying, "Well, do you want to do this . . . or what?" You need to confirm. In most cases, all it takes is confidence in what you have done to ask the question of confirmation. Many lost sales are the direct result of salespeople simply not asking for the order, and so confirming is essential to the MEDIA system.

Confirmation Questions   You attempt to confirm when the client is displaying favorable attitudes and body language toward you and your proposal and you feel certain he or she wants to buy. You should not attempt a confirming question if you are receiving negative feedback from a client. When this occurs, ask open-ended questions to encourage feedback on what went wrong, how, when, and where.

Let's follow through with our earlier example. After you have fully stressed the benefits during the presentation, created desire for your campaign, and explained the scheduling, cost, and billing procedures, you say: "Based on what you have told me, you can see how this will accomplish your goals, can't you?" If the answer is "Yes," you ask a confirming question with no hesitation. Following are several questions you could ask to

would you like to start

confirm that the client wants your proposal and will buy what you have presented.

"Fine. May I then have this opportunity to work with you?" This is a genteel confirmation and as polite a one as you could ever come up with. "No" to this one is difficult if it is delivered with confidence and sincerity.

"Fine. We can start your schedule this Monday or would you rather begin it over the weekend?" This is the alternate choice confirmation. The client is given the choice of starting times rather than a choice between acceptance and rejection.

"Fine. If you'll OK this order, we'll get our creative department working on your copy right away." With this instructional confirmation, you simply instruct the prospect to sign an agreement. Never say *contract*, which is negative as it implies lawyers and technicalities.

"Fine. Do you believe your phone number would be important in the copy?" An affirmative answer to a minor point confirms the fact that the prospect has bought your presentation.

"Fine. Would you like us to mention your large selection of men's wear or should we just stick with women's fashions?" This is a variation of the alternate choice confirmation.

"Fine. I thought so. I'll be sure to bring a written copy of your commercials so you'll have a record for your files. Now, what brand names did you say you wanted to highlight in the women's department?" This is an example of the assumptive confirmation. You assume that the client has bought. Talk as if the sale has been made and ask for the necessary copy information for the commercials.

"Good. Won't it feel great to receive positive feedback from your friends and customers on your new image?" In this type of confirmation, the salesperson asks a subtle question the answer to which implies that the prospect has already bought.

"Well, in fairness to you, let's take a look at the ideas that might cause you to hesitate about starting this program right away and weigh them against the reasons for going ahead with this now." You then draw a line down the middle of your paper and list on the left the ideas or reasons you have detected during the interview that might cause the prospect to hesitate in buying, such as cost or doubts about results. You then list the reasons for starting your proposal as soon as possible on the right side of the page, such as positive image, increase in traffic and sales, and promotional tie-ins. Make sure you have more pros than cons and then say, "You can see that the reasons for going ahead with this program outnumber the negatives. Remember, I'll give you excellent personal service and exciting copy. Shall we begin the schedule this week or the following week?"

"Where do we go from here?" is an open confirming question that allows the prospect to confirm a schedule after agreeing that your logical proposal will meet real needs or solve problems brought up during the interview segment.

These examples represent good ways to close when selling radio, TV, or cable. The significant point is that you have to *ask* a confirming question. You need not be ashamed or timid when asking for a client's business. You are selling a service that you can be proud of and one that you know will work for your client if it is given a fair opportunity to do so. Radio, as an example, doesn't have to be proven. It's been working for decades to build America's businesses. The job of the radio salesperson is to educate businesspeople on the wise and careful use of this most powerful and cost-effective advertising tool.

Trial Confirmations   There is no strict rule about the best time to close. The best time is when you sense that the prospect is prepared to accept your proposal, which is usually at some point during your second visit or after you've asked your client several questions, if you are attempting a confirmation on the first call. If you develop this sense, you have found a good time to attempt a *trial confirmation*, which is a closing question asked at any time before you actually get to the final step. Confirming early is sometimes to your advantage. You don't want to risk boring the client by talking past this point, and you certainly don't want to oversell your station and your ideas, which may be interpreted as pressure.

As an example of a trial confirmation, when the prospect answers "yes" to a leading question, you could say, "Fine. Would you like the voice of a male or a female announcer on your commercials?" You may attempt as many trial confirmations during the sales interview as you can do comfortably and confidently. You may not be successful at any one of these attempts, but you are not losing anything by trying because other confirming opportunities will occur within the sales interview.

Don't Be Afraid of Silence   After a confirming question, trial confirmation, or assumptive question, a pregnant pause may occur. Remember that silence can be productive. Often, salespeople are made uncomfortable by silence and begin talking themselves out of the sale by creating self-doubt in the mind of the prospect. The salesperson is giving an opinion when none was asked for. This is nothing more than nervous talk to avoid confirming the sale and setting oneself up for possible rejection. As sales trainer Danielle Kennedy has noted, "Talking is an avoidance behavior when we are afraid to ask."

If You are Making a One-Stop Call and You Have the Order, Get the Proper Copy Information!   If you make a one-stop call on a prospect and the prospect turns into a client and agrees to your proposal, you cannot leave before you obtain the proper copy information that will enable either you or the creative department to write appropriate commercials. Since you did not interview and qualify the prospect, the information that an interview would have provided must now be gathered so that effective commercials can be drafted. (Refer to Chapter 2 for discussion of appropriate one-stop calls.)

The Assumptive Question   This assumptive question close is always worded "You do want this, don't you?" for example, "You do want more young, married women just starting families to shop in your store, don't you?" The prospect who answers "yes" is confirming your proposal. You could also say, "Long-range growth in your business at this location is more important to you than a monthly statement from our station, isn't it?" If the answer is "yes," you have a confirmation.

Sales Resistance   Today's buyer is becoming increasingly discriminating in deciding where advertising money is spent. Sales resistance is higher, and bringing clients to a point of positive decision is more difficult. Therefore, the interview and the proposal leading to a confirmation becomes even more important. Consultants realize that the emphasis is not on closing, but on the entire MEDIA sales process. To again quote Alessandra and Wexler, "The confirmation is just the beginning of a mutual commitment to have an on-going business relationship."[25]

The media salesperson's planning, hard work and careful preparation, and presentation are all designed to confirm the prospect's agreement to buy, so that you can begin solving business-related problems. Your best solutions to a client's problem do absolutely no good if they go unused. Therefore, a confirmation is the climax of the entire sales effort. Because very few prospects volunteer to buy, salespeople have to learn how to conduct a confident confirmation flowing from a competent proposal.

Building the Consultative Relationship

Because a consultant thrives on being able to do more for clients than anybody else is doing, calling on a prospect without the thought of that person becoming either a new client or a better client in terms of an increased advertising program makes little sense. *Current clients are one of the best sources for new revenue.* Even service calls, when new copy is being gathered for a previously sold account, should be selling calls. The salesperson who is establishing a relationship of trust with the businessperson is continually gathering new information about the business that will assist in doing an even better job of selling merchandise for the client; in a sense, the salesperson is always in a state of information gathering similar to the initial visit with the account when prospect knowledge was being gathered for the very first time. As this knowledge accumulates, the salesperson sees how the station can better serve the client, and each service call can be a selling opportunity for additional time on the station. Radio and TV stations usually have certain open time slots that could serve the needs of a particular client, depending on the time of day they want to advertise, the audience they wish to reach, and other variables.

During a service call, you can attempt to add commercials to an existing schedule if the addition of such time fits into the client's overall marketing scheme. Some salespeople shudder at this concept and feel that once a client is sold they are sold, and the salesperson should never again tamper with the schedule. Such a feeling does not do justice to the changing conditions of the marketplace, such as the need for merchants to increase their schedules during certain peak periods of retail activity. Many salespeople are just not confident enough of their service to ask for additional commercials, even though clients may be looking to them for advice. Forget the notion that you are a public relations person. You're there to increase the client's business through advertising.

Another notion to forget is that you are now the client's buddy just because you have sold something to him or her. Your role has not changed from professional salesperson to one engaged in happy talk during your service calls so as not to offend your new "friend" with further attempts at closing or selling. You are no friend at all if you don't continue to identify and solve problems, and you don't do that with inane talk designed to develop superficial, meaningless relationships that are more a cover for your own ineptitude than a genuine striving for friendship. Consultants confirm well because they ask the right qualifying questions initially. Some are confident enough to explain in their opening statements exactly what they intend to do. Their philosophy is to open each sales call with the close in mind: "I am calling on you today with the view of getting your order for my station, provided I can prove its value to you and we can help you with your business."

SUMMARY: CONCLUDING THOUGHTS ON THE MEDIA SYSTEM

You have now been exposd to a selling system that, when used properly, can help you attain the respect and the financial security you seek. Every good salesperson knows that selling is not a hit-or-miss proposition. He or she knows the value of formulas and how to use them to meet the needs of their clients.

You can find this kind of success selling radio, TV, or cable, but the road to sales success is littered with the empty dreams of those who were content with mediocrity and those who felt that the only thing necessary to sales success is a good personality. Many former sales trainees found procedures boring and systems dull. Who needs structure when they're the life of every party and full of natural personality? Everybody who wants to succeed in a sales career.

NOTES

1. *Successful Sales Managing* (New York: Dun and Bradstreet, 1970), p. 81.

2. Robert Miller and Stephen E. Heiman with Tad Tuleja, *Strategic Selling* (New York, Warner Books, 1985), pp. 263–64. © 1985 by Miller Heiman & Associates. By permission of William Morrow & Company.

3. Reprinted by permission of Warner Books/New York from *Winning Moves: The Body Language of Selling* © 1984 by Ken Delmar.

4. Ibid., pp. 37–38.

5. Ibid., p. 251.

6. From the *Non-Manipulative* audiocassette program by Tony Alessandra and Phil Wexler. © ℗ Nightingale-Conant Corp., 7300 No. Lehigh, Chicago, IL 60648.

7. Ibid.

8. Ibid.

9. Excerpts from *Integrity Selling* by Ron Willingham. Copyright © 1987 Ron Willingham. Reprinted by permission of Doubleday, a division of Bantam, Doubleday, Dell Publishing Group, Inc.

10. Ibid., p. 19.

11. Ibid., p. 17.

12. Ibid., p. 20.

13. Ibid., p. 20.

14. Ibid., p. 18.

15. Ibid., p. 21.

16. Mark McCormack, *What They Don't Teach You at Harvard Business School* (New York: Bantam Books, 1984), pp. 130–31.

17. Miller and Heiman, p. 264.

18. Ibid., pp. 26–266.

19. Andrew Giangola and Daniel Flamberg, "Assessing New Retail Research." *Sound Management* (July, 1986): 8–15.

20. William H. Bolen, *Advertising* (New York: John Wiley & Sons, 1984), pp. 4–5.

21. *The New World of Advertising* (Chicago: Crain Books, 1975), p. 17.

22. Giangola and Flamberg, pp. 8–15.

23. Alessandra and Wexler.

24. Ibid.

25. Alessandra and Wexler.

Chapter 7

HANDLING OBJECTIONS AND USING THE MEDIA SYSTEM

All professional salespeople know that objections will be raised sometime during the course of the MEDIA system for sales success. Objections may come in the form of simple questions, or they may take the form of derogatory comments about the service or the station.

WELCOMING OBJECTIONS

Objections are not only to be expected and planned for, they should also be welcomed. They serve as warning signals that the prospect and the salesperson have diverged in their thinking and are on different frequencies. Objections give the consultant the opportunity to determine what went wrong, correct the problem, and set the course for agreement. No one wants a client who still has major doubts or is unsure of the investment being undertaken. Consultants want satisfied clients, not clients pressured into buying something they feel they don't need. Consequently, view objections as routine in the course of the selling process and not as something atypical to be feared or avoided.

Order takers and peddlers fear objections and melt like butter when they encounter them. Media consultants, however, anticipate objections and therefore show little or no emotion when they arise. Handling objections in this stoic, calm manner by actually welcoming them works in favor of the consultant. It establishes a nonthreatening environment in which the problem or question can be talked out and the salesperson has a chance to show the client just why he or she is a consultant by listening, being empathetic, and supporting the client. This further positions the salesperson apart from the order takers and peddlers as he or she and the client begin working together to come up with the best possible solutions for the client's business. During this time, the salesperson demonstrates a personal commitment to the media service being sold, lets the client know that accountability for producing results is expected, and in general shows the client that an entire service system will go into place after the sale.

GENUINE AND HOPELESS OBJECTIONS

With the exception of two types of objections, all objections and feelings can be addressed. Objections that are genuine and objections that are hopeless cannot and should not be overcome. The former deals with business problems and concerns, and the latter involves personal problems that the salesperson must necessarily avoid.

Genuine Objections   business related

Examples of *genuine* problems would be the businessperson filing for bankruptcy, something the salesperson can do nothing about, or a merchant's store burning down. In the case of the ruined store—a case that befalls every salesperson at one time or the other—immediate advertising is the furthest thing from the merchant's mind, even if a reopening is planned. Allow the merchant to collect his or her thoughts and then return when you sense the time is right. In the case of the bankruptcy, a liquidation sale may be possible, but make sure you get your money up front. The point is that sometimes there are genuine objections that the salesperson cannot possibly overcome. Common sense can tell you what is genuine and what is not.

Hopeless Objections   personal

Hopeless objections involve the emotions of the client and deal with personal or family life. When these are genuinely encountered (as opposed to the old "my dog died" routine just to get rid of you), the salesperson should leave, allow the client to work out the problems, and return at a time when the client can concentrate on effectively promoting the business. Situations that prevent the client from making a clear decision include the death of a family member, the arrest of a family member, and an illness or injury befalling a business partner. Common sense tells you to leave when you learn of this information during a sales call and to return at a later date.

HANDLING OTHER OBJECTIONS

However, most objections do not fall in those insurmountable categories. When ordinary objections occur the salesperson can effectively utilize several techniques.

Answering Objections with Questions

Because any one question has multiple answers, asking "who, what, where, when, why" can tell the consultant the specifics of the prospect's feelings at the moment. A direct answer sometimes diffuses an objection but doesn't get at the real issue. Besides, direct answers to objections often turn into a nasty game of one-upmanship. The salesperson fields an objection; the prospect brings up another one. The salesperson fields that and the prospect bats out another one. The business meeting becomes a game of baseball to see if the salesperson can field more objections than the prospect can slug.

Asking questions may be a better way of handling objections than direct answers. An example of answering an objection with a question would be:

Objection: I can't buy. We're going to go out of business.

Answer: Oh? When do you plan to do this? Within six months or is this a long-term situation?

This type of response lets the salesperson know exactly what the client is thinking. Many merchants go out of business for years.

Handling Objections by Welcoming Them

Another method of handling objections is to make a point of welcoming them before you begin asking questions. All objections are based on what clients feel to be valid and objective concerns. Many salespeople empathize with these concerns by agreeing with the client's feelings. Aside from being inoffensive, a salesperson who welcomes an objection tends to disarm the client. Have you ever been in an argument with a friend or a family member and said something like, "I understand how you're feeling. The way I look at it, though. . ." The argument then became more of a conversation. You were not accusatory by welcoming the objection in that manner, nor were you being defensive. You were, knowingly or not, establishing a common ground for further discussion.

The same psychology works with a client. If the client objects to your price or your idea or whatever, your first reaction could be to welcome or cushion this feeling through empathetic attention to the statement: "Many of our current clients have brought up that very objection before they bought . . ." or "I can see why you would say that. Actually, before I started working at the station, I thought the very same thing. . . ." A final example of nondefensive objection handling would be: "I'm glad you brought that up because I felt I may not have fully explained that point earlier. . . ."

If you choose to welcome the objection, don't forget to follow up by asking questions. If you just welcome the objection by saying something like "Many current clients thought the same thing until they bought" and do not follow up, you would be relying on a band wagon effect that "if other people bought after objecting to the same thing I did, then I better buy too!" This attitude closes the opportunity for the salesperson to hear more about the objection from the prospect.

Prospects like questions because this approach shows interest in them. A manipulative sales technique, many feel, is to cushion and then respond without questioning. The client may think, "If this person was really interested, he or she would be asking me questions."

The Kaufman Closing and Objection-Handling Method

In the cassette program *52 Ways to Close Radio Sales*, sales consultant Richard Kaufman explains that any techniques used must be part of the salesperson, not just a memorized pitch, and suggests role playing as the most efficient way to master the confirming and objection-handling stages of the sales process. He recommends that the salesperson carry:

1. A station media kit containing all relevant research on demographics, coverage maps, and promotional literature

2. Testimonial letters and two lists of station advertisers for the past year, one listing in alphabetical order and the other alphabetized by category

3. All relevant RAB material on the limitations of competitive media and Starch research on newspaper advertising readership

With these materials on hand to assist in addressing specific objections and concerns, Kaufman provides an initial word of advice. Whenever an objection is received from a prospect, pause rather than defensively providing an immediate answer. After a few moments:

1. Clarify the objection. Repeat back to the prospect what he or she has just said. If the prospect says that radio is too expensive, first pause and then say, "What you're saying, then, is that you feel this package is too expensive?"

2. Isolate and eliminate all other objections. After the client agrees that the proposal seems too expensive, say, "Aside from this proposal being too

expensive, how does everything else appeal to you?" If everything else is fine, proceed to the next step.

3. The commitment close is: "If I can rework the package so that the cost is more suitable, can we get you started next week?" The client must answer in the affirmative for you to continue. If the answer is negative, then the salesperson must find the other objection(s): "Is there anything else you don't like about this program?" The prospect may say he or she doesn't believe that radio works. In that case, go back to step one and clarify this objection, then proceed again through steps two and three. The salesperson must continually isolate and eliminate all objections. Once the prospect agrees that he or she would start if convinced that radio worked and that it is affordable, the salesperson would proceed to step four.

4. Answer and resolve the objection(s). Each objection must be addressed by using the station and RAB information and whatever else the salesperson has. After you have resolved the objection, proceed to the final step.

5. Have your prospect agree that the objection has been answered: "Now, this falls more into your budget, doesn't it?" or "You can see now how advertising on radio and on my station in particular makes sense, can't you?"

Then, Kaufman suggests, place a pen on your agreement and walk away. Silence would also be effective, as the confirmation is over. You're just waiting for the prospect to become a client by officially signing the station agreement.

The DANCER Approach to Objection Handling

Following a client's objection, the salesperson, after asking any appropriate questions, may wish to satisfy the concerns of the client by fully addressing the objection itself. An easy-to-remember mnemonic can assist the salesperson in overcoming all but the genuine and hopeless types of objections previously discussed.

D. *Deny* the objection or accusation if it is totally unfounded or untrue and then provide a complete follow-up explanation.

Objection:	I wouldn't buy your station. You guys bad-mouth all the other stations and give free advertising to your favorite clients and I know I'm not one of them!
Response:	As much as I respect your opinions, that simply is not the case. . . .

A. *Admit* to what the client says if it is true. When this situation occurs, the client has usually come up with an unsubstantiated accusation that he or she feels is valid.

Objection: I won't buy from your station. You're directional!

Response: That's right. We are directional. And, our directional signal covers the major population areas where your customers live. . . .

N. *Nothing.* Allow for a few moments of silence, and the client may answer his or her own objection.

C. *Call* your sales manager. If an objection is raised to which you cannot honestly respond, don't attempt to bull your way through. Call your sales manager and get an immediate answer. Then ask your prospect, "Are you satisfied that my sales manager has given us the appropriate information for us to continue?"

E. *Explain* the question raised during the objection. Most responses to client concerns contain an element of explanation.

R. *Reverse* the argument or objection. Often an objection can be turned around to the advantage of the salesperson.

Objection: I can't buy your station. Your rates are too high. .

Response: Even though our rates on a per commercial basis seem to be the highest in the area, the station CPM (cost per thousand) is lower than any other station and the local newspaper. So, the fact that the rates are high is a reason to buy, because those rates translate into more people reached for the money spent.

Don't Ask Why   When responding to objections of any type, do not ask a prospect why he or she feels a particular way. A *why* question causes a person to respond with defensive behavior and often rationalizations for having a certain feeling. Forcing someone to explain feelings is not fair, but asking *what* a reason might be to cause a certain way of thinking is reasonable and allows a direct reason to be given as an answer.

Ask what the reason is that makes a prospect feel a certain way or what makes them feel that way. Such questions are more likely to be answered directly and nondefensively.

Addressing Hidden Objections

Effectively handling objections enables the salesperson to create the proper environment in which feelings and objections can be discussed. Once an objection is answered to the satisfaction of the client, the salesperson may still not have completed the transaction, as the client may have more deeply hidden objections. As noted in Kaufman's technique, the salesperson must continually isolate and eliminate all objections.

A prospect may raise an objection because he or she may feel uncomfortable about bringing up what is viewed as a key or central issue. The salesperson then needs to ask the client if anything else could prevent approving the proposal and beginning the campaign to solve whatever the problem is as soon as possible. If not, the client is probably ready to buy. Stalling or hemming and hawing probably means the businessperson has an uncomfortable feeling about something but doesn't want to take the time to discuss it with the salesperson.

Letting the Client Say "No"   If a presentation has gone this far, the media consultant has an opportunity to smoke out the real objection the client has by asking a very basic and straightforward question. Because you know that the client feels uncomfortable about something and you know that businesspeople basically dislike saying "No" to a salesperson, the sales representative can say, "I understand that you have some apprehensions about some of the things we are discussing here today. Please, if you are uncomfortable in any way about this proposal or my station, feel free to say 'no' to me so I won't have to take up any more of your time."

The salesperson who leaves with any answer other than "yes" has left with "no." A callback is almost always a "no," and the salesperson who leaves with a promise to return after the client has "thought about it" leaves with no opportunity to isolate and answer what may be the biggest objection the client has. By giving the client permission to say "no," the salesperson enables the prospect to feel more comfortable and off the hook.

The salesperson can then say, "Fine. Now exactly what is it that caused you to reject this proposal?" The client tends to respond with whatever feeling has been harbored. The salesperson who is able to respond to that feeling still may be able to make a sale and therefore a new client that day. If not, what to work on in the interim before another call is made on the client is apparent.

"I Want to Think about It"

We ought to mention well-intentioned clients who tell salespeople that they honestly would like to think about a proposal or a campaign before they begin running it on the air. Those who tell you this after you have specifically designed a campaign for them that addresses itself to the indigenous business problems of that particular business either were not being totally honest with you when they discussed their goals, concerns, and problems during the initial interview, or, for whatever reason, they simply don't want

their problems taken care of in terms of customer traffic responding to a campaign. This latter point is difficult to imagine, but salespeople encounter clients who want to think about it and who can't seem to make a decision during the confirming step.

When this situation occurs, attempting to isolate the real objection is to the salesperson's advantage. Businesspeople, as tied up with details and business concerns as they are, honestly do want to think about a station's proposal because they do want more traffic and sales and a positive image projected in their marketplace. Because they are so busy, however, once the salesperson leaves their place of business, they return to their priorities and forget about the radio or TV station. Even though the client planned on thinking about it or talking with a partner about it, the campaign likely will be forgotten. Then, a few days later, in walks the media rep, all ready for the answer that the client was supposed to have carefully considered and thought about for the past few days.

The prospect may admit that he or she has had no time to consider the proposal due to pressing business concerns, but is more likely to tell the salesperson a little white lie. Not wanting to admit to forgetting about the proposal and not wanting to spend much more time discussing something that honestly was forgotten, the businessperson says, "It's good to see you again. You know, about that proposal we discussed last Tuesday . . . well, you know, I don't think the timing is quite right now. It really sounds interesting, but I think we'll pass this time. I have some money tied up in other areas and it's just impossible to transfer it around. Tell you what. Next time you're in the area or you have some other ideas, come on by and maybe we can do something then."

The salesperson has just lost another sale without any chance of isolating an objection. That's precisely why it is advisable to get either a "yes" or a "no" when asking for an order from the prospect. A chance to overcome real or hidden objections is then possible.

Objections Cultivate Customers

All successful salespeople look forward to objections and use them to cultivate customers and build trust and respect. In *How to Make Big Money Selling*, Joe Gandolfo states:

> Some people have a difficult time making decisions that are out of their field of expertise. This is true even with people who make big decisions every day in their own businesses. For example, I have had surgeons who couldn't decide on a life insurance policy; yet these same individuals make split-second life-and-death decisions in the operating room doing open-heart surgery. . . .
>
> In these cases, the mental gymnastics are "If I don't spend my money, I'm in the same position as before I heard the sales presentation. However, if I do spend my money, there's a chance I might spend it unwisely." It's your job as a salesperson to convince these people that the wrong decision is to do nothing.[1]

Some Callbacks Are Lucrative

However, it would be a mistake to assume that all callbacks are pointless. Salespeople are going to close a certain percentage of callbacks. Jon Doherty's *The Magic of Thinking Big in Selling* states that salespeople can close nine of ten callbacks if they possess the right attitude.

> Here's a simple test item for you to think about: In most instances, if a prospect says to you, "I need the time to think it over. Drop by tomorrow for my answer," you might expect:
>
> a) to make a sale on the following day
> b) to receive a series of stalls by the prospect
> c) to wind up without a sale
> d) to gain a customer for life

The correct answers are both "b" and "c." A "see you tomorrow" response usually means your prospect isn't interested in buying and wants to get rid of you. Remember, a big-thinking salesperson records sales, not stalls or rejections.

So, how do you sell callbacks? By leaving the door open for a return visit. Don't antagonize your prospect by trying to force a decision too soon. Instead, when you return, have something "new" to offer that wasn't a part of your initial proposal—something that shows you have done some research and creative thinking since your initial meeting.[2]

The consultant always answers objections and closes with confidence. Self-confidence is a byproduct of understanding the MEDIA system for sales success. Objections arise, but they can be handled. Problems during the presentation are inevitable, but with self-confidence comes the ability to deal with the unexpected in a mature manner.

Recognize, too, that many merchants and advertising agencies do not have the budget to build immediate frequency, and producing desired results may take longer with some clients than with others. Whether copy is designed to solve an identified and specific area of concern or the client's wish is to advertise for consistent traffic or just a seasonal sale, make sure clients understand that a radio or TV campaign needs a sufficient budget to work most effectively and that a lower budget means taking longer to build the desired frequency to make the number of impressions that produce results.

In other words, be sensitive to clients but answer objections and close with confidence. You have the system to do so successfully.

USING MEDIA IN TV AND CABLE

The MEDIA system for sales success was presented in the previous chapter primarily from the standpoint of the radio salesperson making the sales presentation directly to a local business owner or manager. This method has been chosen because this is the situation that confronts radio salespeople employed by the greatest number of the 8,500 commercial radio stations in the United States.

For example, New York State is home to New York City, the number one radio market in the nation, but the 30 commercial radio stations in New York City account for only about 10 percent of the some 310 commercial radio stations in the state. After New York City, the market sizes in that state drop quickly: Buffalo has 18 commercial radio stations, Syracuse has 16, and Albany and Rochester each have 13. These four markets account for 77 radio stations of the 310 in New York State, leaving 233 radio stations located in smaller population centers.[3]

Los Angeles, the second largest radio and television market in the country, has 37 radio stations listed for its market. San Francisco is next in California in number of radio stations with 26, San Diego has 19, Sacramento shows 18, Fresno has 17, and Santa Barbara and Bakersfield each list 11 commercial radio stations. The commercial radio stations in these seven markets adds up to a total of 139 commercial radio stations. Of the 491 commercial radio stations in California, 352 commercial radio stations are not located in its seven largest markets.[4]

Illinois is home to the third largest radio and television market in the country, Chicago, which has 32 commercial radio stations. After Chicago, market size drops dramatically, with 8 commercial radio stations in Rockford, and 7 each in Springfield, Peoria, and Champaign-Urbana. Thus, 32 of the 271 commercial radio stations in Illinois are located in the very large Chicago metropolitan area, and 239 commercial radio stations are elsewhere in the state.[5]

The Smaller the Market, the Greater the Need for Direct Selling

The larger the market, the less often the radio (or television or cable) salesperson sells directly to the business owner. Conversely, as market size decreases, the more often the broadcast salesperson is called on to sell directly to the individual business owner or manager, rather than through an intermediary such as an advertising agency. An overwhelming number of the more than 8,500 commercial radio stations (AM and FM) are located outside the major population centers of the country in markets with one to seven commercial radio stations in each market. Therefore, broadcast salespeople employed in the majority of radio stations find their sales presentation capability must begin with the face-to-face sales call on the business owner or manager who decides the advertising strategy for the company.

However, the same sales capability that must be learned in order to succeed with the business owner serves the radio, TV, or cable salesperson in good stead when dealing with the business owner's surrogate who is capable of making advertising decisions for the business. The broadcast salesperson dealing with these surrogates adapts the basic process for the level at which he or she is selling. The broadcast salesperson, properly backgrounded and armed with the foundation laid in earlier chapters, can adapt the MEDIA process to the selling task at hand. The first connecting link that must be preserved is the consultant approach, wherein the broadcast salesperson aims at becoming an advertising consultant to the potential advertising client; the second link is in the broadcast salesperson not fearing to make the campaign an accountable one, in which the effect of the advertising may be measured and evaluated as a basis for further advertising decisions.

Such a procedure steers the salesperson toward a client-centered presentation that is backed up by product knowledge, prospect knowledge, knowledge of sales psychology, and enough patience to look toward the long-range benefit and the kind of sale that is a good buy for the advertiser and thus a good sale for the salesperson. Tailoring such an approach is easier when the salesperson is dealing directly with the individual business owner or manager who makes the advertising decisions; however, the basics of the system work as well with sales presentations to others charged with advising the client company, such as advertising agency buyers and account executives or advertising directors.

The Smaller the Market, the Less the Need for Ratings

In selling radio advertising to the individual business owner in a small market, the use of ratings material is less. Less ratings material is available to the small market radio salesperson, and the potential client is less knowledgeable about the meaning of ratings information. Prospects who don't comprehend the significance of ratings material may become defensive and feel they are being pushed into a corner.

By the same token, the small market radio salesperson is not likely to find much success with flip-card presentations of the advantages of the campaign. The small-town merchant is not accustomed to doing business with his or her clientele on such a basis and might regard such attempts to win business from his or her company as high pressure tactics.

The Larger the Market, the More Formal the Presentation

As market size increases, more formality is introduced into the sales process, and flip-card presentations become more usable and valuable to point out the advantages of the salesperson's station and the overall campaign. As the market size increases and the number of competing media outlets increases (radio stations, television station or stations, newspaper), the individual business owner or manager must by necessity become more aware of the costs of competitive media, the makeup of the various audiences offered, and the differences between and within competitive media.

When the market size is large enough to have television stations in addition to radio stations and newspapers, the television salesperson can use audience breakdown figures for various spot announcement availabilities and introduce comparative measures such as gross impressions to be gained by a campaign, and cost per rating point. (These and other elements of the broadened sales campaign are discussed in chapter 5.)

The larger the market, the more money is involved in an advertising campaign, due to higher media rates for delivery of larger audiences. The amount of good research information available about the salesperson's own broadcast outlet is greater, as is the competition for the potential client's advertising budget. The broadcast salesperson likewise tailors a more sophisticated presentation with flip-cards, advertising success stories, and research information to bolster the sales effort.

Selling Cable

The cable television salesperson in all of these markets focuses more on the overall medium's capability for audience and points out the audience's long, daily exposure to the overall television medium and thus to the various cable channels. With the scarcity of definitive ratings research information, the cable television salesperson focuses more on the concept of television advertising and the ability to purchase television exposure at low price in availabilities that are adjacent to advertising slots bought by national advertisers. By association with these national advertisers, who have large budgets and the capability to pick and choose their advertising outlets, the cable availabilities look more promising to the local businessperson. If a local business's commercials are alongside the commercials of General Motors, Beatrice, and United Airlines, the client is inclined to feel that the advertising times must be good because these companies with very large advertising budgets do not intentionally waste advertising dollars. The cable television salesperson also focuses on the relative cost of cable television channel advertising as compared with the cost of broadcast television advertising in the same market, assuming the market has a television station or stations.

Dealing with Advertising Agencies

Thus far we have dealt mainly with the retail division of the local sales portion of the overall broadcast sales field. As market size increases, a larger and larger share of the sales presentations are made through advertising agencies employed by the client businesses to handle their overall advertising needs. The basic tenets of the MEDIA process continue to direct the salesperson's efforts, but the approach and method must vary because of the third party involved.

The Media Buyer   The first person with whom the broadcast salesperson is likely to deal at the advertising agency (whether local, regional, or national in scope) is the *media buyer*. The task of this person is to know or learn the media in the markets that have been chosen for advertising buys and to purchase time or availabilities on the proper mix of media outlets to accomplish the advertising aims set by those who decided the campaign goals and limits. In a local agency, the media buyer purchases media advertising capability in that market only, and the media buyer may also be the account executive for the client business; in fact, the buyer may be a partner or owner of the agency.

If the local businesses are represented by advertising agencies, the broadcast salesperson deals with the agency to achieve a share (or a greater share) of the client's business. The media buyer determines which media outlets are purchased by the agency on behalf of the client, and no media salesperson wishes to antagonize a media buyer who can shut out the salesperson's station or cable system from future advertising buys not only for that client but also for other agency clients. Therefore, the broadcast salesperson must call on the media buyers at the advertising agencies representing clients on his or her account list.

For the first call and subsequent calls on the media buyer, the broadcast salesperson should follow the basic tenets of the MEDIA process with minor alterations. The broadcast salesperson wants to be known to the buyers and wants to be sure the media buyers have the latest information on his or her station in order to put the station in a favorable position on upcoming buys. Each such call is a subtle reminder that the salesperson's firm is ready and willing to be the advertising outlet for the client. At the same time, the salesperson attempts to gain, through a modified client interview, information about the needs of the businesses represented by the particular advertising agency. This information goes into the salesperson's file on that client (and agency) so the next call can take advantage of the information already gained.

The Agency Account Executive   Working through the media buyer, the broadcast salesperson wishes to expand direct contact to the next level in the agency, the account executive in charge of the advertising accounts of the particular business. The *account executive* is the individual at the advertising agency who supervises the agency's efforts on behalf of the client's advertising—planning the campaign, gaining the advertiser's business, proposing and developing the advertising campaigns, seeing that these campaigns are implemented through the step of selecting the media mix for the campaign, and working with the media buyer to see that the campaign aims are carried out.

The more involved the broadcast salesperson can become in dealing with the account executive for the particular client on the account list, the more capability the broadcast salesperson has to influence the allocation of advertising campaign expenditures. Moreover, the broadcast salesperson who has begun to deal with the account executive can learn more about the advertiser's problems and needs and become more capable of helping to generate specific campaigns.

Through the rapport built with the account executive, the salesperson builds a bridge that he or she hopes can be crossed to gain access to the advertising director for the business and perhaps to other management personnel to gain more information about the client business plans, as well as needs and areas where the knowledgeable broadcast salesperson can interact better and begin to employ a more consultative approach to the client business advertising. The more involved the broadcast salesperson can be be with the central portion of the business's advertising, the more beneficial the salesperson's input into the advertising process can be and the more financially rewarding that client account can be to the salesperson's revenue.

Perseverance   The broadcast salesperson working through advertising agency personnel has to persevere to get centrally involved in the business's advertising budget and plans. The system is built one step at a time, with each step dependent on the sure foundation of the previous step, in the same manner the salesperson builds a relationship with the retail client. The salesperson has to proceed from being just another seller to the position of advertising consultant working for the good of the business to provide effective advertising that meets problems and needs of the client.

SUMMARY

Handling objections need not be threatening nor intimidating. Objections are a normal and expected part of the selling process. By utilizing the approaches discussed in this chapter, the media consultant should be prepared to effectively answer all but the most genuine and personal of objections. Trained professionals always answer objections and confirm the sale with confidence by using the MEDIA system in direct selling situations with either local or regional clients or media buyers at advertising agencies.

NOTES

1. Joe Gandolfo, *How to Make Big Money Selling* (New York: Harper & Row, 1984), pp. 123–24.

2. From *The Magic of Thinking Big in Selling,* by Jan Doherty with Robert G. Hoehn, © 1983. Reprinted by permission of the publisher, Prentice-Hall, Inc., Englewood Cliffs, N.J.

3. *Broadcasting/Cablecasting Yearbook, 1984,* (Washington, DC: Broadcasting Publications, 1984), pp. B170–80.

4. Ibid., pp. B22–40.

5. Ibid., pp. B75–85.

Chapter 8

PROFESSIONAL COPYWRITING, CLIENT SERVICE, AND INTEROFFICE RELATIONSHIPS

EFFECTIVE COMMERCIALS

When the broadcast salesperson has completed the sale of time for presentation of the advertiser's message, the focus of attention then shifts to the message that will occupy that time. Whether the broadcast outlet is a radio station, a television station, or a cable television system, this advertiser message is the star of the entire sales process. This commercial is expected to do one or more of the following:

- Gain listener or viewer attention
- Inform listeners or viewers
- Make a favorable impression for a product or company
- Increase traffic at the sponsor's location
- Change the attitudes of people in the audience

When an advertiser is represented by an advertising agency, the agency determines the content of commercials for the advertiser and either produces them or has them produced. The broadcast salesperson usually does not have input in this process. The advertising agency proposes and carries out the advertiser's advertising campaign.

When the broadcast salesperson deals directly with the advertiser, however, the advertiser may or may not have commercials already prepared. If the advertiser uses prepared commercials, then the salesperson does not get involved.

When the advertiser needs to have commercials prepared by the broadcast outlet employing the salesperson, the broadcast salesperson becomes the client's representative to the people who prepare and produce the advertiser's commercials. In this situation, the salesperson needs to guide the development of commercials that effectively present the advertiser's message to the intended audience.

When a television advertiser does not use an advertising agency, the production cost of the commercials is normally billed to the advertiser as an additional one-time charge separate from the costs for the time slots purchased. Commercials for the retail client may be produced by an outside production company, but more often are produced by the station's staff or an in-house production company owned by the station.

In radio advertising, the radio station staff generally produces commercials for the advertiser who is not represented by an agency. In both television and radio, the salesperson is the link to the client and normally decides which of the suggested approaches best fills client needs or selects the best two or three suggested approaches for submission to the client for approval.

In smaller radio markets, the salesperson may even write the commercials for some clients. Thus, the salesperson who wishes to become an advertising consultant to clients must know what constitutes a good commercial.

It would be impossible for this book to include everything needed to become an adept writer of commercials. Instead, we provide checkpoints for the salesperson who is acting as the advertising client's representative in seeing that effective commercials are written and produced.

Commercial Checkpoints

1. Does the commercial focus on the client's product or service? This question might seem unnecessary, especially as the first checkpoint, but a great many commercials do not adequately focus on the client's product or service.

2. If the commercial really sounds great, could you remove the client product or service and still have it sound great? This question follows up on the first. Too often, those charged with preparation of commercials get so involved with the process of creation that the client product or service takes second place. If the commercial would still sound or look great without the client product or service, too much emphasis is being placed on production and not enough on informing.

3. Does the commercial stand out when run in succession with one or more commercials for other clients? Listen to a radio station, and after a commercial period list the commercials you remember and the reasons why they remain with you. These commercials that have remembrance capability have that something extra that the stock commercials, which slid in one ear and out the other, did not have.

Try the same experiment with television commercials. View a commercial break; then, after the program has resumed, make a list of the commercials on the break and try to analyze why the commercials you remember most favorably made that impression on you.

4. If the radio commercial has a music *bed*, or background, does it add to or distract from the spoken message? Too often a bit of music is placed behind a commercial to make it a "production." The music is brought up between sentences for no good purpose except to fill the time.

5. For radio commercials, are two voices being used simply because too much copy was written for one person to be able to voice it within the time limits? If such is the case, the commercial should be rewritten and re-produced. The task of the commercial is gaining audience attention and understanding.

6. For television commercials, is the commercial just too busy, with too much going on and distracting the viewer from the advertiser's principal message? In this case, the audience gladly lets the commercial pass unobserved and unremembered.

7. For radio and television commercials in which the advertiser is the on-air voice or on-camera spokesperson, does the advertiser's presence aid the commercial's aim—presenting a message to the intended audience—as effectively or more effectively than a professional announcer or actor? Too many broadcast salespeople build a trap for themselves in the act of trying to clinch a sale by suggesting that the advertiser do his or her own commercials. If the resulting commercials are bad and do a bad selling job for the client's business, it is difficult for the salesperson to then suggest that the client be removed from the commercial.

8. Is humor appropriate for the client message? If a humorous approach is appropriate, it can aid attention, receptivity, and remembrance of the commercial. The Dick and Bert radio commercials for K-Mart and other clients, the Jerry Stiller and Ann Meara commercials for office systems, the Federal Express television commercials for "when it absolutely, positively has to get there overnight," the Wendy's television commercials featuring the apparent Russian fashion show, and the Bud Light television commercials were among the most successful.

All commercials are forms of persuasive communication. They should inform, persuade, convince, and sell. The broadcast salesperson dealing with an advertising account whose commercials are produced by his or her broadcasting outlet must represent both the broadcast outlet and the advertiser in getting effective commercials produced to fill the advertiser's time slots. The difference between effective commercials and also-ran commercials can be a satisfied client who renews or expands the advertising time buy instead of a lost client who is disgruntled and convinced that broadcast advertising just doesn't work.

Tom McElligot, a partner in a Minneapolis advertising agency, declared in a 1986 article in *Inc.* that "between 95% and 98% [of advertising] doesn't work." McElligot said most ads are "strategically stupid, or they are executed stupidly, or both" because agencies "play it safe, go with the known quantity, the formula type ad."[1]

Not all advertising executives concur with McElligot's statements, but Steve Brumfield, a partner in a Nashville advertising agency, said he "generally agrees" and cited as evidence a 1984 survey by the *Journal of Advertising & Research* that showed that American businesses paid about $82 billion for advertising. For this amount, these businesses received 200,000 advertising messages per person, or "560 messages every day for every man, woman and child in America." Of these, "the average person noticed only 76 and remembered only 12, three of them negatively—an attrition rate of more than 98%."[2]

Brumfield was one of a group of Nashville advertising executives quizzed by the *Sunday Tennessean* for reaction to the *Inc.* article. While admitting that some ads are stupid and many ads are not targeted well, the group felt all ads have some effect.[3]

All of the Nashville ad executives agreed with one statement by McElligot: "Advertising nevertheless plays an increasingly important role as competing products assume similar characteristics.

> *What determines whether the consumer will buy one brand over another has a lot more to do with likability of the product. They need to have a feeling about the product that they can identify with. And in that context, the advertising, more than the product itself, becomes the point of differentiation.*[4]

The advertising executives' comments refer not only to television and radio advertising but also to print advertising. Three innovative television commercial campaigns come to mind immediately as answers to some of the criticism expressed: The clay animation commercials ("heard it through the grapevine") for California Raisins, the similar technique for the McTonight series by McDonald's, and the Spuds MacKenzie series for Budweiser Light Beer.

Basic Tips for Commercial Writing

Students interested in going into broadcast sales would be well advised to include a course in writing for television and radio within their preparation for the field. This section is not a replacement for such a course but can help the beginning broadcast salesperson who is unfamiliar with such writing.

1. Gather information from the client on the client's need to communicate (advertise): who the client wants to reach and the outcome desired by the client.

2. Select the proper medium for the client's communication need. Presumably, radio or television has been selected with the schedule devised for the sale to the client. After learning from the client the communication need and the target audience, make sure the schedule selected fits that need or suggest minor changes to the schedule.

3. Decide on the principal idea to be communicated via the commercials. Advertising works best when a principal idea is presented and reinforced. Ads that attempt to convey information about everything often fail to promote audience remembrance of anything.

4. Select the appropriate format for conveying the chosen principal idea, such as testimonial, announcer-read, or musical.

5. Is humor appropriate? Humor helps remembrance if it is tastefully and appropriately handled. Tasteless or inappropriate humor damages the communication and makes the commercial less effective and sometimes detrimental to the client.

6. Check the approach with the client. Point out the communication need expressed, the principal idea to be stressed, and the approach to be taken.

7. Write the commercial, keeping in mind its purpose and the time limit into which it must fit.

8. Edit and revise the written commercial to better focus it on its intent.

9. Recheck the commercial to make sure that its focus is on the sponsor or product rather than on the production gimmicks and that it fits comfortably in the time requirement.

10. Produce the commercial (or have it produced) and make a final check to ascertain that it is targeted on the communication need and has the capability to stand out when run within a group of commercials in a commercial break.

SERVICE: THE VALUE-ADDED PROVISION

What a salesperson does for a client after the sale may be more important than the actual sale itself. Long-term clients are maintained and upgraded according to their needs or are lost due to the actual quality of service—the entire value-added system that the station provides the client following the mutual agreement to advertise. The advertising confirmation is the beginning of a mutual commitment to a long-term relationship in which the client has agreed to use your station and you have agreed to produce certain predetermined results that address the existing needs of the client as determined in the interview step (Expressing client interest via interview). This mutual commitment can succeed only by a two-way exchange of information on a regular and monitored basis after the station proposal has been confirmed.

S Stands for Service

The letter *S* could be added to MEDIA to form MEDIAS, with the *S* meaning Service. How important this is cannot be overemphasized. Think of the times when you as a customer became frustrated and began to lose patience, when bank tellers or grocery clerks were more interested in talking to each other than in serving you. Slow or inadequate service is typically the cause of impatience.

We all respond to a lack of service or a perceived lack of service, and we change our buying habits because of it. We go to different restaurants, shop at different stores, and change gas stations in an effort to find and receive better service. Your clients are no different. They expect and should receive excellent service.

Service in the Electronic Media In radio, TV, or cable advertising, service is sometimes the most important feature to the client. Copy often needs to be changed to reflect changes in merchandising; as a certain store-wide clearance or seasonal sale winds down, for example, copy must be changed to reflect that fact. Attention to such value-added service nips many objections in the bud while establishing a client's confidence in the station and its services.

Brilliant on the Basics McKinsey and Company recently researched 11 of the country's top-performing radio stations, all of which

> have been number one in their formats, and the majority number one in their markets, over the last several years. In fact, 50 percent of the sample have dominated their ADI's for over 10 years. . . . We also wanted sample stations to be different so that they could be collectively representative of the wide range of the radio industry. Our 11 were selected . . . from a spread of important variables, including: different formats and market sizes, a balance of geographic locations, and a range of maturity levels.[5]

They found that the sample stations were brilliant on the basics.[6] Service is one of those basics, service to on-air clients and to the community at large as well.

A service orientation pervaded all our sample stations. [The report gives] a myriad of examples on how these stations cater to their listeners, to their advertisers and to themselves in their support for one another among functional units. We have seen that, as the stations mature, their efforts to serve their general community become more and more extensive and generic.

We found that, for most of our stations, the notion of service, just like quality, was also driven by a more powerful subordinate value—something we've called "believing in the license." While this larger value anchored the concept of service, it meant more than the sum total of each of the individual acts of service. . . .

In hundreds of ways, large and small—ranging from founding charitable enterprises . . . to funding community programs that fill voids . . . to hosting talk shows on public responsibility . . . to ensuring the truthfulness of advertising—the excellent sample stations put their commitment to service into larger context and action.

In so doing, they forged the solid alliances with the customers and communities they serve that are so critical to winning sustainable competitive advantage. And, as important, they added meaning to the work of their individual station employees by giving them—as they tell it—the rare opportunity of being "part of something bigger." In our view, this is precisely where "the search for excellence in radio" begins—and ends.[7]

Lack of Service Causes Cancellations

If a station is properly qualified, it loses few accounts due to its inability to perform, unless the total amount invested by the client is not sufficient to produce expected and desired results. The central problem with client attrition can be directly traced to a lack of service or inadequate service on the part of the sales representative responsible for securing the initial advertising confirmation. Once an account has been confirmed, the salesperson and the station immediately begin the initial phase of client service, that of doing what is necessary to produce promised results for the client. This service includes properly analyzing client concerns for unique copy and/or promotional ideas that produce the results the client is paying for and expects.

Too often, a flight of spots goes on the air with little regard for the job they are supposed to do, and the client does not see the station representative until after the schedule is nearly completed or even after it has stopped altogether. By this time, the advertiser may have forgotten about the schedule, has not monitored what has been advertised in relation to what has been sold, and generally does not renew the schedule because he or she has "tried you for a month and now it's time to do something else." The account is lost for want of service and monitoring on the part of the salesperson who should have been checking results, changing copy, and attempting to solve client needs and concerns.

In the scenario just described, the salesperson simply didn't know what to do once the prospect was converted to a customer. Even more serious is the cancellation of a schedule of commercials by the client, because copy that needed to be updated wasn't due to the inattention of the salesperson. Enough cannot be said about the importance of follow-up and account service to the businessperson who is investing in you to provide a professional service. You are obligated personally, professionally, and morally to do all you can for that client to see that whatever commitment you made during the confirmation is acted upon.

In *How to Make Big Money Selling*, Joe Gandolfo notes that many salespeople simply take the money and run or give lip service to service and wonder why they're not as lucky as the big moneymakers.[8] Successful salespeople know how to take care of new clients. New clients should be given a lot of thought and must be glad they met you and be cared for if they are to buy from you again and again. They will, if service is correctly tended to.

> *Shortsighted people think that service is a costly waste of time—like playing a game after you've won it. They're not only shortsighted, they're foolish. Look, you have to believe that each new client is a potential gold mine; that the initial sale, no matter how exciting, is just the beginning. Each customer, properly nurtured by you, can become the base for a whole new customer list. It can build geometrically. You have to earn referrals— they don't come to you as gifts. But, the payoff can be tremendous. Top salespeople depend on it. They expect 80% of their sales income from referrals and repeat business. And, they achieve this by a customer service program that is well thought out and carefully implemented.[9]*

Service as Professionalism

Service is the ingredient that separates one salesperson from another and one radio or TV station from the others. Gandolfo further claims that "there's no such thing as a product (or service) so superior to its competition that outstanding service cannot make a difference."[10]

Plainly stated, a salesperson must be service oriented to be successful. You can't overkill on genuine service, so plan for it and do it well. Don't waste a client's time with buddy-buddy talk that has nothing to do with your business relationship. Your client doesn't have time for this, and you shouldn't show that you do. Call on the client to find out if your station is producing results, if the merchandise is selling, and if customers, friends, or people in general have commented on the new image your station is broadcasting. Don't back away. Give your client so much service that he or she would feel guilty advertising with anyone else.

Never abandon a customer or take one for granted. Too many signals crowd the market today for you to be anything but the best in providing service. The client has too many advertising choices. Make the choice to stay with you an easy one.

RELATIONSHIPS WITH OTHER DEPARTMENTS IN THE STATION

If service is the key element to success outside the station, relationships with colleagues within the station (tending to the needs of station staff or "internal service") is equally important; without internal harmony, the brainstorming and production of programs and ideas to solve client problems are difficult if not impossible. Working in harmony with fellow staff members in other departments of the station necessitates a cooperative spirit of teamwork.

Teamwork is essential to radio and TV stations. In *How to Sell Radio Advertising*, Si Willing wrote,

> *The sales representative must know what the Program Director is planning. The announcers must know how important their work is in relationship to sales and programming. The traffic manager is the nerve center. She (or he) has to have her (or his) finger on the pulse of the entire organization. . . . Not knowing what the other department is up to can result in plenty of disastrous head-on collisions.*[11]

The only way a consultant's clients receive the excellent service we have been emphasizing is by the teamwork of the whole station. Therefore, each individual in the sales office, by necessity, is wholly involved with those in the station's other departments. The traffic department receives all orders from the sales department for logging and scheduling. The creative director or copywriter receives information from the salespeople that they use in creating advertising campaigns and commercials. The program department, which normally oversees production as well as programming, is charged with the responsibility of producing the written copy, thus making it come to life. Announcers prepare spec tapes that the salesperson can take to potential buyers as examples of how a proposed or suggested commercial or campaign would sound on the air. The news department is also important to the sales staff, as a well-known local news team is a prime source of advertising revenue; sponsors request that their commercials be aired on or near a popular news program, as listenership or viewership is at a peak level at that time.

The Receptionist and the Salesperson

The receptionist is a vital link to the success of the salesperson. He or she takes incoming phone messages and passes them along to the appropriate salesperson.

Every so often, a prospect or an advertising agency representing a local, regional, or even national account calls a local station and asks if anyone is present who can help them or leaves a general message for "someone" to contact them concerning a proposed buy. To whom do you think the receptionist gives the message? Obviously, the receptionist tends to favor the salesperson who has established a professional relationship and who values the internal and external services provided by the reception area.

Poor intrastation departmental relationships can just as easily short-circuit an integrated people-oriented system that can function well only if each department cooperates with all others. Because the sales team interrelates with all departments in a station's operations, sales personnel must demonstrate total cooperation, dependability, and flexibility in their dealings with others to maximize station revenues.

SUMMARY

The media consultant must be cognizant of the need to produce creative, effective commercial copy that will stand above the verbal clutter crowding most of the nation's airways. Effective persuasive communication/commercial writing skills can be developed with practice. Such well-written commercial copy creates satisfied clients who renew or expand their advertising time because the commercials produce measurable results.

Such consultants further understand that long-term clients are maintained and upgraded due to the quality of personal service given by the salesperson after the sale is confirmed. Such service, however, is a product of the teamwork generated by the entire station staff. Each salesperson should establish a professional relationship with and value the services provided by all personnel in every department of the radio or TV station.

NOTES

1. Albert Cason, "Ad Executives Agree Many Commercials Fizzle," *Sunday Tennessean*, July 27, 1987, Business Section I, p. 1.

2. Ibid.

3. Ibid.

4. Ibid.

5. McKinsey and Company, "Radio in Search of Excellence: Lessons From America's Best-Run Radio Stations," in *Radio in Search of Excellence* (Washington, DC: National Association of Broadcasters, 1985), p. 3.

6. Ibid., pp. 48–49.

7. Ibid., p. 49.

8. Joe Gandolfo, *How to Make Big Money Selling* (New York: Harper & Row, 1984), p. 148.

9. Ibid., p. 149.

10. Ibid.

11. Si Willing, *How to Sell Advertising* (Blue Ridge, PA: Tab Books, 1970), p. 274.

Chapter 9

SELLING AGAINST

(AND WITH)

OTHER MEDIA

Advertising is big business in the United States. The overall volume of advertising of all types in 1984 was just over $88 billion, according to estimates by McCann Erickson, a major advertising agency. The National Association of Broadcasters, noted that all advertising revenues increased 16.1 percent from 1983 to 1984.[1] In order to competitively sell against, and with, the other media in the advertising marketplace, the broadcast salesperson needs some background on the overall advertising marketplace and on the competitive media.

In the study of 1984 advertising expenditures, the relative positions of advertising media found newspapers recording the highest advertising volume, a total of $23.7 billion dollars, $3 billion of this in national advertising and $20.7 billion in local advertising volume.

Television was in second place in advertising volume with $19.87 billion. This figure includes $440 million in cable television advertising, network television advertising of $8.5 billion, national television spot advertising of $5.5 billion, and local television advertising of $4.9 billion. Syndication barter added another $400 million, almost matching cable.

Direct mail placed third after newspaper and television advertising with a volume of $13.8 billion. Radio followed in fourth place with $5.8 billion. Network radio accounted for $316 million, national spot recorded a total of $1.2 billion, and local radio advertising accounted for $4.1 billion.

Magazines placed fifth in advertising volume, with $4.9 billion. Of the magazine advertising volume, $2.2 billion was accorded to weekly magazines, $1.5 billion to monthly magazines, and $1.2 billion to the specialized women's magazines. Business papers at $2.2 billion, outdoor advertising at $872 million, and farm publications at $181 million completed the list of specified advertising media. In addition, $16.6 billion was spent on miscellaneous other forms of advertising.[2]

The broadcast media, as we have defined them, are television, radio, and cable television. These three media accounted for $25.6 billion in advertising, about $2 billion more than newspapers. When *local* advertising is studied, however, television shows $4.9 billion, radio $4.3 billion, and cable television $40 million, for a total local advertising volume for electronic media of $9.2 billion. The $20.7 billion in local advertising volume for newspapers is more than twice the local advertising volume of all electronic media.

Local advertising is the arena in which most of the broadcast salespeople who work in television, radio, or cable television sales work. Most television sales managers readily list newspaper and direct mail as their biggest competitors for advertising volume. Too many radio sales managers and salespeople regard "the other station," meaning other radio stations, as their principal competition and the opponent they must spend most of their sales time counteracting.

In the study cited, all advertising increased from 1983 to 1984, but in *local* advertising, newspaper local advertising increased by 16 percent, television local advertising increased by 13 percent, radio local advertising increased by 10.9 percent, and cable television local advertising increased by 33.3 percent, a higher increase than other categories but still a minor portion of the overall advertising volume.

RADIO VERSUS OTHER MEDIA

Radio is described as the personal medium with a one-on-one relationship between the broadcast personality or program and the listener. Radio is also a large and persuasive selling tool when managed, programmed, and used properly. With the sales tools available through research, radio salespeople can approach their task with more information and therefore better represent themselves, their station, and in the process their clients.

As of July 1988, there were 4,912 commercial AM radio stations in the United States with 170 construction permits (CPs) granted by the FCC for a total of 5,082. There were 4,058 commercial FM stations with 418 granted CPs for a total of 4,476. This represents a total of 8,960 commercial radio stations actually on the air with another 588 under construction.[3]

Radio's Reach

To receive the product of these radio stations, 355 million radios were found in homes and 118.6 million radios in automobiles in 1983. There also were 117 million battery-powered portable radios in use.

In 1984, RAB reported that radio reaches 88 percent of Americans at home each week, 12 million people with portable radios, and 74 percent by car radios. During the average day, radio reaches 80.7 percent of all American teens and adults, and during each week it reaches 95.7 percent of the American consumers.[4]

Cost-Benefit

In every field of business activity, businesses sell products on the basis of what the product can accomplish for the stated sales price, and the resultant cost-benefit ratio is shown to be beneficial. For the price paid, the merchandise delivered is a positive buy; the user receives sufficient value for money expended, and the transaction is a favorable one for the consumer. In such a situation, repeat business is likely. A consumer satisfied with the results given by the product purchased is a likely customer for another such product when the need arises.

Also in almost any business area, firms place on the market a product that looks like the leading product and seems to perform like it but is considerably cheaper. In too many instances, the purchaser of such a product finds that the item bought does not perform as well as the leading product, last as long, or have the service after the sale that the leading product has. In some way, the cheaper product is likely to be deficient when compared with the leading product.

The same situation prevails in the advertising field. Given the nearly 9,000 commercial radio stations in operation in the United States, some of that number are not as well run, efficiently programmed, or attractive to listeners as others are. With the capability of each station's management to set the rates for advertising time for that station, the buyer must make a decision on which purchase gives the best cost-benefit ratio, that is, which is a legitimately good buy.

Radio Bargains   Radio stations offer sales on their product, advertising time, just as other businesses have sales. A clothing store has a sale when it's overstocked, when it gets into a cash-poor situation, or to clear out end-of-season merchandise that cannot be profitably carried over to the next season. It may also hold a sale when it wishes to increase notice of itself, gain new customers, or establish itself better among its competitors. All are legitimate reasons to lower prices on selected merchandise or the storewide inventory for good business purposes.

However, everyone is aware of a business that is now completing its tenth year of going out of business. Those who patronize such a business can expect to pay a price that allows it to continue into the eleventh year of its "going out of business" sale.

Assessing Competition

The beginning salesperson in radio must expect to encounter competition in product capability, in cost-benefit ratio, and in just plain price-discounting. The beginning salesperson must first of all become familiar with the *direct* competitors—the other radio stations that serve the market in which he or she is selling. The salesperson must be able to assess the value of the product he or she is selling—airtime for advertising—against others who also are selling the exact (or almost exact) same commodity to demonstrate how and why his or her brand of this item will perform better at the projected cost or will be synergistic in combination with the product of one or more other station's product. With the specialized formatting of radio station programming, the addition of your station for an advertising campaign may enhance the effectiveness of spot announcement purchases made on another station.

For example, consider an advertiser to whom you're trying to sell a package of spots. The advertiser perhaps tells you that a package already has been purchased on Station A; therefore, the business already has its radio advertising. Assume that Station A programs a country music format, and your station programs a contemporary music format. Your task is to show the advertiser that the business has bought a station that reaches only a specialized segment of the adult market and that not all of the people within the metropolitan service area (MSA) tune to that station or desire that type of music.

Using demographic material from the ratings research organizations or from your own research, you can show your audience listening habits and your coverage of the market. Stress that the addition of your station adds to the campaign effectiveness more than its cost adds to the advertising bill. One of your key selling points is that the advertiser is trying to reach adults, not just adults who tune to country music or whatever the competing format is.

In many multiple-station markets, the beginning salesperson encounters the radio station equivalent of that business that has been going out of business for the past ten years (and hopes to continue going out of business successfully for the next ten or more years). Some radio stations put together rate cards or rate schedules and then forget the rate schedules and sell their product for whatever they can get at that moment with that particular advertiser. The advertisers become aware of this willingness on the part of the radio station and simply attempt to drive the price down further each time they deal with that station or any other station in the market.

This attempt to drive prices down must be resisted diligently by the salesperson for the legitimate radio station that has priced its rates fairly for the product (airtime for advertising) delivered to the advertiser. Attempts to meet the price offered by the rate-cutting station simply places your station in the same category, after which the advertisers regard your stated prices as simply the start (or maximum) of the bargaining cycle and the price they know they do not have to pay if they press the salesperson hard enough.

Placing a station with a reputation for rate cutting back on a fairly established rate schedule is difficult. Doing so usually requires a complete, well-publicized change at the station, perhaps including format, management, salespeople, and new ratings research information, all of which takes time.

These cautions do not preclude a "sale" of advertising time by a radio station. After all, radio advertising time is a perishable commodity. The unsold spot announcement times for yesterday can never be sold. Unlike many businesses, the radio station's inventory of merchandise cannot be warehoused or carried over for sale later. Once a particular time period has passed, the opportunity to sell advertising time in that period is over, and the product has vanished, never to be recaptured and sold. For this reason, a radio station may become as overstocked as any other business. Sales of radio time may be conducted just as sales are conducted in any other business. These sales are many times called *promotions*, a way of disposing of what might otherwise be perishable overstock.

Packaging

In such instances, the station may offer a *package rate*, which includes a discounted rate for a limited time for a particular package. Such packages normally include some "good" times, along with a number of times from the periods that are too lightly sold. However, the package might include only times from the too lightly sold periods of the day, grouped and priced in such a way as to be attractive on a cost-benefit basis.

An example of such a package involves non-drive-time newscasts. Suppose that the station's morning and afternoon drive-time newscasts are regularly sponsored and have retained the same sponsors for long periods of time, as have the midday newscasts.

Assume also that the newscasts between 10 A.M. and noon and those between 1 and 4 P.M. have a habit of remaining unsold or of achieving only sporadic, short-term sponsorship. The station might group these newscasts into a package and sell group rotating sponsorship to several advertisers. Their advertising would *float*, or rotate over the entire range of these newscast times.

This grouping could be done in one of several ways. Assume that the newscasts in question are the five-minute newscasts at 10 A.M., 11 A.M., 1 P.M., 2 P.M., and 3 P.M., Monday through Friday. The station is seeking five sponsors to share sponsorship of these 5 five-minute newscasts daily, five days per week. Each sponsor would have full sponsorship of one newscast each day, such as the 10 A.M. newscast on Monday, the 11 A.M. newscast on Tuesday, the 1 P.M. newscast Wednesday, the 2 P.M. newscast Thursday, and the 3 P.M. newscast Friday.

That sponsor might then rotate one position to start the next week with the 11 A.M. newscast on Monday, and so on through the week, ending with the 10 A.M. newscast on Friday.

Another alternative is to have one advertiser as the principal sponsor for a newscast, while another occupies the secondary position. Opening and closing sponsorship credits would go to the principal sponsor, along with the longer commercial, while the secondary advertiser would have a shorter commercial late in the newscast.

Promotions

Similar to a sale of advertising time but different in cost and impetus is a category of advertising at other-than-rate-card rates called *Promotions*. The promotion may have the same underlying reason as the sale, that is, gaining more revenue for the station, but it is carried out differently and priced according to the cost of the promotion elements included. Promotions are dealt with more fully in chapter 10.

One example of a promotion features audience registration at all participating sponsors for a drawing to select the winners of an all-expense-paid vacation in some prime location. Sponsors buy participatory rights to the promotion and for this purchase receive advertising time on the station, station spots that promote the participating advertisers, perhaps other promotion (such as billboards, newspaper advertising or television advertising), and the excitement and resultant in-store traffic of being responsible for an attractive giveaway.

The Real Competition

The beginning broadcast salesperson sees selling against the other radio stations or the other television stations easier and more comfortable. That way, audience quantities and audience demographics can be directly compared. However, the most lucrative selling effort can and should be in selling the electronic medium in competition with or in combination with the other types of media. Over the long haul, the creative radio salesperson who can sell clients on increasing radio advertising on the particular station with advertising reallocated from other media is likely to achieve better financial results than the radio salesperson who spends most of the time trying to combat the other radio stations.

The same holds true for the television salesperson who concentrates on trying to snare dollars from another television station. Instead, the salesperson should be showing the client how reallocation of the advertising budget to include more for the television medium, and specifically the salesperson's own station, can gain better results.

RADIO VERSUS NEWSPAPERS

Potential advertisers often tell salespeople for radio, television, and cable that they recognize that radio or television advertising works for some businesses but worry whether anyone will hear or see their particular electronic media ad that passes by so quickly. The newspaper ad stays around, and newspaper space salespeople are noted for emphasizing this point—that the newspaper reader can read the ads at his or her leisure. That tear sheet of the client's ad displayed on the wall is an indication of the longevity of the print ad and a subtle reminder of their fear of the ephemeral nature of the electronic ad.

Strangely enough, more than sixty years after radio came into being, radio as an advertising medium must constantly be sold to potential advertisers in many markets across the country. In most communities, the newspaper, as the oldest local advertising medium, long has garnered the lion's share of the local advertising revenue. Most of the communities across the nation have only one local newspaper company that publishes either morning editions and afternoon editions, a morning *or* afternoon edition, or a semiweekly or weekly edition. Local businesses have traditionally advertised in the local newspaper.

We are not saying that advertising in newspapers is not helpful. It is if properly done. However, advertising in newspapers alone is not normally the most efficient way to spend advertising money. Advertising on radio alone or on television alone may be a more efficient use of the advertising money, or a combination of media may be the best and most productive expenditure for the local advertiser.

The task of the local radio salesperson is to combat the tendency of many local businesses to place their major advertising budget in newspapers as the continuation of a habit of many years and make them consider a radio or television campaign as an alternative or as a necessary component of their advertising strategy.

Newspaper Advertising Claims

What are the major arguments for advertising in the newspaper? Ask any newspaper advertising salesperson: Every other business does. Everybody reads the newspaper. The newspaper stays around for days, and people can and do refer to it much later to find and reread your advertisement. You're assured by the audited circulation figures of how many newspapers are bought, and readership is several times greater than the audited circulation figures, so you're getting a massive audience for your advertisement. People always look in the newspaper first to find something they're looking for.

The above statements contain some truth and have some truths left out of them. Businesses do advertise in newspapers. If they did not, newspapers as an advertising medium would have died long ago. The same statement could be made regarding direct mail or any other advertising medium. However, newspapers' slice of the advertising pie has decreased over the years with the advent of the newer forms of advertising, such as radio and television. The number of daily newspapers published has been decresing steadily within the past two decades.

Does everybody read the newspaper? No, those who do not subscribe or buy the newspaper at the newsstand do not read the newspaper. Do all who subscribe read the newspaper every day? Contrast your own newspaper-reading habits or ask a number of acquaintances about their newspaper-reading habits. Generally, a fair percentage missed reading the paper that day for one reason or another, and others who said they read the newspaper that day meant skimming the front page, the local news page, the sports page, and/or the comics page. If you ask the remaining percentage who said they read the whole paper, "Did you read the ad for Auto Express automotive parts and service on page 16?" the likely response is "Well, no. I wasn't interested in auto parts."

Does the newspaper stay around for days, waiting for the time when those who did not read it earlier pick it up and read it through, page by page? Certainly, it stays around for days but usually in a pile awaiting disposal because it has been replaced by a more current issue. People don't often go back and read old news. The newspaper, like most other advertising media, has its greatest impact when it is current, and that currency is quickly lost.

Audited Circulation   The audited circulation figures show you exactly how many homes the newspaper goes into, how many people or families were exposed to the newspaper and how many had the opportunity to read the paper. Those figures do not in any way indicate how many people read a particular ad or read *any* ads within the newspaper. Again, contrast your own habits when reading a newspaper. How many times do you read the parts of a newspaper that you are interested in without exposing yourself to a single ad or at most seeing the advertiser's name on a full-page or double-truck ad as you blissfully turn the pages faster to get past that ad and on to the things you consider important? You are not unique in your ability to avoid ads as you read the parts of the newspaper that interest you; millions of people do it daily.

Most people do not buy a newspaper or subscribe to it for the advertisements. These advertisements become a necessary hindrance to skip unless one piques your interest as you are turning past it. Purchase a metropolitan Sunday newspaper and read it as you normally would. Then go back to the paper, and page by page note every ad that you did not notice or read thoroughly your first time through, including the classified advertisements. Keep a separate list of the ads you noticed or read thoroughly your first time through. Research shows that your longest list will be the ads you did not read thoroughly the first time through and your next longest list will be the ads you noted in passing but did not stop to read. Your short list will be the ads you read thoroughly. As a beginning broadcast salesperson is more conscious of advertising than the average person, your lists might well indicate a higher percentage of ads read or noted.

Newspaper Advertising as Information   Do people look first in the newspaper when they need to buy something? Perhaps. Many look in the Yellow Pages. Others watch for the advertisements (sometimes called *throw-*

aways) that are stuffed in with the mail daily. Others visit stores to compare prices on whatever it is they want to buy. Some listen more avidly to radio or watch more closely to see if the item they need is advertised on television.

We do not mean to indicate that newspaper advertising is wasted money. Any advertising is better than no advertising. We intend to place newspaper advertising in a clearer perspective than that in which it is commonly placed by newspapers and their advertising salespeople, who naturally are partisans of their product.

Broadcast salespeople as well should be partial to their medium and believe that it is the best advertising medium when all factors are considered, but they should not believe that their medium is the only workable medium for advertising. No single advertising medium can accomplish the ultimate results for every advertising need.

Target Audience   The target audience for the intended advertising communication has great bearing on the effectiveness of the advertising medium. Most advertising failures result more from incorrect use of the media than from the ineffectiveness of the media themselves. Like any other tool, they must be used properly for best benefit.

Pricing Differences

Radio and television price their advertising availabilities on the basis of delivery of a potential audience for exposure to the client's advertising message. Print media normally base their pricing structure for advertising on *circulation*—the units of the print publication that are distributed in some manner to potential readers. The basic definer of circulation for print publications is the Audit Bureau of Circulation (ABC), which audits the numbers of the print publication actually distributed to people out of the larger total number of publications printed. This ABC figure is important to an advertiser because it indicates the maximum potential audience for the advertiser's message. Note the words *potential audience,* for not every person who buys a print publication at a newsstand or has it delivered to the home reads every issue of the publication or every page of a single issue.

Imagine for a moment the welter of print material that comes into the possession of the average household: the daily newspaper, the weekly magazines, the monthly magazines, the *shopper's guides*, or publications that are totally or primarily filled with advertising, the advertising inserts in the newspaper, and advertising that arrives by itself in the mailbox. Imagine sitting down with each day's volume of material and reading through each and every page, including every advertisement. Print advertising is sold on the basis of circulation, but the truly important figure for the advertiser in print publications is the readership, particularly the readership in terms of ad size, the placement of ads, and the remembrance of ads noted.

Circulation versus Reach   The broadcast salesperson should re-member that the circulation figures for a print publication correspond roughly with the reach of an electronic medium—the maximum number of audience members capable of being reached by that medium. In the case of a radio station, that is the number of homes within the area served by a strong, trouble-free signal; in the instance of a television station, the same; for cable television, the number of homes subscribing to the cable television service. Broadcast advertising, however, is not generally sold on reach, but on esti-mates of the amount of the reach audience that is actually deliverable to the advertiser's message at particular times of the day or night.

Calculating Reach and Frequency

Radio Advertising Bureau has published a workbook that allows quick, easy calculations of radio and newspaper reach and frequency. It has formulas that require only a calculator to contrast reach and frequency numbers for the media.

The eight steps of the RAB process begin with calculation of a cume rat-ing, which is the total circulation of the radio station and comparable to the number of people who might look at the newspaper. The formula for this step is station cume divided by the population equals cume rating.

The second step involves finding the gross impressions (as shown in Chapter 5) for a radio schedule and calculating the average quarter-hour au-dience for the schedule of spots by dividing the gross impressions by the number of spots. Step two is completed by calculating the audience turn-over: divide the cume by the average quarter-hour audience.

RAB provides its members with a chart based on the number of spots and turnover rates that gives information for step three. The salesperson re-fers to the chart to locate the number of spots in the campaign and the turn-over rate closest to the turnover rate calculated in step two.

Step four calculates the reach for the schedule (number of people reached) by multiplying the station cume times the percent of cume found in the RAB chart. In step five, calculate the reach rating by dividing the reach by the population. Step six calculates the gross rating points, as shown in Chapter 5. Step seven is the calculation of the average frequency. To do this, divide the gross rating points by the reach.

Calculations following the formulas through step seven would give the salesperson the average frequency information for one station. If more than one station is used for the campaign and the average frequency for the entire campaign on all stations is needed, then the first seven steps would be com-pleted for each station and an eighth step would eliminate duplication.

Step eight gives the formula: station A plus station B minus (A times B) equals an unduplicated audience. The unduplicated audience figure de-rived from the above calculation would become the new station A, and station C would move up to become the new station B. The answer to this calculation would then become the station A figure, and the next station would be moved to the station B calculation.

Then the salesperson can calculate the frequency, that is, how many times each person would hear the spot. To do this, the gross rating points for all stations are added, and this figure is divided by the reach to get the frequency.[5]

Now, go through this process, filling in numbers for the formula steps. Assume the market population is 400,000, and the station cume, which would be shown in the ratings tabulations, is 80,000:

$$\frac{80,000 \text{ Station Cume}}{400,000 \text{ Population}} = .20 \text{ Cume Rating}$$

This .20 becomes a cume rating when the decimal point is moved two spaces to the right.

In step two, RAB suggests the salesperson refer to the ratings report for the market and select the station average quarter-hour audience and the cume that best describe the schedule planned for the advertiser. If spots are to be run in the 6 to 10 A.M., 10 A.M. to 3 P.M., and 3 to 7 P.M. time slots, then use the cume for 6 A.M. to 7 P.M. We can assume that the cume for Monday to Friday 6 A.M. to 7 P.M. is the 80,000 used in step one. Then the salesperson calculates gross impressions as shown in the RAB formula above:

Time Period	Number of Spots Scheduled	×	AQH Listeners	=	Gross Impressions
M–F 6–10 A.M.	10		10,000		100,000
M–F 10 A.M.–3 P.M.	10		6,000		60,000
M–F 3–7 P.M.	10		7,500		75,000
TOTAL	30				235,000

The average quarter-hour audience for the schedule:

$$\frac{235,000 \text{ Gross Impressions}}{30 \text{ Spots}} = 7,833 \text{ Average Quarter-Hour Audience}$$

To find audience turnover:

$$\frac{80,000 \text{ Cume}}{7,833 \text{ Average Quarter-Hour Audience}} = 10.21 \text{ Turnover}$$

At this point, the salesperson would have to refer to the RAB chart of number of spots and turnover rate. In this instance, with 30 spots in the campaign and a turnover rate closest to that calculated above, 10, the schedule of 30 spots would reach 74 percent of the station's cume.

The reach for the schedule:

Station Cume × Percent of Cume = People Reached

The percent of cume above is changed to a decimal figure for this step:

80,000 Station Cume × .74 Percent of Cume = 59,200 People Reached

To achieve the reach rating:

$$\frac{59,200 \text{ Reach}}{400,000 \text{ Population}} = 0.148 \text{ or } 14.8 \text{ Reach Rating}$$

Next, gross ratings points are calculated:

$$\frac{235,000 \text{ Gross Impressions}}{400,000 \text{ Population}} = 0.5875 \text{ or } 59 \text{ GRPs}$$

The salesperson now has two of the three parts of the reach and frequency for the 30-spot schedule—a reach of 14.8 and 59 GRPs.

Average frequency tells the number of times the average person reached by the schedule hears the commercial. This figure is an average. Some people reached hear it more often and some less often. A big one-time sale would need to be heard more often over a short span of time than would an image commercial that is part of an ongoing campaign. The RAB rule of thumb is that a person needs to hear a commercial a minimum of three times to become motivated to act on the information.

$$\frac{59 \text{ Gross Rating Points}}{14.8 \text{ Reach}} = 3.99 \text{ (4.0) Average Frequency}$$

At this point the salesperson has the average frequency information for the 30-spot campaign on one station, indicating that the average listener to that station will hear the campaign commercial four times. If more than one station is being used for a campaign and the average frequency for the entire campaign on all stations is desired, then the procedure we have gone through here using mythical figures for one station in a 400,000 population market would be completed for each station, with an extra calculation to remove duplication among the stations.

To complete step eight of the RAB process, start with the station figures and then insert figures for two other stations. For this step, RAB uses a technique called *random probability*, which assumes that if a station reaches 20 percent of the market, it also reaches 20 percent of every other station's audience. Remember the formula:

Station A + Station B − (A × B) = Unduplicated Audience

Using the figures for the station above, calculate the unduplicated audience in the three-station market example:

Station	Reach	Frequency	GRPs
A	14.8	4.0	59
B	18.0	3.0	54
C	12.4	4.1	51

Part one of the RAB formula with these figures:

14.8 Station A Reach + 18.0 Station B Reach
= 32.8 Gross Added Reach C

Part two:

.148 Station A Reach × .180 Station B Reach
= .02664 (change to rating 2.7) Duplication D

Part three:

32.8 Gross Added Reach C − 2.7 Duplication D
= 30.1 Net Unduplicated Reach

This process is continued, with the net for the first two stations becoming a new station A, and the next station (in our case, station C) becoming station B in the calculation, and so on through all stations involved in the campaign. Continuing the calculations for the model begun:

30.1 New Station A Reach + 12.4 New Station B (Station C) Reach
= 42.5 Gross Added Reach

.320 Station A Reach × .124 Station B Reach = .03968 (4.0) Duplication

42.5 Gross Added Reach − 4.0 Duplication
= 38.5 Net Unduplicated Reach

Thus, the three-station campaign would reach 38.5 percent of the market. Now the number of times the average person hears the spot on all stations can be calculated by adding the gross rating points and dividing by the reach to get the frequency:

Station	Gross Rating Points
A	59
B	54
C	51
Total	164

$$\frac{164}{38.5} = 4.2597 \ (4.26)$$

Therefore, the reach for the three-station campaign is 38.5, the frequency is 4.26, and the gross rating points for three stations equals 164. The three-station campaign can be expected to reach almost 40 percent of the market, excluding duplicated reach, and members of that audience can be expected to hear the radio spots more than four times each on the average.

In order to contrast the radio advertising against newspaper advertising, the salesperson must perform calculations to show the effectiveness of the newspaper advertising. The same Radio Advertising Bureau workbook has a section on calculating the people reached by a newspaper ad. The steps in this process include determining the circulation for the newspaper and the target audience population as step one.

In step two, estimate the readership of the newspaper by multiplying circulation times readers per copy. RAB bases its readers per copy on information from the Newspaper Advertising Bureau and Simmons Market Research Bureau, which shows 2.158 adult readers per copy. Table 9-1 gives demographics of newspaper readership.

As step three, RAB recommends calculating the reader reach rating of target audience potential through the formula

$$\frac{\text{Readers}}{\text{Population}} = \text{Newspaper Circulation Rating}$$

RAB notes that this figure is comparable to a station cume but cautions that this does not indicate that this number of people have been exposed to a specific piece of advertising.

Step four of the process takes a measurement of Starch Ad Noting Scores (Starch INRA Hooper; see Table 9-2), using it in the formula

Target Audience Potential Rating × Ad Noting Factor
= Reach Rating for Newspaper

With the above information, the RAB model calculates the impact of reducing the ad to a smaller size as step five, using the same formula as above, with a different ad noting factor.

TABLE 9-1
National Average Readers Per Copy of a Daily Newspaper

Reader Age	Men	Women	Adults
18+	1.067	1.091	2.158
18–24	.168	.153	.321
25–34	.242	.210	.452
35–44	.182	.181	.363
45–54	.172	.181	.353
55–64	.157	.181	.338
65+	.146	.185	.331

Source: *Radio Memo,* Radio Advertising Bureau, May, 1986. (Figures from *Key Facts about Newspapers and Advertising,* Newspaper Advertising Bureau; Simmons Market Research Bureau.)

In step six, RAB calculates the frequency and gross rating points with the formula

Reach × Frequency = Gross Rating Points[6]

Once the above is accomplished, the broadcast salesperson has the information to show the potential client how reducing the size of the projected newspaper ad (from a full page to a half page, for example) and adding a radio schedule (partially or wholly financed from the drop in cost) can dramatically increase the reach of the advertising campaign and its frequency. RAB demonstrates that cutting a full-page newspaper ad to a half-page ad and adding a 24-spot radio schedule gives the ad 54 percent more reach than the full page achieved and more than doubled average frequency.[7] That increase in impact would be largely financed by the reduction in size of the newspaper ad and give the client more advertising for little or no additional outlay of money.

Newspaper Readership

One key factor in the above calculations is the inclination of the average person approaching any communication medium containing advertising. The average person who turns on a radio does it to be informed or entertained. The same is true of television. The advertisements that appear on the medium while the individual is listening or watching are tolerated as interruptions of the information or entertainment the individual sought from the medium.

The same principle applies to the individual who opens the daily newspaper. Most do not approach the newspaper to see what ads are there. They approach it with the intention of reading the news, the sports, or whatever

TABLE 9-2
Percent Noting Ad Factors

Ad Size	Men	Women	Adults
1 page or larger	.34	.47	.41
³⁄4 page	.31	.44	.38
¹⁄2 page	.31	.35	.33
¹⁄4 page	.23	.30	.27
¹⁄8 page	.21	.27	.24
less than ¹⁄8 page	.14	.15	.15

From: *Radio Memo,* Radio Advertising Bureau, May, 1986. Source: Starch INRA
    Hooper.

interests them. Unless someone is seeking an advertisement for a particular item, the advertising is barely noticed.

Imagine sitting down with your daily newspaper and reading fully every advertisement from the front page all the way through the last page. Have you ever done it? The normal response is to ask why would anyone want to do it.

Therefore, some newspaper ads in the paper are noticed by people as they pass them, some are read by people as they page through the paper, and some are neither read nor noted by people as they pass by them to get to the part of the paper they desire to read. When most of the news columns remain unread by a large percentage of the people who purchase a newspaper, how could we expect those average people to read every advertisement? The broadcast salesperson should make sure that potential advertisers realize how many newspaper readers are apt to ignore their ads.

The RAB workbook uses a chart with information from Starch INRA Hooper on the percent of people noting print advertisements. The Starch information shows that 41 percent of adults who read a newspaper *note* an ad of one page or larger, 38 percent note a three-quarter-page ad, 33 percent note a half-page ad, and 27 percent note a quarter-page ad.[8]

Assuming a newspaper with circulation of 60,000 within the metro survey area of 400,000 population (which may be a high circulation figure) and adult readership of 2.1 adults per newspaper, the paper's readership is 126,000. This figure is readership of the paper and not an indication of how many read any ads. Applying the percentages above, 41 percent of these adults, or 51,660 people, likely noted a full-page or larger ad. Dividing the readers (126,000) by the population (400,000) gives a target audience potential rating of 31.5. Multiplying this by the ad noting factor for adults for a full-page ad (.41), 12.9 is the newspaper reach rating.[9]

The salesperson has in the newspaper reach rating a figure that can be compared with similar figures for the electronic media. The calculations shown here for radio work as well for television and are another part of that base of information that arms the electronic media salesperson in the competition for advertising dollars available in the marketplace.

Qualitative Research

A 1983 NAB research publication points to the need for more and better audience research in order to meet the increased competition. In it, Richard V. Ducey points out:

> *Media planners and buyers are beginning to look at stations that can deliver target audience segments. These target segments need to be described by qualities other than the basic age and sex breakdown typically provided in audience research. To position your station in a competitive market, it may be important for you to describe the quality as well as the quantity of your audience.*[10]

This form of qualitative research information is a further refinement of the station's market placement or positioning. The larger the market, the more vital the information.

Combating Newspaper Orientation

In selling radio advertising against and with newspaper advertising to a very print-oriented client, a head-on assault is not likely to be a winning tactic. The salesperson's aim is to get the client involved in radio advertising so that its effectiveness can be shown and increase the amount of advertising dollars allocated to radio—particularly to the salesperson's own station.

Anthony Segraves, president of Professional Marketing Advisory, has written:

> *For years, I beat my head against the wall attempting to sell against newspaper as a radio salesperson. One thing I eventually had to accept is the fact that advertisers will continue to invest in newspapers. Regardless of technological advances with electronic media, print will continue to be a factor in the multi-media complexity of the advertising market.*[11]

Segraves's advice points out again the most sensible approach: sell radio as an inexpensive expander of newspaper advertising. As the RAB workbook material points out, a reduction in the size of the newspaper ad, augmented with good radio advertising, can reach more of the market better, and most people, including print-oriented advertisers, are interested in getting more for their money.

Segraves has this advice for the radio salesperson:

> *Illustrate the increase of households in your market, preferably over a six- to eight-year period. This is important, because households in most markets have increased*

significantly (depending on the market), and the number of individuals per house is much smaller than in the 1960s and 1970s. Although the population has increased, households (the individual units that "should" subscribe to the local newspaper) have not increased in equal proportion.

- *Show the increase in the ad rates the newspaper has experienced in the same period of time.*

- *Circulation figures should reflect that the newspaper's subscription total has decreased over the same period of time—or that, at the least, the circulation has not kept up with the increase in the trend of the households.*

- *Starch readership figures should be used to illustrate the percent of ad readership and ad noting per ad size.*

- *The combination of a companion radio schedule with a smaller newspaper ad will give the client more reach and more impressions in the market, not including the increase in frequency that would result.*[12]

Newspaper Plus Radio

Radio Advertising Bureau reinforces the concept of selling radio advertising as a low-cost expander of newspaper advertising by pointing out that only two-thirds of adults see a daily newspaper but 83 percent of adults listen to radio on the average weekday. It points to a rise in newspaper CPM of 266 percent between 1967 and 1984, with daily reach declining over that period by 11 percent. In contrast, it says radio's CPM increased only half as fast over the period, while daily reach has remained constant at levels greater than newspapers. RAB also notes that two-thirds of adults spend an average of just 11 minutes per day with the local newspaper, but adults spend more than three hours daily with radio.[13]

Although some advertising sales representatives may attempt to convince potential advertisers that their particular outlet is the only advertising outlet that delivers an audience and therefore the only advertising source the advertiser ever needs or should use, this approach is not recommended for the beginning salesperson in electronic media. A more honest, straightforward approach enhances the credibility of the individual electronic media salesperson and the capability of that salesperson to move toward becoming a consultant to the advertiser. In such an approach, the salesperson demonstrates how his or her electronic media advertising outlet can fulfill its task—delivering potential customers to the advertising firm in the proper volume and at a favorable cost-benefit ratio.

Media Mix   The electronic media salesperson should not become an advocate for any other advertising medium but must recognize reality. The larger the firm and the larger its advertising budget, the more likely it is to use a media mix in its advertising strategy. *Media mix* means that the advertising strategy encompasses the use of more than one type of advertising media to get its message(s) across to the targeted audience. The aim of the electronic media salesperson should be to demonstrate that the salesperson's own advertising media outlet should be included in that media mix and have an increasing or dominant position in it.

Advertising managers of large businesses are not going to be convinced that the expenditure of all of their advertising dollars on one advertising outlet in a particular city can fulfill their company's advertising needs. Recognition of this fact allows the advertising salesperson to plan credible, beneficial advertising programs that can gain larger and larger shares of the media mix by showing results that merit such increasing expenditures.

Recognition of the fact that the larger the firm the more certain it is to use a media mix does not mean the electronic media salesperson must take into account that division of the advertising budget in each individual campaign. The salesperson can and should prepare specialized campaigns for the company during the year, but he or she should also prepare overall campaigns for the advertising budget year in a timely fashion so that these campaigns can be included in the company's overall advertising budget.

The company's advertising budget sets guidelines for amounts to be spent in various media. Although a good campaign idea can be sold to the company during the year, doing so is easier if the company's budget includes that advertising outlet in its overall budget.

Selling Radio First

In selling radio advertising against newspaper advertising competition, the radio advertising salesperson should first sell radio as an advertising medium, with his or her station as the best choice for radio advertising in that locality for the advertiser's particular purpose and audience. Too many radio salespeople spend too much of their time selling down their competitor radio stations in the locality and not enough time selling up radio advertising in general and themselves as the best available expression of radio advertising.

Principal Competition   The long-standing principal competition for radio stations, television stations, and now cable television systems for the advertising dollar has been local newspapers. To sell successfully against newspapers or to sell the salesperson's medium and outlet in combination with the advertiser's use of newspapers, studying the advantages and disadvantages of newspaper advertising is necessary.

Newspaper Advertising Disadvantages

At one time the local newspaper was the principal disseminator of news to the public and thus the principal beneficiary of advertising dollars from firms who wanted exposure to the newspaper readers who purchased the paper for the news it contained. At the present time, a large majority of the population gets its principal news from media sources other than newspapers.

Overall, newspapers have been losing circulation steadily in recent years. Large cities especially have seen mergers, closures, and cutbacks in circulation. Many more cities now than ten years ago have only one major newspaper, and even in these one-newspaper cities circulation of the large daily newspaper has shown downward trends.

As the post office has received heavy competition from the parcel and specialized communication carriers such as United Parcel Service and Federal Express, newspapers have been competing to deliver multipage advertising inserts. The consumer now finds many of these being delivered to the mailbox or hung on the doorknob in a plastic bag rather than delivered inside the newspaper. CPM (cost per thousand exposures) for a newspaper ad usually run much higher than CPM for either radio or television in the same market.

Newspaper Advertising Advantages

For some companies who have been in business for generations, newspaper advertising is the traditional advertising medium, even though the company probably has delegated some of its advertising dollars to the other, newer media. The company that has been in business for a number of years, has used newspaper advertising all this time, is profitable and tends to assume that newspaper advertising has been at least partially responsible for the company's success.

None of us wants to tinker with something that is working, even if it might be made to work better. The fear is that working on it might make it work worse or even break it.

The electronic media are relative infants compared with print media. Most businesspeople are astute enough to know that electronic media advertising works, but some—perhaps a larger number than even those in electronic media realize—fear that they don't know how to use it properly. These businesses make token use of the electronic media, while retaining the comfort of using the familiar medium as their major advertising source.

Changing Attitudes   Retailers, traditionally the major spenders in local newspapers, have been assessing the changes in advertising media. The advertising spokesperson for a major regional department store chain told a 1986 sales seminar:

> *Newspaper spending is declining in all of our markets as penetration drops . . . so, there is tremendous growth potential for radio. . . . Newspaper was there when retailers started, it's traditionally gotten the dollar, so it has worked; and it's hard to get retailers turned on to radio or even television, but . . . it is happening as newspaper continues to lose effectiveness while costing more.*[14]

A partner in an advertising agency told participants in the same seminar:

I'm buying more electronic media and less newspaper . . . retailers are historically newspaper users, but the media mix is beginning to shift. It used to be that retailers were into newspapers 50–60% of their total budget, but this is changing and radio and television are working because they're now getting the budget in some markets.[15]

Retailers' affinity for newspapers has been a long-standing problem and one on which the Radio Advertising Bureau has worked diligently. Electronic media cannot really show the results of newspaper advertising unless and until they are given a sufficient piece of the advertising budget to be able to show dramatic results. Too many retailers have tried radio and television advertising by allocating $500 to radio and $1,000 to television while spending $10,000 on newspaper on the same promotion and then decided they got best results for the promotion from the newspapers.

Psychological Stroking   Another traditional advantage for newspaper advertising has been that the advertiser can pick up the newspaper, turn the pages, and see the firm's advertisement. This is psychological stroking. The advertiser who is looking for the ad sees it and assumes that every other reader of the paper has also seen and read that ad just as carefully. The newspaper delivers to the advertiser a tearsheet (for the larger-volume, regular advertiser) before the ad appears in the paper. The advertiser can hold this ad in hand, look at it, and see its beauty.

The radio station may play back the radio commercial for the advertiser, and the advertiser probably will see the television commercial before it plays, but neither of them can be held, or thumbtacked on a wall as a constant reminder. Although advertisers may hear or see the electronic media commercials, they worry about the number of potential customers who were listening at that time and how quickly the commercial passes by.

Of course, these questions do not plague the large national advertisers who spend millions on electronic media advertising. They have the research facilities to prove that electronic media advertising works and confidently place their advertising dollars on the media mix to achieve the results desired. The local or regional retailer is coming to the realization that electronic media should play a part in the company's advertising plans but still places ads in one newspaper per locality rather than going to the effort of trying to figure out a proper media mix for each market.

Listing Ads   Newspaper advertising has the advantage in listing types of ads and, of course, legal advertisements. Radio and television, as selling media utilizing sound or sight and sound, do not work as well for pure listing advertising. For most purposes, however, listing ads are not the most successful way to advertise a business. Research has shown that *white space,* that space in a newspaper ad that is devoid of words, attracts the reader's eye better than the crowded, prose-filled ad.

So, radio and television most likely will never capture the legal advertising market from newspapers. Anyone who has read these can be glad that this is the case because gaining legal advertising and losing total audience as a result would be no benefit. As for the other listing ads, supermarkets and others have learned that they can sell several priced items on radio and television, but not 30 to 50 items per commercial. If a theme is developed for the flight of commercials and the price items are used as examples with different examples in each commercial, the commercials have an overall continuity and impression of low prices while keeping the number of prices per commercial within the consumer's capability to comprehend.

Positive Radio Selling

The best way to sell radio advertising against newspaper competition is not to make the process an either/or contest, especially to retailers with a history of newspaper as the major or sole advertising source. The best way to sell a particular radio station is for the broadcast salesperson to:

1. Thoroughly know what that radio station is, what its audience composition is, and what the radio station can do best

2. Know the competitive media, the newspaper, the other radio stations, and the television stations, and know what their audiences, prices, and capabilities are

These recommendations reinforce what has been stated in earlier chapters. The professional studies and learns everything possible about his or her area of specialty. Expertise is earned by hard work.

The newspaper has an advantage if it is the only local newspaper or if the morning and afternoon papers are owned by the same company, which is increasingly common. In such instances, the newspaper is all things to all people because it has no daily print competition. Once the decision is made to use print advertising as a part of an advertising campaign in the market, which newspaper to use is not a question.

In the case of markets with multiple radio stations (most of the markets in the country), the advertiser must first make the decision to use radio and choose which station or stations to use. In multiple-station markets, no radio station can be all things to all people. The radio stations specialize, aiming at particular demographic segments of the total audience. The radio salesperson must contrast the demographic segment of the radio station to the aims and target audience of the advertiser to determine how advertising on the radio station can produce optimum results. Knowing one's specialty and concentrating on doing that can provide success; attempting to do a little bit of everything that might come along not only leads to many failures but also takes time that should be spent on attainable objectives. As the advertising spokesperson for a metropolitan bank phrased it, "Know my target customer. . . . My target customer may not listen to or view the most popular shows. If I then buy the most popular shows, I miss my demographics."[16] The advertising spokesperson for the regional department store chain agrees: "I will not see certain salespeople if they represent stations whose demographics don't match our target customer. . . . I know our customer well enough to know exactly whom I want to reach and which stations reach that customer and which do not."[17]

The beginning salesperson for electronic media should not start out with the idea of converting all advertising in the market from all other media to his or her station and put the other advertising media out of business. At the same time, the well-prepared electronic media salesperson can proceed with well-organized plans to meet the advertising needs of potential advertisers and confidently aim at increasing the share of advertising budgets placed with his or her station.

The radio salesperson has to learn the concept of media mix and plan to assure that his or her station gets a substantial part of the media mix. Doing so calls for the radio salesperson to learn not only how to sell against other media but also how to sell the radio station in concert with other media. The radio salesperson should be able to show the advertiser how combining radio (the salesperson's station) with newspaper advertising can enhance the advertising campaign and provide greater potential results than using newspaper only or using newspaper with only a very small radio budget.

Sometimes the salesperson shows the greatly added benefits of adding money for radio advertising. At other times, the salesperson hinges the sales presentation on persuading the advertiser to substitute radio advertising for part of the planned newspaper expenditure by showing the greater potential benefits of the size of the newspaper ads and using that money to fund or partially fund a supportive radio advertising campaign.

Combining Media   The Radio Advertising Bureau should be given credit for shifting many newspaper-oriented retailers into a media mix that has provided untold advertising dollars for radio stations.

RAB has a three-step model for radio salespeople to use in calculating how media (primarily radio and newspaper in this instance) may be combined, the combined reach, and the unduplicated reach.[18]

Step one of the RAB model is the same as that shown earlier to calculate the unduplicated reach for multiple radio stations. The gross rating points of the newspaper ad and of the radio schedule are added and then the duplication is calculated and subtracted to show net unduplicated reach.

Assume a reach of 18 for the newspaper ad and 13.8 for the radio schedule for a gross reach of 31.8. Moving the decimal point two places to the left in each of the GRPs and multiplying gives .18 times .138, a duplication of 2.5. Subtracting this from the 31.8 shows a net unduplicated reach of 29.3.

Step two addresses GRPs and the frequency of the combination of radio schedule and full-page newspaper ad. The newspaper ad has a reach of 18 and a frequency of 1.0 (because it is run once) for total GRPs of 18.0. The radio station schedule of 24 spots has a reach of 13.8 and a frequency of 3.5, for total GRPs of 48. Thus the combination has a reach of 29.3, a frequency of 2.3, and GRPs of 66 (the frequency is determined by dividing the combination GRPs by the combination reach).

Step three of the RAB radio-newspaper combination model shows that replacing the newspaper full-page ad with a half-page ad provides excellent results. Substituting the 14 reach of the half-page newspaper ad and multiplying by the one time it will run reduces newspaper GRPs to 14.0. Completing the calculation with the previous radio schedule figures gives a reach of 25.9 (dropping only 3.4 from the combination with the full-page ad), a frequency of 2.4 (an increase of 0.1), and GRPs of 62 (4.0 below the earlier combination). Thus, the half-page newspaper ad and 24-spot radio campaign achieves almost the results of the full-page newspaper ad and 24-spot radio campaign, at a considerable reduction in advertiser cost.

Overcommercialization One of the charges leveled at radio and television salespeople is *overcommercialization*, the number of commercials and the time they occupy. An enterprising electronic media salesperson would be well advised to take the time to carefully go through an edition or two of the local newspaper and analyze the content on the basis of advertising amount versus news (and all other) content.

An analysis of a local daily newspaper for Wednesday, July 30, 1986, for a city of approximately 50,000 population showed section A had an average of 15 pages with 1,890 column inches available. Of that total, 933 column inches were advertising, for 49.3 percent of the available space. Section B had 16 pages and 2,016 column inches, of which 1,340 column inches, that is, 66.5 percent were devoted to advertising. The two sections combined had 3,906 column inches available; 58.2 percent of this was advertising, 41.3 percent was used for news, editorial page, entertainment page, columns, comics, and the like, and 0.5 percent was used for the newspaper's own promotion.

In addition, three multipage, multicolor inserts inside the paper were not counted in the above advertising-news breakdown. Can 18 minutes of commercials per hour on a radio station (assuming the station is scheduling that amount) compare with the above percentages? Eighteen minutes is 30 percent of 60 minutes. Television's normal maximum, 16 minutes per hour, is 26.7 percent of the hour.

Retail Suggestions for Radio Use   A trade publication for furniture and home furnishings merchants, the NHFA's *Competitivedge*, has some suggestions for its membership in using radio to sell such merchandise.

> *Radio advertising rates are negotiable. Newspapers print only the number of pages that are paid for by advertising. Radio stations, on the other hand, have a fixed number of time slots to be filled every day. Therefore, they will negotiate rates. . . . If you agree to buy 1,000 or more spots in a 12-month period, most stations offer a yearly discount. There are also weekly "packages" of 12, 18, 24, 36 and more spots which are sold at a better rate than an individual spot. The Radio Advertising Bureau cites another popular and efficient way to buy time. It is a Total Audience Plan, or TAP. You can get effective reach and special rates with this plan, which schedules spots throughout the broadcast day.*[19]

The salesperson fearful of selling too big might be interested in the NHFA's recommendation that for the big sale, the retailer should purchase radio schedules of a minimum of 22 spots a day Thursday, Friday, and Saturday and add spots for Sunday also, if the business is open, then plan a schedule of 5 to 10 spots a day during the week, and repeat the minimum of 22 spots per day for the final Thursday through Sunday. It also recommends 60-second spots over 30s or 10s.[20]

Basic Selling Principles

Salespeople for radio advertising must recognize that the job of selling their station rests on these basic principles:

1. Knowing their station's demographic audience
2. Recognizing their station's capabilities
3. Learning the target audience and the needs of the potential advertiser
4. Planning a program of advertising for the potential advertiser that takes into account the second and third principles
5. Working to show how their station can be inserted in a successful media mix
6. Selling the benefits of radio advertising alone or as part of the media mix and selling the station as reflecting those benefits
7. Realizing that the greatest gains come from positive selling of the medium and their station, not negative or defensive selling against their radio competitors

Of course, positive selling of the radio medium and of the salesperson's particular station points out the superiority of the station among the radio stations in the market, but not as a prime focus.

SELLING RADIO AGAINST AND WITH TELEVISION

Radio and television are both electronic communication media, but they differ in many vital ways. Radio communicates through hearing, television through sight and hearing. Each has its unique advantages and some disadvantages when contrasted against the other. Each can successfully carry out the full burden of advertising for a product or company (as can newspapers, magazines, billboards, cable television, direct mail, and others) if that is the chosen direction.

Radio Advantages

The advantages for radio over television include:

1. Radio advertising is less expensive than television advertising when outlets in the same market are compared on a per-spot basis.
2. Radio generally goes wherever people go: in the home, in the car, at work, and elsewhere. It can be heard while the individual is involved in other things.
3. Radio enables an advertiser to utilize a frequency of impressions on the individual consumer that is more difficult and much more costly on television.
4. Radio is very much a one-on-one medium, with the advertising capability more like information from a friend or neighbor.

Television Advantages

The advantages of television over radio include:

1. Television combines sight and sound to bring better potential remembrance of the individual message.
2. People watching television generally are paying closer attention to the medium than they are when listening to radio.
3. Television is still the glamor medium of the advertising media and therefore draws more attention as a medium than does radio.
4. Television viewing is habitual in most American households and is viewed for extensive periods compared with the shorter individual listening periods of radio.

Selling against or in Combination

In selling radio against or in combination with television, the beginning salesperson should not attempt to convince the potential advertiser that television advertising is no good or not productive of results. Because research figures show the effectiveness of television advertising, too many huge, national companies are spending too much money on it for such a tactic to be effective. The salesperson who opens a radio sales presentation in this manner may spend too much time defending that position to get to the positive aspects of the sales presentation. Concentrating on radio's capability is a much better approach.

Radio's Capabilities Radio advertising can either accomplish the total advertising need or serve as an enhancer for the more expensive media, such as television and newspaper. For the cost of one or a few television commercials, a radio campaign can give a much more extensive campaign with more GRPs and much more frequency.

The low cost of a radio advertising campaign with commercials prepared and produced at little or no cost by the radio station makes possible an advertising campaign for a smaller potential advertiser. Purchasing a newspaper ad big enough to bring reasonable reach or purchasing time for television announcements and having to pay production costs for a commercial might well negate the idea of advertising for such businesses. Radio is truly affordable advertising compared with other media in the same market.

Tips for Radio Selling In tips for the radio salesperson seeking to sell radio against or with television, RAB points out that light television viewers, who watch television an average of 34 minutes a day, make up almost 40 percent of the television viewing audience. These light viewers, according to RAB, are 41 percent more likely to have a household income of $30,000 or more per year, 50 percent more likely to have college degrees, 25 percent likely to use major credit cards, and 32 percent more likely to own a late-model automobile than the average consumer.

In contrast, RAB says light television viewers spend more than three hours per day listening to radio. Television cannot reach consumers away from home, but radio is in 95 percent of all cars and 57 percent of all adult workplaces. Television production costs are high; radio has lower production costs as well as lower costs for time purchased. Television commercials are interruptions to the program that give the audience a chance to leave the room; radio commercials are more an integral part of the format, not as clearly separate.[21]

For the advertiser who is using television in a campaign or on a regular basis, radio provides a very low-cost, effective enhancer of the television campaign. Large national advertisers have found that supplementing their television advertising with radio commercials emphasizing the same theme gives them much higher remembrance and a kind of replay of their television commercial message at the very much lower cost of the radio commercial. As in the case of the radio-newspaper combination, radio enhances and creates additional reach and frequency at very low additional cost when it is combined properly with television advertising.

SELLING RADIO AGAINST OTHER ADVERTISING MEDIA

Selling Radio against and with Cable

In selling radio advertising against cable television advertising, the radio salesperson can focus on the long history of successful radio advertising, the demographics of the audience delivered by the radio station, the ratings research information (from companies specializing in that area or from research done by or on behalf of the radio station), the total availability of radio to practically everyone, and the repetition available through frequent contact with the consumer.

In selling radio in combination with cable television advertising, much of what was said about broadcast television applies. First, radio works well as an enhancer of any other form of advertising, adding frequency of contact and remembrance of the advertising campaign at very low cost; second, radio reaches people in its demographic segments that may not be reached at all by the cable television system, which is limited to subscribers whose homes are wired for the particular tier of service purchased.

Radio Advantages over Cable   In selling radio's advantages over cable television, RAB points out that cable television has proliferated the number of television channels available to the public and fragmented viewer loyalties, but radio listeners are loyal to one or two or three radio stations and the dial position instead of specific shows. Also, 51.1 percent of households (45 million) are wired for cable, while 99 percent of U.S. households have radios. RAB notes that "locally produced spots (cable) are frequently amateurish and of poor quality," yet locally produced radio spots can be made inexpensively without appearing to be cheap.[22]

In another publication, RAB attacks cable television's claim of targeting audiences. RAB says cable claims to target specific audiences, but that radio targets better, "attracting bigger, more homogenized consumer groups which are related directly to your marketing needs."[23]

Videotex/Teletext

Another form of advertising emerging on cable television systems is that of videotex or teletext, sometimes called *electronic newspaper* by newspaper companies who have led the way in attempting to develop this service. Normally, the newspaper leases one or two cable channels and then programs the channel or channels with information gleaned from its editions and rewritten to scroll up or down the screen.

Interspersed within these informational segments are text ads (or commercials) for advertisers who have purchased these ad availabilities. In some markets, radio stations have begun operation of these text channels, offering their own radio signal as the background sound while the text is scrolling.

This type of advertising is still experimental, as is the service itself, and not a serious competitor to the previously existing advertising media. One prinicpal drawback is the size of the audience willing to turn the television on, then switch to a text-only channel, and sit watching and reading as the text scrolls past, information and advertising alternating. For the future, a logical, constructive way should develop to use the technical capability to reach a segment of the audience, however small. Continued experimentation along these lines will determine whether the technique is feasible.

Radio versus Direct Mail

In selling radio against direct mail, the salesperson should recognize that direct mail has one of the higher CPMs. It is most effective when directed to an audience that is tightly defined and scattered in that no large number is available in any particular location where other mass media could compete with it in terms of reach, frequency, and CPM. An advertiser wishing to reach 50,000 people with like characteristics and located in all 50 states (such as members of a specific organization) would find direct mail more efficient than advertisements in all newspapers in the fifty states, network television, network radio, or commercials on television and/or radio stations in all 50 states.

When the audience desired is a mass audience, however, any of the other media would be better suited for inclusion in any modern advertising program.

TELEVISION VERSUS OTHER MEDIA

In 40 years, television has become established as an indispensable part of the lives of most Americans. The technical advances in the industry since it began spreading nationwide in the late 1940s have been staggering. From black-and-white pictures of live performers, to videotape, to color, to smaller cameras and portable videocassette recorders, to microwave antennas to allow "live" transmission of pictures, to satellite transmission of events from practically anywhere on the globe, television has become a dominant part of the American culture.

Television Reach

As of July 1988, 540 commercial VHF television stations were in operation, along with 485 commercial UHF television stations, a total of 1,025 television stations on the air and operating (23 CPs had been granted for VHF, 222 for

UHF for a total of 245). In addition, 369 LPTV (low power television) stations were licensed and on the air at that time.[24] How many of these LPTV stations were functioning as low power commercial television stations and how many were in operation for other purposes (such as pay-television outlets) is not known. The focus in this section is on the television outlet that is operating as a television station and furnishing programming that is paid for by advertising revenue garnered by the station (or by the network, if network-affiliated).

The major differences among the VHF, UHF, and LPTV stations that are functioning as commercial television stations are in coverage area, network affiliation, market positioning or placement, and rates charged for availability of their audiences to the advertiser's message.

Coverage Areas   First, we will review theoretical coverage areas, not including carriage via cable television systems outside the metro area. Assume a low-band VHF television station (channels 2 to 6) with 100 kilowatts of visual signal power and an antenna height of 1,000 feet above terrain. The high-band VHF television station (channels 7 to 13) requires 316 kilowatts of visual signal to match the coverage area theoretically. For a UHF television station to match in theory the coverage area of these stations, the UHF station needs a 2,000-foot antenna tower and 5,000 kilowatts or five megawatts (million watts) of visual signal power.

The LPTV station is limited to no more than 10 watts and therefore provides coverage (on its own, without the aid of cable system carriage) to only the inner portion of the metro area. As you can readily see, all television stations are not equal for the potential viewer, or rather, they are equal if received well on the viewer's screen but vary in how many screens on which they appear or how they get to the television screen.

Television's Growth   The laboratory capability of sending a picutre across a room was developed in the late 1920s. Television was demonstrated at the 1939 New York World's Fair, but expansion was put on hold during World War II. The late 1940s and early 1950s saw an explosion of the establishment of many new television stations, the hurried extension of coaxial cable to get network programming out to the new stations, and the exodus of major entertainment shows from network radio to network television.

In that period, many newspapers established television stations under their ownership, and in the words of one anonymous newspaper executive, "They named the most incompetent on the newspaper to run the television station, because even they could only be successful in this new field." Principal reasons were the public clamor for the new medium and the network revenue available to a station as soon as it could get on air and the coaxial cable could connect it to the network.

This profitability held true for the nighttime programming period, but as stations expanded their hours salesmanship was required to sell daytime periods. For many years, independent stations without network affiliation found it a major struggle just to survive.

Television Today   The television industry today has matured into a multifaceted advertising medium composed of network-affiliated television stations, independent television stations, low-power television stations, and cable television. For purposes of sales of advertising time on the medium, we consider cable television separately.

The viewer receiving signals via cable sees no difference among a conventional broadcast television signal, a television signal uplinked to a satellite to be downlinked by satellite-receiving antennas at cable television systems, or a channel filled with programming received through some other method. What matters to the viewer is the content of the program and how interesting the program material is to them.

Television and Viewers   Stepping back in time again to 1950, of the 43 million households in the United States, only 3,880,000 (9 percent) had television receivers.

By 1960 the percentage of U.S. households with television had grown to 87.1 percent, and as of 1984, 98.1 percent of all U.S. households had television, 83.8 million of the 85.4 million households. In fact, 90.5 percent of those television homes have color television sets; in addition, almost 55 percent of them have more than one television set in the home.[25] These television homes spend an average of about seven hours per day viewing television.[26]

Television Revenue   Commercial television stations received some $425 million in compensation from the networks in 1983 for carrying network programming with advertising sold by the networks. In addition, in that same year these stations received $4.3 billion from national spot advertising sales, where the advertising is purchased by national advertisers on a station-by-station basis. The stations in 1983 received $3.6 billion from local advertising sales,[27] which grew to $4.9 billion for 1984. (Total television advertising estimates for 1988 exceed $25 billion.)

This local sales revenue occupies the working life and efforts of a majority of the salespeople at the local television stations in markets from New York, Los Angeles, and Chicago—the three largest television markets—to the television stations in the smallest of the more than 200 recognized television markets. This local advertising revenue actually is made up of two different types of sales activity: *local* advertising, which is that sold through local advertising agencies, and *retail* advertising, which is that sold directly to the advertiser-client.

Television's Power Television is a powerful advertising medium when properly used. It combines sound and sight, with each television commercial essentially a complete minidrama of sorts. The pictures that display (in living color), the voice message that explains and reinforces, and the music (if used) combine to provide a unique method of advertising that can introduce new products, build an image for an advertiser, and create (or awaken a hitherto unknown) desire to buy.

Most people can remember and identify their favorite television commercials of the present or years past, as well as some commercials that were remembered because they were irritating. The standard television commercial length is currently 30 seconds, although 15-second commercials are becoming more frequent. Programming these 15-second commercials adds to the number of advertising impressions given the viewer during a commercial break in the programming. Several national advertising agencies have expressed worry over commercial clutter.

SELLING TELEVISION AGAINST (AND WITH) NEWSPAPERS

Most television sales mangers readily identify newspaper as a principal competitor for the retail and local advertising dollar. Newspapers earn $20 billion in local advertising revenue, and less than $5 billion dollars in local advertising volume goes to television.

The Television Bureau of Advertising (TvB) functions for television stations in the manner that RAB functions for radio stations. TvB furnishes member stations material to help them market their product, the availabilties for advertiser's commercials.

In discussing the pros and cons of competitive media, TvB says television is the

> largest in reach and the time people spend with it, television is also the most creative of all advertising. It combines many of the advantages of other media—words, pictures, sounds, color—and adds motion. Instantaneously available in nearly every household nationwide, it is the one true mass medium, delivering selective audiences within its mass audience. So advertisers using television to its fullest combine reach with frequency to target specific, bulk audiences.[28]

Newspaper Advantages and Weaknesses

Much of what was said about newspapers' advantages vis-à-vis radio applies to television as well. Newspaper is the oldest of the advertising media, and over the years it has become entrenched with advertisers experienced in using newspaper advertising. Newspapers do allow advertisers to present ads in depth—a half-page, a full page, a *double-truck* (two facing pages filled with advertising for the same firm), up to a complete section of a number of pages, if the advertiser desires that much.

Television stations cannot sell the advertiser the time (in one lump) to put all the information appearing in a double-truck ad on television. If that were possible, the audience more than likely wouldn't stay around to watch. That fact, however, leads to a strength of television advertising that is a weakness for newspapers.

Active and Passive Media Television (like radio) is a passive medium. The viewer is not required to do anything but watch and listen, and commercials, which are interruptions of the program, are tolerated because the viewer knows the program will soon return. In the meantime, much or all of the advertising message is ingested, just as the programming material was. The newspaper reader is dealing with an active medium. The reader must open the paper, turn the pages, and read the material. The newspaper reader tends to scan a page for items of interest, bypassing ads in the process, and, in the case of a full-page or double-truck ad, to turn quickly past them with little recognition.

Shrinking Circulation TvB points to newspapers' shrinking circulation and escalating advertising charges as cons for newspaper advertising and notes that newspaper readership is dropping, especially with the younger population. It points to the increased ratio of advertising content to editorial content, which rebuts arguments of television commercial clutter.[29]

Cost Comparison Television is more costly than radio as an advertising medium but less costly than newspapers on a similar reach and frequency basis or on the basis of CPM. However, the average network-affiliated television station just does not have the inventory of spot availabilities for local sale that the average radio station in the same market has due to network commitment and the large number of spot television sales.

Total Market Coverage TvB recommends that local television salespeople familiarize themselves with the term *total market coverage* or *TMC* (TvB also characterizes it as *alternative distribution*). This TMC is the concept under which a daily newspaper publishes some other device to reach all of the households in its market area or all of those that are not subscribers to the newspaper.

As TvB describes it:

> Let's say a daily newspaper reaches 60% of its market. That's not the ADI, of course, but the newspaper's market. If that newspaper also publishes a weekly newspaper . . . and sends it free to all the households in its market . . . it now has 100% coverage. So it promotes and sells this 100% . . . total market coverage . . . concept to advertisers.

> *To achieve this, a newspaper . . . or catalogs, circulars, almost anything . . . can be distributed by the newspaper. They can be carrier-distributed. Or they can be mailed. Sometimes the newspaper will target non-newspaper subscribers. Or it may target more selectively.*[30]

TvB notes 1,200 such TMC systems and cites the reasons for growth of them to fight television: the drop in newspaper circulation, the rise in newspaper rates, and the rise in popularity of direct mail. TvB cites direct mail (which also includes *shared mail*, those inserts for two or more advertisers bundled together and mailed at third class postal rates) as growing fastest of all media. TvB notes

> *First . . . it's very improbable that the people we want to sell . . . local businesses and retailers . . . are going to turn totally away from print. Why? Because "print works" for local businesses and retailers. But, secondly, print works better with television.*[31]

Television with Print Advertising

Television can expand print coverage, expand the readership of print advertising, and help an advertiser overcome newspaper clutter to make the advertiser stand out. TvB identifies the use of television to add to the impact of print—either newspapers or direct mail—as *media synergism*. A publication of that title quotes representatives of various types of businesses on the effectiveness of this blending of television advertising with print advertising.

> *The president of Buffums' 15 department stores in Los Angeles and San Diego states: "I can reach one million people with the* Los Angeles Times. *But I can reach 20 million with television—many of whom haven't heard of my store. Direct mail alone is incestuous because we're talking to ourselves. Newspaper supports our television, the combination expands reach."*
>   *Macy's San Francisco told TvB that television enables them to double the readership of their print ads, and to increase the success of their sales.*
>   *"Television," Macy's explains, "puts your store in the forefront of people's minds. . . ."*
>   *Bargaintown, USA, with 41 stores in Alabama and Georgia uses a synergistic advertising program because, as its advertising manager explains, "It enables us to better target demographics. Today's consumers are very mobile and very diversified, and no one medium can deliver a message effectively. We use television and radio to not only prepare customers for our print, but we also follow-up with broadcast to remind them that our print is out there."*[32]

The television salesperson recognizes that the larger the business, the more it uses a combination of media. The intent of the professional television salesperson is to have television advertising form a major pillar of the advertising campaign, with the other forms of advertising in the media mix becoming more and more the add-ons.

TELEVISION VERSUS RADIO

One of television's strengths in relation to radio is the numbers. Just as more and more markets in the nation have become one-newspaper markets, each market has fewer television stations than radio stations. Choosing a television station is easier than choosing a radio station because the advertiser has fewer options.

Television, although accepted as commonplace in the home, is still the glamor medium, and being on television carries a certain status that being on radio or in the newspaper does not.

> *Many of radio's strengths are also seen as weaknesses. With a great many radio stations, each a different format—and frequently changing formats—often there's no guarantee of deliverable audiences. Radio is almost too select, too narrow. Multiple stations and formats fractionalize audiences. And this means buying radio is difficult—to reach a substantial market requires using numerous radio stations.*[33]

As in the case of the audience estimates, in which each of the stations in the market can find areas in which that station does best and publicize that portion, each medium can readily find those areas in which that medium is best and can and should stress these areas.

TELEVISION VERSUS CABLE AND OTHER MEDIA

Cable television is another form of television except in the concept of sale of advertising time. When a commercial is inserted on a local cable television system for a local advertiser, it is another television commercial to the consumer viewing it. To the television stations in the market, however, it is advertising that has gone to another medium for the advertiser's dollars.

The other differences between the television station commercial and the television commercial on cable television include, as the RAB noted, the amateurish quality of many cable television commercials. When the price of the cable system advertising campaign is relatively small and the advertiser must pay for production of a commercial to use in that schedule, the tendency is to apply a quick-shoot, quick-edit approach that does not stretch the boundaries of professionalism. However, cable system schedules sold to advertisers who already have commercials produced for broadcast television may show commercials with as much professionalism as any others in the market.

Cable television systems' sale of advertising has not become a major competitor to broadcast television advertising sales. The amounts of money involved in the cable advertising sales would purchase little additional broadcast television time in the same market, and the overall amount of money siphoned off by cable advertising sales has been very small in comparison to broadcast television's biggest competitors (print, exemplified by newspapers and direct mail). Moreover, the cable system channels are not yet showing up in sizable numbers on audience estimate reports, and any system that invites the viewer to subscribe has a plethora of channels and a fragmented audience.

By the same measure, LPTV stations, offering one signal among many in the market, try to find a niche in the visual communication field. Their coverage when compared with that of the broadcast television station is similar to a small suburban weekly that competes with the large daily newspaper that dominates the print portion of media in the market.

CABLE TELEVISION VERSUS OTHER MEDIA

Most of the channels of programming offered by cable television companies are free channels offered to the subscriber as part of a tier of service for which one price is paid for all the offerings. In addition, there are the pay channels, such as the Movie Channel, Home Box Office, ShowTime, the Disney Channel, Cinemax, and the Playboy Channel, for which subscribers pay a separate fee.

Initially, many of the free channels listed charged the cable television companies a small fee per subscriber per month. These free channels derive most of their revenue from advertising inserted within their programs, just as advertising is inserted in programming of broadcast television stations.

In recent years cable television companies have begun to receive a form of payment for carrying the signals of these free channels to consumers. In some cases, it takes the form of a monthly payment of a few cents per subscriber to the cable company; in many cases, it comes in the form of advertising minutes within the channel programming that can be sold locally by the cable company for additional revenue. Thus, the local cable television system in many localities has become another competitor for local, regional, and even national advertising dollars.

Local Inserts

Local commercial availabilities on cable systems are more like broadcast television commercials in makeup and reception by the consumer who views them on a television channel, but they are generally more like radio commercials in the manner in which they are sold. Instead of selling a specific commercial availability within a specific television program, as is usually the case with broadcast television advertising, these cable television local commercials often are sold as a rotational package. The package gives the advertiser a spot within a group of advertisers whose commercials then rotate through the available commercial locations on a particular channel, such as

CNN, or through several of these channels, such as a combination schedule offering so many rotational slots through the cablecast day on two or more of the cable channels.

In cost per commercial aired, these cable television commercials are more like radio than broadcast television in most markets. This is due to three factors.

1. The concept of local cable advertising is still fairly new, and rating research information has been sparse on most of the channels.

2. The cable television reach is limited to the wired subscribers, usually a much smaller number than the population that can receive the broadcast television station (or the radio station) in many instances.

3. The cable television system's main attraction is at the same time a drawback to selling specific commercial locations. The cable system's attractiveness is the multiplicity of channels it offers, with a resulting fragmentation of the possible audience split among many channels and lower viewing per channel.

Wired-Nation Concept

Some years ago, cable television was being promoted as the television of the future. When the nation was wired, everyone (or almost everyone) would receive television signals via connection to a cable system. This has not happened; cable as of 1988 had 51.1% penetration nationwide, although in some markets the cable penetration is considerably higher. Cable was being touted as a shop-at-home, bank-at-home, burglar- and fire-alarm system, and home environment control system. Most of these applications are technically feasible, but public demand for them has not followed technical capability.

Nevertheless, cable television is much more than a community antenna system to bring the signals of television stations to people who otherwise would not receive them well. Cable television also brings many more channels of television capability—free channels (paid for by the monthly fee) and the pay channels or premium channels, the price of which is added to the monthly fee.

Shop at Home

The concept of shop at home, envisioned some years ago as a local function, has instead taken off as a national or regional function. As of August 1986, five shopping channels were in operation to offer the cable viewer a variety of merchandise that can be ordered after viewing on the TV, making shopping an armchair exercise. Because of the success of the format, a number of other firms are planning to enter the field.

Tempo Television   Tempo Television of Tulsa, Oklahoma, distributes home-shopping programming as well as nonshopping shows to viewers. Tempo is carried on cable systems that reach more than 13 million people.

Home Shopping Network   Home Shopping Network, one of the big success stories in this field, began its Home Shopping Network 1 in 1985 and added a Network 2 in 1986. The Home Shopping Networks had a 1986 reach of 7.2 million homes of the estimated 40 million homes that receive television programs via cable or satellite antennas. The two networks operate 24 hours a day, seven days a week.

This company also became a major success story on the American Stock Exchange in 1986, when it offered more than two million shares of its stock to the public at $18 per share. The stock opened at $42 per share, and rose as high as $108 per share before market downturns set in.

Viewers of this network, unlike some of the others, may order merchandise only while it is displayed on the screen. The company reported a profit of $11.4 million on sales of $106.8 million in merchandise in the nine months ending May 31, 1986.

Other Shopping Channels   Others in the home-shopping field include Cable Value Network and Tel-Shop, both of which began operation in 1986. At least three others were in planning stages for start at that time. Cable systems derive revenue from these ventures, with some of the shopping channels paying the local systems up to 5 percent of the amount of revenue received from zip codes within the cable system's area.[34]

Local Advertising Sales

Advertising time sales by local cable systems has been underway, exceeding $215 million in national billing in 1987, but the volume of advertising revenue available has been a tertiary priority for most cable systems because of financial considerations.

Addition of more subscribers has been the primary concern for most cable systems, and next has been the addition of more subscribers to the pay channels. These two prospects offer far greater return to the cable television system than local advertising has offered.

Cable television reversed the process of spread that was customary in other electronic media. Cable television began, not in the largest markets, but in the hinterland. It wired homes in areas where television was hard to get or where few television signals were available.

Its spread into the larger markets came late in its development because the larger metropolitan areas had more television signals more easily available for prospective viewers. However, cable systems have learned that additional revenue is available from advertising sales, and they are showing a more concerted effort to go after this extra market now than in previous years.

Audience Research   One of the big stumbling blocks to selling cable advertising locally has been the lack of authoritative audience data. The cable channels are beginning to show up in audience estimates, and the ratings research firms are offering specialized services dealing with audiences for cable systems.

Television ratings are calculated on a metro and an ADI basis, and most television stations sell advertising based on the ADI—the large area they cover best. A local cable system and its channels may fare badly on an ADI-wide survey because the cable system may have the franchise to wire homes in only a small portion of that ADI.

Fragmentation   Robert Alter, president of Cabletelevision Advertising Bureau (CAB), in a 1982 address pointed to cable's diversity of channels as defining new ways for advertisers to reach audiences through television:

> *All news; all sports; cultural; black; Spanish; rock music; country music; weather; self-improvement; game shows and audience involvement; children's; women's services; and other programming that represents an alternative to traditional TV programming choices.*
>
> *How will this kind of cable programming affect the size and distribution of television audiences and advertising strategies?*[35]

Alter contended that the segmentation (fragmentation) of television audiences caused by specialty cable channels would change audience figures for the broadcast television networks and stations and leave the advertiser open to buying the advertiser-supported cable channels in order to reach the proper balance in advertising and marketing.

In the same address, Alter pointed to new commercial opportunities as an exciting possibility for advertisers. The cable-only channels (as differentiated from those that are broadcast channels relayed via cable) are not bound by FCC regulations on commercial content or length. The cable watcher in 1989 can see a number of programs that are really lengthy commercials for selling the product involved, whether it be a home-study course in something or the real estate available on the market in a community. (Some television stations are experimenting with these program-length commercials in the wake of FCC deregulation in a number of areas.)

Infomercials   A new word has been coined for cable's ability to offer longer commercial opportunities. *Infomercial* is a combination of *information* and *commercial* that means a commercial that lasts longer than the norm but is supposed to provide information while selling something. These infomercials may be two, three, five, or thirty minutes long or longer. (The shopping networks provide one example of infomercials because the entire content of the 24-hour programming is the selling of items.)

Cable Advertising Bureau offers a variety of services to help subscribing cable systems sell cable advertising.[36]

Growth of Cable Advertising

Virginia Westphal, vice president of advertising sales for Viacom Cable (MSO), stated that cable ad sales can be said to have succeeded in establishing cable as a feasible local advertising medium and in adding additional revenue to the cable companies.

> *Those who made the commitment to ad sales early have witnessed the number of systems selling local advertising quadruple in just the last three years: from 316 in 1982, to 539 in 1983, to 900 in 1984, and more than 1,200 in 1985. . . .*
>
> *This initial success has been encouraging, yet in terms of the potential of the business, it is a drop in the bucket. The challenge of the cable advertising sales industry has been reworked: today's challenge is to develop the start-up effort into a continually growing and maturing business. The key to meeting this challenge is to make cable a regular part of an advertiser's media mix.*[37]

Cable Size　The 8,000 cable systems operating in the country as of 1988 serve some 45 million subscribers, with perhaps more than 110 million people included in the subscriber units in more than 20,000 communities. The figures represent 51.1 percent of the nation's television households. Commercial rates on the systems accepting advertising range from $2 to $250 per commercial, with this advertising revenue representing less than 5 percent of gross revenue for most of the cable systems.

Ad Revenue　Each year the *Broadcasting/Cablecasting Yearbook* lists cable systems by state. Among the information about each cable system is an annual advertising revenue figure for those cable systems that sell advertising. In the 1984 *Broadcasting/Cablecasting Yearbook*, the largest volume of local advertising reported by any cable system in the country was the $588,000 reported by Palmer Cablevision's Naples, Florida, cable system.

Second in advertising volume at $350,000 annually was Cable TV of Puget Sound in Pierce County, Washington. Reporting $300,000 each annually were Southern Connecticut Cablevision of Bridgeport and NYT Cable TV of Audubon, New Jersey. KBLE Ohio, Inc., of Columbus, Ohio, was fifth with annual advertising revenue of $278,000.[38]

Table 9-3 shows the changes from 1984 to 1986. In the 1986 *Broadcasting/ Cablecasting Yearbook*, Cox Cable of San Diego, which was not among the top 100 cable systems in advertising revenue in 1984, reported annual advertising revenue of $2 million. (The San Diego cable system also ranks as the largest cable system, with more than 258,000 subscribers.)

Second in advertising revenue was Comcast Cablevision of Maryland in Baltimore County with $1.2 million. Four systems tied for third place with reported advertising revenue of $1,000,000: United Cable of Colorado in Englewood; Cox Cable of Jefferson Parish in Louisiana; Warner/Amex Cable Communication, Inc., of Columbus, Ohio; and Arlington Telecable in Arlington, Texas.

TABLE 9-3

Top 10 Cable Systems in Advertising Revenue Reported

1984			1986		
Rank	Amount	Cable System	Rank	Amount	Cable System
1.	$588,000	Palmer Cablevision, Naples, FL	1.	$2,000,000	Cox Cable San Diego, San Diego, CA
2.	350,000	Cable TV Puget Sound, Pierce County, WA	2.	1,200,000	Comcast Cablevision, Baltimore County, MD
3(T)	300,000	Southern Connecticut Cablevision, Bridgeport, CT	3(T)	1,000,000	United Cable of Colorado, Englewood, CO
3(T)	300,000	NYT Cable TV, Audubon, NJ	3(T)	1,000,000	Cox Cable, Jefferson Parish, LA
5.	278,000	KBLE Ohio, Inc., Columbus, OH	3(T)	1,000,000	Warner/Amex Cable Communication Inc., Columbus, OH
6(T)	250,000	US Cable of Lake County, Waukegan, IL	3(T)	1,000,000	Arlington Telecable, Arlington, TX
6(T)	250,000	International Cable, Erie County, NY	7.	750–900,000	Oceanic Cablevision, Honolulu, HI
8.	218,000	Viacom Cablevision, Seattle, WA	8.	700,000	International Cable, North Tonawanda NY
9(T)	200,000	Greater Fall River Cable TV, Fall River, MA	9.	600,000	Fresno Cable TV Ltd., Fresno, CA
9(T)	200,000	Valley Cable TV, Los Angeles, CA	10.	588,000	Palmer Cablevision, Naples, FL
9(T)	200,000	Metrovision SW Cook County, Inc., Hickory Hills, IL			

Source: 1984 Broadcasting/Cablecasting Yearbook
1986 Broadcasting/Cablecasting Yearbook

In the 1986 yearbook, the Naples, Florida, system reported the same $588,000 reported for it in 1984. This amount earned it first place among cable systems in 1984, but only tenth place in the 1986 listings.[39] It was the only repeater among the top ten in the 1986 listings. The top ten systems in advertising revenue in the 1986 report showed a total of just over $9.9 million, still a relatively small amount of advertising volume but a 341 percent growth in two years.

These sums are relatively small in the overall financial picture of the cable system. To a system like San Diego, with more than 258,000 subscribers, the advertising revenue is a nice addition, but the priority in the building period is adding on subscribers. With each subscriber worth, say, $15 to $20 dollars per month in revenue for regular service, plus premium channels, the addition of 10,000 subscribers would contribute as much or more yearly as the advertising revenue. When considered as part of the company's overall revenue or of the advertising volume of the San Diego market, the $2 million in advertising amounts to a drop in the bucket.

Cable Selling Points

How does a salesperson for local cable advertising compete in the marketplace to get advertising dollars from newspaper, television, direct mail, and radio. First, the salesperson has to learn about the product, cable television.

People who subscribe to cable watch television more. The channels available offer diversity and attract segments of audience, similar to the way radio stations do with their different formats for different tastes. In addition, cable now offers its first national "network" with the advent of TNT or Turner Network Television (Ted Turner's superstation, WTBS, Atlanta), which debuted in the fall of 1988.

The salesperson should note the national advertisers on channels on which local advertising is sold. These firms have advertising counsel to help them make good decisions on advertising.

The rotational way in which cable is sold in many markets offers a chance for the local advertiser to get exposure alongside the national advertiser on two, three, or more of the different channels. The advertiser is getting television commercial time at a cost that more resembles radio commercial costs.

The salesperson and the cable system of course use any success stories deriving from local advertising sales as ammunition to gain additional sales.

Disadvantages   The three principal disadvantages for cable advertising, as indicated earlier, are:

1. Lack of good audience estimate data, a problem being addressed by the ratings firms

2. The charge of fragmentation of the audience, which can be countered with good demographic information

3. The charge that many of the commercials are amateurish, which can best be countered by realizing that saving too much money on the cost of producing the commercial can make the advertising itself ineffective

SUMMARY

Learning to effectively sell against and with other media can maximize the monthly, quarterly, and annual revenue generated by a media consultant selling radio or TV. Salespeople must expect to encounter marketplace competition to their service in both product capability and cost-benefit ratio. They must therefore become familiar with all direct competitors (other electronic media outlets as well as all print media) in order to assess the value of their product against others who are selling the exact or a similar commodity. In the long-run, the creative radio or TV salesperson who can show clients the benefit of advertising on a particular station, using advertising reallocated from other media (like newspaper), is likely to achieve better financial results than the salesperson who spends most of the time combatting other radio stations in the market (if selling radio) or other TV stations (if selling TV).

Learning to calculate media reach, frequency and Gross Rating Points (GRPs) will help a salesperson effectively sell against other forms of media and will provide the qualitative information clients need to make a proper buying decision. (See Table 9-4 for a 5-year forecast on the various electronic media.)

NOTES

1. *Broadcast Marketing & Technology News*, August 1985, p. 8.
2. Ibid.
3. *Broadcasting*, July 4, 1988, p. 12.
4. *Radio Facts*.
5. *Radio Memo*, May 1986, pp. 2–6.
6. Ibid., pp. 8–9.
7. Ibid., p. 9.
8. Ibid.
9. Ibid.
10. *Research NAB*, December 1983, p. 1.

TABLE 9-4
Veronis, Suhler & Associates, 5-year forecast

	1987 (000,000)	1992 (000,000)	% increase 1987–1992
Network TV advertising	$8,830	$13,250	8.5%
Spot TV advertising	$6,830	$11,850	11.7%
Local TV advertising	$6,900	$13,200	13.9%
Total TV advertising	$22,560	$38,300	11.2%
Pay cable subscriptions	$3,600	$4,300	3.6%
Basic cable subscriptions	$5,600	$9,200	10.4%
National cable advertising	$865	$1,900	17.0%
Local cable advertising	$215	$550	20.7%
Total cable TV	$10,290	$15,950	9.2%
TV network program buying	$3,610	$5,190	7.5%
TV station program buying	$1,500	$2,370	9.6%
Cable program buying	$2,300	$3,850	10.9%
Total television program expenditures	$7,410	$11,410	9.0%
Network radio advertising	$405	$650	9.9%
Spot radio advertising	$1,320	$2,000	8.7%
Local radio advertising	$5,515	$9,000	10.3%
Total radio advertising	$7,240	$11,650	10.0%

From: *Broadcasting*, July 4, 1988, p. 48

11. Anthony Segraves, "Taking the Color Out of Black and White," *Radioactive* 12:7.

12. Ibid.

13. *The Radio Marketing Consultant's Guide to Combining Media* (New York: Radio Advertising Bureau, Inc.), pp. 10–11.

14. Sandy Keeling, Snyder's Dept. Store, Kentucky Broadcasters Sales Seminar, Louisville KY, June 4, 1986.

15. Tom DeMuth, Schneider DeMuth Advertising, Kentucky Broadcasters Sales Seminar, Louisville KY, June 4, 1986.

16. Jamie Harper, Director of Advertising, Liberty National Bank, Kentucky Broadcasters Sales Seminar, Louisville KY, June 4, 1986.

17. Sandy Keeling, Kentucky Broadcasters Sales Seminar.

18. *Radio Memo*, May 1986, pp. 11–12.

19. *Radio Reprints* (New York: Radio Advertising Bureau), p. 5.

20. Ibid.

21. *The Radio Marketing Consultant's Guide*, pp. 3–4.

22. Ibid., pp. 5–6.

23. *Is Cable Able?* (New York: Radio Advertising Bureau, 1966).

24. *Broadcasting*, July 4, 1988, p. 12.

25. *Trends in Television 1950 to Date* (New York: Television Bureau, Inc., 1984), p. 2.

26. Ibid., p. 5.

27. Ibid., p. 10.

28. *Competitive Media Pros/Cons* (New York: TvB, Inc.), pp. 1–2.

29. Ibid., p. 2.

30. *Print Synergism* (New York: TvB, Inc.).

31. Ibid.

32. *Media Synergism* (New York: TvB, Inc.), inside cover.

33. *Competitive Media*, pp. 1–2.

34. "TV Shopping Malls A Sensation," *The Sunday Tennessean*, August 3, 1986.

35. *Cable & Advertising: Will the Courtship Lead to Marriage?* (New York: Cabletelevision Advertising Bureau, 1982), p. 4.

36. "CAB Sales and Management Services and Key Resources Areas" (New York: Cabletelevision Advertising Bureau).

37. Virginia Westphal, "Making Cable Competitive for Spot Advertising Dollars," *Monday Memo*, February 3, 1986, p. 24.

38. *Broadcasting/Cablecasting Yearbook* (Washington, DC: Broadcasting Publications, 1984), pp., D-7–275.

39. *Broadcasting/Cablecasting Yearbook* (1986), pp. D-7-275.

Chapter 10

PROMOTIONS
AND CO-OP
ADVERTISING

CONTESTS VERSUS PROMOTIONS

The terms *contest* and *promotion* are often used interchangeably in broadcasting but are very different, according to Larry Perry in *Broadcast Promotion Sourcebook*.[1]

> A "contest" is a giveaway or game conducted on the air in conjunction with other station activities in one of several forms: quarter-hour building contests, cume-building contests, image-building contests, seasonal contests, and the like. A "contest" can involve skill or pure luck; the latter more commonly being the case. Contests tend to be relatively short-lived in duration and have a narrow or specific purpose—to attract new listeners, extend existing listenership, or whatever.
>
> A "promotion," however, is a generic activity designed to provide broad-based sampling of your station in a crowded field of competitors. A promotion can be a major, high-visibility stunt. Or, it can consist of a campaign of TV, outdoor, transit ads, or any combination thereof. It can involve a direct mail piece or a newspaper insert. But whatever form a promotion takes, it is broad in purpose: basically, promotions are high-powered, expensive, comprehensive attacks on the competitive marketplace—designed to make people sit up and take notice of your station.[2]

For our purposes in explaining and presenting broadcast promotions and contests, we will use the broader term *promotion* to denote all station activities designed to attract and keep listeners or create general marketplace awareness of a particular station.

From a sales standpoint, all such efforts should contain sponsor tie-ins and, if possible, present reasons why listeners or viewers should visit a sponsoring business—to pick up clues, entry blanks, or game cards, for example. In this sense, we are using the term *promotion* to mean *sales promotion*, which is but one facet of the word; promotion also includes audience promotion (contests) and public relations.

CROSS-INVOLVEMENT

Our working definition of broadcast *promotion* is any portion of a station's on-air programming that creates cross-involvement between the station, its advertising clients, and the audience who listens to or views that station. Cross-involvement occurs, for example, when a station's listeners or viewers go to an advertiser's store to see a station personality in person or register for prizes to be given away by the store and/or the station. The key element is the involvement of the audience-customers in something outside of and in addition to regular attention to the station's programming. Such cross-involvement creates traffic and eventual sales for the client and more listeners or viewers for the station programming the promotion.

Our working definition of *promotion* does not include call letter–inscribed pens, trade journal ads, colorful brochures, bumper stickers, balloons, or business cards, which are examples of station merchandising with no cross-involvement, or contests designed to attract new listeners with no sponsor tie-in. Marketing a station via such examples and engaging in on-air promotions that require direct listener involvement are two separate activities, even though they may be coordinated by the same individual.

PROMOTION AS A PRIMARY MARKETING FUNCTION

In *Strategies in Broadcast and Cable Promotion*, Susan Eastman notes:

> *No longer is promotion a secondary tactical device; it is now a primary marketing function enabling competitive positioning of stations, networks or services in their markets. Because the public regards television programs and radio formats as much alike, management executives must find ways of luring viewers or listeners to their stations or channels. Promotion is an indispensable tool for creating and exploiting differences—that is, for convincing the public that one network, one station, one service or one program differs substantially from its competitors.*[3]

CONTESTS: CUME BUILDERS AND QUARTER-HOUR BUILDERS

Contests usually last for a short time period and are programmed to serve a specific, strategic function with the active involvement of the listener or viewer. They may or may not require skill and may or may not involve sponsorship. We define anything with cross-involvement or sponsorship as *sales promotion*; contests designed to attract audience that are aired without sponsorship are *contests*. When a contest is sold, thus involving a sponsor or business, it becomes a sales promotion.

Attracting Attention: Cume Builders

Larry Perry writes that *cume* is

> *Business shorthand for "cumulative" or unduplicated listenership—the total number of bodies within a demographic category which your station attracts within the measurement period—daily, weekly or monthly. A "cume" builder contest is designed to attract new listeners who previously "cumed" elsewhere—other stations, or perhaps even earlier non-consumers of radio or TV. A contest designed to build "cume" is usually appropriate immediately following a format change, or to introduce listeners to a brand new signal previously not on the air. Thus, "cume" building contests tend to have an intense but brief appeal, and it is up to your station's programming executives to turn new "cume" into prolonged listenership with attractive and entertaining programs.*
>
> *Of course, if market fragmentation is plaguing your station, a combination of cume and "quarter-hour" building contests may be required to increase both unduplicated listeners and time spent listening.*[4]

Samples of cume-building contests include bumper stickers, station call letter (prize) buttons, citizen of the day, coffee clubs, coupon mania, secretary of the day or week, parking meter Good Samaritan, pet patrol, news tip of the day, week or month, flea markets and merchant fairs, station mystery man, and sponsorship of a parade or large community event.

Maintaining Listenership: Quarter-Hour Builders

> *"Quarter-hours" refer to the arbitrary sampling unit of 15-minute segments used as a ratings yardstick to measure prolonged listenership. Of course, "quarter-hour" share determines a station's overall standing in the marketplace and serves as the universal measurement for allocation of advertiser dollars. A "quarter-hour" building contest is really a temporary substitute for a program formula which will maintain listener interest without a prize or cash incentive. Quarter-hour contests can be useful in intensely competitive situations where there is little exclusive cume for any individual competitor or for a station with inferior signal which is forced to compete with the same format on clearly superior facilities . . . quarter-hour building contests are temporary measures which at best will serve to buy a station some time while finalizing a well-rounded program schedule attractive to the target audience.*
>
> *Quarter-hour contests are also useful for relatively new stations which are attracting considerable "cume" but whose listeners have not cemented station loyalties. Such contests can be helpful in developing listening habits which may be continued later once the competitive situation in the market eases and incentives on other stations are removed.*[5]

Examples of quarter-hour-builder contests include music marathons or playing x number of records in a row, cash calls (how much is in the jack-pot?), bonus songs, high-low (like the cash call, only the DJ responds to a guess by saying that the caller is either high or low, so you have to listen to zero in on the correct amount), soap synopsis, mail it in and win (then listen for your name to be called to phone in and win), music polls, mystery voices, and 100 percent music hours with no interruptions.

Sales Promotion in Broadcasting and Cable

We are concerned with promotions as they relate to the selling or revenue-generating process of station operation. Eastman defines this aspect of station promotion as "anything that helps sales executives sell commercial time on the station or network to advertisers."[6] Such a broad-brush approach includes all material prepared on station demographics for client usage, as well as tradeouts with clients. *Tradeouts* (bartering) are an exchange of merchandise or services from a client for a specified amount of airtime, usually amounting to the retail price of the merchandise or services exchanged. The station then uses such merchandise or services to give away to listeners during on-air promotions.

Revenue-Generating (On-Air) Promotions

Revenue-generating sales promotions provide a valuable service for participating clients who can listen to or view such promotions, trace additional traffic through their store during the course of the promotion, and become more personally involved in something more tangible than typical advertising schedules. These newspaper-oriented merchants are not very familiar with the electronic media and the commercial recall research that documents the high recall rate and memorability of radio and TV commercials.

Tangibility in Electronic Media Promotions

Electronic media messages are remembered at least as well as newspaper advertisements. How many people can recite, in its entirety, the famous McDonald's radio and TV campaign from the mid-1970s that was revived again in the mid-1980s: "Two all-beef patties, special sauce, lettuce, cheese . . . ?" Imagine anyone remembering even any part of such a complicated collage of words if such a campaign had been a print ad.

Merchants who are newspaper-oriented are generally unaware of the market penetration of the electronic media as compared to newspaper. Having something—specifically a promotion—to grab hold of makes it easier for them to make a buying decision in favor of the electronic media. Radio and TV promotional activity is easier to sell to some merchants and makes an intangible service seem more "human" and personal to the business person as well as to the listener, who can be personally involved in the promotion and becomes a potential customer for the client sponsoring the promotion.

Sales promotions are scheduled as a regular part of most commercial stations' programming almost on a continuing basis. Radio outlets are heavily involved in promotions because their market is fragmented and promotions serve as a way to attract and hold as large an audience share as possible during a given period of time, especially during a *book* or ratings period. Radio stations also have more time to sell, and promotions, in essence a sale on available product, provide a way to sell unsold time with more commercial inserts.

Hypoing

However, salespeople should be aware that hypoing is prohibited by both the FTC and the Arbitron ratings service. Larry Perry notes that *hypoing* is defined by the FTC and by Arbitron as

> *Activities calculated to distort or inflate such [audience measurement] data—for example, by conducting a special contest, or otherwise varying . . . usual programming or instituting unusual advertising or other promotional efforts, designed to increase audiences only during the survey period. . . .*
>
> *Any station which designs special contests or promotions, outdoor or TV campaigns solely "for the book" is open for a hypoing charge. . . . On the other hand, most stations in competitive markets do design and execute special promotional activities which happen to coincide with survey periods. And, while the FTC has not vigorously enforced the "hypoing" rule [recently] . . . that is no guarantee that there will not be future investigations. . . . Arbitron, of course, will continue to investigate stations accused of hypoing charges in various markets and delete or "sticker" those stations to protect the credibility of its survey reports.[7]*

Promotions Don't Replace Consultancy

Although a necessary and important part of monthly programming at most stations, promotions should never substitute for regularly scheduled, day-to-day, results-oriented advertising designed to address a businessperson's real problems of profitability. Promotions, by and large, are easier to sell than conducting a consultant call, and for that reason many salespeople prefer them.

Promotions are certainly a part of the portfolio that a salesperson should carry to help clients attract customers, but they are not meant to be the meat and potatoes of the sales staff. The best salespeople realize that promotions have their place and are designed to supplement rather than replace client-oriented consultative sales.

Sales consultants know that effective promotions take time and hard work to plan and need to complement the objectives of the station and the marketing goals of management in terms of the community image the station is projecting or wishes to project.

What Sales Promotions Accomplish

A station sales staff has five potential reasons to engage in sales promotion activity.

1. A promotion generates new advertising dollars for the station during the billing month or months it is being run.

2. A promotion attracts new clients to the station roster of current advertisers.

3. A promotion increases the amount of money being spent in a particular month by a current advertiser by adding to what is already committed. The promotion should thus provide added value to a regular schedule.

4. A promotion involves a station's audience, generates a deeper sense of station loyalty, and causes prolonged periods of listening. Such audience involvement also increases call letter exposure, always important, especially during a ratings sweep.

5. A promotion generates internal staff morale at the station with all departments working together to make the promotion a success.

Promotions, then, can be an extremely valuable sales aid to the financial and ratings success of any station and can help secure clients who would otherwise drift to other media outlets that offer their version of promotion and client involvement.

Promotions and Marketing

Complementing these sales-oriented reasons for developing sales promotions, Robert Klein has noted the marketing problems faced by salespeople when dealing with radio or TV promotions.[8]

- The top-rated station may be trying to maintain its leadership despite aging on-air personalities and audience demographics.
- A challenger may be engaged in building and communicating stability, aggressiveness, and identity in the market.
- A station that has radically altered its programming, format, or network affiliation may be trying to reestablish itself.
- A long-time loser may be trying to turn itself around.
- A station with a new manager who wants to change everything may be fluctuating without defined objectives.
- A public television or radio station may be endeavoring to raise enough money to keep out of the red for another season.

■ A newcomer in cable or subscription television may be trying to establish itself in the crowded marketplace.

Thus, the marketing problems faced by the electronic media are to attract audience, maintain audience, increase audience, alter audience demographics, or improve image.[9]

The ultimate objectives of programming a promotion include:

1. *Building program popularity*

2. *Generating loyalty that results in extended viewing and listening*

3. *Appealing to the entire coverage area*

4. *Identifying the specific television or radio station or cable system with the needs and interests of its community*

5. *Developing a competitive position in relation to the growing number of media alternatives in the market.*[10]

Promotional Need in Radio, TV, and Cable

Klein summarizes the need for promotion in all broadcast media:

The problems for network television affiliates in the 1980's (and into the 90's) tend to be concentrated in newscasts, news personalities and news lead-in and lead-out programming. For independents, the challenge is to counter the programming and the promotion of network affiliates. In radio, the problems relate to format and consistency (as in music mix), to on-air personalities, or to overall service. The problems in cable are to get subscribers, keep them, and persuade them to purchase additional services. The problem of public television appears to be survival. At the same time, the television networks are engaged in a three-horse [now, it's four with the Fox Network] race to maintain mass audience numbers with the new specialized media coming up on the outside.[11]

Sales Promotion Planning Questions

Once the station has made the decision to create and schedule an on-air sales promotion, a considerable amount of planning, interdepartmental cooperation, and forethought needs to occur. A general staff meeting for department heads should be scheduled to ask some very basic questions dealing with station, format, audience, and potential sponsoring clients. Among these questions should be:

1. Is the concept of promotions or a particular promotion good for our station? In other words, exactly how will our station benefit?

2. Will the promotion appeal to our audience? Will they become involved? Will nonlisteners tune in to provide an overall net increase in listenership? Is the promotion targeted to our specific demographics?

3. Is the promotion good for our format? Does it lend itself to our format and our targeted listener?

4. Will our advertisers and clients benefit from the promotion? Will participating store management and staff see additional traffic and customers without enduring undue stress and hardship?

If these questions cannot be answered in the affirmative, then the promotion under consideration should not be scheduled. If the promotion is decided to be a positive factor for the station, its clients and potential clients, the station audience, and target listeners, then additional questions need to be addressed.

1. Is the promotion a station or a sales promotion? A sales promotion, which can be sold to a sponsor, possesses the ingredients of cross-involvement and added value. A station promotion, which is actually a contest such as the 25th caller on our Rock Hits line wins a pair of concert tickets, does not.

2. Can we tie a station promotion and a sales promotion together?

3. What are the specific details—all the whos, whats, whys, whens, and wheres? Everything about the promotion needs to be outlined to be sure that NAB guidelines on contests and lotteries have not been violated. Listeners need to know (and the FCC requires that you tell them!) *exactly* how they can win, the dates of the promotion or registration, what the prize will be, when it will be awarded, who is eligible to win—in short, all of the details of the promotion. This is not the time for listener, sponsor, or station confusion.

4. What is the package price to the sponsor?

5. How many packages need to be sold? How many per salesperson?

6. If prizes are involved, will they be obtained by tradeouts or purchases?

7. What is the total cost to the station of running the promotion? If total promotional cost exceeds 10 percent to 15 percent of expected revenue, the venture may be financially unsuccessful.

8. How can this promotion be effectively coordinated with traffic to ensure an "even" sound throughout the day without bunches of call-ins or other business being logged during prime-time hours or drive-time day parts?

9. What have we forgotten to discuss that we should have?

Sources for Promotional Ideas

Where does the sales department look for local promotion ideas once the appropriate questions have been asked, discussed, and answered? The RAB can give any member station dozens of promotional tie-ins that have worked in markets of all sizes across the country. *Chase's Calendar of Annual Events* lists every known holiday and many unknown and obscure holidays and specially designated days for every week and month of the entire calendar year. Many of these special designations, such as Dairy Month or Hot Dog Week, can be effectively tied in to local marketplace promotions, as can the station's local knowledge of civic promotions, school holidays, and special community events.

In addition to sponsor tie-ins with nationally designated days, weeks, or months, most stations develop their own promotions, especially around ratings time, that range from Caribbean vacations and large cash awards to Easter egg hunts (find the "egg" and receive prizes) and movie pass giveaways.

Designing and Selling Promotions

The specific tactics that go into the design of each sales promotion, whether a generic promotion that can be sold to a variety of clients or a custom promotion designed for one individual client, are dictated by:

1. Station and/or client needs
2. Concern for marketplace awareness and audience cross-involvement (listeners or viewers can be attracted to a station due to its promotional efforts and can remain loyal patrons of a particular station due to such promotional effort)
3. The needs of a defined marketplace where media promotions may be nonexistent or conversely saturating the market with cash giveaways and similar promotions

Clients may need the added impact of a generic or custom promotion to meet specific sales goals, as good promotions indeed generate traffic and hence sales. Audiences as well desire promotions; promotions make them feel they are part of a station's programming efforts. A defined marketplace may either need a promotion if none currently exists or need a unique promotion if many are concurrently offered. Promotions offer excitement and a sense of involvement through personal participation and complement a station's efforts toward positive, community-oriented programming.

Selling Promotion Benefits

Radio, TV, and cable promotions are sold by utilizing the MEDIA selling system and by properly qualifying customers during the interview stage, creatively selecting the proper promotion for their marketing needs, and confirming and assuring the buyer that the promotional benefits will indeed generate the needed results of marketplace awareness, traffic, and sales.

Therefore, the promotion must be exciting and timely and offer benefits to the client, the station audience, and the station itself. Organizational concerns should center on the reasons why a listener or viewer should become involved in a particular promotion. What are the benefits to the audience? What will motivate them to participate? If the audience and the clients can both become involved, then the ingredients for a successful promotion are present.

The Ratings Game and Audience Flow

Promotions are offered to audiences during ratings periods, as promotions are proven to attract new listeners or viewers and keep current ones loyal. Harvey Mednick of RKO radio has noted the importance of promotions in those ratings games:

> *The 1970's signaled the frantic diary stage of commercial radio development. On-air promotion shifted toward elevating ratings. Since most markets are rated two or four times a year (six times in the major markets) for a maximum of sixteen weeks, top forty stations began concentrating their promotion during those rating weeks in the early 1970's. This concentration caused a dramtic increase in the size of prizes, since dividing the same total number of dollars among fewer give-aways results in larger amounts per game.*
>
> *As a result of increased audience research in the 1970's, audience flow strategy surfaced in radio. . . . Programmers began looking for ways to recycle their audiences. They wanted 6 to 10 pm listeners to tune in at 7 am in order to build morning drive audiences for advertisers. . . . One objective of flow strategy is to get listeners to cross two quarter hours while staying tuned to one station. This flow increases average quarter-hour ratings and makes the station a more attractive commodity in the marketplace.*[12]

Most promotions today center on audience flow. Announcers constantly promise that "soon another lucky number will be announced" or "on tomorrow's morning zoo show, the crew will be giving away another trip to Disney World." The name of the game is to keep people tuned in all the time, as they never know when they might win. Listening for a previously announced record rotation (usually three songs played in a row in a particular order) is a popular method to keep listeners tuned to a particular radio station around the clock, especially if they think they can be the first to call when they hear the correct sequence of songs and win the $10,000!

SUCCESSFUL RADIO SALES PROMOTIONS

Here are examples of successful media promotions taken from the hundreds that are run across the country in a given calendar year.

"Old times" promotion: Prices in the stores of participating merchants are rolled back to what they used to be 10 or 20 years ago. Usually the station's frequency is tied in: if the station's frequency is 104 FM, many items are priced at $1.04, or $5.80 items are featured if the signal is 580 AM. This idea combines the sales-oriented, client-centered promotion with the station-oriented promotion.

Back to school: Brochures with special sponsor advertising printed on them welcome back university students in a college community. Brochures can be picked up by students and other listeners at participating stores and are distributed to students via the college bookstore. This promotion gives tangibility to participating sponsors, as their message appears *in print* on the brochures and is promoted on the air via station promotional announcements.

Treasure truck: A large truck or a large box built on a flatbed truck is painted with station colors and call letters and displayed at shopping malls, downtown areas, and at special media events with a station personality. Listeners are invited to see the truck on display and register their guess at participating merchant stores as to the exact contents or the total amount of "treasure" in the truck. Clues are given on the air throughout the broadcast day. The treasure can consist of various prizes donated by sponsoring merchants. The closest guess to the retail value (or whoever first guesses the correct contents via on-air clues) wins it all, with provisions made for ties. (If the promotion is designed to have listeners guess the correct contents of the truck, air personalities should take the tenth call or whatever and put the guesses on the air; the first correct guess wins.)

Button or bumper sticker promotion: Buttons or bumper stickers are passed out at sponsor stores. Listeners wear them or put them on their vehicles and station button spotters or bumper spotters stop them to award prizes that were donated by participating sponsors.

The fortune cookie: This promotion is ideal for all types of retail stores, with the possible exception of grocery stores. The station buys 20,000 fortune cookies, each containing the station's call letters and a personalized message. One out of every 100 (or whatever the sales team decides) has a special message indicating that a specific prize (or whatever) has been won. Cookies are distributed to participating sponsors who are promoted on the air in return for buying a specific package of advertising. This promotion is a good way to get 20,000 promotional announcements into the hands of listeners and potential listeners!

Rodeo days: Bring a professional rodeo show to town. Sell merchants a package that includes tickets to be given away free by the merchants. Of course, you'll have to sell enough advertising packages to cover the cost of the rodeo and realize a profit for the station.

Homemaker's show: Contract with a professional home economist to come into a large auditorium and prepare a variety of food dishes as she explains how it is done to the audience. The audience comes to the show free of charge compliments of the sponsoring station and views what the homemaker is actually doing via a large ensemble of mirrors that acts as a TV monitor. At various points throughout the show, have station personalities give away prizes provided by local merchants who have bought into the sponsorship with an advertising package. Sell the package to one merchant in each category for an exclusive, that is, one grocery store, one appliance dealer, one home improvement center, and one ladies wear store. Competing sponsors are undesirable as sponsors are invited to the show and introduced to the audience via a "commercial." The major appliance sponsor provides the appliances used that night, which are given away at the end of the evening as the grand prizes. People in the audience register as they enter the auditorium.

Flea market: Rent a large arena for sponsoring merchants who bring in selected and advertised merchandise to sell at a legitimate 50 percent discount off the regular retail price. Buy a full-page ad in the local newspaper (yes, you should occasionally do this to attract nonlisteners to *your* event) to supplement the radio promotions and tie in a media advertising package for the privilege of having a booth at the market. Don't forget to contact the local police for traffic control, as everyone in town may show up and most merchants will have little, if any, merchandise remaining. This promotion is better than a close-out or end-of-the-season sale for each merchant, as many of them clustered together offering such a discount guarantees a packed house.

Personalized jingle: Have a sales representative from a *quality* production house (like Media General in Memphis or TM in Dallas) make a presentation to the merchant on having a customized musical image (jingle) made exclusively for their store. These are expensive, around $2,000 for a good one. Offer to buy the image package for the merchant in return for an annual advertising contract. Give the merchant the rights to the package to use wherever he or she wants.

Call letter car: Have an auto dealer donate or trade out a new car, on which you employ an artist to paint your call letters all over it as many times as possible at different angles and keep an exact count of the number of times the call letters are actually painted. Drive the car around town (like the treasure truck) and have listeners and others guess the exact number of times the call letters appear on the car. The one who guesses the exact number of times (on the air or through sponsor stores) wins the car. Make a deal with the winner to pay for gas for a month in return for the winner driving around with the call letters still on the car. Of course, you'll have to pay for either a new paint job or a thorough buffing of the car to return it to its original condition.

Now that you have the idea, here are some titles of promotions suggested by RKO Radio. You can figure out what to do with them if you were designing a promotion for your station:

The Perfect Honeymoon, Mother's Day, Football Scoreboards, Soccer Scoreboards, Tennis Scoreboards, Midnight Sale, Vacation Sale, Home Show, Car Show, Golf Tournament, Swimming Tournament, Stars and Celebrities, Juke Box Show, Sock Hop, Sleigh Rides, Four-Leaf Clover, Diamond Mine, Magic Carpet, April Fool, The Great Escape, Orange Tag Days, Easter in New Orleans, Magic Bus, Scrabble, and Backgammon.

With imagination, creativity, and enthusiasm, you can turn radio into an immediate tangible for your clients and listeners and make it an exciting marketing medium at the same time. Just remember to run only one client-oriented and one station-oriented promotion at any one time in order to avoid listener confusion and maximize the results of cross-involvement.

Radio Sales Promotions in the 1990s

Newly developed promotional practices in the 1980s have tapped into the discovery of direct mail in which sweepstakes types of mailings are sent to the general public with winning numbers on selected tickets that are good for instant cash or other announced prizes when the number is aired and the holder of that ticket number calls in within a prescribed period of time. This is a good example of audience flow procedure. Intense competition leads stations to reach potential listeners at home via the mail; a well-put-together brochure can attract attention, be read, and cause more people to listen to the station.

> *The future of radio promotion is tied to the extended measurement techniques of the rating services. Radio is being measured in the top 100 markets on a 48-week-a-year basis (started in 1980) instead of 16 weeks as in the preceding twenty years. The 48-week ratings are designed to remedy the industry practice of hypoing in order to elevate station ratings during Arbitron diary periods. Extended measurement means that top forty, all-news, talk, beautiful music, and classical stations will now have to depend on program/format marketing.*
>
> *Although extended rating measurement is still in its infancy, promotion and programming experts in the industry are already seeking ways to exploit the situation. Several strategies are certain: Giant on-air activities will remain popular because they demand slow movement and can be sustained for a long time. . . . Entertaining games with clues will return along with low-reward, high-energy promotion recycling the audience. Audience flow strategies will be resurrected.*[13]

Good Promotions Influence Station Preference

Promotions, then, are a plus for any station's programming efforts; however, they should never replace progressive, consultant selling. Ruth Hamill has noted that most promotional effort falls short of its potential impact. Listeners are more interested in the particular music a station plays and the information it provides than in why it is fun to listen to. However, if stations give their listeners specific reasons for tuning in, they pay more attention, and a promotion can be a specific reason to tune in to any station. Hamill continues:

> Good radio promotions influence listeners' station preferences. This theory has underscored radio promotions since the first station ran the first contest. Now, a new telephone survey conducted by Frank Magid and Associates offers new insights into how listeners are reached, influenced or converted. The survey charted 1,010 listeners 18 or older who tune in a minimum of 30 minutes on a weekday. The study showed that people are well aware that more than one station in their market can satisfy their needs. . . . The vast majority of the respondents have a favorite station or at least one they listen to more than others. However, loyalty to a particular station is generally not strong. More than half the listeners would switch if a better one came along and 6 percent are actively looking for a better station. . . . While few admit that ads or promotions led to sampling a station, most people are aware of radio stations' promotions and most can recall recent advertisements. . . . Although they pay attention to promotions, the content does little to motivate people to tune in.[14]

LOCAL TELEVISION SALES PROMOTIONS

Television stations, due to their heavy commitment to network scheduling and/or syndicated programming, do not have the airtime to become heavily involved in promotions. Many of them, however, take advantage of what time they have to involve their audience in either sales-oriented or station-oriented promotions.

Much of this activity can be considered public relations. TV stations face far less direct TV competition with three VHFs and maybe a few UHFs in any marketplace, compared to, for example, 64 radio stations in the total surrounding area of San Francisco.

Of course, cable and video tape recorders are competing for the same audience. In general, however, TV stations rely on their networks and the heavy national promotions surrounding new fall programs to attract viewers and engage in far less local promotion than do radio stations.

Successful local promotions for TV stations include:

Runway: a TV fashion show that is sold to various sponsors who show their spring or fall fashions on the program. The program can be repeated for additional exposure and revenue. This promotion can be a good January promotion for those buying dresses and gowns for summer weddings.

Classified ads: Have merchants come in (or the general public for that matter) and do their own commercials to run on all-night TV. The evening audience for this type of program is surprisingly large.

Documentaries: Sell corporate-underwritten inserts in locally produced documentaries; include promotional announcements in news programs to establish the corporation's image in the community. Prior to the airing of the documentary, run a spot schedule to enhance the corporation's image and to remind viewers of their involvement in the upcoming documentary.

Friendship Days: Bowling Green, Kentucky's WBKO sold advertising packages to merchants on a county-by-county basis within the viewing area and promoted a designated day when the staff of the television station gathers in the county seat for a picnic and informal get-together. Viewers can meet the local personalities and win free prizes registered for prior to the event at various local stores. This personalizes the station for many viewers in rural areas where cable has not yet penetrated and only one radio station serves the community.

Sales-oriented promotions include promoting registration at an advertiser's store, usually a grocery store, and drawing out a winning name each week on the air. The viewer can win either a cash prize or free groceries. An attractive in-store display can ensure a high degree of participation and, of course, the person whose name is drawn must be watching TV when his or her name is actually pulled in order to qualify for the prize. An alternative to the "must view" would be that the winner must have had a card punched within the past week at the particular store. This qualification ensures that a registrant must visit that store at least weekly. If the card is punched, it is a winner, whether the entrant is watching or not.

Promotions can be successful on TV as well as on radio, again if the team responsible for putting the promotion on the air demonstrates imagination, creativity, and enthusiasm.

CABLE

At this point, promotions have not been common in cable television programming. What promotions do exist are designed to urge viewers to subscribe to the premium or pay channels; if they do so within a prescribed amount of time, installation of that new or additional channel is free. Cable companies, in essence, are retail outlets selling a service much like a department store sells products. They want more customers or consumers to buy their product, which is the service of cable television. They are in the business of attracting the largest number of subscribers possible, not attracting viewers to the single signal, as is the case with radio and TV stations.

SPECIAL EVENTS

Special community or station events, such as the broadcasting of local sporting events or live remotes, can attract additional revenue dollars to the station. The broadcasting or telecasting of sporting events such as amateur or professional baseball, football, or soccer boasts a small well-defined audience for the advertiser. Live remotes generate audience, sponsor, and station excitement when coupled with special prices, give-aways, and local media representative appearances.

Such special event happenings are nothing more than well-defined promotional activities that offer value-added benefits to the advertisers. Aside from the actual presentation of the sporting event or live remote broadcast, in-store displays offer additional promotional impact. These displays, a form of station merchandising, promote the event (such as the season schedule of the local team and time of broadcasts) as well as the station, its call letters, and air personalities.

Any community happening can be a special event that can be sold to advertisers with mutual satisfaction and benefit, provided proper planning and organizational procedures are followed.

CO-OP ADVERTISING

Co-op is referred to throughout this book. Such an advertising arrangement offers the salesperson an opportunity to increase sales and serve clients more fully than if such advertising did not exist. Of course, such advertising is not available to all advertisers and of those who have access to co-op funds, only a minimal percentage take advantage of them. "Nationwide, more than 15 billion dollars in CO-OP advertising funds are available each year from hundreds of manufacturers. And, each year, more than half that money goes down the drain. . . . Retailers who fail to use the CO-OP funds available to them are, in effect, throwing money away."[15] These unspent dollars that local dealers fail to take advantage of are usually the result of the merchant not being aware of such funds or feeling that dealing with the necessary paperwork is more trouble than it is worth.

Definition of Co-op Advertising

Co-op advertising is the sharing of local advertising costs between the manufacturer of a product and the local distributor or retailer who sells the product in each local market. Such an arrangement benefits both the manufacturer and the retailer. The manufacturer, who wants to sell as much of the product as possible to local retailers across the country, helps the retailer advertise the product to persuade the public to buy more of it. (If the public buys more product, the retailer orders more of it from the manufacturer.) The manufacturer agrees to pay a set portion of a retailer's advertising bill (25 percent, 50 percent, 100 percent, or even more in some cases), based on a percentage of purchases that the retailer makes from the manufacturer.

A Working Example: Levi Strauss For example, Sam's Department Store may be interested in selling Levi jeans. Levi Strauss and Company has a co-op plan that pays 80-20 up to 5 percent on Levis for men. To help Sam's Department Store move as many Levi jeans as possible, the manufacturer (Levi Strauss and Co.) will pay 80 percent of Sam's media advertising bill up to a maximum of 5 percent of his wholesale purchases from Levi. If Sam buys $20,000 worth of Levi jeans from the manufacturer, he has $1,000 in co-op advertising, that is, Levi Strauss will pay 80 percent of Sam's advertising bill up to a maximum of $1,000 on this line of products.

Very few co-op programs reimburse the retailer in cash or pay the station invoice. The manufacturer credits the merchant's account if the advertising is run. In Sam's case, if he used his allotted $1,000, Levi Strauss would invoice him for $20,000 minus the $1,000 in co-op, or $19,000.

Co-op Guidelines

Local merchants qualify for co-op funds by purchasing the manufacturer's product according to the specific guidelines stated by the manufacturer. Because these guidelines vary from company to company, retailers find coordinating any type of meaningful co-op program difficult unless they carry only a few lines or operate as a limited specialty store.

In recent years radio stations have developed the position of co-op coordinator to handle the details of the hundreds of co-op programs and assist retailers in utilizing co-op funds for the benefit of both the business and the station itself. Most local merchants must be assisted in determining the co-op funds they have available and in providing the certification that the advertising actually ran according to the manufacturer's co-op plan. This is normally done through notarizing special co-op copy paper that the commercial script is typed on (ANA/RAB Tear-Sheet) and notarizing the station bill with the exact dates and times of broadcast (see Fig. 10-1).

This verification system, developed by the RAB and the Association of National Advertisers, serves the same purpose as newspaper tear-sheets that prove that a certain newspaper ad was run. It is an affidavit of performance on the actual script used, attached to the station's receipted invoice for the co-op schedule.

Double-Billing Such a procedure prevents *double-billing*, a practice by which stations send a bogus bill to the manufacturer stating that more commercials ran than actually did, thus allowing the retailer to be reimbursed for more than the correct share of the schedule and to make a profit after paying for the advertising program. The FCC has outlawed double-billing.

The RAB publishes *Radio Co-op Sources* semiannually. The book lists every known co-op program from every manufacturer. The information is

FIGURE 10-1

Two examples of ANA/RAB radio tear-sheets

RADIO **W JIL** 1550 Jacksonville	ANA/RAB RADIO "TEAR-SHEET PROCEDURE FORM AT BOTTOM OF SCRIPT CERTIFIES WHICH COPY RAN.
Client:	For:
			Begin:	End:	Date:

STATION DOCUMENTATION STATEMENT APPROVED BY THE CO-OPERATIVE ADVERTISING
COMMITTEE OF THE ASSOCIATION OF NATIONAL ADVERTISERS.

This announcement was broadcast _____ times, as entered in the station's program log. The times this announcement was broadcast were billed to this station's client on our invoice(s) number/dated _____at his earned rate of:

$_____each for _____announcements, for a total of $_____

$_____each for _____announcements, for a total of $_____

$_____each for _____announcements, for a total of $_____

_____
Signature of station official

_____   _____   _____
(Notarize above)   Typed name and title   Station

FIGURE 10-1
(cont.)

KHMO RADIO 1070 AM ☐

THIS AD RAN ON: ☐

ACCOUNT AS PER LOG _____ CO-OP _____

DATES TO RUN _____ / LENGTH: _____ / SALESMAN: _____

1
2
3
4
5
6
7
8
9
10
11
12
13
14
15
16
17
18
19
20
21
22

This announcement was broadcast _____ times, as entered in the station's program log. The times this announcement was broadcast were billed to this station's client on our invoice(s) number/dated _____ at his **earned** rate of:

$ _____ each for _____ announcements, for a total of $ _____

$ _____ each for _____ announcements, for a total of $ _____

$ _____ each for _____ announcements, for a total of $ _____

_____
Signature of Station Official

ED FOXALL, GENERAL MANAGER   KHMO/KIDS
Typed Name and Title   Station

Notarize above

COPYWRITER & DATE _____

timely and accurate, as each manufacturer is contacted immediately before publication. Station salespeople can increase their monthly billings by helping their clients tap into previously unused sources of revenue that defray electronic media advertising costs.

Evaluating a Station's Co-op Program

Co-op is much more difficult to plan and organize than one may initially think. Manufacturers are witnessing a steady increase in the amount of co-op dollars spent by their retailers, and they are demanding a professional approach and well-thought-out programs before they approve the spending of co-op dollars.

Having co-op funds available does not necessarily mean they are automatically approved. Each manufacturer has a set of compliances that must be met and/or approved before such funds are released to offset any bill incurred by advertising on any station. RAB's *How to Profit From Radio Co-op* gives instructions on preparing effective co-op programs.

Generally manufacturers look for five basic ingredients in evaluating a station co-op program for general effectiveness. If any of these points are omitted, the manufacturer, distributor, or retailer may not approve future programs submitted by a station whose sales personnel have not effectively handled an initial co-op program.

1. The right product must be selected for the medium; the product must appeal to the target audience of the station on which it is being advertised.

2. The commercials must be professionally prepared and produced and must meet the needs and specifications of the manufacturer and the retailer.

3. A timely and well-planned schedule must be placed; it cannot sell swimwear in winter or utilize a schedule that misses the desired audience.

4. The retail outlet(s) must be prepared to handle the results of an efficient and effective co-op campaign that brings in a lot of customers to look for and buy what is being advertised.

5. Proper and complete billing procedures must be established with the retailer and/or manufacturer prior to the beginning of the schedule and must be followed up on as agreed.

CO-OP QUESTIONS AND ANSWERS

In *Making Money with Co-op,* former president of the RAB Miles David offers what amounts to a short course in co-op.

Q: What is Co-op?

A: It's the short name for cooperative advertising. Here's the basic definition we'll start with: Co-op is an agreement between the manufacturer of a product and the retailer (and/or wholesaler) to advertise or promote together for their mutual benefit.

Q: Great . . . now, let's get right to the money. Is co-op always a 50-50 split of ad costs between manufacturers and retailers?

A: Many people think so, because historically most co-op plans were based on sharing equally. But the pendulum is swinging in favor of encouraging retailers to take advantage of co-op. Today about 40% of manufacturers pay more than half. In fact, there are over 1,000 plans in which the manufacturer pays 100% of the advertising costs.

Q: You use the term "co-op plan." What does plan mean in co-op?

A: "Plan" describes the manufacturer's offer to share advertising costs with a retailer or wholesaler. The plan explains what the manufacturer will spend. It also tells what the retailer and/or wholesaler must spend. Other rules are also spelled out. For example, the plan usually specifies what product messages must be covered in the advertising. Important point: If the retailer doesn't follow the plan to the letter, the manufacturer may refuse to share the advertising costs.

Q: Are co-op plans easy to get from the manufacturer?

A: For a retailer, it should be easy because the manufacturer is required to provide them with co-op plans or information. Some send plans out to all their retailers, or their traveling sales reps may give plans to the retailer, or describe them. But, if you ask the retailer for the plan, there's a good chance it's been lost, or the rep forgot to cover it with him. When working with a small to mid-sized retailer, you most likely won't find the current year's plan in a nice, neat file.

Q: How about requesting co-op plans without involving the retailer?

A: That's done all the time when there's no time element. Some stations prepare request letters to the co-op contact at the manufacturer. Stations with a word processor can easily turn out 20 letters a week asking for plans, which they add to their library.

Q: Does the plan tell you who to contact for further information?

A: Many plans omit the name of a contact. If you do not have a name, ask for the Co-op Coordinator when you call the manufacturer. The names of thousands of manufacturer contacts and their phone numbers are listed in RAB's *Radio Co-op Sources* and are updated daily on RABCOOP, RAB's national computer network. Occasionally a company will set up a hotline to encourage media participation. The purpose is to give stations current accruals and fast copy approval.

Q: In a way, co-op sounds almost too good to be true for the retailer. For example, if many co-op plans pay 100% of ad costs, don't manufacturers go broke?

A: No, because most co-op plans have a built-in ceiling. The manufacturer usually pays for advertising up to a set percentage of the amount of merchandise the retailer has bought over the past year. For example, a typical plan might call for 5%. This basis for creating a co-op fund is called the *accrual*, one of the most commonly used terms in co-op.

Q: Is co-op designed to get the retailer to buy more merchandise?

A: It often works out that way. In many cases the manufacturer's salespeople (usually called reps), talk about the co-op plan at the time they're selling to the retailer. As part of their sell they offer co-op advertising support to help the retailer move merchandise.

Q: How much of an ad budget does a 5% accrual create?

A: A 5% accrual, on a retailer's $10,000 merchandise buy, accrues $500. If it's a 50-50 plan, the retailer must spend $500 of his own money to get the manufacturer's $500. So, $1,000 worth of advertising is done. If it's a 100% plan, the retailer doesn't have to spend matching money, so only $500 worth of advertising is done. (Of course, the retailer can always add his/her own money on top of this figure to increase total expenditure.)

Q: What do you have to look for when you read a typical plan?

A: There is no typical plan. It's amazing how different they are. Some are written in legal language and fine print. Others are simple, with exciting graphics. There are dozens of specific points in most plans. Unfortunately, the benefits and rules are covered in a different sequence in every plan, and require some digging. Even the terminology changes from one plan to another. We researched these by reading and analyzing hundreds of the most productive co-op plans.

Q: What's in co-op for a salesperson?

A: New money. That's really what it's all about. Because the subject seems complicated, most radio stations haven't scratched the surface in exploiting co-op's potential. And the same is true about a lot of retailers who don't understand co-op. So, sale people who invest even a little time in understanding co-op open up significant new revenue for their stations and them selves.

Q: How much money do manufacturers spend in co-op?

A: Good question. But the fact is you have to work backwards from some known numbers and use judgment to come up with a co-op spending estimate. We'll work with a figure of $5 billion which is about halfway between the highest and lowest published estimates, and the number that appears in a current book written for co-op executives by Edward C. Crimmins. It's called *Cooperative Advertising* and was published by Association of National Advertisers.

Q: That's a lot of money. But what do people mean when they say billions and billions of available co-op dollars go unspent each year?

A: It's true. This "unspent" phenomenon fascinates people more than any other co-op fact. Theoretically, if retailers used every co-op dollar available from manufacturers, an additional $5 billion could potentially be spent in co-op advertising expenditures.[16]

Sample Co-op Solicitation Letter

Probably the most practical portion of Miles David's book is a sample mail presentation to a retailer with little co-op knowledge; most retailers would fall into this category. Even though they may be familiar with the concept, few take the time to remain up-to-date on the many facets of the available programs. You can use the following letter, which is divided into numbered paragraphs for your convenience, to send to a retailer that you feel or know has co-op monies available.

1. The big advantage of advertising is that it brings people to your store to buy. You know that.

2. But advertising needs repetition to be effective. In a word, frequency. Once is not enough. People have to keep hearing about you — your selection, your prices, all the reasons people shop at your store.

3. You're being *outspent* by other retailers who compete with you to sell the same type of merchandise to the same customer. You know how much the big stores spend for advertising.

4. You may have felt you can't afford to increase the size of your advertising budget. All your costs keep rising, and there may not seem to be enough money to cover more advertising.

5. But there is a way to increase advertising without having to take all the money out of your own advertising expense. It's called *cooperative advertising,* or *co-op.*

6. Many of the manufacturers who provide the merchandise you sell also provide allowances to help you advertise.

7. Some may pay for 50 percent, 75 percent, or even 100 percent of the cost of your advertising.

8. Each year $5 billion is spent on co-op advertising.

9. Another $5 billion that could be spent by retailers isn't. Retailers often neglect to use this source of sales power.

10. You can bet that in this market, however, your big competitors don't let much of that advertising money go to waste. They are out-advertising you with the help of manufacturer dollars.

11. One reason they can do it is because they are staffed to handle co-op advertising. In the big stores people check for every potential co-op ad dollar.

12. The question is: Are you going to continue to underspend in the face of increasing competition or would you like to increase your opportunity to grow by increasing your ad budget?

13. At station _____ we're very knowledgeable about co-op and offer a unique service.

14. We will search out the dollars available to you now that you aren't spending.

15. We'll determine how those dollars can fit into your ad plans.

16. We'll handle all the work for you, from checking the amounts of money the manufacturer provides to creating copy.

17. After the advertising runs, we'll even go a step further—we'll see that you don't have to handle the details of getting reimbursed by the manufacturer.

18. Here's how to get started: I need to know which manufacturers are your biggest suppliers of merchandise. And I would like to examine items on your shelves for ideas. Please show me any literature you have received from manufacturers offering advertising support.

19. I will also need your account numbers with manufacturers. I will then be able to save you time in most cases by obtaining information for you from manufacturers on available dollars (based on the amount the merchant has spent; that's why you need the account numbers).

20. After we have the information, you and I will develop a plan for the effective use of these advertising dollars.

David further suggests to have in mind some specific merchandise the business carries so you can begin your letter by saying, "As I came in your store the other day, I noticed you stock a complete line of _____. That company offers to pay 100% of advertising costs; you could have a lot of advertising dollars from that one line alone. . . ."

Do not send this type of letter to a client unless you have first qualified the prospect in some manner to determine whether a demographic match exists between the target customer they wish to reach and the audience your station serves. Unless you have the backup staff (usually a full-time co-op coordinator) or are willing to do the necessary follow-up yourself, never promise the benefits suggested in this solicitation letter.[22]

DISTRIBUTOR DIRECT ADVERTISING

A form of vendor advertising, distributor direct advertising, will be the advertising of the 1990s and promises to surpass co-op in total marketplace impact. Such advertising secures money separate from and beyond co-op funds.

Distributor direct advertising is accomplished through distributor or manufacturer reps who usually have a multistate territory and are therefore difficult to contact. Persistence is a virtue in this case. Besides being able to help the salesperson sell a specific retailer on the idea of co-op advertising, these overtraveled businesspeople have additional promotional budgets available that they can use at their own discretion to move more of their product (appliances, for example) into the marketplace. With such budgets available, these reps often can use assistance in putting together ideas or promotional packages that help them accomplish the goal of placing more product with their retailers and hence into the homes of customers who buy from them.

The budgets these reps have are distinct from advertising but can be spent on advertising at their discretion. If a station salesperson develops a specific, custom promotion designed to promote and advertise, say, General Electric appliances and presented this idea to the manufacturer's rep, the rep would be able to buy it outright as a service to his dealers. The rep with a low or overspent budget could recoup the cost of such a promotion by "charging" his dealers or retailers; the cost would be covered by the rep telling the dealers: "OK, I'll provide this promotion for you and buy all the advertising. You just have to purchase two or three more units from me, so you'll have enough stock to handle anticipated demand." An advertising deal can be struck without involving the retailer that is designed for and directly benefits the retailer through the advertising promotion. No retailer or co-op dollars are involved. The media salesperson has to find the rep or distributor and develop a well-planned, unique idea or promotion to help him or her move more product into the marketplace.

The hottest users of this type of advertising are grocery stores or chains, drug store chains, convenience stores, women's accessories stores, and distributors of perfumes. If the client's store or business has purchased enough merchandise from a manufacture's representative, $50,000 to $75,000 can be generated for a media schedule without the retailer paying one dollar.

Find out about distributor direct advertising. But make sure your demographics are right for the product to be advertised on your station. With your own initiative and the assistance of RAB, co-op advertising and distributor direct advertising can add thousands of dollars to your annual income.

CO-OP GLOSSARY

Definitions of words and terms associated with co-op advertising, compiled by RAB:

Accruals (co-op): Dealer's current earned-advertising fund based on merchandise the dealer has purchased from the manufacturer.

Advertising Checking Bureau (ACB): An auditing company engaged in many advertising services, one of which is to check co-op verification for its manufacturer clients, then to pay their media bills. If ACB is the billing address listed in the manufacturer's plans, the script, affidavit, and receipted invoice must be sent there for manufacturer payment.

Affidavit: Signature by station manager (should be notarized) attesting to the veracity of the radio schedule (dates and times) and spot costs.

Allowance (co-op): Percentage of merchandise purchases the manufacturer agrees to pay to the retailer for cooperative advertising. Percentages range from 50 percent to 100 percent, sometimes even more.

ANA/RAB tear-sheet: A radio co-op verification system serving the same purpose as a newspaper tear-sheet. It consists of an affidavit of performance of the retailer's actual script attached to station's receipted invoice for the co-op schedule.

Billing: In the manufacturer's co-op plan, details of how the manufacturer requires dealers to submit their advertising claims to the company.

Contact: Person employed by the manufacturer to get in touch with for co-op accruals, scripts, tapes, and dealer copy OK.

Co-op advertising: An arrangement by which manufacturers advertise with local dealers for the benefit of both. The manufacturer agrees to pay a set allowance (for example, 50–50 or 100 percent) on a percentage of the dealer's purchases for advertising the manufacturer's products and the dealer's service.

Co-op coordinator: Person in charge of the station's co-op activities. May have marketing or sales or both assignments.

Co-op period: Calendar months in which the manufacturer requires dealers to advertise. Corresponds to prime selling seasons for the manufacturer's merchandise.

Dealer copy: Scripts written by or for the dealer other than manufacturer-supplied scripts. Dealer scripts usually require prior approval by the manufacturer's contact before airing.

Dealer groups: A joint advertising effort by several manufacturer's dealers—usually organized by a radio salesperson and the manufacturer's local rep—in which all dealers share the radio spots and costs.

Distributor: Manufacturer's local or regional outlet that supplies merchandise and sometimes advertising counsel to dealers. In some cases, distributors share in the co-op allowance. An example is one in which the manufacturer pays 50 percent of the cost, the distributor 25 percent, and the dealer 25 percent.

Manufacturer's reps: The manufacturer's local contacts. Salespeople on this level can be very important to radio salespeople in organizing manufacturer dealer groups and in approving distributor direct advertising.

Notarization: Authentication of station management's signature by a notary public (using a notary stamp) as an advertising affidavit.

Proof of performance: Demonstration that advertising ran as claimed by retailer. Usual documents required for radio are scripts, affidavits, and receipted station invoices.

Purchases: Merchandise bought by local dealer on which co-op advertising is usually based. Percent of purchases run from 1 percent to more than 10 percent.

Vendors: Manufacturers. This term is commonly used by department stores and discounters.

Verification: Proof that the radio co-op schedule ran as stated. Most manufacturers require scripts, dates, times, and costs with an affidavit and receipted invoice as verification.

SUMMARY

Although never a substitute for regular client advertising generated from effectively utilizing the MEDIA system, promotions and contests are a proven way to produce additional revenue for any radio or TV station. Promotions, in addition to attracting new advertising dollars and new clients, foster internal staff morale as well as a deeper sense of station loyalty on the part of the station's audience. Such promotional effort, however, needs to be handled with care, with the right planning questions asked and answered and the correct promotion chosen for the objectives desired.

Co-op and distributor direct advertising produce even more revenue for radio and TV stations through the sharing of local advertising costs between the manufacturer of a product and the local or regional distributor/vendor and retailer who supply and sell the product in the marketplace. Co-op copy must be written and verified via notarization on special ANA/RAB "tearsheets" that attest to the actual cost of the schedule run and the exact copy used. Without such proof-of-performance, retailers could not be reimbursed their due percentage by a manufacturer.

The Co-op "Questions and Answers" section and the sample co-op solicitation letter provide any salesperson with all the necessary information to implement an effective Co-op program.

NOTES

1. Larry Perry, Bob Savage, and Don Craig, *Broadcast Promotions Sourcebook* (Oak Ridge, TN: Perry Publications, 1982), p. 15.

2. Ibid.

3. From *Strategies in Broadcast and Cable Promotion*, edited by Susan Eastman and Robert Klein © 1982 by Wadsworth, Inc. Reprinted by permission of the publisher.

4. Larry Perry, Bob Savage, and Don Craig, p. 16.

5. Ibid., p. 11.

6. Susan Eastman and Robert Klein, p. 13.

7. Larry Perry, Bob Savage, and Don Craig, p. 244.

8. Susan Eastman and Robert Klein, pp. 32–33.

9. Ibid., p. 33.

10. Ibid.

11. Ibid.

12. Ibid., p. 181.

13. Ibid., p. 182.

14. Ruth C. Hamill, "Attacking New Listeners," *Sound Management* 3(5): 33.

15. *Nashville Banner*, October 29, 1985.

16. Miles David, *Making Money with Co-op.* (New York: Radio Advertising Bureau, 1986), pp. 2–7, 22–24, 142. © 1986 Radio Advertising Bureau.

17. Ibid., pp. 153–155.

Chapter 11
REGULATION

THE ROLE OF THE FCC

Salespeople in the broadcast industry must necessarily be aware of the legal restrictions under which all stations operate as public trustees of their assigned space on the electromagnetic spectrum. Being granted a broadcast license by the FCC and accordingly offering a service in the public interest that can be consumed by anyone possessing a receiver within signal range dictates that federal regulations are imposed upon that operation. Not only is the broadcaster accountable to the FCC but also other federal regulatory agencies are involved in the business of any licensed operator.

The Federal Trade Commission (FTC) is responsible for eliminating perceived practices of deceptive advertising. The Food and Drug Administration (FDA) may become involved in issues involving the advertising of food products and over-the-counter drugs, and the Federal Aviation Administration (FAA) concerns itself with station antenna height and location.

In addition to these federal agencies, consumer and other interest groups band together to influence station or network programming that they feel affects the cause of their particular group. Organizations such as Action for Children's Television (ACT), Accuracy in Media (AIM), and even the National Organization of Women (NOW) influence the content of network television programming and many local radio and TV programs.

DEREGULATION

Beginning in 1980, through the tenure of Mark Fowler (until 1987), and continuing into the Dennis Patrick administration (beginning in 1987), the FCC adhered closely to the doctrine of *deregulation*—that the marketplace and not Congress or the federal regulatory agencies should decide what stations can and cannot do. The public decides such matters by their listening or viewing habits. Stations or programs that are popular are supported; those that are rejected, for whatever reason, fail due to lack of audience and revenue dollars.

Each fall, many new network TV programs are cancelled because the Nielsen ratings show them to be in the bottom third of all programs run during the week. Programs that attract a smaller audience also bring in fewer advertising dollars. No "higher authority" need intervene because the marketplace decides whose programming is acceptable in an open, competitive environment.

This hands-off approach won widespread industry support as broadcasters in cable, then radio, and finally TV witnessed the elimination of several burdensome regulations; important areas, however, such as the regulation of contests, promotions, and lotteries, remain unchanged. Salespeople must have up-to-date knowledge in these areas. Ignorance of current FCC policy is no excuse if stations are cited for violating written regulations governing station operation and programming.

Cable Deregulation

The deregulation trend began in 1980 when the FCC, by lifting major restrictions, allowed local cable operators to import distant signals (even if they directly competed with local stations) and further allowed exclusivity rights for syndicated programs. (One station could buy a syndicated national "exclusive," as did WGN with their rights to Geraldo Rivera's look into Al Capone's vault. WGN, carried by most cable systems in the country, won the highest rating points ever for a syndicated program. No one else could pick up or rebroadcast that signal. It was an exclusive to WGN with no network competition.)

The cable industry was deregulated even further under the Cable Act of 1984. Beginning in 1987, cable companies could set their own rates for basic service; prior to that time, local governments, who approved of and granted permission to a certain operator to offer cable services within a given market, approved basic cable rates.

Many early companies on the cable scene promised low initial basic service costs to subscribers in order to win approval from local officials, knowing the higher bids of competing cable companies would be rejected. Most of these companies would then raise their subscriber basic service cost after a few months to levels high enough to offset early losses. This practice raised ethical questions about how a cable franchise, worth untold millions in a virtual monopolistic setting after being awarded the right to wire a market, was awarded by local officials. Widespread speculation that some local officials had accepted kickbacks in the form of cash bribes or promises of a percentage return of future profits proved to be true in several markets.

However, local government is no longer involved in the setting of these basic rates, and this remains the main point of contention surrounding this 1984 Cable Act.

Congress intended rate deregulation to occur only in areas where cable companies face "effective competition"—namely, in places where people receive sufficient over-the-air

TV. (In other words, who have a choice between having cable or receiving free over-the-air service.) The lawmakers wanted to keep local officials in charge of cable in places where residents have little choice but to subscribe (no free over-the-air signals penetrating the area due to geographical location, etc.). It fell to the FCC to sort out which communities have good enough reception to warrant deregulation.

The FCC ruled that deregulation could proceed in any place that can get three on-air channels. But the rules the Commission adopted allow for very snowy pictures and a 30-foot-high antenna (lesser signal quality). Further, if as many as half the people can receive broadcast stations only on the clearest days, the area still qualifies for deregulation (letting the local company set its own rates without local government involvement) under the FCC's rules.[1]

According to *Consumer Reports,* many markets, including most of New York City's residents, cannot receive clear TV signals on a consistent basis without cable TV, as so many live in the shadows of the city's skyscrapers that block incoming TV signals. Yet, cable is deregulated in New York City, where the FCC maintains that three or more signals are available.

Dubuque, Iowa, can barely receive one signal due to 1,000-foot bluffs rich in lead deposits. Yet, that market is also deregulated. "New York and Dubuque joined other cities in a suit over the FCC's guidelines. A verdict handed down in July [1987] requires the FCC to issue new criteria to gauge the quality of local reception, but new rules probably won't be issued soon."[2]

With cable deregulation, consumer advocates feel local governments cannot safeguard the interests of cable subscribers in their markets. Should local rates be regulated or should the marketplace do the regulating with the law of supply and demand? As someone who may be selling availabilities for a local cable operator, you be the judge on that one.

Radio Deregulation

In 1981, radio broadcasters nationwide rejoiced when the FCC lifted restrictions on the maintaining of program logs and on the burdensome process of *ascertainment*, the procedure followed to "ascertain" a cross-section of community views to use in making programming decisions. Logs are still maintained for commercial records, but need be stored only two years instead of five; community viewpoints must still be filed but are only required to list the top ten issues over the past three months and how they were covered as determined and reported by the news director. Prior to deregulation, ascertainment was an exhausting process of contacting and interviewing dozens of community leaders, followed by the tabulation and prioritizing of their collective concerns and the station's written response on its plans to address those concerns.

Furthermore, required percentages of nonentertainment programming (news and public affairs) were dropped, as were the hourly limitations on the number of commercials that could be aired. Stations can now run as many commercials as they please, knowing that too many may erode a base audience that would rather be entertained by music or news than by all-commercial radio.

TV Deregulation

In 1983 television was deregulated in much the same way as radio. Other deregulation highlights include the multiple-ownership rule, amended by the FCC in August of 1984 to increase from seven to twelve the number of AM, FM, and TV stations an owner or company may own, "as long as the last [five stations] don't operate in markets collectively containing more than 25% of the nation's television homes."[3]

By August 5, 1985, the FCC had eliminated the rule requiring station buyers to hold their properties for three years before reselling. The rule had previously been in effect to ensure that prospective buyers held or would develop a certain spirit of community interest and involvement in the market of signal origination. Elimination of this rule has led to a rash of non-broadcast-oriented financial groups buying media properties and then reselling them at high profits as soon as they are able to improve market share and, ultimately, the bottom line. These stations spend thousands on promotional activities and want to become a top station in their market, not because they are attempting to gain community favor, but because they are businesspeople seeking a profit. Each time a station is sold in a marketplace, the price increases dramatically. This means that the new owners have a significant debt service to retire. The responsibility for generating the revenue to retire this debt ultimately falls on the shoulders of the station sales department. The salesperson then has increasing pressure to meet a demanding quota and still maintain long-term customer relationships. Whether this practice is in the public interest, or whether anyone but media critics really cares, is a matter yet to be determined.

The Fairness Doctrine

For 38 years the Fairness Doctrine mandated that broadcasters give balanced treatment to controversial issues. It was a product of an earlier era (1949) when television had not yet made an impact on the American scene and when marketplaces were not saturated with media signals. If a so-called controversial issue was given media attention at all, all sides had to be presented in the "public interest, convenience and necessity" (Communications Act of 1934, which established the FCC). Many broadcasters, especially in smaller markets, could not afford costly hearings if a party complained about one-sided programs or issues and felt such obligations actually prevented them from airing open discussion of local issues. Stations, in essence, were not free to air such issues as they viewed them (as newspapers are able to do) but had to go to great effort to present balanced coverage; finding parties willing to present opposing views was often difficult.

Desiring to exercise their First Amendment rights of free press, as newspapers are allowed to do without governmental regulation, broadcasters had long hoped the FCC would grant relief. The FCC and then President Ronald Reagan, himself a former broadcaster, were sympathetic to this posture. Knowing the Commission was considering deregulating the Fairness Doctrine, the House and Senate voted in the summer of 1987 to make the Fairness Doctrine law, but Reagan vetoed the bill. On August 4, the FCC made it official (to the great relief of the NAB and the dismay of some Congressional figures who feel minority viewpoints will now be suppressed) by abolishing the Fairness Doctrine.

Undoubtedly, Congress will again try to codify this doctrine (make it law), and further changes are expected. However, as ABC News President Roone Arledge commented on the day of the decision, "As journalists we've always felt we shouldn't be regulated as a matter of principle. But as a practical matter it's never been a problem."[4]

NAB spokesman Walt Wurfel put the likely effect of this landmark decision in perspective. "The basic effect is likely to be with small market stations that don't have much money. They can't face months or years of legal proceedings. This has inhibited them from doing anything controversial."[5]

Salespeople and the Fairness Doctrine Salespeople should have a working knowledge of the Fairness Doctrine and its status before the FCC, as they, sometimes even more than news or management personnel, have daily contact with local community leaders who may wish to voice their opinions to station personnel. Rather than responding "I don't know about that. You'll have to call the manager," the salesperson should be able to represent the station by giving intelligent and knowledgeable responses. The person with whom you are speaking may know only that you are a media employee and may not care what your specific job responsibilities are.

AREAS NOT AFFECTED BY DEREGULATION

What was not changed or deregulated in the 1980s were the FCC's attitudes toward lotteries, promotions, and contests. No attitudinal changes are expected in these areas in the foreseeable future.

Lotteries

Although legalized in recent years by many states seeking additional sources of revenue, Congress has forbidden radio or TV stations to air any games or contests, sponsored by either the station or its advertising clients, that fall under the definition of the term *lottery*. Lottery-type games, such as bingo, if not against state law, can be sponsored by nonprofit organizations such as churches in your community to raise money for charitable purposes and can even be advertised in the newspaper, as newspapers aren't regulated by the federal government.

However, lotteries or retail sales promotions that are defined as lotteries cannot be advertised on the electronic media, due to the widespread influence and overall community penetration of radio and TV.

Note that the same FCC over-the-air regulations that govern the radio and TV industry do not always apply to cable, as cable is not broadcast but wired. Attempting to advertise defined lotteries on cable, however, would undoubtedly be a violation of state gambling laws and therefore should be avoided by all cable operators.

State-Run Lotteries   However, some exceptions to the lottery prohibition can be advertised on the electronic media.

> On January 2, 1975, Congress exempted lotteries "conducted by a State acting under authority of State law" from the coverage of Section 1304 of Title 18, thereby permitting licensees to broadcast advertisements, lists of prizes and other information concerning a State-conducted lottery. Such broadcasts are permissible only if two conditions are met: (1) the licensee is located in a state which conducts such a lottery; and (2) the lottery information broadcast concerns the lottery in the licensee's home state or in an adjacent state which conducts such a lottery.[6]

Fishing Contests, Horse Racing, Dog Racing, and Jai Alai   A second exception refers to certain sporting events.

> Certain fishing contests have been specifically exempted from the federal prohibitions on broadcasting lotteries . . . the fishing contest [must be] a self-liquidating type of undertaking, whose receipts are fully consumed in defraying the actual costs of operation and are not intended or used for any other collateral purpose such as establishment of a fund for civic, philanthropic, or charitable objects, no matter how benevolent or worthy.
>
> The better's handicapping skill and knowledge in placing a wager have been construed to eliminate the element of chance in horse racing, dog racing and jai alai. Due to this proposed application of skill to determine the winner of these sporting events, such competitions may be broadcast and legally advertised without running afoul of the lottery laws.[7]

Off-Track Betting (OTB) Ads

> In a decision involving the New York State Off-Track Betting Corporation, the Commission held that where a state has established a betting operation for the purpose of raising revenues and combating illegal gambling, broadcast licensees may air "appropriate advertisements." Appropriate advertisements include those which encourage patronage of state-operated off-track operations or explain how to use OTB facilities. . . . The

advertisements must be consistent with the enumerated purposes of the state's program of legalized betting—the raising of funds and the suppression of illegal gambling. . . . The ruling would be subject to further modification if such advertising were to benefit illegal gambling interests.[8]

In addition to these exceptions, a radio or TV station may broadcast lottery information of a news or editorial nature, such as human interest stories about winners or how a certain state's lottery is supporting education, which some are targeted to support.

How the FCC Defines Lottery

Other than these exceptions, the advertising of lotteries is illegal, and the FCC has specifically determined three identifiable criteria that comprise the definition of the term *lottery*. All three elements need to be present for an event to be determined a lottery. If only one or two of these specific elements are present, a lottery would not exist.

Prize, Chance, and Consideration

The three criteria that define a lottery are prize, chance, and consideration. Taking the most common form of lottery that a salesperson would be involved with, the retail sales promotion, *prize* constitutes anything of value offered to a winner or awarded by the retailer, no matter how small or in what form. *Chance* is the random selection of a winner (one who receives the prize) by any criteria of pure luck and fortune. *Consideration* constitutes the exchange of anything of value required to participate in the promotion or contest, usually money expended as in making a purchase or paying an admission fee, but it can also be time and/or effort expended, such as taking a test drive or waiting in long lines to enter a contest. (Time and effort are looked upon by the FCC as commodities of value.) To further clarify *consideration*, it must flow directly to the promoters (in this case, the merchant) for consideration to be present.

If all three elements of prize, chance, and consideration are present, a lottery exists, and the salesperson could not accept such a promotion for advertising purposes on the station. Doing so could result in a substantial fine from the FCC and jeopardize the station license.

Lottery Case Studies

The concept of what constitutes and what does not constitute a lottery is understood best by example, as many fine lines of legal interpretation define *lotteries* in the retail sense. Following are several case studies to help you better understand what a lottery is.

Read them first and then try to determine if and why the particular case does or does not constitute a lottery. Then read the interpretation to see if you were correct.

Understand that the rendered interpretative opinions are only interpretations by the authors and/or the National Association of Broadcasters. Similar cases at your station should be referred to your station's Washington attorney or the enforcement division of the FCC. The FCC holds final jurisdiction in rendering decisions on what constitutes a lottery in specific cases.

It should also be noted that, at the time of publication, the House Subcommittee on Administrative Law and Governmental Relations (Chairman, Barney Frank, D-Massachusetts) just finished discussing the advertising of lotteries by the broadcast media. This broadcast industry-backed Lottery Ad Clarification Act, which was sent to the House and approved, is more than welcomed. Since lotteries, save for the noted exceptions like state-run games, cannot even be mentioned let alone advertised by the electronic media, new legislation may change this. The subcommittee did not change the criteria in any way that define a lottery, but allowed stations to advertise lotteries if such defined lotteries were authorized and not otherwise prohibited. In other words, should this subcommittee be successful in codifying its proposed legislation, which is now before the Senate and is expected to pass, any legalized activity that is defined as a lottery *can* be advertised. A state may, for example, legalize church Bingo games or charitable raffles. Even though these activities are technically lotteries and may not be advertised on radio or TV, they could be advertised if they were legalized under state law. The NAB reported on May 9, 1988 that such legislation would allow broadcasters to advertise lotteries "sponsored by private groups, including charities that raise money through Bingo and raffle. (Such legislation) will modernize and clarify century-old statutes restricting broadcasters's First Amendment freedoms (and will rid the industry of) antiquated, unnecessary, inequitable and confusing lottery laws." The passed House version, however, added an amendment prohibiting advertising for casino gambling.

If this legislation is approved by Congress, broadcasters should check with their state broadcast association for the current status of state laws pertaining to the legality and advertising of lotteries.[9]

Lottery Case Study #1

A movie theater wants to advertise that every tenth ticket buyer will receive a free T-shirt and baseball hat promoting the movie that is being shown.

Can you advertise this promotion? Why or why not?

Interpretation: This is a lottery. The elements of prize (the T-shirt and hat) and consideration (buying a ticket) are apparent. The gray area of concern involves the element of chance. Recipients of the free prizes (winners) are determined by the chance of being the tenth person in sequence. A movie theater (or any other business engaging in a similar promotion) is unlikely to go to the trouble of requiring the ticket seller to call out the number sequences of ticket purchases.

Therefore, the patron's chances of winning the free merchandise are controlled predominantly by chance and a lottery is present.

Lottery Case Study #2

A broadcaster airs a promotion for the city's monthly magazine that reads, "All during this month, you can be one of five dozen lucky winners whose names will be drawn to receive free a year's subscription to our city's monthly magazine. Consult this month's issue of monthly magazine for details."

Is this legal? Why or why not?

Interpretation: Broadcast promotions that are sponsored by the publisher of a newspaper or magazine and that encourage listeners or viewers to purchase the sponsor's publication contain the element of consideration. The prize (the free subscription) and the chance of winning in a drawing are also present. Therefore, because all three elements comprising a lottery are present, a lottery does exist and the promotion cannot be aired.

Lottery Case Study #3

A shoestore wishes to advertise its summer sale with a promotion entitled Break the Bank. A table topped with small, ceramic piggy banks containing various discount amounts is placed in the back of the store. Customers can "break the bank" of their choice and then receive the amount of the enclosed discount on a future purchase.

Is this a lottery? Why or why not?

Interpretation: This particular promotion is not a lottery. Prize and chance are clearly present, but no consideration is involved. Just because a prize is received in the form of a discount does not commit the person winning such a prize to exercise that discount through making a purchase, and no obligation exists to make a subsequent purchase. However, if the customer is allowed to break the bank only after making a purchase or agreeing to make one, the promotion would obviously be a lottery.

Lottery Case Study #4

The Hometown Jaycees have rented the local college fieldhouse for their annual home show. Display booths are rented to participating merchants and organizations. A $3 admission fee is charged to the public, with all proceeds going to the Jaycees to fund their community programs. A local lawn-and-garden tractor business purchases display space and wishes to run a home show promotion with your station. The promotion encourages home show spectators to come by the booth and fill out cards that will be put into a barrel for a drawing on the last day of the show. The winner will receive a free lawn-and-garden tractor. No purchase from the dealer is necessary.

Would you accept this promotion for advertisement? Why or why not?

Interpretation: Such a promotion with your station would be permissible and is not a lottery. Although a person who registers for the free tractor at the display booth must pay a $3 admission fee to enter the home show, the money does not flow to the merchants or organizations who have rented display space from the Jaycees. In this case, the admissions fee flows to the Jaycees and not to the lawn-and-garden business. Therefore, no consideration is present, and the promotion may be advertised.

Lottery Case Study #5

A breakfast food company introduces a new cereal into your market via two contests designed to create product awareness and encourage consumers to buy the product. The first contest offers participants the opportunity to name the animated character appearing in its TV commercials. The best name will be chosen by a panel of judges from the company and its advertising agency. A second winner will be chosen for writing the best commercial jingle on the theme of "Why I like Buffy's Breakfast Bon-Bons." Each winner will receive a $2500 cash prize. Entry forms are printed on the back of the cereal box.

Can you advertise this? Why or why not?

Interpretation: If these types of contests requiring some thinking and/or reasoning skills on the part of the entrants are judged impartially by the judges, they are not lotteries, even though purchase of the product was required in order to enter the contest. In *best* contests, skill and not chance is considered to be involved. Therefore, chance is not present, no lottery exists, and you may advertise the promotion.

Lottery Case Study #6

A local restaurant and bar wishes to run a promotion allowing any customer to win a free meal if he or she can correctly answer two questions. The restaurant and bar asks questions such as:

1. What is the average number of hamburgers served each day in America?
2. How much beer is consumed annually, per person, by the citizens of Liechtenstein?

The contestant is not afforded an opportunity to research the answers to the questions.

Is this a lottery? Why or why not?

Interpretation: In cases like this, the NAB legal department has noted that, at first glance, promotions of this nature might be considered contests involving skill rather than chance, due to the difficult nature of the questions involved. However, the questions are so obscure that they constitute a guessing contest, and the element of chance outweighs the participant's skill in analyzing the questions. Because a purchase is required (patronizing customers) and a free meal is offered, all three elements of a lottery are present. Therefore, you may not advertise the promotion.

However, as the NAB notes, if the contestants were permitted to research the questions before answering, skill and not chance would be present and no lottery would exist.

Lottery Case Study #7

A vacation resort development company wishes to promote its new vacation hideaway on your station. The resort is in the lake country nearly 100 miles from the city. The company wants to hold a drawing and award a prime lakefront lot to the winner. Those who wish to enter would be required to visit the development to fill out an entry form.

Would you accept this promotion for advertisement? Why or why not?

Interpretation: The NAB notes that this is a gray area of the lottery law. Although no purchase would be required, driving nearly 100 miles to the site of the development amounts to a substantial expenditure of time and effort on the part of the contestant. Consideration is also defined in terms of time and effort, not just in monetary terms. Therefore, the element of consideration seems to be present. However, no definitive rule can define exactly how many miles or what type of external factors would constitute substantial hardship to the participant. The broadcaster should contact an attorney when in doubt. This case is probably a lottery.

Contests

On-air contests and the proper management of such audience-flow cornerstones demand nothing more than common sense. The FCC requires all stations to disclose the material terms of all promotions and contests conducted. *Material terms* are "those factors which are significant in defining the operation of the contest."[10] Misleading the public, whether intentional or not, about contest details, prizes, or when prizes will be awarded or not being explicit about the type of prize(s) offered or the details pertaining to it (as in a vacation) can lead to serious trouble with the FCC.

The material terms of on-air contests, according to NAB legal counsel, that salespeople should be familiar with and that must be announced in detail when the public is initially informed on how to participate in the contest, include:[11]

- How to enter or participate
- Eligibility restrictions
- Entry deadline dates
- Whether prizes can be won
- When prizes can be won
- The extent, nature, and value of prizes

- Time and means of selecting prizes
- Tie-breaking procedures

Avoiding Postcontest Complications   To avoid problems that are likely to occur after the contest has run, stations should maintain a thorough contest file that can provide immediate documentation in case of conflict. The NAB recommends that such a file should include:

- The rules and eligibility requirements of the contest, plus verification of when they actually aired
- Promotional material used during the contest, that is, broadcast copy, newspaper ads, billboards, posters, flyers, and direct mail
- A list of prizes awarded and names and addresses of winners; in case of prizes valued at $600 or more, Social Security numbers must be listed
- Prize receipts signed by the winners

FCC Checklist for Deceptive Contests

The FCC has listed a number of misleading practices relating to contests that sales personnel should be aware of. A station involved with any of the following deceptive procedures would raise serious questions about its responsibility as a licensee.[12]

- Disseminating false, misleading, or unclear information regarding the amount or nature of prizes
- Failing to control the contest to assure a fair opportunity for contestants to win the announced prize(s)
- Urging participation in a contest or urging listeners or viewers to stay tuned in order to win, at times when winning prizes is not possible
- Failing to award prizes or not awarding them within a reasonable amount of time
- Failing to disclose fully and accurately the rules and conditions for contests on a continuing basis
- Changing the rules or conditions of a contest without advising the public or without doing so promptly
- Using arbitrary or inconsistent standards in judging entries
- Predetermining winners or providing secret assistance to contestants
- Stating that winners are to be chosen solely by chance when, in fact, chance plays little or no part
- Broadcasting false clues in connection with a contest

■ Conducting contests without adequate supervision from management, sales, or programming personnel

Treasure Hunts

The FCC looks with disfavor upon contests that might constitute a public hazard or cause interference with or destruction to property. Treasure hunts are an example of the kinds of contests or promotions that sometimes cause listeners or viewers to ransack through piles of goods at department stores or dig up public or private property in search of hidden "treasure." Even when stations broadcast that the so-called treasure is not buried, sometimes listeners still find a way to discredit the station by digging up someone's front lawn. These promotions must be run with extreme care and caution.

Contest Summary

Providing salespeople, program directors, and top management are ethical in their conception, development, presentation, and final airing of any media contest or promotion, problems with the FCC, the local community, or other media are highly unlikely.

POLITICAL ADVERTISING

A boon to broadcasters during election years, political advertising is coveted by media salespeople, as complete payment of planned schedules is payable at least 24 hours in advance of the broadcast date. Most politicians and their campaign managers or treasurers are acutely aware of this fact and are prepared to fill out the NAB Agreement Form for Political Broadcasts. This form is then placed in the station's political file (part of the licensee's public inspection file) for a period of two years. The political file should contain "a list of all requests for broadcast time made by or on behalf of political candidates with a notation showing the disposition of such requests and the charges made, if any. A record of any free time provided must also be kept."[13]

Candidates and Rates

Salespeople should know that all candidates are eligible to pay the lowest unit rate charge that has been offered at the station to commercial advertisers for the same day part and length of commercial 45 days before a primary election and 60 days before a general election. To qualify for this lowest unit rate that the station has offered within the prescribed time limits, the candidate's voice or picture must be present in the commercial in a manner that identifies the candidate to the general public.

In radio, for example, the candidate could tag the commercial message with "Hi, I'm Mr. Candidate. I'd appreciate your vote this Tuesday. Thank you." If the voice were well known or the candidate's picture were easily recognized on TV, no personal identification would even be necessary.

If the voice or picture does not appear and the commercials are hosted by the professional staff at the station or totally packaged by an advertising agency without the appearance of candidate voice or picture, then the normal rates a station would charge for the amount of time purchased and the day part it will be placed in are applicable.

SUMMARY

Successful salespeople are aware of the legal restrictions under which all stations operate. Since 1980, broadcast deregulation has modified the regulatory landscape for radio, TV, and cable. Areas that have not been affected by such deregulation, however, include FCC policies and attitudes toward lotteries, promotions, and contests. Since most lotteries are illegal and are unable to be advertised via the electronic media, the included case studies help define what does and does not constitute a lottery. Political advertising, which is paid for in advance of air date, must be accompanied by a signed NAB Agreement Form for Political Broadcasts and placed in the Nation's political file for 2 years.

NOTES

1. *Consumer Reports Magazine,* September 1987, p. 555.

2. Ibid.

3. *Broadcasting Magazine,* December 31, 1984.

4. *USA Today,* August 5, 1987.

5. Ibid.

6. Cathy E. Blake, *Lotteries and Contests: A Broadcasters Handbook,* (Washington DC: National Association of Broadcasters, 1980), p. 21.

7. Ibid., p. 22.

8. Ibid., p. 24.

9. *Today,* a publication of the National Association of Broadcasters, Washington, DC, May 9, 1988.

10. *Lotteries and Contests: A Broadcasters Handbook,* p. 39.

11. Ibid., p. 39.

12. Ibid., p. 41.

13. Blair, Joyce and Silva, Attorneys at Law, Washington, DC, personal communication, October 1986.

Chapter 12

THE SALES

MANAGERS SPEAK

One of the best ways of gaining additional insight into a particular profession, business, or industry is to talk with the practitioners. These people apply their knowledge everyday in their careers. They know how to begin, carry through, and succeed. However, each person interested in a field cannot, as a practical matter, talk directly at length with several top-flight professionals in that field.

Therefore, we have visited with a number of professionals in electronic media sales—in person and by telephone—in order to ask the questions that beginning broadcast salespeople might wish to ask these professionals. Not only do all of them hold sales management positions, but also they all have experience in selling electronic media. As managers, they know the qualities desired and requirements demanded of people desiring to become salespeople for their particular electronic medium. The same questions were asked of each of these sales managers so that their answers could be excerpted and presented collectively in response to the various questions.

RADIO SALES MANAGERS

To represent radio sales, our respondents include:

Kelly Seaton, General Sales Manager, WGN Radio, Chicago. WGN is a 50 kw, AM radio station owned by the Tribune Broadcasting Company. It operates with an MOR (middle of the road) music and talk format.

Vicki Knight, General Sales Manager, KPLX-FM, Fort Worth, and KLIF, Dallas, Texas. KPLX(FM) is a 100 kw, FM stereo radio station owned by Susquehanna Broadcasting Company, featuring a country-western format. KLIF is a 50 kw day and 5 kw night, AM radio station also owned by Susquehanna. It also features a country-western music format.

Carl McNeil, General Sales Manager, WRVA, Richmond, Virginia. WRVA is a 50 kw, AM radio station owned by Harte-Hanks Radio. It features an adult contemporary music format.

Sandra Kennedy, General Sales Manager, WSM and WSM(FM), Nashville, Tennessee. WSM is a 50 kw, AM radio station owned by Hubbard Broadcasting. It is famous as the home of the Grand Ole Opry and features a country music format. WSM(FM) is a 100 kw, FM station owned by Hubbard. Although it is programmed separately from WSM, it also features country music as its format.

Jeff Kuether, General Sales Manager, WTMJ, Milwaukee, Wisconsin. WTMJ is a 5 kw, AM radio station owned by WTMJ, Inc., and it employs the MOR music format.

The first questions asked of these sales managers dealt with the attributes and the background—education, training, experience—they seek in candidates for sales positions in their markets.

Seaton (Chicago):	Communications background obviously would be somewhat of an asset because students would have been through the basics and have some idea of operation of the station, from the talent, to the news, to the production area. Frankly, communications is an asset, but I'm not sure it's the only one. I didn't take a communications degree, for example. Someone who has a good general education, someone who has a business major and has gotten into this field or has an advertising minor, could equally be a candidate.
	Because this is a major market and it's one of the leading stations in the country, usually we hire someone for an entry-level position with one or two years of outside sales experience that is not necessarily broadcast, for example, someone who has sold newspaper or magazine space or someone who has direct sales experience.
	What they have been doing is not really as important as whether they have answered some basic questions for themselves. Do I like cold calling? Am I able to go out and solicit information? Am I able to go out with no introduction? Just representing myself or my product, am I able to call on someone? That is a very difficult thing for many people to do.
	Our success has been, I think, in entry-level positions. We do train, and, therefore, for that initial sales experience, you had time to make your first mistakes.

Knight (Dallas):

I look for two major goals in a salesperson, which would be ego drive and empathy. And I also look for an energy level. I do look for education and experience, of course, but the first three things outweigh everything else.

Ideally, I look for someone with a communications and marketing background. As far as experience, I like for them to have some small-market radio experience in which they've really had to go out and learn radio—not necessarily in the same market or market size—and know the product very well and what radio is.

McNeil (Richmond):

For a prospect, the first impression is appearance, and after that the appearance of being organized, as well as the intelligence of the person and tenacity. They have to be able to accept rejection and bounce back. They have to be a conversationalist, a person who can strike up a conversation with a bank president or a service station attendant. They have to be able to role play and be an actor in a way.

Some other things I look for: if they're professional; if they have an overall knowledge, not just of radio, but a broad knowledge and a worldly sense of balance.

At WRVA I hire only college graduates. I would rather have a student with a master's degree. I very rarely hire people from other radio stations or other media in the marketplace. I like to hire people who are right out of school and train them the way I feel they should be trained, and I have been very successful at that in the past. So, I look for a college education, preferably a master's degree in business instead of communications. It is a must.

Kennedy (Nashville):

I look for an aggressive person who is truly interested in sales and learning this side of it and will be able to fill the client's needs. They need to be fairly outgoing, confident, self-confident, empathetic. It's very hard to select the right salesperson from meeting someone because they have to have inner drive and self-direction. I think that's difficult to train, if it's not already inherent in the person.

Ideal candidates have schooled themselves, possibly worked their way through college, taking some courses that were on-the-job type of training, where they've worked as part of their coursework. They did some saleswork at a radio station.

I would like for them to just have fairly good grades, at least high Cs, although I prefer a *B* average. Excellent grades aren't necessarily important. Sometimes people with straight *As* are much more oriented, I feel, to be studious, not quite as outgoing, more detail oriented; and sometimes when you get too much detail, you tend to forget what you're doing as far as basic cause.

I feel WSM is a more difficult station to sell because it has a lot of different items, a lot more lines, as far as things that we sell on the Grand Ole Opry and overnight show. It could be confusing, so I prefer that someone appointed by the station begin at a smaller station.

Kuether (Milwaukee):   I just interviewed about 50 people for a position that we had, and the cross-section of people was interesting. A lot of people ask me about formal education, and I think my communication arts advertising major gives me—I graduated from Madison—maybe, a better day-to-day understanding of what I do today, but I don't think that's a necessary part of the job.

Communication skills is number one; you're going to get that with any liberal arts education. Number two is a basic knowledge of sales and sales techniques—how to close, how to read interest, how to gain confidence, how to persuade.

Beyond that, the radio industry can be picked up along the way. The problem right now is that a lot of your students might go to a small market. If by the same token they could come to Milwaukee, which is inundated with radio stations—28 stations broadcasting from Milwaukee, plus Chicago, plus the surrounding areas—you end up starting at the 27th-rated station and stumble through a year there, and then you know what you're doing. Then, you go to the 13th-rated station, and you stumble around, and you start to get to know them, and your skills start to sharpen. Then maybe you go to number 6, and you're making a good living, and you become—by virtue of trial and error and on-the-job experience—a good salesman. It's a kind of scenario that everyone on the sales staff has gone through.

If there were training courses similar to what you mentioned to me, you could eliminate a lot of that stone stepping and stumbling, and get into top management more quickly. Or even start at the 28th station and be a winner right off the bat. Salespersons have to learn the individual idiosyncrasies of the radio station that they work at, and every station has selling points. Every station has a selling point, and you should be able to pick those up. If you're not number 1 at something, you ought to go off the air.

Question: What ongoing training or education does the professional broadcast salesperson need? How much, if any, do you provide for your sales staff?

Knight: They need continual training. We start out with the basics of radio, and when I hire people, no matter what experience level they have, I put them through the very basic course of how to sell radio at a fast pace.

This gives them the basics: "What is FCC?"; "What is our product all about?"; and "How did radio really begin?" From that time on, I feel that salespeople continually need some kind of motivation-in-selling training to keep them on the track.

We provide it. We have a weekly sales meeting that is strictly training, and we go six to eight weeks at a time with a different kind of training; part of our strategic plans for the year . As we go into the year, we know what we're going to do, how we're going to do it, and how to set up and use quarters for our training.

McNeil: What's needed is an intense, one-month training period with the sales manager and with the different managers of the station that goes over exactly what is each manager's job and teaches as much about the business as possible.

Here at WRVA, we have three half-hour training sessions a week—Monday, Wednesday, Friday—the first thing in the morning at 8:00. In these meetings we watch sales training videotapes, we go over RAB information, and we have outside speakers come in—advertising agency presidents, buyers, retailers—to talk with us about their business.

The ongoing training is the most important part of what we do in sales management. If folks aren't trained and knowledgeable about what we're doing, they'll fail every time.

We pay for Dale Carnegie; we pay 100 percent of any outside training that I feel will help our sales staff. We attend all RAB seminars, all seminars on retailing. You know, we're in every club and organization imaginable, from the Chamber of Commerce all the way to the Frozen Food Brokers Association.

Kennedy: They need constant review on the statistical part of their business, constant review on their product. At WSM, we have training sessions once a week for about an hour.

Many times, salespeople don't need to use their selling tools because the people that they deal with are very naive about the business. Then, when they call on someone who does know what they're talking about as far as the statistical part of the business, they no longer have those tools available to them. Motivational kinds of training—general sales, sales technique, and telephone technique—should never stop.

The station provides 90 percent of this continuing education or training. We use outside training from time to time, but I've found that we can do it best inhouse.

Kuether: I'm always looking for good seminars to go to, but training alone can be as good as a seminar.

Seaton: Continuing education is, I feel, very important at all levels. When RAB has an appropriate class which will fit either one or more of the sales staff, we make it available to them. Here in Chicago, Broadcast Advertising Club is an extremely active group. They do many seminars, approximately an hour and a half in length.

Managers can attend particular sessions that we feel would be important in the NRBA or the NAB, instead of going to the whole convention. We have done time management programs with other organizations. We also work with a managerial consultant.

In terms of entry-level people, one-on-one counseling is crucial. I would rather take someone with limited experience and watch them grow and develop. That's where your next managers come from. You should do as much as possible in promoting from within. That takes education as well as experience. We have not at this point asked people to go back to college and take higher education degrees, but if that were warranted, I would, for a particular individual. A number of agencies, including RAB, have dealt with the need for more professional, better-prepared salespeople in broadcasting, especially in radio, by indicating that a small minority of salespeople make a large majority of the sales, usually stated as "about 15 percent of the salespeople making about 85 percent of the sales."

Question:	What, in your opinion, separates the 15 percent of broadcast salespeople who account for 85 percent of the sales from the 85 percent of broadcast salespeople who account for 15 percent of the sales?
McNeil:	I think it's the sales manager's fault; we don't push the other group to obtain these high levels of performance. We as sales managers have taken the easy way out and have let our long-term salespeople keep the big accounts, whether they are working them or not.
Kennedy:	Industry-wide? There're a couple of things that go into that. Part of it is the stations themselves. The better product is going to be higher priced and easier to sell. I think there's a little bit of exaggeration in the statement in your question, but certainly the top three stations in a market are going to have the lion's share of all the billings in the city, so their salespeople naturally have more sales to bill a market.
	The good salesperson is one who has drive. They have direction from their management. They're aware of everything that's going on there; they're aware of the possibilities. They read the papers; they keep their eyes open. Everything they learn, they apply for their clients. They give the clients something the clients don't get otherwise. It consequently benefits the station.
Kuether:	Attitude and desire. You can lead a Monday morning sales meeting and have all great ideas, but if someone already has a preconceived notion, "Well, that's how

he used to do it. That's not going to work for me," or "It's Monday. I can't wait to get to lunch"—something like that—that person is not going to hear what you're saying. I think the basic difference is really the drive and determination.

Seaton: Motivation obviously has to be a key. The best salespeople I have found are people who treat their own list or their own business development as their own private business, and therefore they act like they are self-employed. That means that they are responsible for their work beyond the tasks that you give them. They are the people who are well organized, who have a game plan to start out their week, their day, and their month; people who, as far as possible, follow that game plan. Every station has a different kind of compensation program, and if you are money motivated, how much you earn in this business is directly related to how much you invest in yourself.

Knight: If only 15 percent of people on your staff are making most of the sales, then you need to get rid of the other 85 percent and replace them with people like the 15 percent. Sales managers must initiate good training and demand good discipline from their people.

Question: What advice would you give the beginning broadcast salesperson or the person training to become a broadcast salesperson?

Kennedy: I would advise them to keep a very positive attitude. It's not a business where you can take things personally. Learn from every call. Go in and realize that the client may not be shutting the door on you personally; perhaps you just have not interviewed him well enough. It's a difficult business because of the different types of personalities you have to go in to. Some people are so very negative, and if you take that negativism personally, it beats you.

Have confidence in your product and realize there have to be lots of roadblocks in every calling. Benefits will pay off down the road.

Each client will give you clues on how to sell them and what their needs are. When they tell you what their needs are, you will find out how to sell them. A person has to develop confidence in a salesperson, and that's not done in one meeting. Sales-people need to continually work, do what they say, always follow through on appointments, and put the interests of the client uppermost, and it will pay off in big dividends.

Kuether: I strongly believe that enthusiasm and determination are the two most important parts of any job. If you can take that enthusiasm and determination, and couple that with some learning, selling skills, and an interest in the media, I think you could be successful.

If one or more of those components are missing, maybe it's not the ideal occupation for you, and maybe then it isn't a career for you. But the bottom line is: Everything is there to make this an excellent occupation, and the more professional people that are in it, the better it's going to be for everybody. The rates will go up, and the respect for the job title will go up, and we'll have a lot better profession.

Seaton: Invest some time in yourself. I suggest that you potentially have four entries into this particular area. First and foremost, remember, when you get to the objective line in your resume, list one of those four areas. If you're going to interview in all of four areas simultaneously, have four different resumes.

You could get into this business by getting into an entry level in the advertising business in the media department. At any level that you can get in—whether it be research, or as an assistant buyer, as an estimator it allows you to get some perspective on what it is you might want to do and learn a little bit about the business at the same time. It also gives you an opportunity, after you've been there several months, to meet some salespeople, developing impressions, and make contacts.

If you get into a broadcast-only group, you will at least have some exposure to radio and some exposure to television. Certainly if you get into the sales field out of that area and you're sitting on the other side of the desk, it's going to give you an insight into the person you're calling on at that point.

You can get into other sales. That could be with a local newspaper selling retail space, going through whatever training programs they have. By the time you invested your year or year and a half at the most, you could go to a local radio or television station and say, "I have sales experience; I did this."

You could go into smaller stations and smaller markets. Don't look for number 1 necessarily. Get yourself in the door, and that's the key. If it's the number 3 station in the market, stay there long enough to learn whether you can do what you think you can do or whether you're going to like it, and you have time to build up some kind of track record. Use that track record to get you your next step. If you get your foot in the door and you're as good as you think you are, you can demonstrate that to the management of the station. One of two things will happen: the management will help you grow and give you more opportunity, or you stay long enough to get a predictable track record.

Knight: This business is not brain surgery. It just takes a lot of hard work, honesty, and initiative. You have to be a highly energetic person who wants to go out and really work hard and learn the ropes. When I'm training new people, and I feel they have those attributes, I want them to understand this is not an easy business, and it takes a long time to become a professional. So, you have to work real hard and be honest.

McNeil: Get with the best broadcasting company in the marketplace. Not necessarily the best radio station, but the best company that provides ongoing training over a long-term period. The worst you could ever do is get with a company that gives you the yellow pages and tells you to hit the streets.

The other thing I would suggest is to learn as much as you can, on a day-to-day basis. One of the problems we have in the broadcasting business is that after we've been in it for a short while, we think we know it all. But the real successful folks in our profession are continually training and upgrading their knowledge of the broadcasting industry.

Question: Would you give us your assessment of broadcast sales as a lifetime professional career?

Kennedy: It's an exciting business. There isn't a day that goes by when you don't learn something new. So, if you're the outgoing person, and you're looking for a constant challenge, it's a terrific business. And the financial rewards are there, so it's interesting. You have a chance to help people grow in their businesses, to show them better ways.

Broadcasting is getting more and more sophisticated—more professional. Twenty years ago, when I started in the business, there was a lot of back slapping and personality appeal. Now you need to know what you're talking about to sell people, because the buyers have become more sophisticated.

Kuether: I look at it as a career. My short-term goal is to do the best I can in this office, and I have set goals to accomplish that. Beyond that, I guess that the income or the earning potential and the fact that it is show business and it's fun are the other sides of it. But it's time consuming. To get to the top you can expect to work 60 hours a week, and that's a trade-off an individual has to weigh. Hopefully, we have some people who are willing to make that sacrifice.

Seaton: It's really a marvelous field. I don't know whether sales is still suffering from the perception of being "Johnny Jones Used Car Lot" or not, but it truly is not that. I have found people in this business to be fun. You're always dealing in a time situation. Time is perishable. You're selling an intangible, you have to be pretty good at what you're doing if you're going to be successful.

It is a career in which there isn't really any bias that I have found. I have found women do just as well as men. I think there could be more opportunities made for ethnic groups, especially Hispanics and blacks.

In terms of a career, it's a very lucrative one. Someone who is starting out at a decent station can earn somewhere between $12,000 and $25,000 in the first year. A reasonable expectation might be $25,000 to $35,000 in the second year. The third year should have no ceiling. There are people who make $80,000 a year in this business in a major market. The cost of living in a major market is higher, so that might translate into a smaller market at 60 or 50, but the relationship should be the same.

Knight:	It's always best to work for the right people, have the right company, and always seek self-improvement through training and motivational classwork.
McNeil:	I feel that a lifetime career in broadcasting is very rewarding, both financially and from a personal standpoint. You really make your own breaks. You can make a failure a success, and vice versa. It's one of the few industries today, I think, where there is that entrepreneurial spirit.
Question:	Would you describe the chief responsibilities of a sales manager in broadcast sales?
Knight:	My chief responsibility is to finance the radio station. I am the head of two major stations in Dallas, Texas—KPLX and KLIF. I'm responsible for all sales, so there's a lot more to it than just motivating people. It's also a look at how to work smart instead of harder, how to discipline the salespeople into the right kinds of calls made. My responsibility is to make sure that we get the very most money for the inventory we have on the air. That becomes a harder job than that for a tangible product, because you can't have units of air to show clients.
McNeil:	While the managers' first responsibility is to increase revenue, they also must hire and fire salespeople, set goals, handle accounts receivable, train staff, and do research.
Kennedy:	As sales manager, you should set the direction for all the salespeople. You should be able to analyze the total market and figure out where their station stands in relation to the market. You need to set strategy because the strategies that cause the salespeople to do their best will cause the best revenue return to the station. You should be available to the sales staff to work with them on any problems. You've got to solve the problems; you've got to motivate people. Every salesperson is different, every approach is different, and everyone will be motivated differently. It's not easy, because you tailor your approach to the individual.
Question:	What other advice or counsel would you like to give to people preparing for a career in broadcast sales?

Seaton: There's an old-fashioned work ethic that I think too frequently gets lost. A clue from a cold resume is that if they've been working to support themselves; that's a positive, because that means they cared enough about their education and their future to invest the time. If a person were fortunate enough not to have to do that, you can tell by the number of outside activities that they have.

From an interviewee I'm looking for honesty. I'm looking for someone to show commitment, someone who has a degree of commonsense, and who is articulate. I'm also looking for persistence.

The number of telephone calls that we get from people who want to apply for a job probably averages 40 a week. It's not practical to spend half an hour with each of these 40 people. On the other hand, I feel an obligation to encourage people. There have been occasions when we have said, "We don't have an opening right now, but keep us in mind, keep in contact. Let us know how you're doing," and then gone back four months later through those resumes when we really did have a job opening. We hope they do something constructive with their time in the interim.

I think the individual has to find out what is going to differentiate them from the five other people who are going to come in here, and what is it they need? Communicating motivation is critical. Communicating the fact that you're not going to be buffaloed if I turned around and asked you to do a presentation on something, which I might do. Now, if you don't know this station very well, and you don't know the market very well, that's going to be difficult. Admit the fact. Admit what you don't know, and then ask how you are going to find out the things that you need to know in order to get this done.

The individual has to communicate whatever talents are going to translate into successful sales. That may be different strengths with different individuals. In one case it might be somebody who is extremely—but nicely—aggressive. In another, it might be somebody who has a great deal more information and experience.

Knight: As I mentioned earlier, it's important to learn about radio. I have a lot of people walk in to me and say, "I've just gotten my journalism degree, or I've just gotten my communications degree, and I'm ready to go to work." It's not that easy. I'm looking for someone who has made a commitment to radio and has learned about it.

McNeil: In school, they really need to apply themselves. I've also suggested that they go for internships during the summer with radio and television stations in their particular hometowns: they should work for free if they have to, and get a jump on the rest of the folks.

Kennedy: I guess I would say for them to have a plan of action. In fact, even to get into the industry, they're going to need a plan of action, and they're going to have to be consistent about it. To me, a plan of action would be "Okay, I want into sales." My plan would be to call every sales manager in the city and set up meetings with them. And when they say that there are no openings, say, "Well, I would just like to talk with you in case one should arise." In fact, this is an industry where there is a lot of turnover. Quite often there are openings that the sales manager doesn't even expect.

The same thing applies to their clients. They have that persistence, they have to have a plan, and if the plan works, they've got the business.

TELEVISION SALES MANAGERS

When we talked with television sales managers, we continued to hear references to the need for professionalism and to the changing nature of the electronic media as the business aspect of the field is stressed more. The interviews in this section were carried out individually and the sales managers' answers were then grouped according to the question, as in the interviews with the radio sales managers.

Answering our questions for the television side of the electronic media industry were:

Al Rothstein, General Sales Manager, WTVJ-TV, Miami, Florida. WTVJ is a full-power VHF television station owned by Wometco Enterprises Inc., which owns six television stations in Miami; Grand Rapids, Newark, Smithtown, New York; Asheville, North Carolina; and Bellingham, Washington (Vancouver, British Columbia). It also owns an FM radio station in Asheville and is a cable television MSO (multiple system operator).

Carol Quereau Netter, Director of Sales, WCAU-TV, Philadelphia, Pennsylvania. WCAU-TV is a full-power VHF station located in the fourth-largest television market in the country and a CBS-owned-and-operated television station, one of four such that operate as the CBS stations group.

Tom Bornhauser, Local Sales Manager, WHAS-TV, Louisville, Kentucky. WHAS-TV is a full-power VHF station that until 1986 was co-owned with WHAS-AM and WAMZ-FM by WHAS, Inc., a part of the Barry Bingham, Sr., family ownership, which included the *Louisville Courier-Journal* and the *Louisville Times*. With the sale of all of the Bingham properties in 1986, WHAS-TV was purchased by the *Providence Journal* of Rhode Island.

Larry Shrum, General Sales Manager, KPRC-TV, Houston, Texas. KPRC-TV is a full-power VHF television station owned by H & C Communications, a holding company that also owns stations in Nashville, Orlando, Des Moines, Tucson, and as of 1986, San Antonio.

John F. Lee, General Sales Manager, WBBM-TV, Chicago. WBBM-TV is a full-power VHF television station located in the nation's third-largest television market. It is owned and operated by CBS and is, along with WCAU-TV, one of the four television stations in the CBS stations group.

We asked these television sales heads the same basic questions we asked the radio sales managers. Their answers follow.

Question:	What are the important attributes you look for in a prospect seeking to become a salesperson for your firm?
Rothstein (Miami):	When I look for somebody, I ask myself two questions: One, if I were walking down the street, and I ran into my parents, would I be embarrassed? The second question is, Is this person promotable to the next level?
	The first question may sound a little bit silly. But what a salesperson does is present the face of your television station to the most important part of your community, your advertisers. If we are not setting our best face out there at all times, it's going to cost us money. The nature of television sales is such that it's extremely competitive, and the best-looking, most well-spoken people are going to do the best.

The second question involves hiring people who are promotable. That's a value judgment that I try to make. I want people who try to reach beyond the level they are at. I tell them don't worry about the job that you're doing now. You're capable; you're in the job and you're doing a good job. Show me that you're ready to be promoted. Show me what management capability you have beyond what you're doing in your day-to-day job.

So, those are the two things. One, what kind of face do they show; and two, can I promote them? If I get yes answers in both of those—that's if enough specifics fall into those general categories—I'm pretty sure I'm going to hire a winner.

Shrum (Houston): The standard answer is that you look for the best-qualified person. Now, what does that entail? You're looking for someone who has demonstrated good work habits, who has a native intelligence that's going to allow them to understand the problems that they are presented with, who is going to have an ability to get along with people, to be able to work with people. Our business has changed a lot, but a lot of times it still comes down to interfacing with a person across a desk. You have to be able to do that.

Netter (Philadelphia): The most important factor would be intelligence. Next would be a desire, an interest, a curiosity about people, an interest in people, a desire to work with people as well as an optimistic attitude that can handle a lot of rejection.

Bornhauser (Louisville): I would say aggressiveness, enthusiasm, ability to communicate, the ability to listen, and the ability to understand a client's—or potential client's—business and needs.

Lee (Chicago): I think you need an independent individual, an individual who can work under his or her own volition, who needs little, or as little direct management day-to-day pushing as possible. We like people who are enterpreneurial, self-starters, aggressive, relatively thick-skinned, those who can take no for an answer, go back for more, and make the close for the sale.

We look for someone who has good communication skills, who can relate on the phone as well as during stand-up presentations, someone who is personable and can identify the merits of any given situation, that is, to read the person across the desk from him or her. I think a lot of the success of any salesperson relies on the instinct to measure a situation and measure the viability for a sale in that given situation, by understanding what the person across the desk is telling them. So, you also obviously have to be a good listener and be able to use deductive reasoning.

Question: What background—education, experience, training—do you seek in an ideal candidate for sales in your market?

Shrum: I think our business is changing. For a number of years, it was very incestuous in terms of where we would get our salespeople from. They would come from agencies or other TV stations or possibly have sold radio, but they would have a pretty set background.

Our business is changing. We're having to do more things today than we've ever had to do before, so we're looking for people outside of the business more often than we used to. We're looking for people who have sales experience, possibly with a Fortune 500 company, maybe someone who has been through the Xerox training program. Those types of professional selling environments are beginning to give us some of our new salespeople.

Regarding educational background: Obviously, you're looking for somebody who has the intelligence to do the job. So, you're going to look primarily for a college graduate. But that's not necessarily an absolute requirement to get into broadcast sales. A lot of times, it depends upon the intelligence that the person demonstrates, how professional a job they do in selling themselves. As you get into management, the additional education can help, but I don't think that's necessary in the beginning.

Netter: I'd like to be a bit of a rebel. I do not necessarily seek a degree in communications. As a matter of fact, I sometimes consider that a detriment, because I'm

not sure that the business, at least the way we operate, really parallels textbook situations. I would look,
in terms of education, for a business background
because we are a business. We could be selling wid-
gets, we could be selling cars, we could be selling
stocks and bonds. The profession that we're developing here is one of sales, not necessarily one of
broadcast sales.

I would look for general understanding of business and economics. In terms of experience, because
we are the fourth-largest market, we have the luxury
of enough candidates wanting to come here that we
can afford to hire people with experience. I would
look for experience, either in radio sales or independent television.

Bornhauser: Frankly, the background can come from a myriad of
directions. I believe that a business background,
business major, or business degree background is
excellent because so few people come out of college
understanding how businesses work. But I would
also make the point that a good liberal arts education—an emphasis on English, possibly—the ability
to communicate, a communications degree could
equally be a strong plus for a potential candidate.
There's no one correct path to be successful in the
broadcasting business.

Lee: I won't use requirement, because it's certainly not a
requirement, but in the four CBS-owned-and-operated facilities, it's been my experience that we look
for someone with a college degree, and not necessarily in communications or journalism. From actual
sales training experience, I look for people who have
had, first, prior television sales experience, preferably in the Chicago market, because it certainly helps
to have someone who can identify all the agencies
and their locations and some of the players in the
market. Second, I would look for someone with
radio background who had called successfully on
some of the larger agencies in this market. Third
would be television background outside of the market; fourth would be radio background outside the
market. But those are the primary training requirements.

Rothstein: When I interview, I'm not that impressed by re-sumes. Several successful people that I've dealt with in business had no college or just barely got through. But the one thing that all of these people had was a great passion in their gut, and their training was pretty much on the job. They all found out that they had ability to be convincing to other people, and they presented wonderful arguments. They had the ability to overcome any objection anybody could ever think of.

On the other hand, the first person I ever hired in the business was a straight-A student from Yale. I hired him to be assistant media buyer when I was at Grey Advertising. The background didn't seem to make any difference. He just had a desire.

It's an individual thing. If a student goes to a university, has an interest in broadcasting, and takes broadcasting and marketing courses, that's terrific, because that shortens the amount of time that it takes to be trained. Maybe it can get them into a position more quickly. But in general, it just shortens the training that they'll have to go through.

The people that I've been interviewing most recently have come from schools around this state. Although these students come out of their production courses very well equipped to get involved in that area of the television station, they don't come out as well equipped to get involved in a management area or in a sales area. I don't know why that is.

One piece of background that is excellent is to become a summer intern. Working inside the sales department for a few months you get a feeling for the job. You have salespeople who do the ten things that salespeople are supposed to do on a presentation, and yet they'll fail. And then someone else is a spectacular success in the same kind of an instance, with the same buyer, the same client, same everything. The difference is that one person goes by the numbers and there's something that's missing from the gut that gives life to their sales effort. When somebody tells me they don't want to buy what I'm selling, I am personally affronted by it. I can't understand why they won't buy what I'm selling. If you don't feel that way, I don't think you can be a good salesperson.

Question: What ongoing training or education do professional broadcast salespeople need?

Netter: We've been real pleased with the courses that, for example, TVB offers, which I think are supported by the Sterling Institute. I think Dale Carnegie is good for some, but you have to tailor it. If you have somebody who's got the intelligence and background, but maybe is a little nervous in front of large groups, you might want to send that person to a Dale Carnegie situation in order to develop confidence in public speaking.

There are a number of really good CBS courses that are offered to us as a member of the CBS group. I encourage our account executives to take those seminars; and they range in subject matter, everything from dealing with stress, to how to put together a role-playing presentation, to finance for the nonfinancial manager.

I think it's important that when you are selling time to somebody, you understand their business. You cannot sell to somebody if you haven't identified and understood their needs, because you obviously then can't meet their needs. And you need a general education in business. Knowing how a business operates comes from studying economics, studying business. I encourage all of our account executives to be very current on the trade press, so they are aware of current trends.

I also like them—on their own—to read such books as *In Search of Excellence* and *Megacapital*. I get them on tape and listen to them in my car, since I have no reading time and then I pass them around.

Bornhauser: They need direction, supervision from management, and a continual training as to what the product is that they're selling. More importantly, good salespeople are totally informed about a thousand different topics of what's going on in our society. At one point they may be dealing with the soft drink bottler and the next minute, a fashion retailer, later with a religious broadcaster; they have to be able to deal with people on many different levels. Consequently,

	they have to be as well informed as anyone. I require that my people subscribe to many publications, just so they know what's going on in the world.
Lee:	From a CBS standpoint, we have our own specific systems and research and computer information that people need to be trained in on an ongoing basis. We really don't offer courses per se; we do offer, through our regular sales meetings and regular get-togethers that we have with the local salespeople, ongoing training with respect to any new systems, with respect to any new information that is transmitted out of New York. Most of the salespeople rely on their fellow account executives for updated information with respect to market knowledge, competitive rates and ratings, any kind of local situation that will make them better salespeople on a day-to-day basis.
Rothstein:	When I was at the Petry company, I worked with management consultants, and had them work out case studies which were related to the broadcast industry that relayed the basics of salesmanship and management. I didn't want my people talking about the Ford Motor Company. I wanted them talking about WTVJ in Miami, or about WXYZ in Detroit, or things that occur within our own business. We would have quarterly training sessions for two or three or four days, depending on what the nature of the topics were that were involved.
	There would always be a revisitation to basics of selling. Then we tried to teach them a little bit more about how to read clients, how to confront problems, how to deal with the truth. I find that in management training, many people can't deal with the truth.
	That's what you would try to do, ideally. However, a small broadcasting company may not be able to handle that expense, unfortunately. What we do from time to time is look for TVB things which are inexpensive, which are not always of the best quality. But at least, we're giving our people some training from time to time.
Shrum:	In the past we have done very little in the way of training. I believe that is changing as our business

changes. We're going to be seeing more and more training programs geared for salespeople.

Question: How much of this training, if any, do you provide to your sales staff?

Bornhauser: Well, we have an ongoing training program, as far as in our sales meetings, obviously. We also utilize the Television Bureau of Advertising's annual regional seminars, and of course, all the publications and videotapes. In sales meetings we utilize role playing, let the salespeople make presentations to us before they make presentations to the clients.

Lee: Not really any through any specific and rigid training programs. Most of that is gleaned from day-to-day situations where—and I have to be very adamant about this—communication and byplay takes place, not only the account executives amongst themselves, but among the management and the sales management at the station and the account executives to provide any and all information that we can to make them better account executives.

Rothstein: Nothing that costs us any money directly. We use some TVB materials and hold special sales meetings on things that are pertinent, when they become available to us. We generally have at least one sales meeting a week, sometimes more.

We do a lot of role playing when special occasions come up, like when the fall is coming up, and we re-estimate our entire fall schedule, because we'll have some new programming for 4:00 through 8:00 and the network programs change. What we'll do for a solid week is have the salespeople practice the new fall presentations. During that time that they're making a presentation, we're training the salesperson to get back to the basics of the pitch, and we're also refining the presentation at the same time.

That's the training session for us. There's always 10 or 15 minutes in every weekly sales meeting that are related directly to sales-related problems, and overcoming difficulties within the market.

Shrum: We're starting to do that now, with the Fortune sales training course that we're taking on. We also have a manual to help people understand the inner workings of the television station: how the departments work together to put the end product on the air, buzzwords that we use, an in-depth discussion of the research that we use and how that applies to selling situations.

Netter: We send every account executive to the TVB Sterling Institute courses. We also provide a lot of training internally at CBS. We have a very good tuition plan if somebody wants to go to school at night, if the course is at all job related. I would certainly endorse studying certain psychology courses or economics courses.

Question: Where do you recommend they get the rest of this continuing education or training?

Shrum: Before, people would work their way up into the system. That was how they acquired their knowledge necessary to sell.

Today, as we look outside of our business, we're trying to find people that have sales training in other areas, and then we adapt that training to our individual needs. What I'm recommending is that if somebody can come to us with a good sales background outside of our business, and an understanding of retail, an understanding of how that side of the business works, that can be more beneficial to us than anything else.

Netter: They should attend school on their own with the support of the station. I also set up many seminars within the structure of our sales meetings. For example, once a month we'll have an outside speaker come into the sales meeting for the purpose of educating the sales staff on how differernt clients work. One might be a merchandise VP from a department store, talking about how to penetrate a department store, where the dollars come from, their television advertising, how they go after supportive campaigns.

The next time, somebody talks about how the automotive dealer groups function, who makes the decision, who's on the advertising committee, how do you penetrate that. Another topic might be the structure of a major advertising agency, how do you get entrenched in an advertising agency without offending anybody along the way? So, we have our own internal miniseminar sessions.

Bornhauser: I think I did already answer that, as far as being as well rounded and well informed as possible. Obviously, they can get it through normal educational channels. They can continue their education in the form of a master's degree. But again, it's a matter of maintaining a level of awareness and consciousness of what's going on around them, specifically inside the industry, from a technical standpoint, from a marketing standpoint, and what's going on outside the specific industry.

Lee: I'd endorse any local universities, any local programs that teach marekting, management, any advanced courses in those areas, as well as possible courses that TVB might offer, or any media-type training programs on selling, closing, meeting the objections of the sale, things like that.

I think, though, that the key here is the fact that they should be able to be implemented on a day-to-day basis. Media sales is very difficult to teach, per se, until you get into the actual situation, and if you can provide on-the-job training, or training outside of the job that can be implemented on a day-to-day basis, it's very important.

Question: It has been said that on an industry-wide basis about 15 percent of the broadcast salespeople make about 85 percent of the sales, while the other 85 percent of the broadcast salespeople make the remaining 15 percent of sales. Radio Advertising Bureau has used these or similar figures to stress the need, especially in radio sales, of increased professionalism in the field. Although the percentages probably apply more to radio than to television, what in your opinion separates the very good broadcast salesperson from the also-ran or not-so-good salesperson?

Shrum: The account list that they are handling. That's not a fair answer, but if you look historically at a television station, a person comes in and has a very junior list. And that changes over the years as people leave. Their list continues to improve, they acquire the larger accounts.

So, by a process of elimination, by attrition, what happens is that they in fact end up with a premier account list. Now, one of the problems in that is that the premier account list may require less work than any other account list at the television station. And it will draw more money.

So, you see a situation where people billing a lot less money may be the hardest-working people on the staff. So, in the 85-15, it also means when you look at the industry standards, you need to look at all television stations or all radio stations. You have to understand that a lot of people out there that are selling are not in fact selling a product that very many people are buying. So, you have a limited number of people in a market selling at the top station.

That's especially true in radio, where you have 40 or 50 signals in a market, but only 8, 10, or 12 of them are really viable radio stations. They're going to get most of the buys. But all those other stations, in fact, have salespeople out making calls. But, they're not going to be able to generate the kind of money that the top ten stations do.

Netter: The outstanding account executive—that's the cream of the crop—is one who addresses management's priorities. And that means selling specialties, thinking conceptually, thinking big, doing developmental work. All management teams want to see their base of advertisers broadened, because no one advertiser has real superior clout.

Bornhauser: Those figures would not jibe with my personal experience in the business—the television business. The question you're asking is, What really makes the successful salesman? There are different ingredients; one isn't necessarily better than another.

I would say that probably the most important thing is aggressiveness and alertness, awareness. There's an old expression that "Success in life is 90 percent effort and 10 percent smarts," and I would apply those similar percentages to successs in sales. The most successful salespeople are not necessarily the smartest, but the ones that work the hardest.

Lee: We currently have on our staff 12 local account executives, and those 12 account executives account for approximately 55 or 60 percent of our station's billing. We try to suit the needs of the account executive and the needs of our list to that individual. We try not to provide too much billing, or give too much billing to any one particular local account executive. So I would have to say that for WBBM television our top five or six AEs—account for probably 70 percent of the billing. Also, the way that we pay these people is not based strictly on billing for those lists. So, it pays to have all the lists covered equally. We do attach the more experienced account executives—those account executives who've been in the market a long time—obviously, to the major agencies, the major pieces of business.

We have an evaluation system. Each account executive is given a number—an expected-to-earn number—for any given calendar year. So using this as an example, if the expected-to-earn for account executive A is $50,000, out of that $50,000, we'll pay approximately 80 percent of that in 12-month increments, as what you could almost call a salary. The balance of that—the 20 percent—is put into a pool where they will be judged against their peers, with all aspects of account executiveship, from paperwork to discrepancy, to billing, to credits, to meetings, to hero sales, to special sales, to distress inventory sales, sports sales, and things like that. That 20 percent can be judged then on a management basis that will give them their annual number. So they have reasons to cover all the bases.

Rothstein: I really can't answer that because in television, at an individual station, that's not the case. In Miami, we've probably got somewhere around 40 radio stations with an average of four or five salesmen, so you're looking at 200 salespeople in the market. There's probably about 25 or 30 of them—your 15 percent—who are producing most of the money in the market.

Television is different. We've got six television stations here, and each one probably has about seven salespeople. And nobody's going to hold onto a bad salesperson. All of them produce.

Question: What advice would you give the beginning broadcast salesperson or the person training on being educated to become a broadcast salesperson?

Netter: Do internships while you're in college. They make a tremendous difference in terms of finding your way around the station and knowing how to apply for a job once you're out of college. I can't give you percentages—but I would say that a major number of the interns who work here end up ultimately being hired full-time by the station.

So, I would say get an internship in your college years, get your initial training in radio, in small-market television, or in independent UHF, or just independent television. I think all three of those are tough sells, and they provide excellent training ground. As a matter of fact, of the staff I have now—I have 10 account executives—I would say at least 50 percent of them came from radio.

Bornhauser: There's an old expression: "The first sale that you make in the broadcasting business is getting the first job, and the sales manager that hires you may be the toughest sale that you've ever made in your life." So my first piece of advice would be to make that first sale and get that first job. It may not be necessarily in the broadcasting business. As more and more graduates enter the advertising workforce and there are obviously a finite amount of broadcast sales jobs, they're forced to go into related industries.

I have seen quite a few broadcast salespeople evolve from the agency buying side of the desk. As a buyer, you're exposed to all kinds of sales pitches and every advertising medium. It's a terrific opportunity to get an overview of what's good and bad about sales techniques, different messages, what the different media have to offer. Sometimes starting on the media-buying side can be an avenue to sales. In our rep firm in New York, our sales team has six salespeople plus two sales managers. Four of the six salespeople started as media buyers, and the vice-president in charge of the whole team also started as a media buyer. I currently have 10 salespeople, and four of them were media buyers before they got into broadcast sales.

Lee: First of all, I would recommend that individuals who are interested in getting into the business talk to as many people and as many stations and get as much background on the business or the medium that they're interested in that they can. This will give them an idea as to how certain groups operate, how certain stations operate, how the radio versus television business operates.

The next thing is that they must understand that their chances of getting into the business at a major-market television station are very, very small initially. Unless they know somebody, and that happens in the business, they should go into a situation that they can be comfortable with, and usually that's radio, where they're more likely to take a chance on you and where you can prove your worth.

Rothstein: I hope they have done some internship at stations in their community to give them insight into what it really feels like. Secondly, I would tell them to get in touch with the television stations under any circumstances and perhaps radio stations, to go to lunch with some of the sales managers or the salespeople and find out what these people do and find out if they really want to do it. The people in the business make a lot of money, but they pay for it. Everybody's not a great salesperson and everybody doesn't sleep so well every night.

If they decide that they really want to be involved in TV sales, to investigate the companies that they're going to be interviewing with. Every sales department in this market has a different personality, and it's based upon the management style of the general sales manager.

You can give me somebody out of college who is brilliant, has all the potential in the world, but if they can't work under the system of management that I use, they will fail. There's no doubt in my mind. And when I hire somebody, I don't hire anybody to fail. What I'm looking for when I interview somebody is whether or not this person will fit into what we're doing. Now, we are structured. We have strong sales managers. We have a very powerful, experienced sales team. We evaluate people on everything they do, from the time they walk in the building until the time they walk out at night. Can this person stand this kind of pressure? Can they stand the pressure of the 14th television market in the country which, by the way, is the ninth revenue market in the country?

	Can they handle this kind of pressure, or are they going to crumble?
Shrum:	They should take advantage of all the opportunities that are presented to them. By that I mean to really look at this thing called broadcast sales and understand what kind of impact that they can make. Our business is changing dramatically, preparing to go into the 1990s and beyond.
Question:	Would you give us your assessment of broadcast sales as a lifetime professional career?
Bornhauser:	I believe it's an excellent career, obviously, since I have been involved with it. The positive attributes of broadcast sales are the remuneration can be quite good, and it can be an avenue into management, if that happens to be your interest.
	Beyond that, no two days are ever exactly alike. There is no routine, if you will, in broadcast sales. Every client is different. Every minute and hour of the day are different, and it allows a person with creativity and flexibility to use those skills.
Lee:	The first thing that I came to realize is that it's definitely a young person's business. A lot of it has to do with the pace; a lot of it has to do with the preeminence of young people in the business all along, and that doesn't seem to be changing.
	From my own standpoint, what I hope to do is stay in the business long enough to become financially secure and then move on to something somewhat more entrepreneurial, either in the consulting end or maybe another side of the advertising business.
	It's a great career as long as you can maintain your position in it. The other thing one has to keep in mind is does an individual want to be a salesperson for the predominant part of his or her existence in the business, or do they want to move up into management? I've chosen management, which is one opportunity, but we also have salespeople who are basically what one would consider to be career salespeople. You have to make those decisions as to which avenue you'd like to choose. Both can lead down a very successful career path.

Rothstein: I think it would be limiting. One of the beauties in the business is that you learn just everything there is to know about broadcasting and about the entertainment business. You read all the magazines people send to us every week—*Electronic Media*, *Broadcasting*, and *Advertising Age*—you get a smattering of everything. When you go out to sell, you're selling programing, you're selling rating points, you're selling marketing, you're selling movies, you're selling game shows, you're selling everything that goes on within the entertainment business.

I think what people should be thinking to themselves is, I'm in the entertainment business, I'm not just in the television sales business. If I decide to stay in a television station, I want to run the station. If I decide that I want to continue to be a salesperson, do I want to stay in one television market for my whole life, or do I want to try something else? I'd tell them to try something else.

Shrum: I think it's an honorable profession that will continue to be that way well into the year 2000 and beyond. Our business is changing; we're going to be seeing more of the disciplines of a Fortune 500 company applied to broadcast sales. I think it's going to become an even more honorable profession in the years to come than it is now, and to me it's a wonderful way to make a living. So, I would highly recommend it to anyone looking to get into the broadcast business.

Netter: It's a great career if you don't burn out. It's difficult to do sales on a long-term basis without moving on to bigger challenges, whether it's moving up in the markets, moving into a national sales capacity instead of a local sales capacity, or moving into management. However, if somebody finds it rewarding and stimulating enough to be selling on a long-term basis, over 20 or 30 years, that's great.

As long as they're sharp, and they continue to do the job, it can be financially and personally rewarding. For years, broadcasting has moved people around before they become entrenched. As soon as they start to develop strong relationships in the market, we pick them up and move then to another market. Now there's a trend to recognize the value of a long-term salesperson. I've got two or three on my

	staff who are absolutely invaluable, and they continue to be happy selling. They don't have an interest in management, for various reasons, and they're invaluable to the station.
Question:	Would you describe the chief responsibilities of a sales manager in broadcast sales?
Lee:	A sales manager in this business has to be a keeper of all keys, if you will. It has to be someone who can delegate authority. A good sales manager will not get bogged down in day-to-day operations and activity with respect to making rate calls at every turn but will delegate the task to those account executives or the local sales managers or national sales managers who have responsibility.

Ultimately what we'd like to do is have the umbrella system, where the general sales manager will basically be a purveyor of main sales strategies and day-to-day sales strategies and convey that information to the local sales manager and the national sales manager who will carry them out.

At this television station, the one predominant responsibility is that of inventory, what's available to sell, the pricing of that inventory, and how to sell it. Once we've developed the pricing and made available those units that are for sale, then the actual sale can be broken down into the local and the national arenas for those sales managers to handle.

My activity in the local arena when I was a local sales manager included a great deal of contact with each of the local account executives and a great deal of contact with the local marketplace so I could be aware of what was happening. I knew where to go to get money; I knew where to go to get business. Most good local and national sales managers spend a great deal of their time out in the marketplace, so they can be aware of what's going on.

Rothstein:	Fiscal responsibility is number 1. The sales manager is one of the department heads at a station, and they share part of the responsibility with the general manager and with the other department heads for the bottom line. You have to run a fiscally responsible department.

Next, and this is pretty much of an equal importance, is the development of people. I want to hire somebody who can be promoted. Whatever potential they have, it should be developed. I want my sales managers to delegate everything they can to those salespeople, so that the salespeople will get into another area, and will develop.

Shrum: There are three or four areas that are of paramount importance, and one of them is inventory control. The television station only has X number of spots to sell any given day, and that does not change. Depending upon the demand, or the anticipated demand, you have to do your pricing correctly, so that you don't run out of inventory too soon.

Coupled with that, you set the direction for your salespeople, local sales managers, and national sales managers that will allow them to meet their objectives. We look at bringing in other kinds of research, vendor-support programs, new tools that are going to be necessary for the 1990s and beyond. We've got to keep our minds open to the changes taking place in our business.

We have been competing against newspaper for a lot of years, and we still haven't been able to get close to beating them because they do some things better than we do. One of these is that they service the clients better. We have to find new ways to be able to communicate with our clients, and I think that's a very important aspect of a sales manager's job.

Netter: That depends on which position of sales manager, and we have four different ones here. But I would say the responsibilities would be to hire and train good salespeople, to manage by positives, and therefore always keep the staff motivated. Unhappy salespeople don't sell—they can't sell. It's one department that has to always be highly motivated, and they have to be happy people.

Others are the proper management of inventory, strong client contact—putting out any fires before they get out of control and meeting the problems that sometimes exist between a client and the station head-on—and promoting the value of a sales department and its staff to upper management who may have come from a completely different discipline

within the organization and doesn't really understand what the sales department does or how valuable its people are.

Question: How long does your average sales employee remain
with your firm?

Rothstein: It's hard to say because I've only been in a local station for a year and a half. I hope they won't stay any
more than a few years and then develop well enough
so that another station will hire them as a sales manager, or that they'll try something bigger and better.

Shrum: We have one person on staff who's been here 25
years, down to two people that have been on staff for
a year and a half. So, there's really no answer to that.

Netter: It varies. As I said, I've got two or three people who
are long-term professional salespeople in the local
market. They've been in their particular jobs for anywhere from eight to twelve years; that is long-term in
terms of our industry.

　　We really operate very much as a farm team and
training ground for the CBS national sales rep system, since we own our own rep, and I would say 60
percent of our people end up being promoted to our
national sales organization. The people who do that
are probably with us for an average of three to four
years before they move on.

Bornhauser: There are no averages. This particular television station has very little turnover. We had a salesman two
years ago—which is relatively unheard-of in our business—retire as a broadcast salesperson at the normal
retirement age. We have, as I said, 10 salespeople. In
five years in my position here, we have lost one salesperson. The longest tenure we have would be 14
years; the shortest would be a year and a half. If
there's an average length of service, it would be
around five years at this point.

Lee: With CBS, our average tenure is almost 10 years for
this sales staff, and I think you'd find that a little bit
unusual in this business, but here again too, we're an
owned-and-operated station. A lot of our appeal for
an account executive moving up to major market
television is being owned and operated by CBS and
getting the opportunity to represent CBS and the

	stations division. I'd think you would find that the tenure here would be a little bit different than at a small market.
Question:	A final, open-end question: What other advice or counsel would you like to give to people preparing for a career in broadcast sales?
Shrum:	First of all, it's a great industry. We need young, articulate individuals who are highly motivated to come into our business. The opportunity's going to be there for them, if in fact they do make the commitment to the business.

I think the key is to be prepared to work hard and do the job you currently have better than anyone else has done it, so that you're going to be given an opportunity to grow and to prosper with the industry. If you can get some additional sales experience before you come into the business, that's going to be beneficial.

Netter: Think about your long-term goal. Make sure it's something you want because you can't do it half-heartedly. You have to really want to do it in order to be successful. Don't look at it as a way to make fast money, even though salaries escalate pretty quickly in sales, and there are a lot of young people making big dollars. My oldest salesperson on staff is 41 or 42 and the youngest is probably 25, and both make healthy salaries. But they wouldn't enjoy one penny of it if their hearts weren't in it and if they didn't really have the motivation to do it.

I would say, also, develop a long-range plan. Don't just go into it as a job. Figure out where you want it to lead. Do you want to do this forever as a career, or do you want this as a step to sales management, or are you going to spend six years in sales and then make a lateral move into the programming area, spend some years in programming, and then go after a station manager's job? Have a career plan mapped out in your mind.

Keep yourself up to speed. Listen to motivational tapes and selling tapes, things like that in your car; make commuting time productive. Read the trade press. Think bigger than sales; think as a broadcaster.

Bornhauser: It's very difficult to get a starting position in sales without an education, because there are so many people competing for the positions. The person that has demonstrated the discipline of four years worth of degree has an edge over someone with no degree at all. However, that's not absolutely important in the long run if a person is successful in broadcast sales.

As I mentioned before, that first job is the most important thing in the business because once you have that first job, you can have success and demonstrate that success to any potential employer. Tenacity will get you a job ultimately in the business.

A business education background is important. If you don't understand how business operates, you can't possibly do an effective job in dealing with business people.

Lee: You need to be a people person, be able to communicate effectively and concisely and get along with people. You also have to have common sense to be a good salesperson. You've got to have the will to succeed, as well as the ego to succeed.

The other thing that is very important for any sales staff, and for any successful sales operation, is the aspect of teamwork. On a baseball field, you can't have nine pitchers. You can't have nine cleanup hitters. You've got to have a guy that bats first and a guy that bats last, and you've got to have a guy that plays pitcher, catcher, as well as all the other separate positions on the baseball diamond. Once a sales staff is willing to understand that, and an individual understands that he or she can't be the biggest biller, that there are niches for all, then I think you'll find a sales operation that thrives.

Rothstein: Get to know the business. Talk to as many people as you can—everybody's got a television station near where they live. Find somebody that will talk to you, spend as much time with those people as you can, and get a feel for the business.

SUMMARY

Though the comments of the sales managers express their own views, each without having heard the others' comments, there run some central themes.

First, a college degree in a communication field is not a requirement to get a job in broadcast sales or succeed in such a career. Neither is a college degree in any other field a requirement at some stations.

However, the expressions by the sales managers that they want to see intelligent, knowledgeable, outgoing people that have made, or are ready to make, a commitment to professionalism in the field of broadcast sales indicate that the regimen of a four-year college degree will not be wasted. Also, the more knowledge one has about the field, the easier it is to gain the additional learning that goes on beyond the formal classroom.

A good degree in broadcast communication is going to be at least as helpful as just any four-year degree and has the potential of being more helpful than any other degree in preparing those who will be the professionals of tomorrow in the field.

Second, the prospective broadcast salesperson is going to be dealing professionally with businesses of all sorts and thus should plan to include as much background in business as possible within the four-year degree program. This can be accomplished through a minor in business, a second major, or basic backgrounding courses in business to augment the studies in the broadcast field.

Third, the field of broadcast sales is one where learning and application march side by side. Feedback from application of the learning helps the prospective salesperson learn more for renewed application.

Individuals advance better and faster when they have an opportunity to put into practice the things learned as quickly as possible. This can and is being accomplished in four-year college programs through direct lab application while the study is underway, internships with broadcast stations to allow the beginner to work with professional salespeople, and role-playing sessions in which the beginning salesperson attempts to make sales and is critiqued by an instructor, a sales manager, or peers.

Chapter 13

ADAPTING

FOR THE FUTURE

Telecommunications is entering into an era of unprecedented internal competition because of the public availability of an enormous number of media signals. Gone is the isolated market served by only one stand-alone AM signal. Residents of smaller communities or rural areas, more likely than not, can now choose from several regional FM stations; if no satellite dish is sitting in the back yard beaming down 150 or more television signals, residents may have local cable TV service offering 12 or more channels 24 hours per day and own video cassette recorders (VCRs). That stand-alone AM station that once served a sparsely populated area as a comparative electronic monopoly is now competing hard for listenership, even if it still is the only station licensed in that community. The larger the market, the more intense the competition becomes; hence, the total available audience becomes more defined and the more difficult it becomes to convince merchants that *your* station is the one to buy.

EXCELLENCE

Those stations that will survive such intense competition are not just the ones who provide excellence in programming content and engineering. The surviving stations will also, as a necessity, excel in overall station management. Such a management makes real investments in its people as well as in its equipment and recognizes that continuing personal development, at all levels and in all departments, is the central core of an ongoing sales training effort that will allow the station to stay afloat financially despite the proliferation of available signals in the marketplace.

A Daily Commitment to Excellence

Learning the basic ingredients of professional sales contained within the chapters of this book, unfortunately, does not a salesperson make. To compete in this saturated media environment, the salesperson is necessarily involved in a daily commitment to excellence that builds on every potential the salesperson has for personal success in selling. Success comes in stages—by doing what needs to be done and doing things right on a daily basis—not by the crash reading of a book or attending a one-day motivational seminar that teaches "all about sales" in five easy steps. One necessarily becomes one's own coach and develops a mind-set of self-instructed sales training, or, more simply, the salesperson learns to accomplish on a daily basis those things that yield success.

Certainly, the student of electronic media sales could develop a list of what the sales consultant needs to accomplish daily just by referring to this book. Planning your day, organizing it, and properly controlling that plan are likely to be central to the time management of the successful consultant's day.

BECOMING YOUR OWN TEACHER

Learning to accomplish this yourself and monitor yourself is a key ingredient to developing successful, self-instructed sales training. You as a sales consultant cannot always rely on the boss to motivate you, monitor the effects of that motivation, and keep you on a high level of performance at all times. The successful consultant understands that he or she alone is responsible for daily and even hourly productivity by putting into practice what has been learned and by willingly accepting the role of ongoing self-instructor in the sales effort.

By feeling comfortable in his or her role as salesperson and confident in the knowledge of a sales system, the consultant can greet each day as a further challenge. Each day confirms his or her abilities as a continuing resource to clients doing business in a competitive environment. Receiving the client's business confirms to the salesperson that he or she is doing something right in the competitive media marketplace.

Self-Concept

How does one accomplish such an undertaking on a daily basis? How can one build on potential to maximize results? How does one become a self-instructor? What answers exist are not easy. They lie within the complex inner workings of the salesperson's concept of self and the desire to achieve professional respect within his or her business community. Teaching such intangible values is difficult. However, once the career commitment is made and the standards of the consultant are accepted, such questions begin to be answered—on a daily basis.

Self-Employment

A media sales consultant in effect works for himself or herself. Such a person has sole responsibility for a personal account list, a territory, and areas of follow-up responsibility. This self-employment aspect is what makes this position so unique and so full of opportunity in broadcasting. Income potential in markets of all sizes is unlimited, given the support of the entire staff back at the station. In a sense, media sales representatives are truly self-employed, and the only limits placed on productivity are self-imposed.

Perhaps Mark McCormack puts it best:

> *Being self-employed is the purest form of capitalism and the best way I know of getting paid what you are truly worth. It also demands a different mind-set, including an awareness that the number of hours you put in is only meaningful in terms of what you do with them.*
>
> *Most successful entrepreneurs [read* electronic media salespeople*] spend twenty-four hours a day either working or thinking about their business. But it is how they fill those hours that makes the difference between success and failure. The cliche is, "Don't work hard, work smart." The truth is, "work hard, work long, and work smart."*[1]

THE FUTURE MARKETING ENVIRONMENT

Adapting for the future is getting in touch with today's marketing environment. As Kenneth J. Costa of RAB says:

> *There's a world of difference among retail formats today. The local "Supermarket" doesn't exist anymore. We have warehouse-type stores, combination stores, convenience stores and gourmet food stores. A building materials outlet may be a hardware store, a garden supply store or Sears Roebuck.*[2]

A store is not a store is not a store. There are specialty stores, and there are stores with mass market appeal.

> *Paint stores are not alike. While paint represents 47 percent of the store's total sales, it is 65 percent of a manufacturer-owned paint store's sales, 53 percent of a hardware store's paint section sales, and just 26 percent of a department or discount store's paint section sales. The most effective radio campaign should rotate copy with other product lines. A proper mix also enables outlets like manufacturer-owned stores to position themselves as specialists. Retailers devoting enough frequency to creative ads can become specialists in several important categories. . . .*
>
> *Retail and product formats offer unique benefits to different customer groups. The key to effective radio sales is to match your station's format to the client's and to target copy appeal directly to appropriate listeners. The proliferation of consumer choices can be a blessing. There are many kinds of roses in the garden.*[3]

TABLE 13-1
Sales Relationships

Traditional Sales	Progressive Sales
Casual acquaintance	Business friendship
Topics are social or general	Business topics are appropriate
Dialogue is limited	Dialogue is open
Little is known about each other	Mutual professional respect is shown
Attitude is often I win, you lose	Attitude is I win, you win
Personal courtesies are shown	Professional courtesies are shown
Additional meetings are not expected	Follow-through is expected
Interest is sporadic and spontaneous	Interest is shown in needs and goals
Meetings could last any length of time	Meetings are brief and businesslike
Meetings happen at any time	Appointments are made
Disagreements are a threat	Disagreements are opportunities for mutual problem solving

CHANGING THE LANGUAGE OF SELLING

Aside from understanding today's marketing environment, adapting for the future is learning to change the language of selling. *Traditional sales* can be differentiated from *progressive sales*.

> *Progressive sales emphasizes the information-gathering stage whereas traditional focuses on the sales close. In addition, there are differences in sales terms. In traditional sales the vernacular implies manipulation or superficiality (pre-approach, the pitch and closing). Progressive sales terms show concern, preparedness, cooperation and the intent to continue the relationship after the sale (planning, proposing and assuring).*[4]

Specifically, then, how is traditional sales language changed? Table 13-1 from Alessandra and Cathcart shows how.

> *One of the major differences between traditional sales and progressive sales is the amount of study that takes place. The traditional salesperson spends little time studying. The professional salesperson, however, is truly concerned with the prospect's personal style, business needs and objectives, and financial status. This is done by en-*

couraging the prospect to become involved in the sales process. By asking open-ended questions and other probing methods, the salesperson invites the client to provide information that otherwise would remain unknown. In this way, the prospect is able to feel that the sale was a mutual agreement.

Progressive salespeople thrive on satisfied customers because they see them for what they are: assets. Assuring customer satisfaction after the sale means changing hats from salesperson to quality control person. By assuring the satisfaction of each customer, the progressive salesperson builds a clientele that will guarantee future sales and new prospects.[5]

Adapting for the future means leaving traditional sales behind, entering the era of progressive selling, and becoming a consultant of the type described and outlined in this book.

SUMMARY

Adapting for the future of broadcasting in the 1990s and beyond means changing the language of selling and positioning oneself apart from the competition by making a daily commitment to excellence. Productive consultants understand that they basically work for themselves, with sole responsibility for the success of a personal account list. Such successful salespeople adapt to a changing marketing environment and always strive for excellence by remembering the adage, "If it is to be, it is up to me!"

NOTES

1. Mark McCormack, *What They Don't Teach You at Harvard Business School* (New York: Bantam Books, 1984), p. 251.
2. Kenneth J. Costa, "Retail Format Explosion," *Sound Management* (July, 1986), pp. 36–37.
3. Tony Alessandra and Jim Cathcart, "Changing the Language of Selling," *Sound Management* (March, 1986), pp. 30–31.
4. Ibid.
5. Ibid.

Appendix I
RAB
CONSULTANT
CALL INTERVIEW

The contents of this entire book could appropriately be renamed *The Making of a Professional Salesperson*, as the information presented thus far has concentrated on the ingredients that go into the making of a professional media consultant. The student has learned that a media consultant's success depends upon the success of the client whose needs and problems have been predetermined by the consultant prior to any attempt at selling a media schedule. The media consultant who operates as a sustaining resource for clients is the highest level of media sales professional in the market today; the order takers and peddlers who comprise the majority of media salespeople on the streets today are an embarrassment to the industry. Those who have learned to become consultants are looked upon with respect by the business community they serve, and they bring prestige to their stations.

Many of these consultants have graduated to this level of selling by following the guidelines and interview techniques provided by the Radio Advertising Bureau (RAB), the trade association of the radio industry, which has been promoting the consultant form of selling for years.

For those of you with career plans that entail the selling of radio time, this section of the sales text is for you. Other media consultants can certainly learn from the following information, but the concepts have been designed specifically for radio, an industry that employs the vast percentage of media sales personnel in America today. The consultant sell, as it was originally named, was developed by the RAB to help these local station representatives become third-level sales consultants. Recently renamed the consultant call interview, the tool gives each salesperson a blueprint to follow during his or her initial visit with a prospect. This form is printed in its entirety at the end of this section (see pp. 360–363).

Defining the Consultant Call

According to RAB's *Radio Consultant Sales and Marketing:*

> *The Consultant Sell Interview allows you to confirm and expand on your knowledge of a client's business, including products and services, hours, locations, customers, marketing campaigns, current advertising message and the client's position in the marketplace in relation to the competition.*[1]

Combined with knowledge gathered about the business or the industry prior to the initial meeting, the thoroughness of this presentation impresses most clients. The salesperson has positioned himself or herself apart from the unskilled clerks at this point and is beginning to gain the confidence and the trust of the prospect.

After the client interview begins, the first series of questions in the Business/Customer Profile section gives the consultant a complete profile of the prospect's business, competition, and desired customers—the people wanted in the store on a continuing basis. Here the consultant is beginning to see the store and the prospect through the prospect's own eyes and is beginning to understand the prospect's needs through the prospect's point of view. The salesperson also begins to determine whether the customers the business is attempting to reach actually listen to the station the salesperson is representing or view the programs offered by the particular TV station.

In order to help the client with any merchandising efforts, the people wanted as customers must match to some extent the listeners who tune in to the station. Not everybody listens to your station. If your station programs a format heavily favored by males and the business is primarily interested in women 18 to 49, for example, your station may not be the best buy for the client. As the RAB puts it: "Your goal in this part of the interview is to gain enough insight into a prospect's business to determine *which* customers should be addressed and which elements of the prospect's business should be emphasized by your proposed marketing plan."[2] In TV as well, the target customers your client wants to reach must be the target demographic of the program you are trying to sell to that client.

Marketing Strategy

The Marketing Strategy section helps the consultant learn about the potential advertiser's business year—the up and down cycles that profile the normal business climate in any given year. This understanding helps the consultant and the prospect "create a marketing plan responsive to a business climate that shifts throughout the year."[3] A mistake of the nonconsultant in this industry is to attempt to get clients on the air with a "regular" schedule of, say, one or two commercials a day, seven days a week, and 365 days a year.

Regular advertising is essential, but this type of regularity does not allow for the changes that inevitably occur in the business climate. By understanding the cycles of the business, the consultant can devise a schedule that reflects or follows such cycles. He or she may well suggest a regular schedule of two or more commercials daily that is supplemented by increasing the schedule to six or more commercials daily during peak periods of business activity when getting the right customer in the store at the right time is essential to business success.

Advertising and Media

The section on Advertising and Media is a key area that gives you information on how to sell a merchant when you return for your second visit and assists you in planning a new media strategy and budget. You can learn what the client's attitudes toward advertising in general are and, specifically, his or her opinion of the various media.

Such knowledge assists the consultant in helping to improve the client's previous marketing efforts, and at the second call the salesperson will know whether to sell "against" newspaper (which is most often the case), direct mail, billboards, or whatever. Much of this information is estimated or researched before going in for the interview, as you can tell from reading the questions, but this information needs to be confirmed, as you need to understand the way in which the advertiser has planned past campaigns before you can begin developing new strategies for the future.

Find out, if possible, how the annual advertising budget is divided among segments of the year, such as months or quarters, and how much is allocated to the various media in the marketplace. Coupled with the information garnered in the Business/Customer Profile section, the consultant now knows the best and slowest business months, how the advertising budget is allocated during those times, and which media seems to work best at which times. With this information, presenting a customized campaign at the second meeting is much easier.

Conversation

An essential key to success during this entire client interview is to be as conversational as possible with the client. The questions on the form are worded informally for this purpose and are not to be read as an entry-level newscaster would read a TelePrompTer. Be human, genuinely curious, and openly friendly as you engage in a consultant call interview. Otherwise, the station could send out a robot and obtain the same results.

Normally, the entire interview process should not take more than a half hour. Taking up too much of a client's time may easily leave a negative impression; however, too little time spent may give the prospect the impression of disinterest or a general lackadaisical attitude. Ask all the questions because each one may uncover vital information necessary for planning a successful media campaign for the merchant. Keep in mind that you are there to listen, not to talk or to sell the benefits of your station during the initial meeting.

After Completing the Interview

After you've completed the questions, thank the prospect for granting you the time and then set a firm date for your next meeting—no fewer than three business days and no more than ten. Explain that you'll be reviewing the information and consulting resources in order to develop a specific marketing plan that the client can review. Then, politely leave and return to the station for what is perhaps the most difficult part of being a consultant—the preparation of a media campaign that meets the needs of the client and produces tangible, accountable results.

PREPARING AN EFFECTIVE CAMPAIGN BY DETERMINING CLIENT NEEDS

Knowing how to operate as a media consultant is not the same thing as being one. Many students may feel that the basic responsibilities of such a person are essentially completed when the appropriate information has been gathered from the client; however, being a media consultant means total involvement in the preparation of the campaign that will be presented to the client during the second meeting. Asking the questions and obtaining client information are actually the easy part. What to do with that information, that is, how to analyze and process it after you leave the store, is perhaps the single most difficult part of being a media consultant.

Taking Orders Is Easier

You can now see why being a clerk or an order taker is perhaps easier and safer. You just get client copy information and run it on the air—no analyzing, no accountability, and no knowledge of how the copy works in an overall marketing scheme. Sitting down with all the information gathered from an initial client interview and doing something constructive with it is enough to challenge even veteran salespeople.

However, media consultants thrive on the opportunity to organize and

implement a media campaign that has been specifically designed for a particular client because they know that its chances for success are high. When
the client is successful as a result of the help given by the consultant and the
station, the salesperson is successful from a financial standpoint and in gaining the respect of the professional business community.

The Consultant as Client Campaign Manager

Developing a client campaign that actually produces results, as opposed to
just running a flight of spots on any radio or TV station, cannot be done
without first interviewing the client. In this initial stage, the consultant begins to grasp the nature of the prospect's business and develops a feel for
how the business can be successfully promoted in the marketplace. Developing a campaign means either writing copy for a client's products or services or instructing others in the creative department to do so. Either way, the
consultant needs to understand the potential advertiser's products and services, the target customers for those goods, the business itself and its
advantages and disadvantages, the advantages and disadvantages of the
competition, the overall use of current and projected budgets, and the media and creative strategy that have been successful in the past.

Now comes the time to analyze this information so you can return to the
client with confidence, assured that you have developed a solid proposal
that the client will want to run. Regardless of whether you use the consultant
sell interview, ask the series of questions suggested in the second step of the
MEDIA system (expressing interest in the client via interview), or use a combination of both.

Find a Problem or a Need

Review your gathered information to see if you can determine any major
problems the client might have. You won't be able to solve every problem a
prospect perceives, but you might be able to tackle what you feel is a major
problem. Such problems demand immediate attention and have the best
chance of being turned around in the shortest period of time, and your objective is to develop solutions that will produce tangible results as quickly as
possible. Examples of major problems (or opportunities, for that matter)
would be large amounts of unsold inventory, a giant annual sale where the
client must better last year's sales volume, 10,000 pairs of Jordache jeans that
the client just bought at a special price and now has to sell, reduced customer traffic caused by a variety of conditions that you will have to analyze,
and special holiday periods and sales like Christmas and Easter with increased inventories that have to be sold before the holiday period ends.

Assist the Merchant in the Planning Process

Attacking a major problem area is fine, but perhaps what the client needs is just a consistent image in the marketplace or a steady increase in business as the year goes on. In this case, you can help the prospect by assisting with the planning. Advertisers, even though many operate or seem to operate by the seat of their pants, need a quarterly and an annual plan with predetermined goals. You can formulate an annual plan (strategic planning) that is broken down into short-term plans (operational planning) based on quarters or months. These short-term plans should "be developed to allocate and implement the budget into campaigns and promotions . . . including a promotional calendar . . . considering whether various holidays tie in with products and services offered by your client."[4] You can also compare ad investment with peak and slow periods, taking into account the business potential for each quarter, and suggest an annual schedule based on these peak and slower business periods. You may be able to maximize busy periods and attract additional business during slower business cycles.

As the RAB suggests:

> *While some problems can be solved by increasing expenditures in advertising during certain periods of the year, others can be addressed creatively in a marketing campaign that projects a new, fresh image or emphasizes a product or service that might not have been promoted in previous ad campaigns. In formulating solutions to address each peak and valley in a client's business year, remember to retain a picture of the entire year in your mind . . . the best proposal offers solutions to immediate (short term) problems and sets a marketing pattern that will hopefully lead to overall improvements in a client's business.[5]*

The Demographic Fit

Determine a demographic fit (your listeners, the client's customers) and the target customers. Some advertisers actually aim their messages at the wrong people. The RAB's *Instant Background* reveals customer profiles and typical demographics for all stores; see if these match with the perceived target customer group. The client may also be utilizing the wrong media to reach the target customer. If young people are desired and newspaper is heavily used, you'll have to point out that radio can target younger demographics better than the local newspaper. Look for discrepancies in who customers are and how and when the client is reaching them. Maybe you could even introduce a new target customer—your audience! Remember that you can't help if those who listen to your station are not, never have been, and never will be target customers for your client's particular business.

Truly Creative Campaigns

The next step is to conceive and implement the creative strategy and write and produce the commercials for the campaign. All of your thinking and planning will have been totally useless if you do not develop a sound, creative campaign to take back to the merchant. If it's the same old stuff, your campaign will be useless because you are not developing new strategies and new thinking to complement your consultant approach. New commercial ideas and top-flight production must accompany your return visit to the prospect or you will be exposed as a fraud. Solid, creative solutions to the advertiser's marketing problems are what you need. You can write the advertising messages yourself or have your copy people (creative department) write them. Just make sure the commercials address the problem(s) and are creatively different than whatever the merchant has tried before, which probably didn't work that well.

Always return to the client with two very different campaigns, for example, one humorous and one straight. This gives the client a *choice.* He or she can too easily reject out of hand a single campaign, and three campaigns would be confusing. So, return with two different campaigns that address the needs or the new marketing plan you have devised for the advertiser.

Devising Schedules

When you return to the client, have a written schedule or a choice of suggested schedules that you have determined would best target desired customers. Make sure each is large enough to do the job properly. If the client chooses to spend very little money in radio, the impact of the chosen schedule on the desired goals will be negligible. The client needs to give radio a budget in order to produce results. Radio is cost-effective; it is not necessarily cheap. Like newspaper, TV, or any other medium, it needs an adequate budget to be successful, so forget one or two spots a day. If you have the audience that is the client's target customer, 10 or more impressions per day, especially during peak periods, should be planned.

Newspaper is probably not targeting the proper customers, so the client can reduce the size of a newspaper ad to come up with a budget for your radio campaign. Just don't offend a client who has been using newspaper for years; get him or her to examine a media mix concept and see the need for a radio budget to accomplish what the two of you have been discussing during the entire process of the consultant sell.

As the RAB states:

> *if you know your product as you should, you'll demonstrate that radio can offer a wide range of problem-solving ideas. Look for the "soft spot" in the client's current advertising—the area where he seems most vulnerable to competition—and tie your proposed*

schedule on radio to that area. Scheduling, coverage, immediacy, targetability, creativity: keep these radio strengths in mind and possible solutions to a client's needs should come easily. If you come to a problem you can't solve, try brainstorming. Many times others might suggest an idea that eluded you.[6]

Bringing the student to this consultant level of excellence has been the central focus of this entire book. Nobody enters the profession of media sales and automatically begins operating at this level of competence.

From Survival to Professional

All who sell radio, TV, or cable experience what consultant Ken Greenwood calls the four passages of selling.[7] All salespeople begin their careers in the first stage of survival, graduate to the stage of learning, enter a competence phase, and eventually become professional. The survival phase lasts approximately a month, or until the salesperson begins to generate ideas, see relationships, and understand what he or she is trying to do; it is usually at this point that salespeople begin wondering when they'll start to earn more money or go beyond their guarantee. The learning phase continues through the first year. Somewhere between the salesperson's first and third year, the period of competence flowers. The salesperson is confident and competent with the basics of selling, knows what works for him or her, and generally has that warm glow that accompanies a feeling of having made it. After five years of successful selling, Greenwood says the salesperson becomes a professional, and recognition and status are more important than money. The salesperson knows that he or she is good and can sell and that career direction may now be a choice of continuing to sell, moving to a larger market, or going into sales management.

Achieving sales success in media, however, is not an easy task. The student must understand that there are no short-cuts to becoming an invaluable resource to the clients. Generating this level of trust and respect comes from months and, more often, years of putting into practice the theories and guidelines explained in this book and any other sources on sales you may consult. What we have done is to give you a head start, your advantage being the knowledge of a system that can lead you to the highest pinnacle of sales success possible. We have not told you how to sell; instead, we have given you a road map to follow. How you put your personality and your ways of saying and doing things into your presentation and how you follow up with your clients will determine your level of sales success, not your ability to recite a memorized sales pitch. Your success, in a word, depends upon you. You are the one who meets face to face with your clients and prospects each day. You alone have the power to change their lives by helping them with their unique business problems and by doing so, you advance yourself. A more satisfying and exciting career possibility is hard to find.

RAB

Consultant Call

Guidelines For Client-Needs Analysis
To Develop A Marketing Plan.

FIRM NAME: _____ PHONE: _____

MAILING ADDRESS: _____

PRIMARY CONTACT:_____ LOCATION ADDRESS: _____

TYPE OF BUSINESS: _____

NUMBER OF LOCATIONS:_____ ADDRESSES: _____

AGENCY:_____ ACCOUNT EXECUTIVE: _____

Pre-Appointment: By monitoring advertising, visiting the advertiser and calling on various research sources, you can assemble much information about the advertiser's industry and specific business before the interview. This "homework" will impress the client with your thoroughness and professionalism, make it easier to direct the dialogue during the interview, and save time.

Review Marketing Research: Instant Background, Sales Call Guide, Target Marketing, Simmons data, other RAB sources and local information such as Chamber of Commerce, Library, etc. Note research sources:

_____

_____

Advertiser's Business and Competition: List products, services, days/hours open, main competitors, etc.:

_____

_____

Current Media Strategy: Monitor activity in Radio, newspapers, Tv, outdoor, yellow pages, direct mail, etc. and estimate expenditures, if possible:

_____

_____

Impressions From Personal Visit To Store and/or Contacts With Customers: _____

_____

_____

_____

Business/Consumer Profile: In this section you'll confirm and expand upon preappointment research to establish a profile of the advertiser's business, the competitors, the current and potential customers. This information will assist you in developing a marketing plan with good copy points and advertising that targets best prospects. Here are questions to guide you:

Who are your competitors? _____

What are their advantages? _____

What are your advantages over them? _____

_____

In what ways do your competitors' customers differ from yours? _____

_____

What is your primary marketing trade area? _____

From where do other customers come? _____

Who is your typical customer? (**Age range, sex, income, occupation, other demographics, single** or multi-family dwelling?) _____

_____

Does the type of customer differ in your other locations? (If applicable) _____

_____

What other types of customers would you like to attract? _____

_____

Marketing Strategy: A strategic plan is essential to an advertising effort and to your proposal. In this section, you'll establish the client's planning procedures and learn when, how and why the promotional budget is developed. This will help you to time your marketing plan for maximum benefit. The basic questions:

How long have you been in business? _____

Do you use a calendar or fiscal year? _____

How far in advance do you plan marketing/merchandising strategies? _____

_____

Is the plan based on previous years' sales curves or other criteria? _____

Within the plan, do you develop quarterly promotional plans? _____

What are your best months? quarters?

1. _____ ;   2. _____ ;   3. _____ ;

4. _____ . *Why?* _____

_____

Advertising & Media: It's important to establish rapport with the client before getting into the budget area. Some sales managers include this section as part of the initial interview. Others establish this information with a follow-up call. This information will help you develop a profile of the client's current advertising program, confirming budget and media-mix figures, learning attitudes and rationale. This data will help you plan a new media strategy and budget. Questions to guide you:

How do you develop promotional budgets? (percentage of gross sales, by need, based on sales curves, annually, quarterly, etc.) _____

_____

What percentage goes to each quarter? month? How do you determine that percentage? _____

_____

What is your total advertising budget in dollars? _____

What percentage of your budget do you allocate to individual media? (Confirm your preappointment research to establish which media are used, what percentage of the budget each receive.)

_____

Why do you use those media in those proportions? _____

_____

How do you measure the effectiveness of media? _____

_____

In your strongest quarter or month, what was the effect of advertising on sales? _____

_____

Who are other people in your company involved in advertising decisions? _____

_____

_____

(Try to include all decision makers when presenting your marketing plan.)

Co-op: Here you'll establish the role of co-op in current and future advertising and you may find additional funds for your suggested marketing plan.

What percentage of your budget is co-op funded? _____

For which media do you use co-op? _____

Are there other co-op funds available that you haven't yet been able to use?

_____

I've noticed that you carry these co-op brands (see list from preappointment). Are there others?

_____

(Suggestion: Review additional brands in RAB Radio Co-op Sources book.)

Important: Once all information has been gathered, analyze each module to determine client needs and problems. You may find other sources of information* will be helpful. If so, incorporate this data into your analysis. *Then*, structure a marketing plan utilizing Radio to meet these needs and be a solution to the problems. REMEMBER, THE MARKETING PLAN WILL NOT BE A *COST* TO THE ADVERTISER, BUT WILL BE AN *INVESTMENT*!

*From your RAB files or from RAB on request:

- Instant Backgrounds
- Industry Trade Articles
- Case Histories
- Newspaper Circulation Analysis
- Simmons Data
- Starch Slide Rule
- Target Marketing & Special User Tabulations

- Local TV Ratings
- Radio Facts Book
- Sales Call Guide
- Radio Co-op Sources
- Local Market Profile
- Advertiser Category Tape

Call or write RAB Member Service Department for a review of other advertisers in this business who are successfully using Radio.

NOTES

1. *Radio Consultant Sales and Marketing,* © Radio Advertising Bureau, New York.

2. Ibid.

3. Ibid.

4. Ibid.

5. Ibid.

6. Ibid.

7. Ken Greenwood, *Radio in Search of Excellence* (Washington, DC: National Association of Broadcasters, 1985), pp. 74–75.

Appendix II
CONVERSATION
WITH A CABLE
SALES PIONEER

Solicitation of local advertising by cable systems has not been a priority of most of the cable systems until recently, and advertising sales still are not the highest priority for most cable systems because advertising revenue makes up such a small percentage of the systems' gross revenue. However, a substantial effort in local advertising sales has been undertaken in the past three years, and such an effort can be expected to continue as cable systems see their subscriber lists and pay channel subscribers peaking.

Local cable advertising increased 33⅓ percent from 1983 to 1984, from $30 million in 1983 to $40 million in 1984. The top cable system in advertising revenue in the 1986 *Broadcasting/Cablecasting Yearbook* reported well over three times as much advertising revenue as the top cable system reported in the 1984 yearbook. Information from the 1984 report showed just over $6 million in advertising revenue for the top 43 cable systems that were selling local advertising. In the 1986 report, the top 42 cable systems account for a reported $19 million in local advertising.

A noteworthy factor in the growth of cable system advertising sales is that the large MSOs (multiple system operators) and the cable systems in the largest metropolitan areas did not lead the way in development of cable television as a local advertising source. The largest metro areas have been among the later areas to be cabled (because of the multiplicity of signals available, the cost of cabling these huge population centers, and other factors).

Cable systems in less populated areas have achieved something nearer maximum growth in subscribers and, in looking for other revenue sources, have done the missionary work to begin the development of cable as an advertising sales medium in local markets. These pioneers in cable advertising sales showed that, although subscribers' monthly payments for basic and premium services were the more important and larger parts of the cable television system's balance sheet, advertising could be something akin to the frosting on the cake.

The Cable Advertising Bureau (CAB) was brought into existence to help in this pioneering effort toward cable television as an advertising medium. One of the earliest pioneers in cable advertising was Bill Ryan, a founder of CAB and its first chairman, and now president and chief executive officer for Palmer Communications, Inc., in Des Moines, Iowa. Palmer Communications owns two cable television systems, one in Florida and the other in California, in addition to broadcast interests. He became an executive with Palmer Communications when the company bought a radio station and cable system in Florida in which Ryan held an interest. While directing Palmer's Florida interests, Ryan became a pioneer in cable advertising in the early 1970s.

The cable system that led the industry in reported advertising revenue in the 1984 *Broadcasting/Cablecasting Yearbook* with $588,000 is headquartered in Naples, and with several subsidiary offices serves almost 90,000 subscribers in Naples and the surrounding area, Marco Island, Collier County, Pine Island, Captiva Island, Sanibel Island, and Lee County in southwest Florida.

At the time of the 1986 *Broadcasting/Cablecasting Yearbook*, the system reported the same volume of advertising, at that time enough to earn it tenth place among cable systems reporting advertising revenue.

With those advance thoughts, now to a conversation with Bill Ryan.

Satterthwaite:	Do you have one system, Bill, or several satellite systems?
Ryan:	If you're talking about head-ends, there are several. There is one general manager, one business manager, and one chief engineer for the whole thing. They, in turn, operate out of about three or four offices. We have systems serving a string of communities in southern California.
Satterthwaite:	You have been president of Palmer Communications how long?
Ryan:	I've been president of Palmer Communication for four years and CEO for the last two and a half years.
Satterthwaite:	Palmer has been one of the pioneers in cable advertising. When did you first get involved in the idea of cable advertising?
Ryan:	It was in the early seventies. Palmer Communications purchased two radio stations in Naples and a little cable system in which I had personal owner-

| | ship. I don't think we had more than about a thousand subscribers. A few years before that, Palmer Communications had purchased the Naples system, which had started to do some local programming. I had a television broadcast background, having worked in television production some years earlier. We thought that the radio station would be the appropriate vehicle to do the local programming and sell advertising. The first programming we went about was a local news show. |

Satterthwaite: What year was this?

Ryan: This would be about 1971. We put on a local newscast every evening. In that day, it was in black and white, and we had no videotape to begin with, although we got that soon thereafter. The evolution from black and white to color and the improved technical facilities came about over a period of time. But the very early news telecasts were crude.

Satterthwaite: This was before Sony introduced the videocassette format.

Ryan: Right. We were using a reel-to-reel tape. It was not two-inch or anything like that; it was a narrower band, and the format is long gone, because it wasn't that good.

Satterthwaite: Probably half-inch, reel-to-reel, black-and-white videotape. Ampex and several others made it then.

Ryan: That's probably what we were using. So, from there, it evolved, and we started out using the radio news people—this was a relatively small-market radio station, but it had a couple of people in its news department. It didn't take very long, however, to start expanding and hiring people just for the television aspect of it; and over a period of time, it got to the point where they were totally separate.

Satterthwaite: About how long did this take? You mentioned starting about 1971. About when did you become totally separate?

Ryan: I'd say 1982. But the overlap between radio and television was limited to just reporters and on-air performers. All the production people were obviously separate; the sales departments were separate.

Satterthwaite: You began, in essence, a radio newscast on television in 1971.

Ryan: That's right. We tried to use pictures. We used Polaroids, and so we tried to add some visuals.

Satterthwaite: And you sold the advertising separately, for the cable channel?

Ryan: That's correct, sold totally separate.

Satterthwaite: What kind of success did you have initially?

Ryan: We thought we were doing great. We were very enthused, very excited, and you must remember the market at the time. There was no local television station, so we had an exclusive opportunity to provide local news.

Satterthwaite: Do you think that you had an opportunity there that you might not have had if you'd been in a larger market?

Ryan: No question about it. If it's a very cohesive community that's interested, as a lot of towns are obviously, in all the local happenings and political activities, there's an opportunity there. As the market community gets bigger and becomes part of a larger metropolitan area, the barriers break down, it blends into one bigger city, and there's less interest in that kind of thing.

I might tell you, that in recent years, we have cut back on the news aspect of this. All three of the affiliates in the market have either opened bureaus or have some news coming out of Naples every night in their newscast. As the local guys were slicked up and got better looks, we found ourselves competing toe to toe with the broadcast program. Although our technical facilities have improved enormously, and we now have excellent broadcast quality facilities, we found the cost kept going up, skyrocketing, and the revenue just wasn't there to justify it.

Satterthwaite: This was your start—local origination. What did you go on to from newscasts?

Ryan: There was one other show that accompanied the newscasts. It was a telephone interview talk show. It was right after the news, and it was called "Page Two," because the channel was Channel 2.

Satterthwaite:	So, you started out programming one hour a night?
Ryan:	That's correct. Gradually, we went into other things. We did special-interest kinds of shows, tennis shows, golf shows.
Satterthwaite:	How did you first decide, or when did you first decide, that advertising on this system in south Florida can be not only a feasible, but a profitable enterprise?
Ryan:	You know, this was a long time ago. If the whole thing were to start up today. . . .
Satterthwaite:	You might not do it again?
Ryan:	I think we'd do it again; we'd do it differently. But things have changed dramatically from those days. Don't forget that we had no network—that is, cable-oriented network programming.
Satterthwaite:	You had only off-air signals plus what you put on?
Ryan:	We had off-air signals, plus what we could produce locally or buy in the syndicated marketplace. We tried that. We ran feature films, for example. We tried to program a small independent.
	Now, with the advent of CBN, CNN, USA, ESPN and all, the picture is totally different. We now have good-quality programming with local availabilities in it to sell. Advertising revenue as a profit center is there now because we don't have to pay much for programming. As cable operators, we have to buy the programming. We have to buy USA whether we sell advertising in it or not. Although the costs are there—and I might add the costs are going up rapidly, for programming on cable—fact is as a subscription service, we have to have it. Therefore, this advertising revenue is "found money," to at least help offset those programming costs.
Satterthwaite:	And the availabilities of approximately two minutes per hour delivered back to you by USA and others like it give you a chance to insert local commercials and not only make back what it costs you to carry it, but a little profit in addition?
Ryan:	Hopefully, that's the case. What makes it nice is that there's automated equipment today that's quite good; earlier, we had to have somebody sit there, and when a cue came along, they'd have to push a

button to insert into the network. Now not only is the equipment automated, but the logging and the billing as well.

Satterthwaite: When did you first start importing the cable network signals, and when did you first decide that there's an opportunity to sell these availabilities too?

Ryan: We were trying to program a channel in Naples. At first, we'd do the news and the talk show in a character-generated environment, so you'd see an alphanumeric. In the very early days, they called this a weather scan, and you may recall it was a black-and-white scan back and forth across weather instruments, which was pretty crude.

So, we programmed our hour, and then we went back to the weather scan. Well, we realized that people don't sit and watch a weather scan.

We began to build a schedule around that 6:00 hour. We added syndicated material and feature films, and we gradually looked for more program product to fill up more hours. When the opportunity to carry a satellite service came along—USA was the first that we used, I believe—we immediately made that service available.

We got an exception in the contract which allowed us to retain our window of local programming. We would do our local news, then after our talk show, we'd go to USA for major league baseball, and then we'd do something else. That's how it evolved. As soon as the satellite services were available, we saw the advertising.

Satterthwaite: You were a spokesperson, Bill, for advertising on cable long before many, if any, other cable systems began to do this to any great extent. I remember reading comments that came from you, or from your operation in Naples, Florida, in *Broadcasting* and in the other cable-oriented magazines, urging people in cable to get involved in this business of advertising. Why?

Ryan: I had come out of the broadcast side of our business, while most people at that point in the cable industry had come out of the hardware side. The first people in management were technical people, the ones who built the original systems. That was still largely the case in the seventies: the technical people were running the cable business.

So, the few broadcasters who had any involvement were pretty much in the minority. And to us in broadcasting, it's a very obvious opportunity to sell advertising, because really, it's television programming. As it's oftentimes been said, the viewer doesn't care how you deliver the programming, whether it's over the air or on a wire, it's still television programming. So, it's a very logical extension to sell advertising.

But the average mentality of the people managing cable systems was from the technical side, and they didn't see that. Importantly in their defense, the big problems and the big revenue sources were not from advertising, but from subscription increases and subsequently premium pay services.

Satterthwaite: If you can add a few additional subscribers at ten or fifteen dollars a month, figured up over the basis of a year, that takes the place of an awful lot of advertising sales effort?

Ryan: That's right. Advertising is not the highest priority. In our case, we enjoyed a rather good subscriber saturation. It's one of the so-called classic cable markets. So, we didn't have as much of a problem trying to get basic subscribers. Maybe we concentrated on these other revenue streams a little earlier.

Satterthwaite: You were one of the organizers as well as the first chairman of the Cable Advertising Bureau, were you not?

Ryan: That's correct.

Satterthwaite: Why was Cable Advertising Bureau organized?

Ryan: I was a member of the Cable Television Administrative Marketing Society, and Tom Johnson was president at that point. Tom asked me to chair an advertising committee. We met on a couple of occasions, and we jumped into some of the major shows—major meetings. The momentum and the enthusiasm that evolved out of this moved very quickly, snowballed.

I'd say in a period of a year, or a year and a half, it was obvious we were going to have a cable advertising bureau. There was support for it. So, we set out to create a cable version of the TVB.

In the very beginning, it actually was called the CTVB, the Cable Television Bureau. The major MSOs were all highly supportive. It was a grass-roots deal. We all put in seed money.

Leonard Rensch, who was with Cox but had subsequently retired, and I were part of the screening committee; Leonard and I were the ones that cut the deal with Bob Alter. Now, Bob Alter at the time was the number two guy at the Radio Advertising Bureau. When Bob came aboard, he picked up the baton and ran it from there. He's the guy that cleaned it up from the CTVB, to the CAB, which is much more appropriate, and put the office in New York.

When we structured it, we were sensitive to the fact that we had a couple of constituencies—one was the cable networks and the other was the cable systems. We thought that we also had to have a room there for cable reps.

At the time, we thought that local sales would be more than they are at the moment. It's turning out that the Cable Advertising Bureau, although it has a local committee and is doing a lot to support local advertising sales, is also very, very helpful and very important to the networks, because this is how they all get together and make their pitches a lot of times.

Satterthwaite: This is helping them on a national scene sell large advertisers?

Ryan: Yes, and they may be getting a little more benefit than the local systems are. The rep aspect of the business never got very big. There are a couple of reps still there, but unlike television where national business is very important to a television station—as you know, in many markets it's well over half the business—in the cable business, spot buying on a cable system is very, very rare, with the exception of a few of the larger interconnects.

Interconnects are very, very important in a metropolitan market. There are five cable operators serving a particular metropolitan market. It's incumbent on them all to get together. It's happening slowly, but it's happening.

Satterthwaite: Let's take a system like San Diego. A cable system there reported in the 1986 *Broadcasting/Cablecasting Yearbook*, $2 million annual advertising revenue. Two million dollars is a lot of money in advertising revenue, but at the same time, with 258,000 or more subscribers, it's a drop in the bucket, about 5 percent of their total revenue billing.

Ryan: If you're looking at it another way, it's a drop in the bucket in terms of the revenue generated in the San Diego television market.

Satterthwaite: Yes, and yet it is—when you reach a figure like $2 million in advertising revenue—significant, even if it is a drop in the bucket.

Ryan: San Diego is another system that has done this from way back. They have had a solid subscriber base.

Satterthwaite: On a local scene, whether you're in a large interconnect area or in Naples on an independent system, how do you answer the question posed by many potential advertisers—"You've got 12, 15, 35 channels and you're spread all over. How do I know that my ad will ever appear before anybody?"

Ryan: You're talking about ratings. Ratings are a very difficult thing for cable people to use. The shares that you have on most satellite services are miniscule compared to the broadcast stations. One little trick, is called *roadblocking*, whereby, for example, you go to the client and say, "OK, we'll roadblock at eight o'clock tonight, we'll give you five networks all at the same time." You may come up with a number that's at least a little stronger compared to one of the affiliates in the market. But, it's a tough sell, frankly, and difficult to prove the circulation.

Satterthwaite: When you sell radio, you're basically selling in the spot mode; you're selling on the basis of either a block-time period, like drive time, midmorning, early afternoon, or you're selling a float through various time periods. When you sell television, you're selling on the basis of a specific availability. What's the best way to sell cable?

Ryan: My feeling is it's a heavy tonnage of run of schedule, or some sort of a rotation plan.

Satterthwaite: Not only run of schedule, but run of network, too?

Ryan:	You have to take your demographics. For MTV, you obviously have a special kind of demo. You need to look at Lifetime as a different demo.
	Arbitron doesn't measure every town, obviously, so you get into unrated markets. We have one or two radio stations. They use little ratings services, which have no credibility on Madison Avenue, but they're OK in Main Street.
	There are ways of doing some things, and they're legitimate. For example, if you have a big event in a small town—this works best in small towns where there is no local television—like a high school football game, especially a championship game, and you promote it a little bit, you could get megabucks for those spots compared to what you can get normally. Use a telephone coincidental. We used to have Nielsen do a lot of telephone coincidentals for us that were very effective.
	If I was spending my money, advertising a business that I owned, I would be very cautious about cable. I think it's a great business for us as cable operators but we have to be realistic that it's a difficult sell, because you've got low ratings, low shares.
	The network share has been declining over the past years. Over the long haul I think we're going to see an increase in the viewing levels on cable channels. If you can get more and more people to view these channels, it will help the program product; it's going to get better.
Satterthwaite:	Would you say that somewhere down the road the system operators, MSOs, and others are going to change their orientation from digging for new subscribers and try to cultivate existing possibilities like cable advertising.
Ryan:	Oh, yes. More and more companies are setting up people to sell advertising.
	But I think we have to be realistic as to what advertising can do. For example, it makes absolutely no sense for a national advertiser, except for doing some little experimenting, test marketing something, to buy advertising on a local cable system.
Satterthwaite:	Buying it on the national networks apparently does make sense for them, however, because they're do-

ing it. Let me take you real quickly to the year 2000. What's the cable system going to be like then, in terms of local programming, local advertising, and things of this sort?

Ryan: I don't see a lot of local programming. You know, everybody's talking about how cable is going to be the access for the local people to express themselves. And I think those few people that want to have an opportunity to access channels. But they have extremely low viewership, and the broadcast television business is driven by the numbers and the ratings. I don't know if cable is going to change that. I think that advertisers are still going to want to get results, and they want measurable results, which is cash registers ringing up, and they need to have eyeballs watching their programming for it to work.

We might see a few more program channels, but I don't think we'll see three or four times as many channels of additional so-called basic programming. We'll see better programming; quality-wise production values and the content will be much better than it has been, and it's pretty good now.

I think you'll see a few things outside the area of our discussion. There will be a consolidation of cable companies, especially in markets. I think most metropolitan areas will have an evolution toward one operator serving the whole area. That's happening now, there are trade-offs, buying and selling. I know our company's philosophy is to concentrate in these markets.

So, one operator will be serving hundreds of thousands of subscribers. It will be a much more sophisticated, highly computerized business. Addressable boxes will be working, and they will work very well; you will order a service, and it will be there instantaneously. In theory, that's happening now, but it isn't really working. The equipment is not debugged, but all that will be behind us in future years.

As far as where the premium services are going to go, I don't know. The pay per view is going to be an interesting experiment, to see what happens to that.

SUMMARY

Other cable television authorities concur with many of the things Bill Ryan has said. Certainly all of those in cable are interested in upping the penetration rate of cable systems and raising it above 51.1 percent now to much closer to the concept of the wired nation, about which so much was heard a few years ago.

While continuing this as top priority, efforts are going forward to build and increase a local advertising sales effort, primarily for the local, retail business. Without the ratings the television stations have to aid their selling, local cable selling will continue to be on a conceptual basis: television exposure to segments of the overall market at radiolike prices.

If and as programming quality increases on the cable channels and more people begin watching cable channels so that ratings books show better numbers, and interconnects and mergers increase the size of the cable system (in numbers of subscribers reachable with one cable advertising buy), cable advertising sales can become a higher priority for the cable television systems.

Until that time, many cable systems will continue development work to see how local cable—especially those advertising minutes available for local sale on the cable channels—can be turned into additional profits for the system.

An advertising medium that has increased in volume by a third in one year—even though still small when compared to the giants of advertising—is a possibility that will not be discarded.

Appendix III
COLLECTIONS

All broadcast advertising salespeople soon learn that an integral part of their job as a business consultant necessarily involves the collection of revenue from station accounts that are past due in payment of their monthly invoices, usually by 90 to 120 days. As the person who has an established relationship with a past due account, the account executive who originally sold and has serviced that account is most often expected by station management to request payment. Such collection procedures on the part of the salesperson are the last resort in a station system that normally involves monthly statements and reminders of past due amounts mailed at the end of the calendar month to all clients.

Many stations build in a collections incentive to a salesperson's commission structure by deducting 15 percent, or whatever percentage is paid the salesperson, of the unpaid 90 to 120 past due amount from the salesperson's paycheck. This approach assumes that the salesperson has already received commission payment from the original sale. The point is, becoming involved in the collections process is expected from most managers today.

The thought of "asking for money" creates fear in many entry-level and veteran account executives who fear such a request will bring anger and/or embarrassment that will lead to cancellations or future loss of business. Consultants, however, recognize that the client is fully aware of the responsibilities of a business relationship, which include obligations for payment. Such consultants, who have done the job of interviewing, qualifying and preparing a customized media campaign that has been accepted by the client and aired for a period of time, are not intimidated by the thought of asking their client for a check to make such an account current or, at the very least, take it out of the 90 to 120 day column on the station's accounts receivable list.

Many clients unofficially operate on "90 day money," preferring to pay supplier/vendor accounts first (the "necessities") while leaving advertising invoices (the "extras") until last, and need only a reminder that they are in arrears in order to produce a check. Some clients simply find it convenient to wait until a request is made before they write a check. Others are simply not good bookkeepers and need to be constantly reminded to keep their account current and on the air. (Most stations will cancel the advertising of any business whose past due amounts exceed 120 days.)

Collecting from a client who is past due is very similar to the confirmation of the original sale. Few consultants confirm a sale without asking; hence, few checks are received from past due accounts without directly asking the client for payment.

Suggested Readings

Mortimer J. Adler, *How to Speak, How to Listen* (New York: Macmillan, 1983).

Roger Ailes, *You Are The Message: Secrets of the Master Communicators* (Homewood, IL: Dow Jones–Irwin, 1988).

Tony Alessandra and Phil Wexler, *Non-Manipulative Selling.* (Nightingale-Conant audiocassette program).

John C. Aspley, *The Dartnell Sales Promotion Handbook* (Chicago: Dartnell Corporation, 1966).

William Behrmann, *Advertising Opportunities in Cable Programming* (Chicago: Ogilvy and Mather, 1981).

James F. Bender, *How to Sell Well* (New York: McGraw-Hill Book Co., 1961).

Frank Bettger, *How I Raised Myself from Failure to Success in Selling* (New York: Simon & Schuster, 1981).

Frank Bettger, *How I Multiplied My Income and Happiness in Selling* (Englewood Cliffs, NJ: Prentice-Hall, 1982).

Robert Blake and Jane Mouton, *The Grid For Sales Excellence: Benchmarks for Effective Salesmanship* (New York: McGraw-Hill, 1970).

Leo Bogart, *Strategy in Advertising* (Chicago: Crain Books, 1984).

William H. Bolen, *Advertising* (New York: John Wiley & Sons, 1981).

David M. Brownstone, *Sell Your Way to Success* (New York: John Wiley & Sons, 1979).

John J. Burnett, *Promotion Management* (St. Paul, MN: West Publishing Company, 1984).

V. R. Buzzota, R. E. Lofton, and Manuel Thorberg, *Effective Selling through Psychology: Dimensional Sales and Sales Management Strategies* (Cambridge, MA: Ballinger Publishing Company, 1982).

Dana Cassell, *How To Advertise and Promote Your Retail Store* (New York: American Management Association, 1983).

Jim Cathcart and Tony Alessandra, *Selling Smart* (Nightingale-Conant audiocassette program).

Kenneth Cooper, *Nonverbal Communication for Business Success* (New York: AMACOM, 1979).

Terrence E. Deal and Allan A. Kennedy, *Corporate Cultures: The Rites and Rituals of Corporate Life* (Reading, MA: Addison-Wesley, 1982).

Gillian Dyer, *Advertising as Communication* (New York: Methuen, 1982).

Susan Eastman and Robert Klein, eds., *Strategies in Broadcast and Cable Promotion* (Belmont, CA: Wadsworth Publishing Company, 1982).

Paul W. Farris and John A. Quelch, *Advertising and Promotion Management: A Manager's Guide to Theory and Practice* (Radnor, PA: Chilton Book Company, 1983).

Alan D. Fletcher and Thomas A. Bowers, *Fundamentals of Advertising Research* (Columbus, OH: Grid Publishing, 1974).

William Frank and Charles Lapp, *How to Outsell That Born Salesman* (New York: Colliers, 1979).

Alan Garner, *Conversationally Speaking* (New York: McGraw-Hill, 1981).

Harold Gash, *New Concepts in Selling* (Nightingale-Conant audiocassette program).

Joe Girard, *How to Sell Yourself* (New York: Warner Books, 1981).

Rolf Gompertz, *Promotion and Publicity Handbook for Broadcasters* (Blue Ridge Summit, PA: TAB Books, 1977).

Guidelines for Radio: Promotion (Washington, DC: National Association of Broadcasters, 1981).

Mark Hanan, James Cribbin, and Howard Berrian, *Sales Negotiation Strategies* (New York: AMACOM, 1977).

Mark Hanan, James Cribbin, and Herman Heiser, *Consultative Selling* (New York: AMACOM, 1970).

Richard Jackson Harris, ed., *Research in Advertising* (Hillsdale, NJ: Lawrence Erlbaum Associates, 1983).

Fred Herman with Earl Nightingale, *Keep It Simple, Salesperson!* (Nightingale-Conant audiocassette program).

Mel J. Hickerson, ed., *How I Made the Sales that Did the Most for Me* (New York: John Wiley & Sons, 1981).

How to Profit From Radio Advertising (New York: National Retail Merchants Association, 1975).

Jacob Jacoby and Samuel C. Craig, *Personal Selling: Theory, Research and Practice* (Lexington, MA: D.C. Heath, 1984).

Jerome A. Jewler, *Creative Strategy in Advertising* (Belmont, CA: Wadsworth Publishing Company, 1985).

Kerry Johnson, *Subliminal Selling Skills* (Nightingale-Conant audiocassette program).

Spencer Johnson and Larry Wilson, *The One Minute $ales Person* (Nightingale-Conant audiocassette program).

George N. Kahn, *The 36 Biggest Mistakes Salesmen Make and How to Correct Them* (Englewood Cliffs, NJ: Prentice-Hall, 1981).

Kenneth L. Kanady, *The Essence of Professionalism: A Handbook for the Sales Practitioner* (Indianapolis, IN: R & R Newkirk, 1985).

Jack Kinder, Jr., Gary D. Kinder, and Roger Staubach, *Winning Strategies in Selling* (Englewood Cliffs, NJ: Prentice-Hall, 1981).

Otto Kleppner, *Advertising Procedure* (Englewood Cliffs, NJ: Prentice-Hall, 1973).

Alan Lakein, *How to Get Control of Your Time and Your Life* (New York: David McKay Company).

Legal Guide to FCC Broadcast Rules, Regulations and Policies (Washington, D.C.: National Association of Broadcasters, 1977.

Kenneth A. Longman, *Advertising* (New York: Harcourt, Brace, Jovanovich, 1971).

Lotteries and Contests: A Broadcaster's Handbook (Washington, DC: National Association of Broadcasters, 1980).

John J. McCarthy, *Secrets of Super Selling* (New York: Boardroom Books, 1982).

Jack McDonald, *The Handbook of Radio Publicity and Promotion* (Blue Ridge Summit, PA: TAB Books, 1970).

Anthony F. McGann and Thomas J. Russell, *Advertising Media: A Managerial Approach* (Homewood, IL: Richard D. Irwin, 1981).

Og Mandino, *The Greatest Salesman in the World* (New York: Bantam Books, 1974).

G. Manning and B. Reece, *Selling Today—A Personal Approach* (Dubuque, IA: William C. Brown Publishers, 1987).

George Mazzie, *The New Office Etiquette* (New York: Poseidon Books, 1983).

Albert Mehrabian, *Silent Messages: Implicit Communications of Emotions and Attitudes* (Belmont, CA: Wadsworth Publishing Company, 1980).

David W. Merrill and Roger H. Reid, *Personal Styles and Effective Performance* (Radnor, PA: Chilton Book Company, 1981).

Robert L. Montgomery, *How to Sell in the 19$0's* (Englewood Cliffs, NJ: Prentice-Hall, 1980).

Jonne Murphy, *Handbook of Radio Advertising* (Radnor, PA: Chilton Book Company, 1980).

William G. Nickels, *Marketing Communication and Promotion* (New York: John Wiley & Sons, 1984).

David Ogilvy, *Ogilvy on Advertising* (New York: Random House, 1983).

On-Air Promotion Handbook (Lancaster, PA: Broadcasters Promotion Association, 1980).

Vincent Pesch, *A Complete Manual of Professional Selling: The Modular Approach to Sales Success* (Englewood Cliffs, NJ: Prentice-Hall, 1983).

Thomas Peters and Nancy Austin, *A Passion for Excellence* (New York: Random House, 1985).

Thomas Peters and Robert Waterman, *In Search of Excellence* (New York: Harper and Row, 1982).

Daniel Pope, *The Making of Modern Advertising* (New York: Basic Books, 1983).

Barbara A. Pletcher, *Saleswoman: A Guide to Career Success* (Homewood, IL: Dow Jones–Irwin, 1978).

Radio In Search of Excellence: Lessons from America's Best-Run Radio Stations (Washington, DC: National Association of Broadcasters, 1985).

Eugene Raudsepp and Joseph C. Yeager, *How to Sell New Ideas, Your Company's and Your Own* (Englewood Cliffs, NJ: Prentice-Hall, 1981).

Ross R. Reck and Brian G. Long, *The Win-Win Negotiator* (Nightingale-Conant book and audiocassette program).

Michael Schudson, *Advertising, The Uneasy Persuasion* (New York: Basic Books, 1984).

Roger W. Seng, *The Skills of Selling* (New York: AMACOM, 1977).

Connie M. Siegel, *Sales, The Fast Track for Women* (New York: MacMillan, 1982).

Loy Singleton, *Telecommunications in the Information Age* (Cambridge, MA: Ballinger Publishing Company, 1983).

Jack Z. Sissors and E. R. Petray, *Advertising Media Planning* (Chicago: Crain Books, 1976).

Brian Tracy, *The Psychology of Selling* (Nightingale-Conant audiocassette program).

Charles Warner, *Broadcast and Cable Selling* (Belmont, CA: Wadsworth Publishing Company, 1986).

Frederick E. Webster, Jr., *Field Sales Management* (New York: John Wiley & Sons, 1983).

Joel Weldon, *Sell It! with the Million Dollar Attitude* (Nightingale-Conant audiocassette program).

Nicholas C. Williamson, *Salesperson Motivation and Performance: A Predictive Model* (Ann Arbor, MI: UMI Research Press, 1982).

Wilson Learning Corporation, *Managing Interpersonal Relationships* (Minneapolis: Wilson Learning Corporation, 1980).

Carly Winter. *Present Yourself with Impact* (New York: Random House, 1983.)

William K. Witcher, *Effective Advertising* (Nightingale-Conant audiocassette program).

Zig Ziglar, *Sell Your Way to the Top* (Nightingale-Conant audiocassette program).

INDEX